LARO_ _ _ _

Dictionary of

BRITISH
HISTORY

LAROUSSE
Dictionary of
BRITISH
HISTORY

Editor
Min Lee

LAROUSSE

LAROUSSE
Larousse plc
43–45 Annandale Street, Edinburgh EH7 4AZ
Larousse Kingfisher Chambers Inc.
95 Madison Avenue, New York, New York 10016

First published by Larousse plc 1994

10 9 8 7 6 5 4 3 2

Copyright © Larousse plc 1994

British Library Cataloguing in Publication Data
for this book is available from the British Library

Library of Congress Cataloging in Publication Data
for this book is available from The Library of Congress

ISBN 0-7523-0004-0

Cover design: Paul Wilkinson, Larousse plc

Typeset from author-generated disks by BPC Digital Data Ltd
Printed in Great Britain by Clays Ltd, St Ives plc

Preface

This book provides a concise overview of the history of Britain from earliest times to the present day. It is based on the work compiled by the extensive team of contributors and consultants for the *Dictionary of World History*, and has been updated and added to where appropriate. Like that work, it concentrates on the main diplomatic, military and political, rather than the cultural and social, landmarks. The selection of events and people has been made on the basis of the influence which they have exerted on British history; thus Napoleon and Hitler feature in these pages along with Wellington and Churchill.

Reference to the information contained here will be swift and easy, because all articles follow a strict alphabetical order. Within an article, the highlighting of a word or phrase in bold type indicates that a full reference to it can be found elsewhere in the book. The presence of additional information on any topic is indicated by the symbol ▷ at the end of each entry.

The strength of a small book such as this lies both in the accuracy and relevance of each short entry, and in its careful and accurate cross referencing. For the first stage I thank the contributors, and for the second the two editors, Angela Cran and Alison Jones, who have endlessly searched the editorial database.

Min Lee
June 1994

Acknowledgements

Grateful acknowledgements are due to all contributors and consultants to *Dictionary of World History* and especially to Bruce Lenman the Consultant Editor and Katharine Boyd the Managing Editor of that title.

A

Abercromby, Sir Ralph (1734–1801)
British general. He studied law at Edinburgh and Leipzig, then joined the Dragoons in 1756 and fought in the **Seven Years War**. He became an MP in 1774, later serving in Holland and the West Indies, capturing Trinidad (1797). In 1801 he commanded the expedition to the Mediterranean, and effected a successful landing at **Aboukir Bay**, but was mortally wounded in the ensuing battle.
▷ Napoleonic Wars

Aberdeen, George Hamilton Gordon, 4th Earl (1784–1860)
Scottish politician and Prime Minister of Britain. He succeeded to his earldom in 1801, and became a Scottish representative peer (1806), Ambassador to Vienna (1813–14), and Foreign Secretary (1828–30 and 1841–6). From 1852 to 1855, he headed a coalition ministry, which for some time was extremely popular. However, vacillating policy and mismanagement during the **Crimean War** led to his resignation.

Aboukir Bay, Battle of (Aug 1798)
A naval battle during the War of the Second Coalition, in which the British Admiral **Nelson** destroyed the French fleet under Brueys off the coast of Egypt; the engagement is also known as the Battle of the Nile. This victory forced **Napoleon I** to abandon his Egyptian campaign, aimed at threatening British territory in India, and return to France.

Abraham, Plains/Heights of, Battle of (1759)
The site of a battle in Quebec City, Canada, in which British forces under James **Wolfe** defeated a French/Canadian force under Montcalm and Vaudreuil, and gained control over Quebec. Wolfe and Montcalm were both killed in the battle.

Adams, Gerry (Gerald) (1948–)
Northern Irish politician, born in Belfast. He became politically active at an early age, joining the Irish nationalist party, **Sinn**

Féin, the political wing of the **IRA**. During the 1970s he was successively interned and then released because of his connections with the IRA, and in 1978 was elected vice-president of Sinn Féin and later president. In 1982 he was elected to the Northern Ireland Assembly and in the following year to the UK parliament as member for Belfast West, but has declined to take up his seat at Westminster. He has been frequently criticized for his association with the IRA, and the UK government protested when he was granted a visa to visit the USA in 1994.

Adams, John (1735–1826)

US politician and 2nd President. Educated at Harvard, and admitted to the Bar in 1758, he emerged as a leader of US resistance to Britain's imposition of the **Stamp Act** (1765), and led the debate that resulted in the **Declaration of Independence**. He served in Congress until 1777, after which he had an extensive diplomatic career in Europe. He took part in negotiating a peace treaty with Great Britain, then served as Minister to Great Britain (1785–8). He became the first US Vice-President, under George Washington (1789) an office he found frustrating. Both were re-elected in 1792, and in 1796 Adams was elected President with Thomas Jefferson as Vice-President. Adams's presidency was marked by factionalism within his cabinet and his party, especially over the issue of war with France. Adams opposed a war, which made him an unpopular president, and he was defeated by Jefferson on seeking re-election in 1800. He retired to his home at Quincy, where he died.

Adams, Will(iam) (1564–1620)

English sailor. He was pilot of a Dutch ship stranded off Japan in 1600, and was kept by Tokugawa Ieyasu, the first Shogun, as an adviser on such areas as shipbuilding, navigation, gunnery, foreign relations, and trade. He built the first European type of ocean-going vessel in Japan. The first Englishman to enter the service of a Japanese ruler, he lived at Edo (now Tokyo), where he was given an estate by Ieyasu. He is buried at Pilot Hill, Yokosuka, and is commemorated by monuments at Ito and Tokyo.

Addison, Joseph (1672–1719)

English essayist and poet. In 1708–11 he was Secretary to the Lord-Lieutenant of Ireland, where he formed a warm friendship with Alexander Swift. He became an MP, and contributed largely to the *Tatler*. In 1711 the *Spectator*, 274 numbers of which were his work, was founded. He was satirized by Pope in the famous character of Atticus. Addison was made a commissioner for trade and the colonies, and in 1717 was appointed Secretary of State, but a year later resigned his post on health grounds.

Addled Parliament
The name given to the brief parliament of Apr–June 1614 which saw disputes over money between **James VI** and the House of Commons. The Commons attempted to coerce the King into giving up prerogative revenue from 'impositions' on goods entering and leaving the country. The King dismissed the parliament, which passed no legislation.

Adrian IV (Nicholas Breakspear) (c.1100–59)
English Pope (1154/9). The only Englishman to hold the office, he became first a lay brother in the monastery of St Rufus, near Avignon, and in 1137 was elected its Abbot. His zeal for strict discipline led to an attempt to defame his character, and he had to appear before Eugenius III at Rome. Here he not only cleared himself, but acquired the esteem of the Pope, who appointed him Cardinal Bishop of Albano in 1146. As Pope, he is said to have granted Ireland to **Henry II** of England.

Adullamites
A nickname coined by the radical Liberal MP John **Bright** to describe those in his party who opposed **Gladstone**'s parliamentary reform bill in 1866. Bright's reference was to the 'Cave Adullam' in the First Book of Samuel which housed 'everyone that was in distress ... and everyone that was discontented'. The Adullamite leaders, Robert Lowe and Lord Elcho, succeeded in bringing down the Liberal government (1866). ▷ **radicalism**

Afghan Wars (1838–42, 1878–80 and 1919)
A series of wars between Britain and Afghanistan, prompted by the British desire to extend control in the region to prevent the advance of Russian influence towards India. The treaties which followed the third Afghan War (1919) reinforced the country's independent political status.

Africa, Partition of

The division of the continent of Africa into colonial territories, which occurred in the last three decades of the 19c. Europeans had traded with Africa for several centuries, using a series of coastal settlements. Portuguese efforts to penetrate the interior in the 16–17c had largely failed, and only the Dutch at the Cape had been able to establish a dynamic permanent settlement. In the course of the 19c, efforts to abolish the **slave trade**, missionary endeavours, and optimistic views of African riches helped to encourage colonial ambitions. The countries involved in the Partition included Britain, France, Germany, Portugal, and Italy, as well as the Boers in the south, and (in his private capacity) King Leopold of the Belgians. When the French and the Italians completed the Partition of North Africa in the years before **World War I**, only Liberia and Ethiopia remained independent. At the end of the two World Wars, a repartitioning occurred with the confiscation of German and Italian territories. Most of the countries created by the Partition achieved independence in or after the 1960s, and the Organization of African Unity pledged itself to the maintenance of the existing boundaries.

Agincourt, Battle of (1415)

A battle between France and England during the **Hundred Years War**. **Henry V** of England was forced to fight near Hesdin (Pas-de-Calais) by the French who, ignoring the lessons of the Battles of **Crécy** and Poitiers (1356), pitched cavalry against dismounted men-at-arms and archers. Though heavily outnumbered, the English won another overwhelming victory, and returned in 1417 to begin the systematic conquest of **Normandy**.

Agricola, Gnaeus Julius (AD40–93)

Roman general. Rome's longest-serving and most successful governor in Britain (78–84), he skilfully implemented a two-pronged policy, of conquest in the north and Romanization in the south. He subdued northern England and Lowland Scotland, and actively encouraged the development of Roman-style towns in the south. Though his plans to conquer the extreme north of Scotland and Ireland came to nothing, the circumnavigation of Britain by his fleet greatly impressed contemporaries. Recalled c.84 by Emperor Domitian, probably out of jealousy, he lived quietly in retirement in Rome until his death.

Agricultural Revolution

The name popularly given to a series of changes in farming practice occurring first in England and later throughout Western Europe. Some historians date these as far back as the end of the 16c, but the term usually covers the period 1700–1850. The main changes included: greater intensity of productive land use; the reduction of fallow land and waste lands; the introduction of crop rotation; the development of artificial grasses; and scientific animal breeding. Many such changes were facilitated by the replacement of open fields by enclosures. They also depended upon tenant farming and market production replacing subsistence and peasant agriculture. The widespread use of mechanized farming techniques, such as threshing machines and mechanical ploughs, mostly post-dated the changes of this agricultural revolution. ▷ **Industrial Revolution**

Alabama Claims (1869–72)

A diplomatic dispute in which the USA held Britain accountable for damage inflicted to the Union during the American Civil War by Confederate naval vessels (the *Alabama*, *Florida* and *Shenandoah*) built in Britain. The dispute was resolved in 1872 when an international tribunal (Italy, Switzerland and Brazil), ruled that Britain should pay an indemnity to the USA of US$15 500 000. ▷ **Washington, Treaty of**

Alanbrooke (of Brookeborough), Alan Francis Brooke, 1st Viscount (1883–1963)

British field marshal and leading strategist of **World War II**. He joined the Royal Field Artillery in 1902, and fought in **World War I**. He commanded the 2nd Corps of the **British Expeditionary Force** in France (1940), and later was Commander-in-Chief Home Forces. Chief of the Imperial General Staff 1941–6, he was Winston **Churchill**'s principal strategic adviser at the conferences with Roosevelt and Stalin. He was created baron (1945) and viscount (1946).

Albany Congress (1754)

A meeting in Albany, New York, of representatives from seven British colonies in North America at which Benjamin Franklin proposed his 'plan of union' to unite the separate American British colonies. The Albany Plan of Union was rejected by the Colonial governments and the Crown. However, the plan served as a model for the joint action of the mainland colonies in the **American Revolution**.

Albert (1819–61)

Prince Consort of Queen **Victoria**. The youngest son of the Duke of **Saxe-Coburg-Gotha**, he married his cousin, an infatuated Queen Victoria, in 1840. He became her chief adviser, first as Consort (1842), then as Prince Consort (1857). Ministerial distrust and public misgivings combined to obstruct his interference in politics, but he developed a congenial sphere of self-expression by encouraging the arts and social and industrial reforms. It was largely on his initiative that the Great Exhibition of 1851 took place.

Alcock Convention (1869)

A proposed treaty agreed upon by the British ambassador to China, Sir Rutherford Alcock, and Chinese officials in Beijing. Reflecting the British government's view that undue pressure to extract greater trade concessions should not be exerted on the Chinese government, the proposed treaty allowed the Chinese government to increase import duties on opium and export duties on silk, as well as to open a consulate in the British colony of Hong Kong. However, due to protests from British merchant interests eager for a considerable expansion of commercial opportunities in China, the treaty was not ratified by the British government.

Alexander I (c.1077–1124)

King of Scots (1107/24). He ruled north of the Forth–Clyde line while his younger brother David (later **David I**) controlled southern Scotland in his name. The second of the three sons of **Malcolm III, 'Canmore'** and Queen (later St) Margaret to become king, he succeeded his brother, Edgar. He founded an Augustinian monastery at Scone, and maintained friendly relations with England by marrying Sybilla, an illegitimate daughter of **Henry I**, and fighting alongside Henry in Wales (1114). ▷ **Margaret, St**

Alexander II (1198–1249)

King of Scots (1214/49). The son and successor of **William I, 'the Lion'**, he supported the English barons against King **John**, later

concluding a peace treaty with **Henry III** (1217), and marrying Henry's eldest sister, Joan (1221). In 1239 he married Marie, the daughter of Enguerrand de Coucy. His reign represents an important landmark in the making of the Scottish kingdom. He renounced his hereditary claims to Northumberland, Cumberland, and Westmorland by the Treaty of York (1237), and concentrated on the vigorous assertion of royal authority in the north and west. He died of a fever on Kerrera, near Oban, while leading an expedition to wrest the Western Isles from Norwegian control.
▷ **Barons Wars**

Alexander III (Rolando Bandinelli) (c.1105–81)
Italian Pope (1159–81). He taught law at Bologna, and became adviser to Pope **Adrian IV**. As pope, he was engaged in a struggle with the Emperor Frederick I, 'Barbarossa' who supported antipopes against him. The Emperor was finally defeated at the Battle of Legnano (1176) and peace was concluded by the Treaty of Venice (1177). The other notable conflict of church and state in which he was involved was that between **Henry II** of England and Thomas à **Becket**. He also called the third Lateran Council (1179).

Alexander III (1241–86)
King of Scots (1249/86). The son of **Alexander II** of Scotland, in 1251 he married Princess Margaret, eldest daughter of Henry III of England. Soon after he had come of age, he defended the kingdom against the Norwegians, who were routed at Largs (1263). By the Treaty of Perth (1266), Scotland gained the Hebrides and the Isle of Man. In the later part of his reign, the kingdom enjoyed a period of peace and prosperity. He was killed in a riding accident.

Alexander (of Tunis), Harold Rupert Leofric George, 1st Earl
(1891–1969)
British field marshal. In **World War I** he commanded a brigade of Irish guards on the Western Front, and in 1940 was the last officer out of Dunkirk. He served in Burma, and in 1942–3 was Commander-in-Chief, Middle East, his **North African Campaign** being one of the most complete victories in military history. Appointed field marshal on the capture of Rome in June 1944, he became Supreme Allied Commander, Mediterranean Theatre, for the rest of the war. He later became Governor-General of Canada

(1946–52) and Minister of Defence (1952–4), and was created Viscount (1946) and Earl (1952). ▷ **World War II**

Alfred, 'the Great' (849–99)

King of **Wessex** (871/99). He was the fifth son of King Ethelwulf. When Alfred came to the throne, the Danes had already conquered Northumbria, East **Mercia**, and East Anglia, and threatened to subdue Wessex itself. He inflicted on them their first major reverse at the Battle of **Edington** in Wiltshire (878), and began to win back Danish-occupied territory by capturing the former Mercian town of London (886). He stole the military initiative from the Danes by reorganizing his forces into a standing army, building a navy, and establishing a network of burhs (fortified centres). These developments were complemented by his revival of religion and learning, a programme designed to win God's support for victory over the pagan Danes and to consolidate loyalty to himself as a Christian king. He forged close ties with other English peoples not under Danish rule, and provided his successors with the means to reconquer the **Danelaw** and secure the unity of England. The famous story of his being scolded by a peasant woman for letting her cakes burn has no contemporary authority, and is first recorded in the 11c. ▷ **Anglo-Saxons; Athelstan; Edward the Elder; Vikings**

Alinagar, Treaty of (7 Feb 1757)

The treaty concluded by **Clive of Plassey** following his recapture of Calcutta from the Nawab of Bengal, **Siraj ud-Daula**. Under its terms, Calcutta was returned to the British **East India Company**, its privileges were renewed and the rights to fortify the town and mint money were secured. This absolutely secured a bridgehead from which to increase the Company's power in Bengal.

Allenby, Edmund Henry Hynman, 1st Viscount (1861–1936)

British field marshal. As Commander of the 3rd Army during the Battle of Arras (1917), he came close to breaching the German line. He then took command of the Egyptian Expeditionary Force, and conducted a masterly campaign against the Turks in Palestine and Syria, capturing Jerusalem (1917), Damascus and Aleppo (1918), and securing an armistice. He was made a viscount in 1919. ▷ **World War I**

Allied Intervention in Russia (1918–22)

The term refers to the intervention of foreign troops in Russian affairs following the Bolshevik October Revolution (1917). France, Britain, Japan and the USA were initially concerned to stiffen resistance to Germany by landing contingents in the north and the south of Russia and in eastern Siberia. Before these could become effective, Lenin had concluded the separate Treaty of Brest-Litovsk (Mar 1918), and they got drawn instead into the Russian Civil War on the side of his opponents. This did nothing to help defeat Germany and soured Western-Soviet relations for years to come. Most of the troops had been withdrawn by 1920, but it was Oct 1922 before the Japanese left Vladivostok.

American Revolution (1775–83)

The war that established the 13 American colonies as independent from Britain, often called the American War of Independence. In the years 1763 to 1775 relations between the North American colonies and Britain became increasingly strained as Britain began taking measures to tighten control over the colonies. Colonial resistance was especially high over the issue of whether the British parliament had the right to tax the colonies without their representation. Anti-British sentiment was more organized in the major port towns, with considerable support coming from the elected assemblies. The tension during this period was reflected in the **Stamp Act** crisis (1765–6), resistance to the **Townshend Acts** (1767–70), the **Boston Massacre** (1770), the burning of the customs cruiser *Gaspée* (1772), and the **Boston Tea Party** (1773). The British Parliament's passage of the **Intolerable Acts** (1774) to punish Massachusetts for the Tea Party led to the calling of the First Continental Congress (1774). In Apr 1775 fighting broke out between British troops and the colonial militia known as the Minutemen at the Battles of **Lexington and Concord** in Massachusetts. Other military engagements followed, including the colonial capture of Fort Ticonderoga (May 1775), the Battle of **Bunker Hill**, and the unsuccessful colonial expedition in Quebec, Canada. In June 1775 the Second Continental Congress elected George Washington to command the Continental Army and in July adopted the **Declaration of Independence**. Following the British evacuation of Boston in May 1776, the main theatre shifted to New York, New Jersey, and Pennsylvania. Washington's troops suffered a number of defeats in the New York area, including the Battle of Long Island (Aug 1776), but his surprise attacks at

Trenton (25 Dec 1776) and Princeton (Jan 1777), New Jersey, though small victories, did much to reinvigorate the colonial cause. In the Battle of Brandywine (Sep 1777) in Pennsylvania, however, Washington's troops were once again defeated. In June 1777 British troops had begun to move down from Canada and at first seemed assured of victory, but shrewd American man-oeuvring resulted in defeat of the British and the surrender of Burgoyne following the Battle of Saratoga in upstate New York. This American triumph convinced the French to enter the war officially, bringing to the colonists badly needed material support, troops, monetary credit, and a fleet. During the winter of 1778 Washington's troops suffered great hardship while wintering in Valley Forge. By the spring the colonial forces had regathered their strength and Washington's men made a good showing at the Battle of Monmouth (June). Later that year fighting shifted southward, when Sir Henry Clinton commanded an invasion of South Carolina. Clinton's successor, Lord **Cornwallis**, led the army gradually north until Washington and the French Admiral de Grasse trapped him on the Yorktown Peninsula in Virginia, where he surrendered in 1781. The defeat resulted in the fall of the British Prime Minister, Lord North, who had prosecuted the war, and ended British will for further fighting. After almost two years of negotiating, the Treaty of Paris was signed in Sep 1783, recognizing the independence of the USA. The revolution had an impact felt far beyond the battlefield. Although support had not been universal — many loyalists fled at the war's end and became the core of English-speaking Canada — the various coalitions uniting entrepreneurs, professionals, planters, farmers, and urban working people had given form to the most advanced political hopes of their time. The newly created republic was an institution that political thinkers of the day had doubted was capable of governing a large area or of even surviving at all. The new country, founded by a democratic movement and based on an ideology of 'equal rights' opened the way for the long-term decline of mon-archy in the rest of the world. ▷ **Camden, Battle of; Charleston, Battles of; Cowpens, Battle of; Gaspée; Sugar Act; Yorktown Campaign**

Amherst, Jeffrey, 1st Baron (1717–97)
British general. He successfully commanded an expedition against the French fortress at Louisbourg (Nova Scotia) in 1758. After the fall of **Quebec** the following year, he completed the conquest

of Canada by taking Montreal in 1760. He became a peer in 1776, and served as Commander-in-Chief of the British army.

Amiens, Treaty of (1802)
A treaty between Britain and France, marking the end of the first stage of the wars with revolutionary France. Most of the conquests made by either power since 1793 were agreed to be returned. The peace held for only a brief period; war broke out afresh in 1803, and continued until 1815. ▷ **Napoleonic Wars**

Amnesty International
A British-based pressure group, founded in London in 1961, that campaigns for the release of any person detained for their political or religious beliefs or who has been unjustly imprisoned for any other reason.

Amritsar Massacre (13 Apr 1919)
On 10 Apr 1919 riots broke out in Amritsar in the Punjab in the course of an agitation for Indian self-rule. A gathering assembled three days later at Jallianwalla Bagh, a public park, on the festive occasion of Baisakhi. While they were being addressed, General Dyer, the local British commander, marched in. With barely a warning to the assembly and leaving no adequate means for the crowd to disperse, he ordered his troops to fire on the unarmed crowd, which included women and children, killing 379 Indians and wounding nearly 1 200. A government commission of inquiry severely censured Dyer and he had to resign his commission. Back in England, however, the House of Lords passed a motion approving of his actions and Dyer was widely acclaimed as 'the man who saved India' (the *Morning Post* launched a fund for him, raising £26 000 towards his retirement). The long-term effect of the massacre was the reverse of what Dyer had intended: many Indians were driven into supporting the Indian National Congress, and M K **Gandhi** himself became convinced of the impossibility of just rule under the British and the necessity for Indian independence.

Angevins
The name conventionally given to the English monarchs from 1154 to 1216: **Henry II** and his sons, **Richard I** and **John**. It derives from the lordship of the medieval county (and later, duchy) of

11

Anjou in western France via Henry, son of Geoffrey Plantagenet, Count of Anjou. Henry created a wider 'Angevin Empire' comprising also Normandy, Maine and Aquitaine. The Angevin line continued as Plantagenets after the death of John, although John is usually considered the last Angevin king because it was during his reign that Anjou was lost to the French. ▷ **Plantagenet Dynasty**

Angles

A Germanic people from the southern Danish peninsula and neighbourhood. With the **Saxons**, they formed the bulk of the invaders who, in the two centuries following the Roman withdrawal from Britain (409), conquered and colonized most of what became England. Anglian rulers were apparently dominant by the 8c, and the Angles ultimately gave their name to England, its language and people. ▷ **Anglo-Saxons**

Anglesey, Henry William Paget, 1st Marquis of (1768–1854)

English field marshal, who commanded the British cavalry at the Battle of **Waterloo** (1815), where he lost a leg. He sat in parliament at various times between 1790 and 1810, succeeding his father as Earl of Uxbridge in 1812. He served in the army with distinction in Flanders (1794), Holland (1799), and the **Peninsular War** (1808–14), and was made Marquis of Anglesey for his services at Waterloo. He was Lord Lieutenant of Ireland (1828–9 and 1830–3), where he supported Catholic emancipation, and Master-General of the Ordnance (1846–52).

Anglo-Burmese Wars (1824–6, 1852–3 and 1885)

Three wars which secured British control of Burma: the first (1824–6) brought control of Arakan and Tehnasserim; the second (1852–3) led to the occupation of Pegu; the third (1885) saw the occupation of Upper Burma, and in 1886 all Burma was proclaimed a province of British India.

Anglo-Dutch Wars (1652–4, 1665–7, 1672–4 and 1780–4)

Four naval wars fought between the Dutch Republic and England caused mainly by commercial and colonial rivalry between the two great sea powers. The first three, in the second half of the 17c, did not result in the supremacy of either nation; the fourth (1780–4), shortly before the French revolutionary period, was heavily lost by the Dutch, and signalled the end of their claims to commercial domination. The wars were the occasion of great naval heroics on both sides, for instance in the persons of Robert **Blake**, Maarten and Cornelis Tromp, and Michiel de Ruyter.

Anglo-Egyptian Treaty (1936)

In 1922 the British government had issued a declaration which recognized Egypt as an 'independent sovereign state', but retained for Britain control of the Suez Canal, the right to keep troops in the Canal Zone and the condominium in the Sudan. The 1936 treaty gave more of the substance of independence to Egypt. British residents in Egypt lost their legal and financial privileges, the British occupation was formally ended and Egypt gained control of her armed forces for the first time since 1882. In wartime, the British had the right to reoccupy the country, a right they exercised in 1939.

Anglo-Iraqi Treaty (1930)

This treaty prepared the way for ending Britain's mandate in Iraq. The two countries formed a 25-year alliance in which they agreed to consult each other where they had common interests in foreign policy. Britain would retain the use of some air bases in Iraq and would train the Iraqi army. In 1932 Iraq became independent and joined the **League of Nations**.

Anglo-Irish Agreement (1985)

A joint agreement allowing the Irish Republic to contribute to policy in Northern Ireland for the first time since 1922, signed (15 Nov 1985) by the British and Irish Prime Ministers, Margaret **Thatcher** and Garrett Fitzgerald. It established an inter-governmental conference to discuss political, security, and legal matters affecting Northern Ireland; early meetings focused on border cooperation. Both governments pledged not to change the status of Northern Ireland without the consent of the majority. The agreement was opposed by the Irish Republic's opposition party, **Fianna Fáil**; in Northern Ireland, Unionist leaders withdrew cooperation with ministers and boycotted official bodies.

Anglo-Japanese Alliance (1902)

The first modern alliance between a Western and Asian power, which lasted until 1921. It reflected the anxiety both countries felt at increasing Russian encroachment in Manchuria. The alliance took account of each country's interests in China, as well as Japan's interests in Korea, and provided for joint action in the event that either of the signatories was involved in war with more than one power in East Asia. Each signatory would remain neutral if the other fought only one power. The alliance was renewed twice (1905 and 1911), extending its scope to the protection of Britain's interests in India and recognizing Japan's annexation of Korea in 1910. Although the alliance brought benefits to both countries, the irrelevance of Russia as a threat in East Asia after 1918 and persistent US hostility led to its replacement in 1921 at the Washington Conference by a much looser consultative Four-Power Pact (USA, Britain, France and Japan).

Anglo-Russian Entente (1907)

A crucial settling of differences between Russia and Britain which in the event almost amounted to an alliance. The Russian and British empires had been rivals in the Near, Middle and Far East for at least a century. However, they were gradually brought together by mutual distrust of an aggressive Germany and mutual interest in friendship with a worried France, with which Russia had had an alliance since 1894 and Britain an entente since 1904. Neither was prepared to sink their differences so far as to conclude a treaty. However, agreeing their respective spheres of influence, particularly in Persia, enabled them to operate as a diplomatic bloc that went to war in 1914.

Anglo-Saxons

A term probably first used to distinguish the **Saxons** of England from those of the Continent; occasionally adopted by the 10c English kings for all their subjects, though 'English' was preferred; now commonly employed for the entire Old English people from the incoming of **Angles**, Saxons, and **Jutes** in the 5c to the **Norman Conquest**. Among the main themes in Anglo-Saxon history are the emergence of the early kingdoms, their conversion to Christianity, their response to attacks by the **Vikings**, and their eventual unification in the 10c into a single realm, England, literally 'land of the Angles'. The Anglo-Saxons left an enduring legacy, including a developed system of government and a rich economy. ▷ **Alfred, 'the Great'; Athelstan; Edgar; Edward the Elder; Offa; Wessex**

Anglo-Tibetan Agreement (1904)

The agreement reached in Lhasa between Tibetan officials and a British expeditionary force (under Sir Francis Younghusband) fearful of potential Russian influence. Tibet recognized British overlordship of Sikkim and agreed to open relations with India. Trade marts were also to be opened in Gyantse and Gartok (western Tibet), where British officials and troops could be stationed. This agreement was virtually repudiated by the British government when it signed a convention with China in 1906 reaffirming China's position in Tibet and promising not to interfere in Tibetan affairs, in return for China's guarantee to keep Tibet free from encroachment by a third power.

Angry Brigade

A left-wing group with anarchist sympathies, active in Britain in the 1960s and early 1970s, which took sporadic violent action against representatives of the establishment in the name of the working class. Its leaders were tried and imprisoned for a bomb attack on the home of Robert Carr, Secretary of State for Employment, in 1971.

Anne (1665–1714)

Queen of Great Britain and Ireland (1702/14). The second daughter of **James VII and II**, she was the last Stuart sovereign. In 1672 her father became a Catholic, but she was brought up in the Church of England. In 1683 she married Prince George of Denmark (1653–1708); and Sarah Jennings (1660–1744), the wife of Lord Churchill (afterwards 1st Duke of **Marlborough**), was appointed a lady of her bedchamber. Lady Churchill speedily acquired supreme influence over her, which she exerted in favour of her husband. During her father's reign, Anne lived in retirement, taking no part in politics, but later was drawn into intrigues for his restoration, or to secure the succession for his son. She was herself childless when she succeeded to the throne in 1702. She bore 17 children, but only William, Duke of Gloucester, survived infancy. The influence of Marlborough and his wife was powerfully felt in all public affairs during the greater part of her reign, which was marked by pronounced party political conflict between **Whigs** and **Tories**, the Union of England and Scotland (1707), and the long struggle against Louis XIV of France known as the War of the **Spanish Succession**. Towards the end of her reign she quarrelled with the Marlboroughs and **Godolphin**, her

Lord Treasurer. Anne found a new favourite in Abigail Masham, and under her influence appointed a Tory government (1710); but quarrels between the new ministers prevented her securing the succession for her brother. ▷ **Stuart, House of; Union, Acts of; Whigs**

Anne of Cleves (1515–57)

Lutheran princess. She became the fourth queen of **Henry VIII** of England in Jan 1540, as part of Thomas **Cromwell**'s strategy of developing an alliance with German Protestant rulers. The marriage was declared null and void, on grounds of non-consummation six months afterwards. On agreeing to the divorce, Anne was given a large income, and she remained in England until her death.

Anti-Corn Law League (Sep 1838)

An association formed in Manchester, largely under the patronage of businessmen and industrialists, to repeal the British **Corn Laws**, which imposed protective tariffs on the import of foreign corn. League propaganda aided the growing movement for free trade in early 19c Britain, and the league was an influential political pressure group with many supporters in parliament. The Corn Laws were repealed by Robert **Peel** (1846). ▷ **Bright, John**

Antonine Wall

A defensive frontier barrier commissioned by the Roman Emperor Antoninus Pius in AD142, which extended the northern limit of Roman Britain into Scotland. Constructed of turf upon a foundation of cobbles, guarded by 19 forts, and with a ditch in front and a military road behind it, the 'wall' extended from the Forth estuary to the Clyde. ▷ **Britain, Roman**

Anzio Landing (22–3 Jan 1944)

Landing by 50 000 US and British troops during **World War II** at a small port 60 miles behind the German defences of the so-called Gustav Line. Although the Germans were taken by surprise, they were able to confine the Allied troops and prevent them from using Anzio as a bridgehead. In late May the forces at Anzio eventually made contact with the advancing troops of General Alexander who had overrun the Gustav Line.

appeasement

A foreign policy based on conciliation of the grievances of rival states by negotiation and concession to avoid war. The term is most often applied to the unsuccessful British and French attempts before **World War II** to satisfy **Hitler**'s demands over German grievances arising out of the Treaty of **Versailles**. As a result, Hitler remilitarized the Rhineland, secured Anschluss with Austria, and gained the Sudetenland from Czechoslovakia. ▷ **Chamberlain, Neville**

Arab Revolt (1916)

The result of British negotiations with Sharif **Husayn ibn 'Ali** of Mecca, in part at least encouraged by the **Husayn–McMahon Correspondence**, the revolt was led by the Sharif's son, Faysal. Attached to the Arab forces during the revolt was T E **Lawrence** ('Lawrence of Arabia'). Amongst the achievements of the revolt was the destruction of the Hijaz Railway between Ma'an and Medina, and the capture of Aqaba. Essentially a revolt against Turkish occupation, the Arabs were also under the impression that a greater Arab nation had been promised them by the British. The revolt cleared the way for British troops under **Allenby** to advance northwards into Syria, where the capture of Damascus effectively brought Turkish hegemony to a close. Unsurprisingly, the Arabs felt aggrieved, if not betrayed, by the provisions of the subsequent **Balfour Declaration** (providing for a national home for the Jews in Palestine) and by the provisions for British and French 'spheres of influence', initially negotiated by Sykes and Picot and confirmed after **World War I** by the **League of Nations**. ▷ **Sykes–Picot Agreement**

Arbroath, Declaration of (6 Apr 1320)

A response by Scottish barons, with the support of the Church, to a demand from Pope John XXII that the Scots make peace with England. The Pope did not recognize Robert **Bruce** as King of Scotland. Almost certainly written by Bruce's Chancellor, Bernard de Linton, also Abbot of Arbroath, the declaration asserted the separate nationhood of Scotland and the integrity of its 'uninterrupted succession of 113 Kings, all of our own native and royal stock'. The declaration, a skilful and effective piece of anti-English propaganda, declared that the signatories would never 'consent to subject our selves to the dominion of the English' and urged the Pope to take note of the wrong and calamities to the Church and state which had been wrought by the English incursions. Unsurprisingly, it has since become a key document for supporters of a separate Scottish nation.

Arlington, Henry Bennet, 1st Earl of (1618–85)

English statesman. A member of the **Cabal** ministry under **Charles II**, and Secretary of State (1662–74), he was created Earl of Arlington in 1672. In 1674 he was impeached for embezzlement, and although cleared, resigned and became Lord Chamberlain. He negotiated the Triple Alliance against France (1668), and helped to develop the English party system.

Armada, Spanish

A fleet of 130 Spanish ships, commanded by Medina Sidonia, carrying 20 000 soldiers and 8 500 sailors, sent by **Philip II** of Spain to invade England in 1588. The invasion was in retaliation for English support of Protestant rebels in the Netherlands, the execution of **Mary, Queen of Scots** (1587), and raids on Spanish shipping, such as **Drake**'s at Cadiz (1587); Philip's aim was to gain control of the English Channel. The fleet, hampered by orders to rendezvous with Spanish forces in the Netherlands, was routed by English attacks off Gravelines (28–9 July 1588); 44 ships were lost in battles and during the flight home around Scotland and Ireland. Although a victory for the English, counter-armadas were unsuccessful, and the war lasted until 1604. ▷ **Elizabeth I**

Army, (British) Indian (1748–1947)

British-controlled and officered military force in India in which the rank and file were recruited from the native populace, although some purely European regiments existed until 1860. The Indian Army served abroad as well as in India, and was a mainstay of the Pax Britannica. It was originally formed from guards used to protect properties of the British **East India Company** and Indian soldiers known as sepoys. In 1748 the growing French presence in Madras and continuing bad relations between France and Britain caused the Company to organize a permanent military force in India. Until 1759, when the size and organization of units were standardized, the armies of the Bengal, Bombay and Madras presidencies developed entirely independently, and expanded at different rates. By 1796, when two-battalion native infantry regiments were instituted, Bengal had 12, Madras 11, and Bombay 6. Bengal and Madras also had cavalry regiments, although these were less strictly regulated and sometimes amounted to elite private units raised and commanded by enthusiastic Company officials. The growth of the military reflecting the Company's increased territorial acquisitions and responsibility for what had been Mughal administration. For all its size, the Indian Army in the first half of the 19c was inefficient and amateur; defects became apparent especially amongst the exclusively European officer cadre. Following the mutiny of the Bengal army and the **Indian Uprising** of 1857–8, the East India Company was dissolved and the Indian Army became the property of the Crown; by 1861 European regiments had been transferred to the British Army. The main functions of the Army between 1858 and 1914 were guarding the North-West Frontier and maintenance of order, although it was designed to be used in emergencies between Suez and Hong Kong. In 1895, the armies of the three Presidencies were amalgamated into one British Indian Army. In 1903 Lord Kitchener administratively combined the Staff and Troops, and renamed the force the Indian Army. Because of their performance during **World War I** and the changing political climate, Indians became eligible for the King's Commission in 1917. In 1922 the army was again reorganized and 'Indianization' of the officer corps was accelerated. By 1924 there were 8 wholly Indian units and in 1934 an Indian Military Academy for the training of officers was opened at Dehra Dun. In **World War II** units of the Indian Army were employed throughout the world in the Allied cause, although the bulk of the force fought in Burma and remained in India to maintain order. With Indian independence in 1947, the British Indian Army ceased to exist, its resources having been divided equally between India and Pakistan. ▷ **British India**

Arnhem, Battle of (Sep 1944)

A major confict in occupied Dutch territory towards the end of **World War II**, in which the German forces thwarted Allied attempts to break through. Operation 'Market Garden' was designed by Field Marshal **Montgomery**, and involved the largest airlift operation of the war, parachuting 10 000 troops on 17 Sep 1944 into the Dutch rivers area, to take key bridges over the Rhine, Maas and Waal. Allied forces advanced to Nijmegen, but at Arnhem met the 9th and 10th German Panzer divisions, which successfully resisted attack and eventually forced an Allied withdrawal on 25 Sep to behind the Rhine River.

Arrow War (Second Opium War) (1856–60)

A conflict between Britain and China, which began when the Hong Kong-registered ship *Arrow*, flying the British flag, was boarded at Canton (Guangzhou) by the Chinese, who arrested most of the crew for piracy. British warships and troops then attacked Canton and were initially repulsed, but a combined British and French force took it the following year, and proceeded north, threatening Beijing. The Treaty of **Tianjin** (Tientsin) that concluded hostilities opened additional **treaty ports** to foreign trade, legalized the opium traffic, and facilitated Christian missionary activity. ▷ **Opium Wars**

Arthur (?6c)

A probably legendary king of the Britons. He is represented as the unifier of the British tribes against the pagan invaders (5–6c AD), and as the champion of Christianity. It is very doubtful that he actually lived: he is claimed alike as a prince in Brittany, Cornwall, Wales, Cumberland, and the Lowlands of Scotland. His story passed into literature and many legends became interwoven with it, including those of the Round Table and the Holy Grail (both from the 12c–13c). The stories were developed by French writers (notably Chrétien de Troyes), and Lancelot, Percival, and the Grail were added. Malory's English version, *Morte d'Arthur*, was the final medieval compilation from which most later retellings are derived.

Arthur (1187–1203)

Claimant to the English throne. He was the posthumous son of Geoffrey (**Henry II**'s fourth son) by Constance, Duchess of Brittany. On the death of **Richard I** (1199), Arthur claimed the English crown; and the French King, Philip II, for a while supported his bid for the throne. However, King **John** had him captured and murdered.

Arundel, Thomas (1353–1414)

English prelate and statesman, third son of Robert Fitzalan, Earl of Arundel. He became Archdeacon of Taunton and Bishop of Ely (1373), then Archbishop of York (1388), and finally of Canterbury (1396). He supported the nobles opposed to **Richard II**, who banished him (1397), but he returned to help seat Henry of Lancaster on the throne (1399). He was a vigorous opponent of the **Lollards**.

Ashdown, Jeremy John Durham ('Paddy') (1941–   )

English politician. After a career in the Royal Marines (1959–71) and the diplomatic service (1971–6) he entered politics, becoming Liberal MP for Yeovil (1983). He was Liberal spokesman on trade and industry (1983–6) and succeeded David **Steel** as leader of the Social and Liberal Democrats (1988). ▷ **Liberal Party**

Asquith, H(erbert) H(enry), 1st Earl of Oxford and Asquith
(1852–1928)

English Liberal politician and Prime Minister of Britain. He was called to the Bar (1876), and became a QC (1890) and MP (1886), Home Secretary (1892–5), Chancellor of the Exchequer (1905–8), and Premier (1908–16). His regime was notable for the upholding of free trade, the introduction of old-age pensions, payment for MPs, the Parliament Act of 1911, Welsh disestablishment, suffragette troubles, the declaration of war (1914), the coalition ministry (1915), and the **Sinn Féin** rebellion (1916). His replacement as Premier by Lloyd George provoked lasting bitterness; in 1918 he led the Independent Liberals who rejected Lloyd George's continuing coalition with the Conservatives. He was created an earl in 1925. ▷ **Liberal Party; suffragettes**

Assemblies

A unique feature of the 'Old Representative System' which existed in the pre-19c British West Indies colonies. When the previous proprietary system of government was abolished in 1663, real legislative and financial power quickly devolved on to a forum of the unrepresentative, rich plantocracy, whose wealth made London's responsibility for the administration somewhat illusory. Aping the powers and prerogatives of the House of Commons in England, the Assemblies resisted progressive legislation and imperial edict and countered all attempts to abolish them. So obstructive, oligarchic, self-interested and obscurantist had the Assemblies become, that when Britain took over Trinidad, Berbice-Essequibo and St Lucia after the **Napoleonic Wars**, they were incorporated into the empire under **Crown Colony Government**. Jamaica gave up its assembly after the Morant Bay Rebellion (1866), but Barbados maintained an assembly until 1966.

Assize Court
A legal system in England and Wales, dating from the time of **Henry II** of England, which was abolished by the Courts Act, 1971. Assize courts were presided over by High Court judges, who travelled on circuit to hear criminal and civil cases. The functions of Assize courts continue to be exercised by High Court judges sitting in Crown Courts throughout England and Wales.

Astor, Nancy Witcher Langhorne, Viscountess (1879–1964)
Conservative politician. The first woman MP to sit in the House of Commons (1919–45), she succeeded her husband as MP for Plymouth in 1919, and became known for her interest in women's rights and social problems, especially temperance.

Athelstan (c.895–939)
King of England (927/39). The son of **Edward the Elder**, and the grandson of **Alfred, 'the Great'**, he was elected King of **Wessex** and Mercia on his father's death in 924. He built upon his predecessors' achievements by invading **Northumbria**, securing his direct rule over it, and thus establishing himself as effectively the first King of all England (927). He stabilized his position by defeating a powerful coalition of enemies at Brunanburh (location unknown) in 937. ▷ **Anglo-Saxons**

Atlantic, Battle of the (1940–3)
The conflict arising out of German attacks on shipping in the Atlantic during **World War II**. The German strategy was to cut off Britain's supplies of food and munitions by submarine action. Only at the end of 1943 were the attacks countered, and the threat brought under control.

Atlantic Charter (Aug 1941)
A declaration of principles to govern the national policies issued by US President Franklin D Roosevelt and British Prime Minister Winston **Churchill** after a secret meeting off the Newfoundland coast. Echoing Woodrow Wilson's **Fourteen Points**, and the **Four Freedoms** of Roosevelt's Jan 1941 State of the Union Address, the charter called for the rights of self-determination, self-government and free speech for all peoples, promised a more equitable international economic system, and called for the abandonment of the use of force, pending the establishment of a system of general

security. After the entry of the USA into the war, the charter was endorsed internationally by the inclusion of its provisions in the Declaration of the United Nations signed by the USA, Great Britain, the USSR and China, on 1 Jan 1942, and by 22 other states on the following day. It served as an ideological basis for Allied cooperation during the war. ▷ **World War II**

Attlee (of Walthamstow), Clement (Richard), 1st Earl (1883–1967)
English politician and Prime Minister of Britain. Early converted to **socialism**, he became the first Labour Mayor of Stepney (1919–20), an MP (1922), Deputy Leader of the Opposition (1931–5), and then Leader (1935). He was Dominions Secretary (1942–3) and Deputy Prime Minister (1942–5) in Winston **Churchill**'s war cabinet. As Prime Minister (1945–51), he carried through a vigorous programme of nationalization and social welfare, including the introduction of the National Health Service (1948). His government granted independence to India (1947) and Burma (1948). He was Leader of the Opposition again (1951–5) until he resigned and accepted an earldom.

Auchinleck, Sir Claude (John Eyre) (1884–1981)
British field marshal. He joined the 62nd Punjabis in 1904, and served in Egypt and Mesopotamia. In **World War II**, he commanded in northern Norway and India, and then moved to the Middle East (1941). He made a successful advance into Cyrenaica, but was later thrown back by Rommel. His regrouping of the 8th Army on **El Alamein** is now recognized as a successful defensive operation, but at the time he was made a scapegoat for the retreat, and replaced (1942). In 1943 he returned to India, serving subsequently as Supreme Commander India and Pakistan (1947). ▷ **North African Campaign**

Augsburg, League of (1686)
The alliance against French territorial expansionism (the *réunion* policy of Louis XIV), formed by Emperor Leopold I, Spain, Bavaria and various circles of the empire. The accession to it of England, the Netherlands and Savoy during the subsequent War of the League of Augsburg (1688–97, also known as the War of the Palatinate Succession) created the so-called Grand Alliance. Following the devastation of the Palatinate (1689) and a joint English–Dutch naval victory at the Battle of La Hogue (1692), the eventual peace treaty (Treaty of **Rijswijk**, 1697) restored the

independence of Lorraine but confirmed France's possession of Alsace.

Augustine, St (d.604)

The first Archbishop of Canterbury. He was prior of a Benedictine monastery at Rome, when in 596 Pope **Gregory I** sent him with 40 other monks to convert the **Anglo-Saxons** to Christianity. He was kindly received by **Ethelbert**, King of Kent, whose wife was a Christian, and the conversion and baptism of the King contributed greatly to his success. Augustine was made Bishop of the English in 597, and established his church at Canterbury. His efforts to extend his authority over the native Celtic Christianity were less successful. He died at Canterbury, and in 612 his body was transferred to the abbey of Saints Peter and Paul, now the site of St Augustine's Missionary College (1848).

Axis Powers

The name given to the co-operation of Nazi Germany and Fascist Italy (1936–45), first used by **Mussolini**. In May 1939 the two countries signed a formal treaty, the Pact of Steel. In Sep 1940, Germany, Italy and Japan signed a tripartite agreement, after which all three were referred to as Axis Powers. ▷ **World War II**

B

Babington, Antony (1561–86)

English Roman Catholic conspirator. He served as a page to **Mary, Queen of Scots**, when she was a prisoner at Sheffield. In 1586, he was induced by John Ballard and others to lead a conspiracy towards **Elizabeth I**'s murder and Mary's release (the Babington Plot). Cipher messages were intercepted by **Walsingham** in which Mary warmly approved the plot, and these were later used against her. Babington fled, but was captured and executed with the others.

Bacon, Francis, Viscount St Albans (1561–1626)

English philosopher and statesman. He became an MP in 1584, and was knighted by **James VI and I** in 1603. He was in turn Solicitor-General (1607), Attorney-General (1613), Privy Counsellor (1616), Lord Keeper (1617), and Lord Chancellor (1618). He became Lord Verulam in 1618, and was made viscount in 1621. However, complaints were made that he accepted bribes from suitors in his court, and he was publicly accused before his fellow peers, fined, imprisoned, and banished from parliament and the court. Although soon released, and later pardoned, he never returned to public office, and died deeply in debt.

Baden-Powell, Robert (Stephenson Smyth), 1st Baron (1857–1941)

British general. Educated at Charterhouse, he joined the army, served in India and Afghanistan, was on the staff in Ashanti and Matabeleland, and won fame as the defender of Mafeking in the second Boer War. He founded the Boy Scout movement (1908) and, with his sister Agnes (1858–1945), the Girl Guides (1910). ▷
Boer Wars; Mafeking, Siege of

Bagehot, Walter (1826–77)

English economist, journalist, and political theorist. He studied mathematics at London, and spent some time as a banker in his father's firm, then became editor of the *Economist* in 1860. His *English Constitution* (1867) is still considered a standard work. His *Physics and Politics* (1872) applied the theory of evolution to politics. He advocated many constitutional reforms, including the introduction of life peers.

Balaclava, Battle of (25 Oct 1854)
A battle fought between British and Russian forces during the early stages of the **Crimean War**. The Russian attack on the British base at Balaclava was unsuccessful, but the British sustained the heavier losses. ▷ **Charge of the Light Brigade**

Baldwin (of Bewdley), Stanley, 1st Earl (1867–1947)
English politician and Prime Minister of Britain. He worked in his family business before becoming a Conservative MP in 1908. He was President of the Board of Trade (1921–2) and Chancellor of the Exchequer (1922–3), and then unexpectedly succeeded Bonar **Law** as Prime Minister. His periods of office (1923–4, 1924–9 and 1935–7) included the **General Strike** (1926) and was interrupted by the two minority Labour governments of 1924 and 1929–31. During the **MacDonald** coalition (1931–5), he served as Lord President of the Council. He played a leading role in arranging the abdication of **Edward VIII** in 1936. He resigned from politics in 1937, when he was made an earl. ▷ **Conservative Party**

Balfour, Arthur James, 1st Earl (1848–1930)
Scottish politician. He entered parliament in 1874, becoming Secretary for Scotland (1886) and Chief Secretary for Ireland (1887–91), where his policy of suppression earned him the name of 'Bloody Balfour'. A Conservative, he was Prime Minister (1902–5) and First Lord of the Admiralty (1915–16). As Foreign Secretary (1916–19), he was responsible for the **Balfour Declaration** (1917), which promised Zionists a national home in Palestine. He resigned in 1922, was created an earl, but served again as Lord President (1925–9). ▷ **Zionism**

Balfour Declaration (2 Nov 1917)
A short communication from the British Foreign Secretary, A J Balfour, to Lord Rothschild, expressing the British government's disposition towards a Jewish national home in Palestine. The central portion reads: 'His Majesty's Government view with

favour the establishment in Palestine of a national home for the Jewish people ... it being clearly understood that nothing shall be done which may prejudice the civil and religious rights of existing non-Jewish communities'. Britain having received the Mandate for Palestine in 1920, the vagueness of the Balfour Declaration was clarified in 1923: Jewish immigration was to be encouraged; an appropriate Jewish body formed to that end; the rights of non-Jews were to be protected; and English, Hebrew and Arabic were to be given equal status. However, the ensuing two decades showed Britain to be either unwilling or unable to deliver its promise to the Jews, especially in view of increasing Arab hostility to Jewish immigration. ▷ **Haganah; Irgun; Zionism**

Balliol, Edward (c.1283–1364)

King of Scots (1332/56). He was the elder son of John **Balliol**. In 1332, accompanied by the 'disinherited barons' bent on recovering their forfeited Scottish estates, he landed with 3 400 followers at Kinghorn, Fife; and at Dupplin Moor, Perthshire, on 12 Aug, surprised and routed the Scottish Army under the new Regent, the Earl of Mar. On 24 Sep he was crowned King of Scotland at Scone. Less than three months later, he was himself surprised at Annan and fled across the Border on an unsaddled horse. Two further incursions into Scotland, in 1334–35, were unsuccessful and he resigned his claims to the Scottish throne to **Edward III** in 1356. He died without heirs.

Balliol, John (c.1250–1313)

King of Scots (1292/96). On the death of Margaret, the 'Maid of Norway' in 1290, he became a claimant to the crown of Scotland; and was supported by **Edward I** of England against Robert **Bruce**, Lord of Annandale. Balliol swore fealty to Edward before and after his investiture at Scone (1292) and was forced to repudiate the Treaty of Bingham of 1290 with its guarantees of Scottish liberties. By 1295 a council of 12 of the magnates had taken control of government out of his hands and concluded an alliance with France, then at war with England; Edward invaded Scotland, took Balliol prisoner, and forced him to surrender his crown (10 July 1296). Balliol was confined for three years at Hertford and in the Tower; in 1302 he was permitted to retire to his estates in **Normandy**.

Bannockburn, Battle of (21 June 1314)
A battle fought near Stirling between English forces under **Edward II** and the Scots under Robert **Bruce**. It resulted in a decisive victory for the Scots. The English Army was largely destroyed, and many English nobles were killed or captured. The battle made Bruce a national hero, and inspired Scottish counter-attacks against northern England.

Barebone's Parliament (4 July–12 Dec 1653)
The English 'Parliament of Saints', nominated by the Council of Officers of the Army to succeed the **Rump Parliament**; named after radical member Praise-God Barebone. It instituted civil marriage and sought legal reforms; but collapsed after disagreements over the abolition of tithes and lay patronage in church.

Barons Wars (1215–17 and 1263–7)
Two wars in England during the reigns of **John** and **Henry III**. The first came about after the sealing of **Magna Carta**: many barons still defied John, and offered the crown to Prince Louis (later Louis VIII) of France. After John's death, the French and baronial army was routed at Lincoln (May 1217), and the war was effectively ended by the Treaty of Kingston-on-Thames (Sep 1217). The second war broke out after the Provisions of Oxford failed to achieve a settlement, and some barons led by Simon de **Montfort**, captured Henry III at Lewes (1264). Earl Simon was killed at Evesham (1265), and the King was restored to power by the Dictum of Kenilworth (1266). ▷ **Oxford, Provisions of**

Barrier Treaties (1697, 1709 and 1715)
A series of agreements giving the Dutch Republic the right to garrison certain towns in the southern Netherlands as a protection against potential French encroachments. The first was signed between the Dutch and Spain in 1697, the second between the Dutch and the English in 1709, and the third between the Dutch, the English, and the Austrians in 1715. In the War of the Austrian Succession (1740–8) the towns were overrun by the French; in 1781 Emperor Joseph II declared the treaties void and returned the garrisons to the Netherlands.

Beaton (Bethune), David (1494–1546)
Scottish statesman and Roman Catholic prelate. He resided at the French court (1519) and was appointed Bishop of Mirepoix

by Francis I (1537). In 1525 he took his seat in the Scots parliament as Abbot of Arbroath and became Privy Seal. Elevated to cardinal (1538), and made Archbishop of St Andrews (1539), he championed French interests at the expense of English influence. A persecutor of the Scottish Protestants, he had the reformer George Wishart burnt at St Andrews (1546), but was murdered in revenge three months later by a group of Protestant conspirators. ▷ **Reformation** (Scotland)

Beatty, David Beatty, 1st Earl (1871–1936)

British admiral. He served in the Sudan (1896–8), and as battleship commander took part in the China War (1900). At the outbreak of **World War I** he steamed into Heligoland Bight, and destroyed three German cruisers. He later sank the *Blücher* (Jan 1915), and took part in the Battle of **Jutland** (May 1916). He became Commander-in-Chief of the Grand Fleet in 1916 and First Sea Lord in 1919, when he was created an earl.

Beaufort, Henry (1377–1447)

English cardinal and political figure. He studied at Oxford and Aix-la-Chapelle, was consecrated Bishop of Lincoln (1398) and Winchester (1405), and became a cardinal in 1426. He was Lord Chancellor on three occasions (1403–5, 1413–17, 1424–6). In 1427 the Pope sent him as legate into Germany, to organize a crusade against the Hussites; this undertaking failed, and he fell from papal pleasure. During the 1430s he controlled the government of the young King **Henry VI** of England. He retired from politics in 1443. ▷ **Hussite Wars**

Beaufort, Margaret (1443–1509)

Daughter of John, 1st Duke of Somerset, and great-granddaughter of **John of Gaunt**, Duke of Lancaster. She married Edmund Tudor, Earl of Richmond (1455), and became the mother of **Henry VII**, to whom she conveyed the Lancastrian claim to the English crown. She was twice widowed before her third husband, Thomas, Lord Stanley, was instrumental in helping Henry VII assume the crown. She was a benefactress of William Caxton, and of Oxford and Cambridge.

Becket, St Thomas (à) (1118–70)

English saint and martyr, Archbishop of Canterbury. The son of a wealthy Norman merchant, he studied canon law at Bologna and Auxerre. In 1155, he became Chancellor, the first Englishman since the **Norman Conquest** to hold high office. A skilled diplomat and brilliant courtly figure, he changed dramatically when created Archbishop of Canterbury (1162), resigning the chancellorship, and becoming a zealous ascetic, serving the Church as vigorously as he had **Henry II**. He thus came into conflict with the King's aims to keep the clergy in subordination to the state. He unwillingly consented to the Constitutions of Clarendon (1164) defining the powers of Church and state, but remained in disfavour. He fled the country after having his goods confiscated and the revenues of his sees sequestered. After two years in France, he pleaded personally to the Pope, and was reinstated in his see. In 1170 he was reconciled with Henry, and returned to Canterbury, amid great public rejoicing. New quarrels soon broke out, however, and Henry's rashly-voiced wish to be rid of 'this turbulent priest' led to Becket's murder in Canterbury cathedral (29 Dec 1170) by four of the King's knights. He was canonized in 1173, and Henry did public penance at his tomb in 1174.

Bedchamber Crisis

A political crisis which occurred in May 1839, after **Melbourne**, Prime Minister in the Whig government, offered to resign, and advised the young Queen **Victoria** to appoint **Peel** and the **Tories**. The Queen refused to dismiss certain ladies of the Bedchamber with Whig sympathies, whereupon Peel refused office and the Whig government continued. ▷ **Whigs**

Bede (St Baeda or the Venerable Bede) (c.673–735)

Anglo-Saxon scholar, historian and theologian. He studied as a child at the Benedictine monastery at Wearmouth under Benedict Biscop, and in 682 moved to the new monastery at Jarrow, where he was ordained. He remained there the rest of his life, writing homilies, lives, hymns, epigrams, works on chronology, physical science and grammar, and commentaries on the Old and New Testament. His greatest work is the *Historia Ecclesiastica Gentis Anglorum* (Ecclesiastical History of the English People), the source of almost all our information on the history of England before 731, said to have been translated into English by **Alfred, 'the Great'**. He was canonized in 1899.

Bedford, John of Lancaster, Duke of (1389–1435)

English general and statesman. He was the third son of **Henry IV**. In 1414 his brother, **Henry V**, created him Duke of Bedford, and during the King's campaigns against France he was appointed Lieutenant of the Kingdom. After Henry's death (1422), he became Guardian of England and Regent of France. When Charles VI died, he had his nephew proclaimed King of France and England as **Henry VI**. In the **Hundred Years War**, he defeated the French in several battles, notably at Verneuil (1424), but an army under **Joan of Arc** forced him onto the defensive (1429).

Beecroft, John (1790–1854)

British trader, explorer and consul. He was influential in promoting the conquest of Lagos in 1851. Beecroft arrived in West Africa in 1828 as a trader on the island of Fernando Po, which the British occupied as a naval base and settlement for freed slaves during the period 1827–34. He administered the island under the Spanish flag, but later he explored the Niger Delta and in 1849 was appointed Consul for the Bights of Benin and Biafra. He promoted legitimate commerce and the suppression of the slave trade.

Benbow, John (1653–1702)

British admiral. His main engagements were in the Nine Years War (1690, 1693 and 1694) and the War of the **Spanish Succession**, when he came upon a superior French force in the West Indies (1702). For four days he kept up a running fight from Santa Marta, almost deserted by the rest of his squadron, until he was wounded. He was forced to return to Jamaica, where he died.

Bengal Presidency

The original British **East India Company** designation for lands around Calcutta under its direct administrative control. The Bengal Presidency bordered Bihar and Orissa to the west, Sikkim and Bhutan to the north and Assam and Burma to the east. It was from the Bengal Presidency that the Company's greatest expansion of influence and control took place in the 18c and 19c, and it was also from there that most of the old Mughal Empire was informally controlled until 1858. The Bengal Presidency was the senior administrative area, and the Governor of Bengal was in fact the Governor-General of British India. The term and administrative area of the Bengal Presidency remained current even after the dissolution of the Company.

Ben-Gurion, David (1886–1973)
Israeli politician. Born in Poland, he emigrated to Palestine in 1906. Expelled by the Turks during **World War I**, he recruited Jews to the British Army in North America. In Palestine in 1919 he founded a socialist party and became Secretary to the Histadrut in 1921. He led the Mapai Party from its formation in 1930 and headed the Jewish Agency in 1935. Ben-Gurion moulded the Mapai into the main party of the Yishuv during British rule and became Prime Minister (1948–53) after independence, when he was responsible for Israel absorbing large numbers of refugees from Europe and Arab countries. He was Prime Minister again from 1955 to 1963.

Benn, Tony (Anthony (Neil) Wedgwood Benn) (1925–   )
English politician. The son of Viscount Stansgate, he became a Labour MP in 1950 but was debarred from the Commons on succeeding to his father's title. He renounced his title, and was re-elected in a by-election in 1963. He held various government posts under Harold **Wilson** and James **Callaghan**, notably Minister of Technology (1966–70), Secretary for Industry (1974–5) and Secretary for Energy (1975–9). He was the main focus for the left-wing challenge to the Labour leadership in the late 1970s and 1980s which ultimately failed but which persuaded some on the right to leave the party and form the **Social Democratic Party**. ▷
Foot, Michael; Kinnock, Neil; Labour Party

Bentham, Jeremy (1748–1832)
English writer on jurisprudence and utilitarian ethics. He was called to the Bar in 1767, though he never practised, being more interested in the theory of the law. His publications include *A Fragment on Government* (1776), and *Introduction to the Principles of Morals and Legislation* (1789), which present his theory of hedonistic utilitarianism. He held that laws should be socially useful and not merely reflect the *status quo*, and that all actions are right when they promote 'the happiness of the greatest number' (a phrase which he popularized). He travelled widely on the Continent. Supporters of his utilitarian ideas (the Benthamites) attempted to apply them to public policy (1830s and 1840s). He was also a founder of University College, London, where his skeleton, dressed in his clothes, is preserved.

Bentinck, Hans Willem, Baron (1649–1709)

Friend, confidant and agent of Stadholder William III (later King **William III** of England). Bentinck was a page to William III, and in time took on vital missions for his master, such as the marriage negotiations between William and Princess Mary, daughter of **Charles I** of England, and the role and input of Amsterdam in the invasion of England by William's forces in 1688. When William had succeeded to the English throne, he made Bentinck the first Duke of Portland in 1689; Bentinck remained a key figure at William's court, in war, peace and diplomacy. ▷ **Glorious Revolution**

Bentinck, William Henry Cavendish, 3rd Duke of Portland
(1738–1809)

English politician. He entered Lord **Rockingham**'s cabinet in 1765, and succeeded him as leader of the Whig Party. Although twice Prime Minister (1783 and 1807–9), he is best remembered as Home Secretary, in what was effectively a Tory government, under William **Pitt**, 'the Younger', with charge of Irish affairs (1794–1801). ▷ **Whigs**

Bentinck, William (Henry Cavendish), Lord (1774–1839)

English soldier and Governor-General of India. The second son of the 3rd Duke of Portland, in 1791 he became an army officer. Appointed Governor of Madras in 1803, he was recalled from India following a mutiny of native soldiers, and commanded troops during the **Napoleonic Wars** in Spain and Sicily. A liberal Whig in his political sympathies, in 1811 he was entrusted with reorganizing Sicily where he forced a constitution on the reactionary Bourbon King, Ferdinand I. In 1814–15 he championed the cause of Italian independence and constitutional government but was unable to persuade the authorities in Britain to share his vision. On his return to Britain he was elected to parliament. He later became Governor-General of India (1828–35), where he introduced important administrative reforms.

Berwick, James Fitzjames, 1st Duke of (1670–1734)

French and Jacobite general. He was the illegitimate son of James VII of Scotland and II of England. Educated in France as a Catholic, he was created Duke of Berwick (1687), but fled from England at the Glorious Revolution. He fought in his father's

Irish campaign (1689–91), and then in Flanders and against the Camisards. In 1706 he was created a Marshal of France, and in Spain established the throne of Philip V by the decisive victory of Almansa (1707) in the War of the **Spanish Succession**. Appointed Commander-in-Chief of the French forces (1733), he was killed while besieging Phillippsburg. ▷ **James VII and II; Jacobites**

Besant, Annie (1847–1933)

British theosophist and social reformer. Brought up in Harrow, she married the Rev Frank Besant, but was separated from him in 1873. From secularism and **Bradlaugh** she passed in 1889 to Madame Blavatsky and theosophy, becoming its high priestess from 1891. In her later years she went to India, where she championed the causes of nationalism and education.

Bevan, Aneurin (1897–1960)

Welsh politician. One of 13 children, he worked in the pits on leaving school at 13, and led the Welsh miners in the 1926 **General Strike**. He entered parliament for the **Independent Labour Party** in 1929, joining the **Labour Party** in 1931. He established a reputation as a brilliant, irreverent, and often tempestuous orator. As Minister of Health (1945–51), he introduced the National Health Service (1948). He became Minister of Labour in 1951, but resigned in the same year over the National Health charges proposed in the Budget. From this period dated 'Bevanism', a left-wing movement to make the Labour Party more socialist and less 'reformist'. He married Jennie **Lee** in 1934, and died while still an MP. ▷ **socialism**

Beveridge, William Henry Beveridge, 1st Baron (1879–1963)

British economist, administrator, and social reformer. He entered the Board of Trade (1908) and became the Director of Labour Exchanges (1909–16). He was Director of the London School of Economics (1919–37) and Master of University College, Oxford (1937–45). He is best known as the author of the *Report on Social Insurance and Allied Services* (The Beveridge Report, 1942), which provided a blueprint for the creation of the welfare state. He was knighted in 1919, became a Liberal MP (1944–6), and was made a baron in 1946. ▷ **Liberal Party**

Bevin, Ernest (1881–1951)

English politician. Orphaned by the age of seven, and self-taught, he early came under the influence of trade unionism and the Baptists, and was for a time a lay preacher. A paid official of the dockers' union, he gained a national reputation in 1920 when he won most of his union's claims against an eminent barrister, earning the title of 'the dockers' KC'. He built up the National Transport and General Workers' Union, and became its General-Secretary (1921–40). In 1940 he became a Labour MP, Minister of Labour and National Service in Winston **Churchill**'s coalition government, and was Foreign Secretary in the Labour governments (1945–51). ▷ **Labour Party**

Bill of Rights (1689)

A Bill to enact the **Declaration of Rights** (1689), it asserted that **James II** (of England) had abdicated, established **William III** and Mary II as monarchs, forbade Roman Catholics from succeeding to the throne, and declared illegal exercise of royal power, such as the maintenance of an army in peacetime, without the consent of parliament.

Birkenhead, Frederick Edwin Smith, 1st Earl of (1872–1930)

English politician and lawyer. A Conservative, he entered parliament in 1906, where he became known as a brilliant orator. In the Irish crisis (1914) he supported resistance to **Home Rule**, but later helped to negotiate the Irish settlement of 1921. He became Attorney-General (1915–19) and Lord Chancellor (1919–22) and was made an earl in 1922. His conduct as Secretary of State for India (1924–8) caused much criticism, and he resigned to devote himself to a commercial career. ▷ **Conservative Party**

Bishops Wars (1639–40)

Two wars between **Charles I** of England and the Scottish **Covenanters**, caused by his unpopular policies towards the Scottish Kirk. They resulted in English defeats, and bankruptcy for Charles, who was then forced to call the Short and Long Parliaments (1640), bringing to an end his 'personal rule' (1629–40). ▷ **Long Parliament; Short Parliament**

Black and Tans

Additional members of the Royal Irish Constabulary, recruited by the British government to cope with Irish nationalist unrest in

1920. The shortage of regulation uniforms led to the recruits being issued with khaki tunics and trousers and very dark green caps, hence their name. Terrorist activities provoked severe and brutal reprisals by the Black and Tans, which caused an outcry in Britain and the USA.

Black Death
The common name for the virulent bubonic and pneumonic plague that swept through West and Central Europe from Asia (1347–51). It reached England in 1348. Approximately 25 million people, about a third of the European population, perished; in England it has been estimated that the population in 1400 was aproximately half that of a century earlier, and about 1 000 villages were destroyed or depopulated. With the reduction of labour available to cultivate the land, land-owners were forced to offer wages in place of the old feudal traditions to keep their tenants and this, coupled with generally higher rates charged by the remaining craftsmen and traders, brought the possibility of social change to a hitherto strictly stratified society. The consequences of the plague varied from region to region (the economy of southern England continued to thrive, for example) and the subsequent pandemic recurrence of the plague (eg in 1361–3, 1369–71, 1374–5, 1390 and 1400) proved equally important in initiating social and economic change.

Black Hole of Calcutta
A small badly-ventilated room in which surviving British defenders were imprisoned following Calcutta's capture (June 1756) by **Siraj ud-Daula**, Nawab of Bengal. It was claimed that only 23 out of 146 prisoners survived. Following possibly self-serving publicity by J Z Holwell, the incident became famous in the history of British imperialism, but the circumstances are controversial, and the total number of prisoners was probably much smaller.

Black Saturday (26 Jan 1952)
After guerrilla attacks on their bases in Egypt, the British acted against suspects, including the Egyptian police. British forces surrounded police headquarters at Ismailia and called on the police to surrender; they refused and 50 were killed in the attack on their headquarters. The next day — Black Saturday — Egyptian crowds, led by the Muslim Brotherhood, burnt down British and

foreign shops and restaurants in the centre of Cairo. Egyptian troops did not intervene to bring the situation under control until evening. King Farouk and the government blamed each other for the delay and there began a period of ministerial instability, as governments followed one another rapidly. This led the Free Officers to bring forward the coup they were planning for 1954 or 1955 to July 1952, when army units seized key points in the capital and Farouk was forced into exile.

blackshirts
The colloquial name for members of Oswald **Mosley**'s British Union of Fascists (BUF), formed in Oct 1932. It derived from the colour of the uniforms worn at mass rallies and demonstrations organized by the BUF on the model of European fascist parties. After clashes and disturbances in Jewish areas of London (1936), the Public Order Act prohibited the wearing of uniforms by political groups. ▷ **Union Movement**

Blake, Robert (1599–1657)
English admiral. He lived in Oxford as a quiet country gentleman until he was 40. In 1640 he was returned for Bridgwater to the **Short Parliament**, and later served in the **Long Parliament** (1645–53) and the **Barebone's Parliament** (1653). In 1649 he blockaded Lisbon, destroying the squadron of Prince **Rupert**, and in 1652–3 routed the Dutch in several battles. His greatest victory was his last, at Santa Cruz, when he destroyed a Spanish treasure fleet off Tenerife; but he died on the return journey to England. ▷ **Anglo-Dutch Wars; English Civil Wars**

Blenheim, Battle of (1704)
The greatest military triumph of **Marlborough** and his Imperial ally, Prince Eugene of Savoy, in the War of the **Spanish Succession**. Fought on the Danube to prevent a combined Franco Bavarian thrust on Vienna, it marked the first major defeat of Louis XIV of France's armies, and the first major English victory on the European mainland since the Battle of **Agincourt**.

Bligh, William (c.1753–c.1817)
English sailor. He sailed under Captain James **Cook** in his second world voyage (1772–4), and in 1787 was sent as commander of the *Bounty* to Tahiti. On the return voyage, the men mutinied

under his harsh treatment. In Apr 1789, Bligh and 18 men were cast adrift in an open boat without charts. In June, after great hardship, he arrived at Timor, near Java, having sailed his frail craft for 3 618 miles. In 1805 he was appointed Governor of New South Wales, where his conduct led to his imprisonment for two years. He was promoted admiral in 1811.

blitz

The colloquial name for the series of air raids on British cities by the German Air Force (Sep 1940–May 1941). The purpose of the raids was to weaken British resistance to projected invasion. The cities of London and Coventry were particularly badly affected.
▷ **Luftwaffe; World War II**

Blood, Thomas (c.1618–80)

Irish adventurer. Celebrated for his activities during the **English Civil Wars** and **Restoration**, his most famous exploit was the attempt, disguised as a clergyman, to steal the crown jewels from the Tower of London (May 1671). After nearly murdering the keeper of the jewels, he succeeded in taking the crown, while one of his associates bore away the orb. He was pursued, captured, and imprisoned, but later pardoned by King **Charles II** of England.

Bloody Assizes

The name given to the western circuit assizes in England in the summer of 1685, presided over by Lord Chief Justice George **Jeffreys** after the defeat of the Duke of **Monmouth** at the Battle of **Sedgemoor**. About 150 of Monmouth's followers, mostly poorer farmers and clothworkers, were executed, and 800 transported to the West Indies.

Bloody Sunday (13 Nov 1887)

The name conventionally given to clashes between police and demonstrators in Trafalgar Square, London, at a meeting called to protest against a ban on open-air meetings and to call for the release of an Irish MP who had been supporting a rent strike. Two demonstrators were killed. The meeting took place against a background of economic depression, widespread unemployment and Irish nationalist unrest.

Bloody Sunday (30 Jan 1972)

The name given, especially by Republicans in Northern Ireland, to events occurring during a Catholic civil rights protest march in Londonderry. The British Army opened fire, killing 14, mainly young, demonstrators. This action led to increased support for the **IRA** and to many more deaths from political violence. Indirectly, it led to the ending of the **Stormont** parliament and the reimposition of direct rule by the British government over Northern Ireland.

Blücher, Gebbard Leberecht von, Prince von Wahlstadt

(1742–1819)

Prussian field marshal. He fought against the French in 1793 and 1806, and completed **Wellington**'s victory at the Battle of **Waterloo** by his timely appearance on the field.

bluestockings

A nickname, usually with derogatory connotations, for educated women. The term was widely used when opportunities expanded for the education of middle-class women in the late 19c, but it originated in the Blue Stocking Club at Montagu House, London, c.1750.

Blunt, Anthony (Frederick) (1907–83)

British double agent. An art historian, he became a Fellow at Trinity College, Cambridge (1932), where he shared in the left-wing communist-respecting tendencies of the time, and first met **Burgess**, **Philby** and **Maclean**. Influenced by Burgess, he acted as a 'talent-spotter', supplying to him the names of likely recruits to the Soviet communist cause, and during his war-service in British Intelligence, was in a position to pass on information to the Soviet government. Although his spying activities appear to have ceased after the war, he was still able to assist the defection of Burgess and Maclean in 1951, although suspected by British Intelligence. In 1964, after the defection of Philby, a confession was obtained from Blunt in return for his immunity, and he continued as Surveyor of the Queen's Pictures until 1972. His full involvement in espionage was made public only in 1979, and his knighthood (awarded 1956) was annulled.

Boadicea ▷ Boudicca

Boer Wars (1880–1 and 1899–1902)
Two wars fought by the British and the Boers for the mastery of southern Africa. The British had made several attempts to re-incorporate the Boers, who had left the Cape Colony in the **Great Trek**, within a South African confederation. The first Boer War ended with the defeat of the British at **Majuba Hill**, and the signing of the Pretoria and London Conventions of 1881 and 1884. In 1896 the **Jameson Raid** was a clumsy private effort to achieve the same objective. The second Boer War can be divided into three phases: (1) (Oct 1899–Jan 1900) a series of Boer successes, including the sieges of **Ladysmith**, **Kimberley**, and **Mafeking**, as well as victories at Stormberg, Modder River, Magersfontein, Colenso, and Moderspruit; (2) (Feb–Aug 1900) counter-offensives by Lord **Roberts**, including the raising of the sieges, the victory at Paardeberg, and the capture of Pretoria; (3) (Sep 1900–May 1902) a period of guerrilla warfare when **Kitchener** attempted to prevent Boer commando raids on isolated British units and lines of communication. The Boers effectively won the peace. They maintained control of 'native affairs', won back representative government in 1907, and federated South Africa on their terms in 1910. On the other hand, British interests in South Africa were protected and, despite internal strains, the Union of South Africa entered both **World War I** and **World War II** on the British side. ▷ **Vereeniging, Peace of**

Boleyn, Anne (c.1504–36)
Queen of England. She was the second wife of **Henry VIII** and the daughter of Sir Thomas Boleyn by Elizabeth Howard. Secretly married to Henry (Jan 1533), she was soon declared his legal wife (May); but within three months his passion for her had cooled. It was not revived by the birth (Sep 1533) of a daughter (later **Elizabeth I**), still less by that of a stillborn son (Jan 1536). She was arrested and brought to the Tower, convicted of treason on fragile evidence, and beheaded (19 May). Henry married Jane **Seymour** 11 days later.

Bolingbroke, Henry St John, 1st Viscount (1678–1751)
English politician. After travelling in Europe, he entered parliament (1701), becoming Secretary for War (1704), Foreign Secretary (1710), and joint leader of the Tory Party. He was made a peer in 1712. On the death of Queen **Anne** (1714), his Jacobite sympathies forced him to flee to France, where he wrote *Reflec-*

tions on Exile. He returned for a while to England (1725–35), but unable to attain political office he went back to France (1735–42). His last years were spent in London, where his works included the influential *Idea of a Patriot King* (1749). ▷ **Tories**

Bombay Presidency
The original British **East India Company** designation for lands around Bombay under its direct administrative control. The Bombay Presidency bordered Baroda and the Rajput States to the north, the Central Provinces, the Principality of Hyderabad to the east and Mysore to the south. The term and administrative area of the Bombay Presidency remained current even after the dissolution of the Company. ▷ **British India**

Boniface, St (originally, Wynfrith) (c.672–754)
English Benedictine missionary, known as the 'Apostle of Germany'. He became a monk in Exeter, and in 718 was commissioned to preach the Gospel to all the tribes of Germany. He met with great success, and was made Bishop, Primate of Germany (732), and Archbishop of Mainz (746). His work in christianizing Bavaria paved the way for its being incorporated into the Carolingian Empire. He enjoyed the whole-hearted support of Charles Martel, Carloman and Pepin the Short, who used the discipline of the Church as a means of subduing rebellious magnates. The opposition this aroused forced Boniface into a less prominent role after 747 and he was killed by the heathen in Frisia in 754.

Boston Massacre (5 Mar 1770)
The first bloodshed of the **American Revolution**. In an atmosphere of intense resentment against British troops and regulations, on 5 Mar 1770 British guards opened fire on an unruly crowd, killing five. Of the nine British soldiers tried for murder, seven, including the commander, were acquitted and two were found guilty of manslaughter.

Boston Tea Party (1773)
During the **American Revolution**, the climactic event of resistance to British attempts at direct taxation, resulting in the destruction of 342 chests of dutied tea by working men disguised as Indians. Other ports had refused to let the tea ships enter. ▷ **Intolerable Acts**

Bosworth Field, Battle of (22 Aug 1485)

The battle which put **Henry VII** on the English throne after victory over **Richard III**, who died in the conflict. Henry Tudor's forces were possibly inferior in number, but proved more loyal; they received crucial support from the Stanley family, who had feet in both camps. ▷ **Tudors, House of**

Bothwell, James Hepburn, 4th Earl of (c.1535–78)

Scottish nobleman and third husband of **Mary, Queen of Scots**. One of the greatest nobles in Scotland, he was held responsible for the abduction and murder of Mary's second husband, Lord **Darnley** (1567). He was made Duke of Orkney, then married Mary, but faced opposition from the nobles. He fled to Denmark after Mary's surrender to rebel forces at Carberry Hill, and was imprisoned in Dragsholm, where he died insane.

Boudicca (also known as Boadicea) (1c AD)

Warrior-queen. She was the wife of Prasutagus, King of the **Iceni**, a tribe inhabiting what is now Norfolk and Suffolk. On her husband's death (AD60), the Romans seized her territory and treated the inhabitants brutally. She gathered a large army, destroyed the Roman colony of Camulodunum, took Londinium and Verulamium, and put to death as many as 70 000 Romans. Defeated in battle by Suetonius Paulinus, she took poison.

Bouvines, Battle of (27 July 1214)

The battle near Valenciennes in northern France, at which King Philip Augustus of France defeated the armies of the Holy Roman Emperor Otto IV, the Count of Flanders, and King **John** (Lackland) of England. This victory consolidated the power of the French monarchy over its vassals, led to Otto's deposition as Emperor, to the loss of **Normandy** by King John, and probably contributed to his acceptance of **Magna Carta** (1215).

Boycott, Charles Cunningham (1832–97)

English soldier. As land agent for Lord Erne in County Mayo, he was one of the first victims in 1880 of **Parnell**'s system of social excommunication. His name is the source of the word 'boycott' in English.

Boyne, Battle of the (12 July 1690)

A battle fought near Drogheda, County Louth, Ireland, between Protestant forces under **William III** of Great Britain and smaller Catholic forces led by **James VII and II**. William's decisive victory enabled him to capture Dublin, and marked a critical stage in the English reconquest of Ireland. It ended James's campaign to regain the English throne. The anniversary is celebrated annually by Protestant marches in Northern Ireland.

Bradlaugh, Charles (1833–91)

English free-thinking social reformer. He became a busy secularist lecturer, and a pamphleteer under the name of 'Iconoclast'. In 1880 he became an MP, and claimed the right as an unbeliever to make affirmation of allegiance instead of taking the parliamentary oath; but the House refused to allow him to do either. He was re-elected on three occasions, and finally was admitted (1886). ▷ **Besant, Annie**

Breda, Peace of (31 July 1667)

The treaty which brought an end to the second of the **Anglo-Dutch Wars**, following hard on the heels of Michiel de Ruyter's raid on Chatham Docks (June 1667). This improved the terms of the peace for the Dutch Republic: they lost their North American colonies to England (New Amsterdam became New York, after James Duke of York, the King's brother and future monarch himself), but the Dutch retained Surinam in South America and the English gave up their claims to the Moluccan islands in the East Indies. The English Navigation Acts were also relaxed to allow more Dutch trade into England. ▷ **Chatham, Dutch Descent on**

brehon laws

A corpus of ancient Irish customary law written down by the 8c; the name derives from Irish *breitheamh*, 'judge'. Following the Anglo-Norman invasion of Ireland in the late 12c, Irish law gave much ground to English common law. It was finally abolished by statute in the early 17c.

Bright, John (1811–89)

British politician and orator. A quaker, he worked in his father's cotton mill, and took an interest in public questions. He became a leading member of the **Anti-Corn Law League** (1839), and engaged in free-trade agitation. A radical-Liberal, he was MP for Durham (1843), Manchester (1847), and Birmingham (1857), and was closely associated with the Reform Act of 1867. He later held several government posts, until his retirement in 1882. ▷ **Reform Acts**

Britain, Battle of (1940)

The name given to the air war campaign of late summer 1940 in which the German **Luftwaffe** attempted to destroy the Royal Air Force (RAF) as a prelude to the invasion of Great Britain. The aerial offensive began in Aug, the German bomber aircraft and fighter escorts concentrating on wiping out the RAF both by combat in the air and by bombing their vital airfields in the south of the country. British resistance proved stubborn, with the Spitfires and Hurricanes of RAF Fighter Command being directed by radar onto the incoming bomber streams. Badly mauled, the *Luftwaffe* switched their offensive from attacks on airfields to attacks on British cities (the '**blitz**'), losing their opportunity to gain true air superiority. Between 1 July and 31 Oct the *Luftwaffe* lost 2 848 aircraft to the RAF's 1 446. ▷ **World War II**

Britain, Roman

Known to the Graeco-Roman world from the late 4c BC, Britain escaped invasion until the time of Julius **Caesar** (55–54BC) and conquest until the time of Emperor **Claudius** (AD43); Roman military occupation then followed, the main garrison towns being Lincoln, York, Caerleon on the Usk, and Chester. Conquest of the whole island was initially intended, but the fierce resistance of the tribes in the north (Caledonia) ruled this out. Instead, defensive barriers were erected in northern England and southern Scotland: **Hadrian's Wall** (AD122–9) and the **Antonine Wall** (c.150 AD). To the south, control was exerted through the army and the policy of Romanizing the natives. Military occupation lasted until c.400, when troubles elsewhere in the Empire forced the withdrawal of the garrison troops. ▷ **Iceni; Picts**

British Empire

There were in fact several British Empires: the empire of commerce and settlement in the Caribbean and North America, founded in the 17c and partly lost when the 13 colonies declared their independence in 1776; the empire in the East, founded in the 17c but developed through the extensive conquest of India (1757–1857) and the acquisition of islands, trading posts, and strategic positions from Aden to Hong Kong; the empire of white settlement in Canada, Australia, New Zealand and the Cape in South Africa, each of which had been federated as 'dominions' by 1910; and the 'dependent territories' in Africa and elsewhere acquired during the 'New Imperialism' of the last few decades of the 19c. To this must be added the British 'informal empire': territories which the Empire did not rule directly, but which fell under its influence because of its industrial and commercial power. These included parts of South America, the Middle East, the Persian Gulf and China. In 1919 the Empire reached its fullest extent through the acquisition of mandates over German and Ottoman territories in Africa and the Middle East. It was this diversity which gave rise to such famous phrases as 'the empire on which the sun never sets'. By the late 19c the empire was bonded together not only by industrial strength, but by Britain's vast merchant marine and powerful navy. After **World War I** it was apparent that Britain could not control such an extensive empire: the dominions secured effective independence in 1931; the Middle Eastern mandates were virtually lost by **World War II**; India gained her independence in 1947, and the other Asian colonies soon followed; while most of the rest of the Empire was decolonized in the 1960s. Many of the countries of the Empire remained in the British **Commonwealth of Nations**.

British Expeditionary Force (BEF)

An army, first established in 1906, sent to France (Aug 1914 and Sep 1939) to support the left wing of the French armies against German attack. In **World War II** its total strength was 394 000, of whom 224 000 were safely evacuated, mainly from Dunkirk, in May–June 1940. ▷ **French, John; Haig, Douglas; Marne, Battle of the; World War I**

British India

The term commonly used to designate the whole of India during the period of British hegemony, more properly it refers to those districts of India under direct British rule. This area may be said to have varied from the first granting of Zamindari rights over 24 parganas near Calcutta to the British **East India Company** in 1701. By 1766 the Company directly ruled the area around Madras, the Northern Circars and a sizable area of Bengal and Bihar, while the Crown had control of the city of Bombay. More properly, British India came into being in 1858 when the Company was dissolved and its lands taken over by the crown. At its height, just before independence in 1947, British India included North-West Frontier province and the provinces of Baluchistan, Sind, Punjab, Ajmer, Merwara, Delhi, United Provinces, Bombay, Coorg, Madras, Ceylon, Central Provinces, Bihar, Orissa, Bengal and Assam; Sikkim and Bhutan were protectorates. Although not officially part of British India, there were also many princely states which are often viewed as part of British India. Though nominally independent vassal states of the Crown, the princely states were watched over by British Residents and advisers. All control over foreign affairs and policy, and a wide variety of continent-wide matters were ceded by princely states to the government of British India, under informal terms of para-mountcy by which Britain had filled the vacuum left by the Mughal Empire. Although India moved gradually toward representative government between 1858 and 1947, British India was effectively governed by a viceroy or governor-general and some sort of advisory council throughout the period. Along with a small elected assembly, this was the government of India. The viceroy was responsible only to the Crown and the government of England. Below the government of India was the small but effective bureaucracy of the **Indian Civil Service** (ICS), which was focused on provincial centres, with district commissioners in rural areas. The ICS was supported by the local police forces under its control. The entire government was supported by the British Indian Army which was an integral part of both government and society, especially after the **Indian Uprising** (1857–8).

British–Iraqi Treaty (1930)

This treaty carried, amongst others, clauses providing for mutual assistance between Iraq and Britain in time of war and special rights for Britain in respect of 'essential communications' through Iraq and was, in effect, the treaty which brought to a close the British mandate in Iraq. It also granted Britain two air bases on the condition that these were not in any way to be regarded as constituting an occupation; nor were they to be seen as interfering with the principle of Iraqi sovereignty. The treaty, therefore, although ending the mandate and securing full independence for Iraq, bound Iraq to Britain in what was de facto a military alliance, due under the treaty to last for 25 years.

British North America Act (1867)

An act passed by the British parliament which sanctioned the Confederation of Nova Scotia, New Brunswick, Quebec and Ontario, thus giving rise to the **Dominion of Canada**. In 1982 it was renamed the Constitution Act (1867).

British South Africa Company

A company, formed by Cecil **Rhodes**, which used a series of concessions from King Lobengula and other Central African chiefs to secure a Royal Charter from the British government in 1889. Mashonaland was invaded in 1890 and by 1900 the Company ruled much of Central Africa despite considerable African resistance. In 1923–4 its territories were divided into Northern Rhodesia (Zambia after 1964) and Southern Rhodesia (Zimbabwe after 1980). It retained extensive mineral rights.

British Union of Fascists ▷ Blackshirts

Brooke, Sir James (1803–68)

English soldier, and Rajah of Sarawak. He sailed in 1838 in a schooner-yacht from London for Sarawak, on the north-west coast of Borneo, with the object of putting down piracy. Made Rajah of Sarawak (1841) for assisting the local sultan against Dayak rebel tribes, he instituted free trade, framed a new code of laws, declared the Dayak custom of head-hunting a capital crime, and vigorously set about suppressing piracy. In 1857 Brooke repelled, with native forces, a series of attacks by a large body of Chinese, who had been irritated by his efforts to prevent opium-smuggling. He was succeeded as rajah in 1868 by his nephew, Sir Charles Johnson, who changed his name to Brooke. He was succeeded in turn in 1917 by his son, Sir Charles Vyner, who in 1946 ceded Sarawak to the British crown.

Brookeborough, Basil Stanlake Brooke, 1st Viscount (1888–1973)

Irish politician. He was elected to the Northern Ireland parliament in 1929, became Minister of Agriculture (1933), Commerce (1941–5), and then Prime Minister (1943–63). A staunch supporter of union with Great Britain, he was created viscount in 1952, and retired from politics in 1968.

Bruce, Robert (1274–1329)
King of Scots (1306/29) and hero of the Scottish War of Independence. As Earl of Carrick, in 1296 he swore fealty to **Edward I** of England, but soon joined the Scottish revolt under **Wallace**. In 1306 he quarrelled with John Comyn, his political rival, stabbing him to death; then assembled his vassals and was crowned king at Scone. He was forced to flee to Ireland, but returned in 1307 and defeated the English at Loudoun Hill. After Edward's death (1307), the English were forced from the country and all the great castles recovered except Berwick and Stirling. This led to the Battle of **Bannockburn** (1314), when the English were routed. Sporadic war with England continued until the Treaty of Northampton (1328), which recognized the independence of Scotland and Bruce's right to the throne. He was succeeded by **David II**, the son of his second wife. ▷ **Scottish War of Independence**

Bruges, Treaty of (15 Aug 1521)
The agreement between King **Henry VIII** of England and the Emperor Charles V against France, despite the Anglo-French friendliness of the **Field of the Cloth of Gold** the year before. The treaty meant that England was involved in long campaigns in northern Europe in support of the Emperor.

Bryce, James, 1st Viscount (1838–1922)
British politician. He entered parliament in 1880, and was made Irish Secretary (1905) and Ambassador to the USA (1907–13). As chairman of the Bryce Commission (1894–5), he recommended the establishment of a Ministry of Education. His best-known work is *The American Commonwealth* (1888).

buccaneers
The term used to denote legalized pirates operating in the Caribbean in the period 1650–98. The name derives from the French *boucanier* ('buyer of smoked beef'). The initial buccaneer stronghold was the island of Tortuga off Hispaniola, but this transferred itself to Port Royal after the English capture of Jamaica in 1655. As with the privateers a century earlier, the home governments often used the buccaneers as instruments of policy, issuing them with Commissions of Reprisal entitling them to attack Spanish shipping and settlements. The most infamous buccaneers were the Frenchmen L'Ollonais, Du Casse and De Maintenon and the

Welshman Henry **Morgan**. English buccaneering was ended by the Treaty of Madrid (1670).

Buchan, John, 1st Baron Tweedsmuir (1875–1940)

Scottish author and politician. During **World War I** he served on HQ staff (1916–17), when he became Director of Information. He was MP for the Scottish Universities (1927–35), when he was made a baron, and became Governor-General of Canada until 1940. In 1937 he was made a Privy Councillor and chancellor of Edinburgh University. Despite his busy public life, Buchan wrote over 50 books, especially fast-moving adventure stories, such as *Prester John* (1910) and *The Thirty-Nine Steps* (1915).

Buchanan, George (1506–82)

Scottish humanist and reformer. He was imprisoned for a satirical poem on the Franciscans. He escaped to France (1539), and taught at Bordeaux, Paris, and Coimbra, Portugal (1549), where he was arrested as a suspected heretic. Released in 1552, he returned to Scotland in 1561, and was tutor to **Mary, Queen of Scots**. Abandoning Mary after the death of **Darnley**, he became tutor to James I of England, and Keeper of the Privy Seal (1570–8). His European reputation rested mainly on his skill in Latin poetry; his Latin paraphrase of the Psalms was used as a textbook until the 19c. ▷ **James VI and I**

Buck, Edward Charles (1838–1916)

British Indian administrator. Buck, a graduate of Clare College Cambridge, joined the **Indian Civil Service** in 1886, being immediately posted to Bengal. Having proved a great asset to the Bengal Civil Service, Buck moved through the ranks and eventually became Secretary of the government of India in 1882, a post he held until his retirement in 1897. In 1886 he represented the government of India at the Great Colonial Exhibition. In 1897, marking both his retirement and Queen **Victoria**'s diamond jubilee, Buck was made a Knight Commander of the Star of India.

Buckingham, George Villiers, 1st Duke of (1592–1628)

English statesman and court favourite. He was knighted by **James I** (of England), and raised to the peerage as Viscount Villiers (1616), Earl of Buckingham (1617), Marquis (1618), and Duke (1623). In 1623 he failed to negotiate the marriage of Prince

Charles to the daughter of the Spanish King, but later arranged the marriage to Henrietta Maria of France. The abortive expedition against Cadiz (1625) exposed him to impeachment by the Commons, and only a dissolution rescued him. An expedition against France failed (1627), and while planning a second attack, he was assassinated at Portsmouth by John Felton, a discontented subaltern.

Buckingham, George Villiers, 2nd Duke of (1628–87)

English statesman. After his father's assassination, he was brought up with **Charles I**'s children, and went into exile after the royalist defeat in the **English Civil Wars**. His estates were recovered at the **Restoration** and he became a member of the **Cabal** of **Charles II**. He was instrumental in **Clarendon**'s downfall (1667), but lost power to **Arlington** and was dismissed in 1674 for alleged Catholic sympathies.

Bulge, Battle of the (1944)

The last desperate German armoured counter-offensive through the Ardennes in **World War II** (beginning 16 Dec), to prevent the Allied invasion of Germany. It achieved early success, but ground to a halt, and the Germans were then pushed to retreat by the Allies by the end of Jan 1945.

Bunker Hill, Battle of (1775)

The first pitched battle of the **American Revolution**, technically a US defeat. The British garrison dislodged New England troops from their position overlooking occupied Boston, but very high British casualties demonstrated American fighting capacity, and forbade attempts on other American emplacements. The battle was actually fought on Breed's Hill, above Charlestown, not on nearby Bunker Hill.

Burgess, Guy (Francis de Moncy) (1910–63)

British double agent. Recruited as a Soviet agent in the 1930s, he worked with the BBC (1936–9), wrote war propaganda (1939–41), and again joined the BBC (1941–4) while working for MI5. Thereafter, he was a member of the Foreign Office, and second secretary under **Philby** in Washington in 1950. Recalled in 1951 for 'serious misconduct', he and **Maclean** disappeared, reemerging in the USSR in 1956. He died in Moscow. ▷ **Blunt, Anthony**

Burgh, Hubert de (d.1243)
Justiciar of England under King **John** and **Henry III** (1215–32). He is chiefly remembered as the jailer of Prince **Arthur**. He was created Earl of Kent in 1227, but was imprisoned after falling from favour (1232–4), then pardoned.

Burgoyne, John (1723–92)
British general. He entered the army in 1740, and gave distinguished service in the **Seven Years War** (1756–63). He then sat in parliament as a Tory, and in 1777 was sent to America, where he led an expedition from Canada, taking Ticonderoga, but being forced to surrender at Saratoga. He later joined the **Whigs**, and commanded in Ireland (1782–3). ▷ **American Revolution; Tories**

Burke, Edmund (1729–97)
Irish politician and political philosopher. He began in 1750 to study law, but then took up literary work. His early writing includes his *Philosophical Inquiry into the Origin of our Ideas of the Sublime and Beautiful* (1756). He became Secretary for Ireland, and entered parliament in 1765. His main speeches and writings belong to the period when his party was opposed to Lord **North**'s American policy (1770–82). His *Reflections on the French Revolution* (1790) was read all over Europe. ▷ **American Revolution; Hastings, Warren**

Buss, Frances Mary (1827–94)
English pioneer of higher education of women. She founded the North London Collegiate School for Ladies, which became a model for the High Schools of the Girls' Public Day Schools Company. She also campaigned for women to be admitted to university.

Bute, John Stuart, 3rd Earl of (1713–92)
Scottish politician and Prime Minister of Britain. After early court appointments, he became a favourite of **George III**, who made him one of the principal Secretaries of State (1761). As Prime Minister (1762–3), his government was highly unpopular. Its principal objective was the supremacy of the royal prerogative, and he was soon forced to resign. From 1768 his life was chiefly spent in the country, where he engaged in scientific study.

Butler, R(ichard) A(usten), Baron (1902–82)
British politician. He became Conservative MP for Saffron Walden in 1929. After a series of junior ministerial appointments, he became Minister of Education (1941–5), introducing the forward-looking Education Act of 1944, and then Minister of Labour (1945). He became Chancellor of the Exchequer (1951), Lord Privy Seal (1955), Leader of the House of Commons (1955), Home Secretary (1957), First Secretary of State and Deputy Prime Minister (1962). He narrowly lost the premiership to Douglas-Home in 1963, and became Foreign Secretary (1963–4). He was appointed Master of Trinity College, Cambridge (1965–78), and was made a life peer. ▷ **Butskellism; Conservative Party; Home of the Hirsel, Baron**

Butskellism
A compound of the names of Conservative politician R A **Butler** and the Labour leader Hugh **Gaitskell**, used in the 1950s and early 1960s to imply a high degree of similarity between the policies of the two main parties. 'Mr Butskell' was first referred to in *The Economist* (Feb 1954).

Byng, George, 1st Viscount Torrington (1663–1733)
English sailor. He joined the navy at 15, and gained rapid promotion as a supporter of William of Orange. Made rear-admiral in 1703, he captured Gibraltar, and was knighted for his gallant conduct at Málaga. In 1708 he defeated the French fleet of James **Stuart**, the Pretender, and in 1718 destroyed the Spanish fleet off Messina. He was created viscount in 1721. ▷ **William III**

Byng, John (1704–57)
English sailor. He was the fourth son of George **Byng,** 1st Viscount Torrington. He joined the navy at 14, and was rapidly promoted, becoming admiral in 1756. For his failure to relieve Minorca, blockaded by a French fleet, and for retreating to Gibraltar, he was found guilty of neglect of duty, and shot at Portsmouth.

Byng (of Vimy), Julian Hedworth George, 1st Viscount
(1862–1935)
British general. He commanded the 9th Army Corps in the **Gallipoli Campaign** (1915), the Canadian Army Corps (1916–17), and

the 3rd Army (1917–18). After **World War I** he became Governor-General of Canada (1921–6) and Commissioner of the Metropolitan Police (1928–31), and was made a viscount in 1928 and a field marshal in 1932.

C

Cabal

An acronym taken from the initials of the five leading advisers of **Charles II** of England between 1667 and 1673: **C**lifford, **A**rlington, **B**uckingham, **A**shley Cooper (Shaftesbury), and **L**auderdale. The name is misleading, since these five were by no means Charles's only advisers; nor did they agree on a common policy. Arlington and Buckingham were bitter rivals. ▷ **Arlington, Henry; Buckingham, George Villiers, 2nd Duke of; Lauderdale, John; Shaftesbury, Anthony Ashley Cooper, 1st Earl of**

Cade, Jack (d.1450)

Irish leader of the insurrection of 1450 against **Henry VI** of England. After an unsettled early career he lived in Sussex, possibly as a physician. Assuming the name of Mortimer, and the title of Captain of Kent, he marched on London with a great number of followers, and entered the city. A promise of pardon sowed dissension among the insurgents; they dispersed, and a price was set upon Cade's head. He attempted to reach the coast, but was killed near Heathfield, Sussex.

Caesar, in full **Gaius Julius Caesar** (c.100–44BC)

Roman statesman, whose military genius enabled Rome to extend her empire permanently to the Atlantic seaboard, but whose ruthless ambition led to the breakdown of the Republican system of government at home. In 60BC he joined with Pompey and Crassus (the so-called First Triumvirate) to protect his interests in the state. Between 58 and 50BC he conquered northern Gaul, greatly extending the empire's north-western frontiers, and made two raids into Britain (55 and 54BC). Although these raids had little military importance, they are significant as the first Roman contact with barbarian Britain. In 49BC Caesar led his army across the River Rubicon into Italy and plunged the state into civil war, winning sole control at Rome. He did not disguise his absolute power, and was eventually assassinated by a group of Republican-minded Romans under the leadership of Brutus and Cassius. His brief period of power left him with little time to carry through the many reforms, social, economic and administrative, that he had intended. ▷ **Britain, Roman; Cassivellaunus**

Callaghan, (Leonard) James ('Jim') (1912–)

English politician and Prime Minister of Britain. After a secondary education, he joined the Civil Service (1929), and in 1945 was elected Labour MP for South Cardiff. As Chancellor of the Exchequer under **Wilson** (1964–7), he introduced the controversial corporation and selective employment taxes. He was Home Secretary (1967–70) and Foreign Secretary (1974–6), and became Prime Minister (1976–9) on Wilson's resignation. He resigned as Leader of the Opposition in 1980. ▷ **Labour Party**

Camden, Battle of (1780)

A battle of the **American Revolution**, fought in South Carolina. After the British capture of **Charleston**, Camden was the first major battle of the Southern campaign. Americans under Horatio Gates were defeated by British troops under Lord **Cornwallis**.

Campbell, Sir Colin (Baron Clyde) (1792–1863)

British field marshal. He fought in the **Peninsular War** against **Napoleon I**, where he was twice badly wounded, and after 30 years of duty in various garrisons, fought in China (1842) and in the second of the **Sikh Wars** (1848–9). In the **Crimean War** he commanded the Highland Brigade in a campaign which included the renowned repulse of the Russians by the 'thin red line' at the Battle of **Balaclava** (1854). During the 1857–8 **Indian Uprising** he commanded the forces in India, and effected the final relief of Lucknow. He was created baron in 1858.

Campbell-Bannerman, Sir Henry (1836–1908)

Scotish politician and Prime Minister of Britain. He became a Liberal MP in 1868, was Chief Secretary for Ireland (1884), War Secretary (1886 and 1892–5), Liberal leader (1899), and Prime Minister (1905–8). A 'pro-Boer', he granted the ex-republics responsible government, and his popularity helped to reunite a divided **Liberal Party**. He supported the Lib–Lab pact of 1903, which played a part in the Liberal landslide of 1906. ▷ **Boer Wars**

Camperdown, Battle of (1797)

A naval battle fought between British and Dutch fleets off Texel Island, Holland. Admiral Adam Duncan (1731–1804) virtually destroyed the Dutch fleet, frustrating the attempt to disable the British North Sea squadron and thus facilitate the invasion of Britain.

Canning, Charles John, 1st Earl (1812–62)

English politician. He entered parliament in 1836 as Conservative MP for Warwick, but next year was raised to the Upper House as Viscount Canning by his mother's death, both his elder brothers having predeceased her. In 1841 he became Under-Secretary in the Foreign Office, and in 1856 he succeeded Lord **Dalhousie** as Governor-General of India. The war with Persia was brought to a successful close in 1857. In the same year (10 May), the **Indian Uprising** began with the outbreak at Meerut. Canning's conduct was described at the time as weak — he was nicknamed 'Clemency Canning' — but the general opinion later was that he acted with courage, moderation and judiciousness. In 1858 he became the first Viceroy of India, and in 1859 was raised to an earldom.

Canning, George (1770–1827)

English politician. He entered parliament for Newport, Isle of Wight (1794) as a supporter of **Pitt,** 'the Younger'. He became Under-Secretary of State (1796), Treasurer of the Navy (1804–6), and Minister for Foreign Affairs (1807). His disapproval of the Walcheren expedition led to a misunderstanding with **Castlereagh**, which resulted in a duel. He became MP for Liverpool (1812), Ambassador to Lisbon (1814), President of the Board of Control (1816), and MP for Harwich (1822). Nominated Governor-General of India (1822), he was on the eve of departure when Castlereagh's suicide saw him installed as Foreign Secretary. In this post he gave a new impetus to commerce by advocating tariff reductions. He was the first to recognize the free states of Spanish America; promoted the union of Britain, France, and Russia in the cause of Greece (1827); protected Portugal from Spanish invasion; contended earnestly for **Catholic Emancipation** (1829); and prepared the way for a repeal of the **Corn Laws**. In 1827 he formed an administration with the aid of the **Whigs**, but died the same year.

Canute (c.995–1035)

King of England (1016/35), Denmark (1019/35) and Norway (1028/35). The younger son of **Svein I Haraldsson, 'Fork Beard'**, he first campaigned in England in 1013, and after his father's death (1014) successively challenged **Ethelred the Unready** and **Edmund II, 'Ironside'** for the English throne. He defeated Edmund in 1016 at the Battle of Assandun, secured Mercia and Northumbria, and became King of all England after Edmund's death. In 1017 he married Emma of Normandy, the widow of Ethelred. He ruled England, according to the accepted traditions of English kingship, and maintained the peace throughout his reign. He died at Shaftesbury, Dorset. The story of his failure to make the tide recede was invented by the 12c historian, Henry of Huntingdon, to demonstrate the frailty of earthly power compared to the might of God. ▷ **Anglo-Saxons**

Cape St Vincent, Battle of (1797)

A naval battle fought between British and Spanish fleets. Admiral Sir John Jervis (1735–1823) defeated a numerically superior Spanish force, thus preventing French plans for the assembly of a combined invasion fleet to conquer Britain. ▷ **French Revolutionary Wars**

Caractacus (Caratacus or Caradoc) (1c AD)

Chief of the Catuvellauni. The son of Cunobelinus, he mounted a gallant but unsuccessful guerrilla operation in Wales against the Romans in the years following the Claudian conquest (AD43). Betrayed by the Brigantian queen, Cartimandua, he was taken to Rome (AD51), where he was exhibited in triumph, pardoned by **Claudius**, and later died. ▷ **Britain, Roman**

Cardigan, James Thomas Brudenell, 7th Earl of (1797–1868)

British general. He entered the army in 1824, and purchased his promotion, commanding the 15th Hussars (until 1833), and then the 11th Hussars (1836–47). He commanded a cavalry brigade in the Crimea, and led the fatal charge of the Six Hundred (the **Charge of the Light Brigade**) against the Russians at the Battle of **Balaclava** (25 Oct 1854) in the **Crimean War**. He then became Inspector-General of Cavalry (1855–60). The woollen jacket known as a cardigan is named after him.

Cardwell, Edward, 1st Viscount (1813–86)

English politician. He became a lawyer (1838) and an MP (1842). First a Peelite, then a Liberal, he served as President of the Board of Trade (1852–55), Chief Secretary for Ireland (1859–61), Chancellor of the Duchy of Lancaster (1861–4), and Colonial Secretary (1864–6). As Secretary for War (1868–74), he carried out a major reorganization of the British Army. He was made a peer in 1874.

Carleton, Sir Guy (Lord Dorchester) (1724–1808)

Acting Governor (1767–70) and Governor (1786–91) of Quebec and Governor-in-Chief of British North America until 1798. General James **Wolfe**'s quartermaster at the capture of **Quebec** in 1759, he realized during his first tour of duty as Governor that the 13 North American colonies were close to rebellion and that British imperial authority would require a base which he set out to establish in Quebec. His belief that the maintenance of the seigniorial system would ensure French-Canadian loyalty was embodied in the **Quebec Act** of 1774 which, despite protests from the increased English-speaking population, was pushed through the House of Commons against bitter opposition. Carleton refused to consider the English speaking settlers' demands for *habeas corpus* and other aspects of English law, but in spite of resentment against this, it was they who took up arms against the US rebels when they invaded in 1775–6. Carleton's successful defence, however, was criticized for the slowness with which he pursued the rebels and he resigned. Sent out as Governor of Quebec again in 1786, he became Governor-General after the Constitutional Act of 1791. He disliked the division of Quebec into Upper and Lower Canada, and the introduction of elected assemblies, but his advice that Montreal be retained within Lower Canada was accepted. His continued concern for the military defence of Canada was illustrated by the inflammatory speech he made to Indians just before **Jay's Treaty** was signed in 1794, when he was sure that war with the USA was imminent. He resigned in 1794 and left the province in 1796. ▷ **Loyalists**

Caroline (of Brunswick), Amelia Elizabeth (1768–1821)

Wife of **George IV**, the daughter of **George III**'s sister, Augusta. She married the Prince of Wales in 1795; but the marriage was disagreeable to him, and although she bore him a daughter, the Princess Charlotte, they lived apart. When George became King (1820), she was offered an annuity to renounce the title of Queen and live abroad; when she refused, the King persuaded the government to introduce a Divorce Bill. Although this failed, she was not allowed into Westminster Abbey at the coronation (July 1821).

Carrington, Peter (Alexander Rupert), 6th Baron (1919–)

English politician. A Conservative, he held several junior posts in government (1951–6), before becoming High Commissioner to Australia (1956–9). He then served as First Lord of the Admiralty (1959–63) and Leader of the House of Lords (1963–4). He was Secretary of State for Defence (1970–4) and briefly for Energy (1974), and also Chairman of the Conservative Party organization (1972–4). Upon the Conservative return to office he was Foreign Secretary (1979–82), until he and his ministerial team resigned over the Argentinian invasion of the Falkland Islands. He later became Secretary-General of **NATO** (1984–8), and **EC** mediator during the crisis in Yugoslavia (1991–2). ▷ **Conservative Party**

Carson, Edward Henry, Baron (1854–1935)

Irish-born politician and barrister. He became a Conservative MP (1892–1921), a QC of the Irish Bar (1880) and English Bar (1894), and in 1895 became known for his successful prosecution of Oscar Wilde. He was Solicitor-General for Ireland (1892) and for England (1900–6), Attorney-General (1915), First Lord of the Admiralty (1916–17), and Lord of Appeal (1921–9). Strongly opposed to **Home Rule**, he organized the Ulster Volunteers. ▷ **Conservative Party**

Carteret, John, 1st Earl Granville (1690–1763)

English politician. He entered the House of Lords in 1711, and became Ambassador to Sweden (1719), Secretary of State (1721), and Lord-Lieutenant of Ireland (1724–9). Chief Minister from 1742 to 1744, he was driven from power by the Pelhams (1744) because of his pro-Hanoverian policies, though from 1751 he was President of the Council under Henry **Pelham**, and twice refused the premiership. ▷ **Pelham, Thomas; Walpole, Robert**

Casablanca Conference (Jan 1943)

A meeting in North Africa between Franklin D **Roosevelt** and Winston **Churchill** during **World War II**, at which it was decided to insist on the eventual 'unconditional surrender' of Germany and Japan. Attempts to overcome friction between Roosevelt and the Free French under de **Gaulle** had only limited success. The combined Chiefs of Staff settled strategic differences over the projected invasion of Sicily and Italy.

Casement, Roger (David) (1864–1916)

British consular official. He acted as Consul in various parts of Africa (1895–1904) and Brazil (1906–11), where he denounced the Congo and Putumayo rubber atrocities. Knighted in 1911, ill health caused him to retire to Ireland in 1912. An ardent Irish nationalist, he tried to obtain German help for the cause. In 1916 he was arrested on landing in Ireland from a German submarine to head the **Sinn Féin** rebellion, and hanged for high treason in London. His controversial 'Black Diaries', revealing, among other things, homosexual practices, were long suppressed by the government but ultimately published in 1959.

Cassivellaunus (1c BC)

King of the Catuvellauni, a British tribe living in the area of modern Hertfordshire. He led the Catuvellauni in resistance to Julius **Caesar** on his second invasion (54BC). ▷ **Britain, Roman**

Castle, Barbara Anne (1911–)

English politician. She became Labour MP for Blackburn (1945–87) and was Chairman of the Labour Party (1958–9), Minister of Overseas Development (1964–5), and a controversial Minister of Transport (1965–8), introducing a 70 mph speed limit and the 'breathalyser' test for drunken drivers. She became Secretary of State for Employment and Productivity (1968–70) and Minister of Health and Social Security (1974–8). She then returned to the backbenches, but became Vice-Chairman of the Socialist Group in the European Parliament in 1979, when she became an elected member of that body, a post she held until 1985. ▷ **Labour Party; socialism**

Castlereagh, Robert Stewart, Viscount (1769–1822)

British politician. The son of an Ulster proprietor, he became Whig MP for County Down in 1790, turning Tory in 1795. He was created Viscount Castlereagh in 1796, and became Irish Secretary (1797), President of the Board of Control (1802), and Minister of War (1805–6 and 1807–9). His major achievements date from 1812, when, as Foreign Secretary under Lord **Liverpool**, he was at the heart of the coalition against **Napoleon I** (1813–14). He represented England at Chaumont and the Congress of Vienna (1814–15), Paris (1815), and Aix-la-Chapelle (1818). He advocated 'Congress diplomacy' among the great powers, to avoid further warfare. Believing that he was being blackmailed for homosexuality, he committed suicide at Foots Cray, his home in Kent. ▷ **Tories; Whigs**

Catherine of Aragon (1485–1536)
Queen of England. The fourth daughter of and Isabella I, 'the Catholic' of Spain, she became the first wife of **Henry VIII**. She was first married in 1501 to Arthur (1486–1502), the son of **Henry VII**, and following his early death was betrothed to her brother-in-law, Henry, then a boy of 11. She married him in 1509, and bore him five children, of whom only the Princess Mary (later **Mary I**) survived. In 1527 Henry began a procedure for divorce, which he obtained in 1533, thereby breaking with the Pope, and starting the English Reformation. Catherine then retired to lead an austere religious life until her death. ▷ **Reformation** (England)

Catherine of Braganza (1638–1705)
Wife of **Charles II** of England. The daughter of King John IV of Portugal, she was married to Charles in 1662 as part of an alliance between England and Portugal, but failed to produce an heir. She helped to convert him to Catholicism just before his death, after which she returned to Portugal (1692), where she died.

Catholic Emancipation (1829)
A reluctant religious concession granted by the Tory government, headed by the Duke of **Wellington**, following mounting agitation in Ireland led by Daniel **O'Connell** and the Catholic Association. Roman Catholics were permitted to become MPs; and all offices of state in Ireland, except Viceroy and Chancellor, were also opened to Catholics. ▷ **Tories**

Cato Street Conspiracy (Feb 1820)
A plot formulated by Arthur Thistlewood (1770–1820) and fellow radical conspirators, to blow up the Tory cabinet as it attended a dinner at the house of the Earl of Harrowby. The plot was infiltrated by a government agent, and the leaders were arrested and hanged. ▷ **radicalism; Tories**

Cavalier Parliament

The name given to the English parliament of 1661–79. Until the crisis over the **Popish Plot** it usually supported the King, its name deriving from royalist support during the **English Civil Wars**. It passed legislation in the 1660s and early 1670s to strengthen the Church of England and to discriminate against Puritans and Nonconformists who had been dominant during the English revolution. ▷ **Charles II; Puritanism**

Cavaliers

Those who fought for **Charles I** in the **English Civil Wars**. The name was used derogatorily in 1642 by supporters of parliament to describe swaggering courtiers with long hair and swords, who reportedly welcomed the prospect of war. Similarly, the parliamentarians were labelled 'Roundheads' by Cavaliers, dating from the riotous assemblies in Westminster during **Strafford**'s trial in 1641, when short-haired apprentices mobbed Charles I's supporters outside the House of Lords.

Cavendish, Spencer Compton, 8th Duke of Devonshire

(1833–1908)

English politician, known as the Marquis of Hartington. A Liberal, he entered parliament in 1857, and between 1863 and 1874 was a Lord of the Admiralty, Under-Secretary for War, War Secretary, Postmaster-General, and Chief Secretary for Ireland. In 1875 he became leader of the Liberal Opposition during **Gladstone**'s temporary abdication, later serving under him as Secretary of State for India (1880–2) and as War Secretary (1882–5). He disapproved of Irish **Home Rule**, and, having lead the breakaway from the **Liberal Party**, became head of the Liberal Unionists from 1886, serving in the Unionist government as Lord President of the Council (1895–1903).

Cavendish, William, Duke of Newcastle (1592–1676)

English soldier and patron of the arts. He was created Knight of the Bath in 1610, Viscount Mansfield in 1620, and Earl (1628), Marquess (1643), and Duke (1665) of Newcastle. He gave strong support to **Charles I** in the **English Civil Wars**, and was general of all forces north of the Trent. After the Battle of **Marston Moor** (1644) he lived on the Continent, at times in great poverty, until the Restoration. A noted patron of poets and dramatists, he was himself the author of several plays, and of two works on horsemanship.

Cecil, Robert, 1st Earl of Salisbury (c.1563–1612)

English minister, son of William **Cecil**, 1st Baron Burghley. He entered parliament in 1584. He became a Privy Councillor (1591) and was appointed **Elizabeth I**'s Secretary of State (1596). His years of control in the last years of the reign helped to smooth the succession of James VI of Scotland to the English throne. James maintained him in office and he negotiated peace terms ending the long war with Spain (1604). He was an efficient administrator and financial manager who fought a losing battle against mounting royal debts. ▷ **James VI and I**

Cecil, Robert (Arthur Talbot Gascoyne), 3rd Marquis of Salisbury (1830–1903)

English politician and Prime Minister of Britain. He became a Conservative MP in 1853. In 1865 he was made Viscount Cranborne, and in 1868 Marquis of Salisbury. He was twice Indian Secretary (1866 and 1874), became Foreign Secretary (1878) and, on **Disraeli**'s death (1881), Leader of the Opposition. He was Prime Minister on three occasions (1885–6, 1886–92 and 1895–1902), also serving much of the time as his own Foreign Secretary. He resigned as Foreign Secretary in 1900, but remained as head of government during the **Boer Wars** (1899–1902). He retired in 1902.

Cecil, William, 1st Baron Burghley (Burghleigh) (1520–98)

English statesman. He served under Somerset and Northumberland, was made Secretary of State (1550) and knighted (1551). During **Mary I**'s reign he conformed to Catholicism. In 1558 **Elizabeth I** appointed him chief Secretary of State, and for the next 40 years he was the chief architect of the Elizabethan regime, controlling the administration, influencing her pro-Protestant foreign policy, securing the execution of **Mary, Queen of Scots**, and preparing for the Spanish **Armada**. In 1571 he was created Baron Burghley, and in 1572 became Lord High Treasurer (an office he held until his death).

Celts

Different groups of prehistoric peoples who all spoke Celtic languages and lived in most parts of Europe from the Balkan regions to Ireland. Most powerful during the 4c BC, they probably originated in present-day France, southern Germany, and adjacent territories during the Bronze Age. Celtic-speaking societies developed in the later first millennium BC, expanding through armed raids into the Iberian Peninsula, British Islands, Central Europe, Italy, Greece, Anatolia, Egypt, Bulgaria, Romania, Thrace, and Macedonia. They were finally repulsed by the Romans and Germanic tribes, and in Europe withdrew into Gaul in the 1c BC. Celtic tradition survived most, and for longest in Ireland and Britain. They were famous for their burial sites and hill forts, and their bronze and iron art and jewellery.

Cetewayo (c.1826–84)
King of the Zulu (1872/9). In Jan 1879 he defeated an entire British regiment at Isandhlwana, but was himself overcome by British forces under Sir Garnet **Wolseley** at Ulundi in July of the same year. However, so eloquently did Cetewayo present his case in London, that in Jan 1883 he was restored by the British as ruler of central Zululand. Shortly thereafter, though, he was driven out by his subjects, and died at Ekowe.

Chamberlain, (Arthur) Neville (1869–1940)
English politician and Prime Minister of Britain. He was the son of Joseph **Chamberlain** by his second marriage. He was Mayor of Birmingham (1915–16), a Conservative MP from 1918, Chancellor of the Exchequer (1923–4 and 1931–7), and three times Minister for Health (1923, 1924–9 and 1931), where he effected notable social reforms. He played a leading part in the formation of the National Government (1931). As Prime Minister (1937–40), he advocated '**appeasement**' of Italy and Germany, returning from Munich with his claim to have found 'peace in our time' (1938). Criticism of his war leadership and initial military reverses led to his resignation as Prime Minister (1940), and his appointment as Lord President of the Council. ▷ **Conservative Party; Munich Agreement; World War II**

Chamberlain, Joseph (1836–1914)
English politician. He entered the family business at 16, and became Mayor of Birmingham (1873–5) and a Liberal MP (1876). In 1880 he became President of the Board of Trade, but in 1886 resigned over **Gladstone**'s **Home Rule** Bill, which split the **Liberal Party**. From 1889 he was leader of the Liberal Unionists, and in

the coalition government of 1895 took office as Secretary for the Colonies. In 1903 he resigned office to be free to advocate his ideas on tariff reform, which split the Conservative and Unionist Party. In 1906 he withdrew from public life after a stroke. ▷ **Chamberlain, Austen; Chamberlain, Neville; Conservative Party; radicalism**

Chamberlain, Sir (Joseph) Austen (1863–1937)
English politician. The eldest son of Joseph **Chamberlain**, he was elected a Liberal Unionist MP in 1892, and sat as a Conservative MP until his death in 1937. He was Chancellor of the Exchequer (1903–6 and 1919–21), Secretary for India (1915–17), Unionist leader (1921–2), Foreign Secretary (1924–9), and First Lord of the Admiralty (1931). He received the 1925 Nobel Peace Prize for negotiating the Locarno Pact. ▷ **Conservative Party**

Charge of the Light Brigade
An incident during the Battle of **Balaclava** (1854), when the Light Brigade, under the command of the Earl of **Cardigan**, charged the main Russian artillery. The charge involved massive loss of life. It resulted from the misunderstanding of an order given by the commanding officer, Lord **Raglan**, to stop guns captured by the Russians being carried away during their retreat.

Charles I (1600–49)
King of England and Ireland (1625/49). He failed in his attempt to marry the Infanta Maria of Spain (1623), marrying instead the French princess, Henrietta Maria (1609–69). This disturbed the nation, since the marriage articles permitted her the free exercise of the Catholic religion. Three parliaments were summoned and dissolved in the first four years of his reign; then for 11 years (1629–40) he ruled without one, making much use of prerogative courts. He warred with France (1627–9), and in 1630 made peace with Spain, but his growing need for money led to unpopular economic policies. His attempt to anglicize the Scottish Church brought active resistance in the **Bishops Wars** (1639–40), and he then called a parliament (1640). Having alienated much of the realm, Charles entered into the First of the **English Civil Wars** (1642–6), which saw the defeat of his cause at the Battle of **Naseby**, and he surrendered to the Scots at Newark (1646). After many negotiations, during which his duplicity exasperated opponents, and a second Civil War (1646–8), he came to trial at Westminster, where his dignified refusal to plead was interpreted as a confession

of guilt. He was beheaded at Whitehall (30 Jan 1649). ▷ **Long Parliament**

Charles II (1630–85)
King of England and Ireland (1660/85). He was the son of King **Charles I**. As Prince of Wales, he sided with his father in the **English Civil Wars**, and was then forced into exile. On his father's execution (1649), he assumed the title of King, and was crowned at Scone (1651). Leading poorly organized forces into England, he met disastrous defeat at the Battle of **Worcester** (1651). The next nine years were spent in exile until an impoverished England, in dread of a revival of military despotism, invited him back as King (1660). In 1662 he married the Portuguese Princess **Catherine of Braganza**. It was a childless marriage, though Charles was the father of many illegitimate children. His wars against the Dutch (1665–7 and 1672–4) were unpopular, and the first of these led to the dismissal of his adviser, Lord **Clarendon** (1667), who was replaced by a group of ministers (the **Cabal**). He negotiated subsidies from France in the Secret Treaty of Dover (1670), by which he also promised Louis XIV to make England Catholic once more. He negotiated skilfully and sometimes unscrupulously between conflicting political and religious pressures, and, during the **Exclusion Crisis** (1678–81) refused to deny the succession of his Catholic brother, James. For the last four years of his life, he ruled without parliament. ▷ **Anglo-Dutch Wars; Popish Plot**

Charles (Philip Arthur George), Prince of Wales (1948–)
Eldest son of HM Queen **Elizabeth II** and HRH Prince Philip, Duke of **Edinburgh**, and heir apparent to the throne of Great Britain. Duke of Cornwall as the eldest son of the monarch, he was given the title of Prince of Wales in 1958, and invested at Caernarvon (1969). He served in the RAF and the Royal Navy (1971–6), and in 1981 married Lady Diana Frances, younger daughter of the 8th Earl Spencer, from whom he separated in 1992. They have two sons, Prince William Arthur Philip Louis and Prince Henry Charles Albert David. In the 1980s he made a number of controversial statements about public issues, including architecture and educational standards.

Charleston, Battles of (11 Feb–12 May 1780)
During the **American Revolution**, the victorious British siege of Charleston, South Carolina, which marked the beginning of the

Southern phase of British strategy. At a small cost, the troops of Sir Henry Clinton (c.1738–95) captured a 5 400-strong American garrison and a squadron of four ships.

Chartered companies

A series of companies chartered to rule colonies in late Victorian times, designed to produce imperialism on the cheap. The idea for these companies was based upon the monopolistic ventures of the mercantilist period, like the East India Company of 1599 and the Hudson's Bay Company of 1670, whose charters had been abrogated in the 19c. The British North Borneo Company was chartered in 1882 and survived until the Japanese invasion of 1941. The Royal Niger Company ruled in Nigeria between 1886 and 1898; the Imperial British East Africa Company was chartered to run British East Africa (Kenya and Uganda) from 1888 to 1893; and the British South Africa Company received a charter to rule in Southern and Northern Rhodesia between 1889 and 1923.

Chartism ▷ Chartists

Chartists

Supporters of democratic political reform, most active between 1838 and 1849. Their name derives from the 'People's Charter' presented twice to parliament (1839 and 1842) which called for universal manhood suffrage, voting by secret ballot, the abolition of property qualifications for MPs, payment for MPs, equally-sized constituencies and annually elected parliaments. All but the last of these were obtained but this movement, largely of working people, threatened and occasionally alarmed the authorities, who arrested and imprisoned its leaders during the main phase of the agitation. Chartism was an important cultural and educational force in working-class development. ▷ **O'Connor, Feargus**

Chatham, Dutch Descent on (17–24 June 1667)

A Dutch naval expedition at the end of the second of the **Anglo-Dutch Wars**, which had the effect of forcing the hand of the English at the negotiations for the Peace of **Breda**. The Dutch Pensionary Johan de Witt sent the expedition under his brother, Cornelius, and Admiral Michiel de Ruyter; they sailed up the Thames and captured the fort at Sheerness. They proceeded up

the Medway to the Royal Docks at Chatham, destroyed a number
of ships, and carried off the English flagship the *Royal Charles*,
causing panic in London. Traditionally, this event is under-
reported in English history books. ▷ **Chatham, Dutch Descent on**

Chefoo Convention (1876)

An agreement signed by the British Minister to China, Thomas
Wade, and Li Hongzhang, representing the Chinese government.
The previous year a British consular official, Margary, was killed
in south-west China en route to meet a British expedition from
Burma. The agreement both provided for Chinese government
compensation and an official mission of apology to Britain, as
well as stipulating that four more **treaty ports** were to be opened.
In return, however, the Chinese government was allowed to
increase taxes on opium imports and could impose the *likin*
(internal transit tax) on foreign goods outside the treaty ports.
These two concessions outraged British mercantile opinion, and
the convention was not ratified until 1885.

Chesterfield, Philip Dormer Stanhope, 4th Earl of (1694–1773)

English politician, orator, and man of letters. He studied at Cambridge, made the Grand Tour, became an MP (1715), and in 1726
succeeded his father as Earl. A bitter antagonist of **Walpole**, he
joined the **Pelham** ministry (1744), became Irish Lord-Lieutenant
(1745), and one of the principal Secretaries of State (1746–8).

Childers, (Robert) Erskine (1870–1922)

Irish nationalist and writer. He fought in the **Boer Wars** and
World War I, and wrote a popular spy story, *The Riddle of the
Sands* (1903), and several works of nonfiction. After the establishment of the **Irish Free State**, he joined the IRA, and was active
in the civil war. He was captured and executed at Dublin. His
son, Erskine Childers (1905–74), was President of Ireland in
1973–4.

Chiltern Hundreds

A legally fictitious office of profit under the crown: Steward or
Bailiff of Her Majesty's Chiltern Hundreds of Stoke, Desborough,
and Burnham. To accept this office disqualifies an MP from the
House of Commons. As an MP cannot resign, application to the

Chiltern Hundreds is the conventional manner of leaving the Commons.

Christian, Fletcher (fl.18c)

English seaman. He was the ringleader in the mutiny on the *Bounty*, which sailed to Tahiti 1787–8. In 1808 his descendants were found on Pitcairn Islands. ▷ **Bligh, William**

Churchill, Lord Randolph (Henry Spencer) (1849–95)

English politician. He was the third son of the 7th Duke of Marlborough, and the father of Winston **Churchill**. He entered parliament in 1874, and became conspicuous in 1880 as the leader of a ginger group of Conservatives known as the 'Fourth Party'. He was Secretary for India (1885–6), and for a short while Chancellor of the Exchequer and Leader of the House of Commons. His powers rapidly diminished by syphilis, he resigned after his first budget proved unacceptable, and thereafter devoted little time to politics. ▷ **Conservative Party**

Churchill, Sir Winston (Leonard Spencer) (1874–1965)

English politician, Prime Minister of Britain, and author. The eldest son of Randolph **Churchill**, he was gazetted to the 4th Hussars in 1895, and his army career included fighting at Omdurman during the 1898 Nile Expeditionary Force. During the second Boer War he acted as a London newspaper correspondent. Initially a Conservative MP (1900), he joined the Liberals in 1904, and was Colonial Under-Secretary (1905), President of the Board of Trade (1908), Home Secretary (1910), and First Lord of the Admiralty (1911). In 1915 he was made the scapegoat for the **Dardanelles** disaster, but in 1917 became Minister of Munitions. After **World War I** he was Secretary of State for War and Air (1919–21), and (as a 'Constitutionalist' supporter of the Conservatives) Chancellor of the Exchequer (1924–9). In 1929 he returned to the Conservative fold, but remained out of step with the leadership until **World War II**, when he returned to the Admiralty; on Neville **Chamberlain**'s defeat (May 1940) he formed a coalition government, and, holding both the premiership (1940–5) and the defence portfolio, led Britain through the war against Germany and Italy with steely resolution. Defeated in the July 1945 election, he became a pugnacious Leader of the Opposition. In 1951 he became Prime Minister again, though he was less effective after a stroke (1953) which was concealed from the public.

From 1955 until his resignation in 1964, he remained a venerated backbencher. He achieved a world reputation not only as a great strategist and inspiring war leader, but as a classic orator with a supreme command of English, a talented painter and a writer with a great breadth of mind and a profound sense of history. He was knighted in 1953, and won the Nobel Prize for Literature the same year. ▷ **Boer Wars; Conservative Party; Liberal Party**

Cinque Ports
Originally, the five southern English coast ports of Dover, Hastings, Hythe, Romney, and Sandwich, associated by royal authority (under **Edward the Confessor**) to provide ships for naval defence; Rye and Winchelsea were added later. They received royal privileges, including (from 1265) the right to send barons to parliament, and charters, the first dating from 1278; they were governed by a Lord Warden who was also Constable of Dover Castle. Their role declined with the growth of the navy under the Tudors and Stuarts, and the status was abolished in 1835. ▷ **Stuart, House of; Tudor, House of**

civil disobedience
A political strategy adopted by **M K Gandhi** and his followers in India in 1930, in opposition to Britain's imperial rule: launched by a march to the coast in order to break the law symbolically by making salt (on which tax was payable), it was a non-violent, mass, illegal protest, intended to discredit the authority of the state. The movement was banned, and many were arrested, including Gandhi; but a pact was reached in 1931, and Gandhi then participated in the second of the **Round Table Conferences**.

civil rights
The rights guaranteed by certain states to its citizens. Fundamental to the concept of civil rights is the premise that a government should not arbitrarily act to infringe upon these rights, and that individuals and groups, through political action, have a legitimate role in determining and influencing what constitutes them. Historically, civil rights in England have been protected by the **Magna Carta** and in the USA by the Constitution and Bill of Rights. In common usage, the term often refers to the rights of groups, particularly ethnic and racial minorities, as well as to the rights of the individual.

Clarendon, Edward Hyde, 1st Earl of (1609–74)
English statesman and historian. He trained as a lawyer, and in 1640 became a member of the **Short Parliament**. At first he supported parliamentary claims, but in 1641 became a close adviser of **Charles I**, and headed the royalist opposition in the Commons until 1642. He was knighted in 1643, and made Chancellor of the Exchequer, became High Chancellor in 1658, and at the **Restoration** (1660) was created Baron Hyde and (1661) Earl of Clarendon. In 1660 his daughter Anne (1638–71) secretly married the King's brother, James (later **James VII and II**). Unpopular as a statesman, Clarendon irritated Cavaliers and Puritans alike, and in 1667 he fell victim to a conspiracy at court. Impeached for high treason, he left the country for France, where he died. ▷ **English Civil Wars**

Clarendon Code
A series of Acts passed by the **Cavalier Parliament** (1661–79) between 1661 and 1665 which reasserted the supremacy of the Church of England over Protestant nonconformity after the collapse of the 'Puritan Revolution' in 1660. The most important were the Corporation Act (1661) and the Act of Uniformity (1662). Nonconformity was recognized as lawful, but severe restrictions were placed on the activities of Nonconformists. ▷ **Puritanism; Uniformity, Acts of**

Clarendon, Constitutions of (1164)
A written declaration of rights claimed by **Henry II** of England in ecclesiastical affairs, with the purpose of restoring royal control over the English Church. Promulgated at Clarendon, near Salisbury, the Constitutions (especially Clause 3, which jeopardized benefit of clergy and threatened clerical criminals with secular penalties) brought Thomas Becket and Henry II into open conflict. ▷ **Becket, St Thomas (à)**

Claudius (10BC–AD54)
Roman Emperor (AD41/54). He was the grandson of the Empress Livia, brother of Germanicus, and nephew of the Emperor Tiberius. Becoming Emperor largely by accident in the chaos after Caligula's murder, he proved to be an able and progressive ruler. He extended the Roman Empire by his annexation of Britain, Mauretania and Thrace.

Clayton–Bulwer Treaty (19 Apr 1850)
A US–British agreement on the terms for building a canal across Central America. It remained in effect until 1901, when it was superseded by the Hay–Pauncefote Treaty. Its major provision was to forbid either party to exercise exclusive control or to build fortifications. The parties involved were the US Secretary of State, John M Clayton, and the British Minister to Washington, Sir Henry Lytton Bulwer. The Panama Canal was not completed until 1914.

Clive of Plassey, Robert (1725–74)
British soldier and administrator. In 1743 he joined the British **East India Company** in Madras, and took part in the campaigns against the French. In 1755 he was called to avenge the so-called **Black Hole of Calcutta**, and at the Battle of **Plassey** (1757) defeated a large Indian force — much of which defected to the British side following the offer of inducements to the commanding general, Mir Jaffar, and the payment of bribes by Indian merchants to the soldiers of the Mughal Nawab (Governor), **Siraj ud-Daula**. For three years, Clive was sole ruler in all but name of Bengal. In 1760, he returned to England, entered parliament, and was made a baron (1762). In 1765 he returned to Calcutta, effectively reformed the civil service, and re-established military discipline. His measures were seen as drastic, and he became the subject of a select committee inquiry upon his return to England in 1767. He committed suicide in London.

CND (Campaign for Nuclear Disarmament)
An organization formed in 1958 to oppose Britain's development of a **nuclear weapons** programme. It organized annual Aldermaston marches and briefly persuaded the Labour Party to declare a policy of unilateral disarmament in 1960, only to see it effectively reverse that decision a year later. An effective pressure group in the 1960s, its popularity and influence had already begun to decline before the signing of nuclear non-proliferation pacts in the 1980s, although supporters agreed that as part of a European movement it played a part in halting the arms race.

Coastal Command
A separate functional Command within the British Royal Air Force (1936–69). Moves to transfer it to the Royal Navy caused

a political storm in 1958–9. During **World War II**, the Command destroyed 184 German U-boats and 470 000 tonnes of enemy shipping, and played a decisive role in winning the Battle of the **Atlantic**.

Cobbett, William (1763–1835)

English journalist and reformer. The son of a farmer, he moved on impulse to London (1783), spent a year reading widely, and joined the army, serving in New Brunswick (1785–91). In 1792 he married and went to the USA, where he wrote fierce pieces against the native Democrats under the name 'Peter Porcupine'. Returning to England in 1800, he was welcomed by the **Tories**, and started his famous *Weekly Political Register* (1802), which continued until his death, changing in 1804 from its original Toryism to an uncompromising radicalism. In 1810 he was imprisoned for two years for criticizing the flogging of militiamen by German mercenaries, and in 1817 he went again to the USA, fearing a second imprisonment. Returning in 1819 he travelled widely in Britain, and finally became an MP (1832).

Cobden, Richard (1804–65)

English economist and politician. He worked as a clerk and commercial traveller in London, then went into the calico business, settling in Manchester. He visited the USA in 1835, and the Levant in 1836–7, after which he published two pamphlets preaching free trade (thus earning the nickname 'the Apostle of Free Trade'), non-intervention, and speaking against 'Russophobia'. A radical-Liberal, in 1838 he helped to found the **Anti-Corn Law League**, becoming its most prominent member. He became an MP in 1841. His lectures and parliamentary speeches focused opinion on the **Corn Laws**, which were repealed in 1846.

Coke, Sir Edward (1552–1634)

English jurist. He became Speaker of the House of Commons (1593), Attorney-General (1594), Chief Justice of the Common Pleas (1606), Chief Justice of the King's Bench (1613), and Privy Councillor. He vigorously prosecuted **Essex**, **Raleigh**, and the **Gunpowder Plot** conspirators, but after 1606 increasingly supported the idea of national liberties vested in parliament, against the royal prerogative. He was dismissed in 1617, and from 1620 led the popular party in parliament, serving nine months in prison. The **Petition of Right** (1628) was largely his doing. Most of his epoch-making Law Reports were published during the period 1600–15.

Cold War

A state of tension or hostility between states that stops short of military action or a 'hot' war. The term is most frequently used to describe the relationship between the USSR and the major Western powers following **World War II**. Tension was particularly high in the 1960s when the nuclear 'arms race' intensified. The process of detente, begun in the late 1960s, led through two decades of arms reduction and control negotiations to the 'end' of the Cold War in 1990, mainly as a result of a dramatic change in the Soviet attitude under Mikhail Gorbachev.

Colenso, Battle of (1899)

A reverse suffered by the British in the Boer War. General Sir Redvers Buller (1838–1908), fearing that his forces might be cut off in his efforts to relieve Ladysmith, changed his plans and attempted to take Colenso, an important crossing-point on the Tugela River. He was defeated by Boer force under Louis Botha.
▷ **Boer Wars**

Collier, Jeremy (1650–1726)

English bishop. He became a priest in 1677, and refused to take the oath of allegiance to **William III** and Mary II (1689). Arrested in 1692 on suspicion of being involved in a Jacobite plot, in 1696 he was outlawed for giving absolution to two would-be assassins on the scaffold. Returning to London, he continued to preach to a congregation of those who had not taken the oath (nonjurors), and was consecrated bishop in 1713. He was also the author of a celebrated attack on the immorality of the English stage (1698).
▷ **Jacobites**

Collingwood, Cuthbert, Baron (1750–1810)

British admiral. He joined the navy at 11, and from 1778 his career was closely connected with that of **Nelson**. He fought at the Battles of Brest (1794), **Cape St Vincent** (1797), and **Trafalgar** (1805), where he succeeded Nelson as commander. He was created baron after Trafalgar, died at sea, and is buried beside Nelson in St Paul's Cathedral, London.

Collins, Michael (1890–1922)

Irish politician and **Sinn Féin** leader. He was an MP (1918–22), and organized the nationalist intelligence system against the British. With Arthur Griffith, he was largely responsible for the negotiation of the treaty with Great Britain in 1921. Commander-General of the government forces in the civil war, he was killed in an ambush between Bandon and Macroom.

Colonial and Imperial Conferences

A series of conferences at which representatives of the British colonies and dominions discussed matters of common imperial concern; usually held in London. The first Colonial Conference was held in 1887, and this was followed by others in 1894, 1897, 1902 and 1907. They were particularly concerned with defence, although they also dealt with issues of trade and communications. The first Imperial Conference was held in 1911, the change of name implying a new status for the colonies, and was followed by others in 1921, 1923, 1926, 1930 and 1937, mainly concerned with constitutional changes and economic matters. After **World War II** they were replaced by the Conferences of Commonwealth Prime Ministers, now by the Commonwealth Heads of Government meetings. ▷ **British Empire; Commonwealth of Nations**

Colonial Development and Welfare Acts

(1929, 1940, 1945, 1949 and 1950)

A series of acts designed to offer funds for the development of British colonies. They represented a departure from the notion that colonies should be self-supporting and a recognition that development might serve to combine colonial idealism with British economic self-interest. The 1929 act made available £1 million; the 1940 act was partly a response to riots in the West Indies and partly designed to encourage sympathy and loyalty during **World War II**. £20 million was set aside, but only £3 million was spent in the first four years. The principle was extended in the post-war climate of trusteeship when £120 million was invested under the three acts introduced by Clement **Attlee**'s Labour government.

colonialism

A form of imperial domination of one country (the colonial power) over others (its colonies) for political, economic, or strategic purposes. The main period of colonial rule was 1870–1960, when Western European powers 'scrambled' to gain control over territories in Africa, Asia and the Far East. The French and British had the largest colonial empires. Colonialism is said by some to have established a system of 'dependency' in the colony, whose economy and political administration served primarily not its own needs but those of the colonial power. This has made it difficult for the colony to develop on its own terms and in its own direction. This situation is said to prevail even after the granting of 'independence', and these dependent countries make up the 'underdeveloped' Third World.

Combination Acts (1799 and 1800)

British legislation which prohibited the coming together ('combination') of workers in trade unions. The Acts were part of anti-reformist legislation passed by the Pitt government during the French wars, though combinations in many trades were already illegal. The Acts were repealed in 1824–5, and trade unions, though under severe restrictions, legalized. ▷ **Pitt, William, 'the Younger'**

Combined Operations Command

A British force established in 1940 when Winston **Churchill** appointed Admiral of the Fleet Lord Keyes to coordinate British commando raids against German-occupied Europe. Keyes's successor Lord **Mountbatten** (1941–3) directed larger operations involving all three Services, and prepared for the eventual Allied invasion of France, in which Combined Operations techniques were to play a crucial role. ▷ **D-Day; World War II**

Commons, House of

The lower, and effectively the ruling, chamber of the bicameral legislature of the UK. It contains 650 members, elected by universal adult suffrage, each representing a single constituency. The Commons is elected for a maximum period of five years, though the prime minister may call an election at any time within that period, and the government is drawn from the party that wins the majority of seats. The ascendancy of the House of Commons over the House of Lords began during the 16c, and was completed with the passage of the Parliament Acts of 1911 and 1949. The Commons is dominated by a disciplined party system, which means that governments are generally assured of a majority in the passage of legislation. In this sense the Commons serves a legitimizing rather than a legislating function. ▷ **Lords, House of**

Commonwealth

English republican regime created by Oliver **Cromwell**, based on the **Rump Parliament** established in 1649, which lasted until the Instrument of Government created a **Protectorate** in 1653. It failed to achieve political settlement at home, but its armies pacified Scotland and Ireland. The Navigation Acts (1650 and 1651) and the **Anglo-Dutch Wars** (1652–4) fostered overseas trade and colonies. ▷ **English Civil Wars**

Commonwealth of Nations

A voluntary organization of autonomous states which had been imperial possessions of Britain. Its head is the reigning British monarch. It was formally established by the Statute of Westminster (1931) and meets frequently to discuss matters of mutual interest and concern. While most states, on independence, chose to become members of the Commonwealth, three have left (Irish Republic, 1949; Pakistan, 1972; Fiji, 1987). South Africa left in 1961 but rejoined in 1994. ▷ **Westminster, Statutes of**

communism

A political ideology which has as its central principle the communal ownership of all property, and thereby the abolition of private property. Although examples of early social and religious groupings based upon communal sharing of property have been cited, modern communism is specifically associated with the theories of Karl Marx. Marx saw the emergence of a communist society as being the final stage in a historical process that was rooted in human material needs, preceded by feudalism, capitalism, and (a transitional stage) socialism. Communism, according to Marx, would abolish class distinctions and end the exploitation of the masses inherent in the capitalist system. The working class, or proletariat, would be the instrument of a revolution that would overthrow the capitalist system and liberate human potential. A fully developed communist system would operate according to the principle of 'from each according to his ability, to each according to his need', and as there would be no need for the state to regulate society, it would 'wither away'. Marx's writings have provided a powerful ideological basis for communist and many socialist parties and governments, which have legitimized the implementation of their policies by reference to Marxism or some variant of it.

Communist Party of Great Britain

Formed in 1920 through the merger of various leftist groups, it acknowledged from its inception the authority of Moscow. Its fortunes improved with Soviet intervention in **World War II,** but it never won more than four seats in parliament, and the 1956 Hungarian Uprising saw many defections. Unlike many European parties, its influence was minimal long before the collapse of the USSR (1990–1). ▷ **communism**

Compton, Spencer, Earl of Wilmington (1673–1743)

English politician. He was Paymaster-General from 1722 to 1730 and **George II** attempted to make him his First Minister on succeeding to the throne (1727), but was outmanoeuvred by **Walpole**. Compton remained a strong supporter of the King as Walpole's popularity waned after the outbreak of war with Spain (1739). As First Lord of the Treasury (1742–3), he was leader of the administration in name only, being overshadowed by Thomas **Pelham**-Holles, 1st Duke of Newcastle, and **Carteret**. ▷ **Whigs**

Condominium (Anglo/Egyptian Sudan)

After the defeat of the Mahdist forces by **Kitchener**, the area of the Upper Nile was linked with Egypt, named the Anglo/Egyptian Sudan and controlled nominally by Britain and Egypt as a 'condominium'. In practice, though, real power lay in British hands as Britain was, at the time, in effective control of Egypt. The period of the condominium, initially both economically and socially advantageous to the Sudan, led (through the development of an educated class) to a desire for independence. Some progress was made and in 1948 Britain recognized the validity of these aspirations. However, the movement of the Sudanese towards independence received a setback when, in 1951, King Farouk of Egypt proclaimed himself also King of the Sudan. Farouk's subsequent fall led to Egypt's recognition, in principle, of the Sudanese right to independence, and full independence was declared in 1955.

Confederation Movement

Canadian political movement for unification within the British North American provinces. Prefigured at various times from the

American Revolution onwards, consideration of the project by Earl **Grey**, the British Colonial Secretary (1846–52), set in train discussions within the maritime provinces. At the same time a growing paralysis of government was becoming evident within the Province of Canada. A T Galt's entry into the Cartier–Macdonald government in 1858 was only secured on condition that it sought confederation, which was rapidly being seen as a necessity. The English-speaking business community believed it to be essential for economic growth and expansion to the west against American competition, while the threat to reciprocity demanded closer trading links between Canada and the Maritimes. The British government's commitment to Canadian defence had been called into question since the Oregon dispute, and with the onset of the American Civil War, the provinces became aware that they were very vulnerable to retaliation from the Northern states because of British policies and because Confederates were ready to use Canada as a base for raids. In 1864 the 'great coalition' of Canadian reformers and conservatives under the leadership of Sir Étienne-Paschal Tache broached the idea of a general union at the Charlottetown Conference called by the Maritimes. Discussions continued at the Quebec Conference, where agreement was quickly reached. Acceptance by the provincial legislatures was much more difficult to obtain, and was achieved in Canada (where it needed all George Étienne Cartier's political acumen to persuade the French-Canadians) only after lengthy debate. In the Maritimes, Newfoundland and Prince Edward Island rejected confederation, but Samuel Tilley and Charles Tupper eventually secured its adoption in New Brunswick and Nova Scotia. The final resolutions were agreed at the London Conference of 1866 and embodied in the **British North America Act** of 1867. ▷ **Dominion of Canada**

conscription

The practice of compelling young men of eligible age and fitness to serve by statute in the armed forces of a nation. To meet the huge manpower needs of **World War I**, conscription was introduced in Great Britain in early 1916. Conscription was again enforced in Britain from 1939 to 1945, continuing in peacetime as National Service, which was finally abolished in 1962.

Conservative Party

One of the two major political parties in the UK, its full name being the Conservative and Unionist Party. It developed from the

Tory Party during the 19c and pursued policies, first under **Peel** and then **Disraeli**, designed to broaden its appeal beyond the English landowners and supporters of the Church of England. It has largely succeeded in this, having been in power either solely or as the dominant element in coalitions for approximately two-thirds of the period since Disraeli's election victory of 1874. Its main support, however, has remained English rather than British and the party is stronger in rural than in urban areas. ▷ **Tories; Whigs**

Constantinople Agreements (Mar–Apr 1915)
Britain and France feared that Russia would make a separate peace with Germany unless she was offered significant territorial gains. They secretly agreed, therefore, that after **World War I** Russia should receive Constantinople (Istanbul) and land along the Straits. This was a remarkable change in British policy particularly, as throughout the 19c Britain had opposed Russia gaining control of the Straits. After the October Revolution of 1917, however, the Bolsheviks rejected all agreements made by the Tsarist government.

Cook, James (1728–79)
English navigator, born at Marton, Yorkshire. He spent several years as a seaman in North Sea vessels, then joined the navy in 1755, becoming master in 1759. He surveyed the area around the St Lawrence River, Quebec, then in the *Endeavour* carried the Royal Society expedition to Tahiti to observe the transit of Venus across the Sun (1768–71). He circumnavigated New Zealand and charted parts of Australia. In his second voyage he sailed round Antarctica (1772–5), and discovered several Pacific island groups. Thanks to his dietary precautions, there was only one death among the crew. His third voyage (1776–9) aimed to discover a passage round the north coast of America from the Pacific; he was forced to turn back however, and on his return voyage was killed by natives on Hawaii.

Cooperative Party
A political party which grew out of the ideas of voluntary mutual economic assistance developed in the 19c by Robert Owen (1771–1858). Established in 1917, one candidate, who joined with the parliamentary **Labour Party**, was elected to the House of Com-

mons in 1918. Thereafter it became closely integrated with the Labour Party.

Copenhagen, Battles of (1801 and 1807)
British naval operations aimed at preventing Danish neutrality from benefiting France during the **Napoleonic Wars**. The first engagement (Apr 1801), led by Admirals Hyde Parker (1739–1807) and **Nelson**, resulted in Denmark's withdrawal from the Armed Neutrality. After the bombardment of Copenhagen (Sep 1807) by Admiral James Gambier (1756–1833) and Arthur Wellesley (later Duke of **Wellington**), the Danes surrendered their fleet and stores.

Corn Laws
Legislation regulating the trade in corn. This was common in the 18c, but the most famous Corn Law was that enacted by Lord **Liverpool**'s government in 1815. Passed at a time when market prices were dropping rapidly, it imposed prohibitively high duties on the import of foreign corn when the domestic price was lower than 80 shillings (£4) a quarter. Widely criticized by radical politicians as legislation designed to protect the landed interest at the expense of the ordinary consumer, the Corn Law was amended in 1828, with the introduction of a sliding scale, and duties were further reduced by **Peel** in 1842. The Laws were repealed in 1846.
▷ **Anti-Corn Law League**

Cornwallis, Charles, 1st Marquis (1738–1805)
British general and politician. He served in the **Seven Years War**, although he was personally opposed to taxing the American colonists, accepting a command in the war. He defeated Gates at Camden (1780), but was forced to surrender at Yorktown (1781). In 1786 he became Governor-General of India, where he defeated Tippoo Sahib of Mysore, and introduced the series of reforms known as the Cornwallis Code. He returned in 1793, to be made marquis. He was Lord-Lieutenant of Ireland (1798–1801), and negotiated the Peace of Amiens (1802). Reappointed Governor-General of India (1804), he died at Ghazipur.

Corporation Act (1661)
An Act passed by the **Cavalier Parliament** (1661–79), soon after the **Restoration** of **Charles II**. Office in municipal corporations

was restricted to those who took the sacrament according to the usage of the Church of England. Part of the reassertion of Anglican supremacy represented by the **Clarendon Code**, the Act remained on the statute book until 1828.

Cosgrave, William Thomas (1880–1965)

Irish politician. He joined the **Sinn Féin** movement at an early age, and took part in the **Easter Rising** (1916). He was elected a Sinn Féin MP (1918–22) and, after holding office as first President of the **Irish Free State** (1922–32), became Leader of the Opposition (1932–44). His son, Liam, was Leader of the **Fine Gael** Party (1965–7) and Prime Minister (1973–7).

Covenanters

Originally, signatories (and their successors) of the National Covenant (1638) and the **Solemn League and Covenant** (1643) in Scotland, who resisted the theory of 'Divine Right of Kings' and the imposition of an episcopal system on the Presbyterian Church of Scotland. When declared rebels, they resorted to open-air preaching. Until **Presbyterianism** was restored in 1690, they were savagely persecuted, with imprisonment, execution without trial, and banishment (eg to Holland or the USA).

Cowpens, Battle of (1781)

During the **American Revolution**, an engagement in South Carolina in which a small American army under Daniel Morgan (1736–1802) defeated a British force under Banastre Tarleton (1754–1833).

Cox, Percy (1864–1937)

British diplomat. After receiving his military training, he served in India. During his time there, he left the army to work in the Indian political service in the Persian Gulf area; he was subsequently made Foreign Secretary in India but his major work was in Iraq, where he moved in 1914. He attended the Cairo Conference of 1921 which resulted, on his returning to Iraq, in his supervision of the emergence by resolution of the Council of Ministers of the Amir Faysal, second son of Sharif **Husayn ibn 'Ali** of Mecca, as King of Iraq (as Faysal I), a resolution which was ratified by a referendum upon which Cox insisted. Given his military background, he was also tasked with supervising the creation of an army for the country, and with looking after its constitutional arrangements. His last act in Iraq was his signature on behalf of the British of a Protocol to the 1922 Anglo-Iraqi Treaty which, amongst other things, reduced the effective period of the Treaty to four years, a provision which was welcomed by the King and a majority of the politicians.

Craig, James, 1st Viscount Craigavon (1871–1940)

Ulster politician. His early career was as a stockbroker. He was MP in the UK parliament (1906–21) where he vigorously campaigned to preserve the Act of Union against the Irish Nationalists. After Northern Ireland refused to join the South in 1921, he worked as its first Prime Minister (1921–40) to maintain order in the Province and then to develop social and educational services under powers devolved to **Stormont**. His Unionist beliefs ensured that the interests of the Protestant majority in Northern Ireland would be paramount. While still in office, he died suddenly. ▷
Carson, Edward

Craig, James Henry (1748–1812)

British soldier and colonial administrator. He fought in the **American Revolution**, being wounded at the Battle of Bunker Hill (1775) and serving with distinction in the invasion of the Hudson River Valley. After playing a prominent part in the capture of the Dutch colony of the Cape of Good Hope, he was made the colony's temporary governor from 1795 to 1797. After further commands in India, England and in the **Napoleonic Wars**, he became Governor-General of Canada (1807–11). There, with the backing of London and the English-speaking Montreal merchants, he sought to anglicize the province. To that end he dissolved the assembly, and cashiered many French officers from the militia. In 1810 the printers and proprietor of the critical newspaper, *Le Canadien*, were arrested for treason and, when war broke out with the USA, he introduced a special Act which enabled him to suppress the newspaper altogether. This provoked both riots and the election of an increased number of radical French-Canadian deputies. The British government drew back from its policy and Craig was recalled. His name is still hated in the province, and the period of his governorship is known as the 'Reign of Terror'.

Cranmer, Thomas (1489–1556)

Archbishop of Canterbury. His suggestion that **Henry VIII** appeal for his divorce to the universities of Christendom won him the

King's favour, and he was appointed a royal chaplain. He was made Archbishop of Canterbury in 1533, making allegiance to the Pope 'for form's sake'. He later annulled Henry's marriages to **Catherine of Aragon** (1533) and to Anne **Boleyn** (1536), and divorced him from **Anne of Cleves** (1540). He was largely responsible for the Book of Common Prayer (1549 and 1552). On Henry's death, Cranmer rushed Protestant changes through. He had little to do with affairs of state, but agreed to the plan to divert the succession from Mary to Lady Jane **Grey** (1553), for which he was later arraigned for treason. Sentenced to death, he retracted the seven recantations he had been forced to sign, before being burnt alive. ▷ **Reformation** (England)

Crécy, Battle of (1346)
A battle between France and England in the **Hundred Years War**. Using tactics perfected against the Scots, **Edward III** routed a larger French Army, mainly cavalry, near Abbeville (Somme). It was a classic demonstration of the superiority over mounted knights of a coordinated force of dismounted men-at-arms, and archers providing offensive fire-power.

Crimean War (1854–6)
A war fought in the Crimean Peninsula by Britain and France against Russia. Its origins lay in Russian successes in the Black Sea area and the British and French desire to prevent further expansion into the **Ottoman Empire** by the Russians, since this would threaten the Mediterranean and overland routes to India. Major battles were fought in 1854 at the River Alma (20 Sep), **Balaclava** (25 Oct), and Inkerman (5 Nov). The war was notable both for the nursing exploits of Florence Nightingale at Scutari and the pioneer war reports of W H Russell in *The Times*. The fall of the Russian fortress at **Sevastopol** (Sep 1855) led to peace negotiations. Under the treaty finally agreed at Paris (Mar 1856), Russia returned southern Bessarabia to neighbouring Moldavia and had to accept the neutralization of the Black Sea; Moldavia and Wallachia were soon to unite as an independent Romania. Shattered by its defeat in the war, Russia turned to overdue internal reform.

Cripps, (Richard) Stafford (1889–1952)
English politician. He made a fortune in patent and compensation cases. In 1930 he was appointed Solicitor-General in the second

Labour government, and became an MP in 1931. During the 1930s he was associated with several extreme left-wing movements, and was expelled from the **Labour Party** in 1939 for his 'popular front' opposing Neville **Chamberlain**'s policy of **appeasement**. He sat as an independent MP during **World War II**, was Ambassador to the USSR (1940–2), and in 1942 became Lord Privy Seal, and later Minister of Aircraft Production. In the 1945 Labour government, he was readmitted to the party and appointed President of the Board of Trade (1942–5). In 1947 he became Minister of Economic Affairs and then Chancellor of the Exchequer, introducing a successful austerity policy. He resigned due to illness in 1950.

Cromer, Evelyn Baring, Earl (1841–1917)

British colonial administrator. He was private secretary to his cousin, Lord Northbrook, when Viceroy of India (1872–6), British Controller-General of Egyptian Finance (1879–80), Finance Minister of India (1880–83), and Agent and Consul-General in Egypt (1883–1907). Effectively the ruler of Egypt, he reformed its administration and agricultural policies, and put its finances on a good footing.

Cromwell, Oliver (1599–1658)

English soldier and statesman. A convinced Puritan, after studying law in London, he sat in both the **Short Parliament** and the **Long Parliament** (1640), and when war broke out (1642) fought on the parliamentary side at Edgehill (1642). He formed his unconquerable Ironsides, combining rigid discipline with strict morality, and it was his cavalry that secured the victory at the Battle of **Marston Moor** (1644), while under **Fairfax** he led the **New Model Army** to decisive success at **Naseby** (1645). He quelled insurrection in Wales in support of **Charles I**, and defeated the invading army of Hamilton. He then brought the King to trial, and was one of the signatories of his death warrant (1649). Having established the **Commonwealth**, Cromwell suppressed the **Levellers**, the Irish (1649–50), and the Scots (under **Charles II**) at **Dunbar** (1650) and Worcester (1651). Using the power of the army, he dissolved the Rump of the Long Parliament (1653), and after the failure of a nominated **Barebone's Parliament**, then established a **Protectorate** (1653). As Protector (1653–8), he refused the offer of the crown (1657). At home he extended religious toleration, and gave Scotland and Ireland parliamentary representation. Under him the

Commonwealth became the head and champion of Protestant Europe. ▷ **English Civil Wars**

Cromwell, Thomas, Earl of Essex (c.1485–1540)

English statesman, known as *malleus monachorum* ('the Hammer of the Monks'). He served as a soldier on the Continent (1504–12), then entered **Wolsey**'s service in 1514, and became his agent and secretary. He arranged **Henry VIII**'s divorce with **Catherine of Aragon**, and put into effect the Act of Supremacy (1534) and the dissolution of the monasteries (1536–9). He became Privy Councillor (1531), Chancellor of the Exchequer (1533), Secretary of State and Master of the Rolls (1534), Vicar-General (1535), Lord Privy Seal and Baron Cromwell of Oakham (1536), Knight of the Garter and Dean of Wells (1537), Lord Great Chamberlain (1539), and finally Earl of Essex (1540). In each of his offices, he proved himself a highly efficient administrator and adviser to the King; but Henry's aversion to **Anne of Cleves**, consort of Cromwell's choosing, led to his ruin. He was accused of treason, sent to the Tower and beheaded. ▷ **Reformation** (England)

Crosland, Tony (Charles Anthony Raven) (1918–77)

English politician. He taught in Oxford after serving in **World War II**. Elected as a Labour MP in 1950, he became Secretary for Education and Science (1965–7), President of the Board of Trade (1967–9), Secretary for Local Government and Regional Planning (1969–70), Environment Secretary (1974–6), and Foreign Secretary (1976–7). A strong supporter of Hugh **Gaitskell**, he was a key member of the revisionist wing of the **Labour Party** aiming to modernize socialist ideology, and wrote one of its seminal texts, *The Future of Socialism* (1956). ▷ **socialism**

Crossman, Richard (Howard Stafford) (1907–74)

English politician. He became a philosophy tutor at Oxford, and leader of the Labour group on Oxford City Council (1934–40). In 1938 he joined the staff of the *New Statesman*. In 1945 he became a Labour MP, and under **Wilson** was Minister of Housing and Local Government (1964–6), then Secretary of State for Social Services and head of the Department of Health (1968–70). He was editor of the *New Statesman* (1970–2). His best-known work is his series of political diaries, begun in 1952, keeping a detailed, and frequently indiscreet, record of the day-to-day workings of government and political life. They were published in four volumes (1975–81), despite attempts to suppress them. ▷ **Labour Party**

Crown Colony Government

Imperial system of trusteeship government in which full executive power was vested in the Governor. Introduced into Trinidad and St Lucia in 1797 and 1803 respectively, 'the direct protection of the Crown of the unrepresented classes, which takes the place of representation' was meant to be a panacea to cure the evils of the **Assemblies**. The elective principle was absent from the constitution, the Governor's Executive Council being composed of his chief officials and the Legislative Council which, while it had nominated unofficial members, possessed an unofficial majority. The system was in place in most of the British West Indies by 1898 and, although reformist and impartial, it excluded the rising coloured middle-class from the decision-making process and was viewed as imposed, alien and paternalistic.

Crusade, Third (1189–92)

This was proclaimed by Pope Gregory VIII following the defeat by Saladin of the field army of the Latin Kingdom of Jerusalem at the Battle of Hittin (July 1187), and his subsequent capture of the Holy City itself (Oct 1187). Led by the three great rulers of Western Christendom, Frederick I, 'Barbarossa', Philip II of France and **Richard I, 'the Lionheart'**, the Crusade promised much. It did not, in the event, live up to this promise. Barbarossa perished by drowning in the River Cydnus in Anatolia before even arriving in the Holy Land, with the consequent disintegration of the German effort; the leisurely outward progress of Philip and Richard, the pillaging and capture of Cyprus from their thoroughly disillusioned Byzantine co-religionists, and the scarcely-veiled hostility between the French and English (which led to Philip's early return to France and Richard's subsequent pre-occupation with affairs at home and his own departure in 1192) meant that the Crusade failed in its objective of regaining Jerusalem. It did, however, bring Guy of Lusignan's siege of Acre to a successful close in 1191 and gained, if not an overwhelming, at least morale-lifting victory over Saladin's forces at Arsuf in the same year. Richard managed to achieve a compromise settlement whereby pilgrimage to the Holy Places was safeguarded and the Crusaders maintained their position on the Levantine littoral with the Muslims (in this case the Ayyubid Dynasty) controlling the hinterland.

Culdees

Originally, monks in the Irish church in the 8c and the Scottish Church in the 9c, who later became secular clergy. In Scotland, they were respected for their high ideals and spirituality, and survived in St Andrews until the 14c.

Culloden, Battle of (16 Apr 1746)

A battle fought near Inverness, the last major battle on British soil, which marked the end of the Jacobite **Forty-Five Rebellion** led by Charles Edward **Stuart**. His force, mainly of Scottish High-landers, was crushed by a superior force of English and lowland Scots under the Duke of **Cumberland**. ▷ **Jacobites**

Cumberland, William Augustus, Duke of (1721–65)

British general. The second son of King **George II**, he fought in the War of the Austrian Succession (1740–8), in which he was wounded at Dettingen (1743) and defeated at Fontenoy (1745). He crushed Charles Edward **Stuart**'s rebellion at the Battle of **Culloden** (1746), and by his harsh policies against the Highland clans thereafter earned the lasting title of 'Butcher'. In the **Seven Years War**, he surrendered to the French (1757), and thereafter retired.

Curzon (of Kedleston), George Nathaniel, Marquis (1859–1925)

English politician. He became an MP in 1886, and travelled widely in the East. He became Under-Secretary for India (1891–2), and for Foreign Affairs (1895), and in 1898 was made Viceroy of India and given an Irish barony. He introduced many social and political changes, establishing in the interests of imperial security a new North-West Frontier province (1901) under a Chief Commissioner responsible to the government of India alone. He also partitioned Bengal (1905). He resigned after a disagreement with Lord **Kitchener** (1905), returning to politics in 1915 as Lord Privy Seal. He became Foreign Secretary (1919–24), and was created a marquis in 1921.

Cymbeline (d.c.43 AD)
Pro-Roman King of the Catuvellauni. From his capital at Camulodunum (Colchester), he ruled most of south-east Britain. Shakespeare's character was based on Holinshed's half-historical Cunobelinus. ▷ **Britain, Roman; Caractacus; Cassivellaunus**

D

Dáil Eireann

The lower house of the parliament of the Irish Republic. Unlike the upper house, the Senate (*Seanad Eireann*), which is appointed, the Dáil is elected by universal suffrage by proportional representation for a period of five years. It nominates the Prime Minister for appointment by the President. There are 144 members, who are called *Teatcha Dala*.

Dalhousie, James Andrew Broun Ramsay, 1st Marquis of

(1812–60)

British politician and colonial administrator. He became an MP in 1837, was made Earl of Dalhousie in 1838, and President of the Board of Trade in 1845. As Governor-General of India (1847–56), he encouraged the development of railways and irrigation works. He annexed Satara (1847) and Punjab (1849), but the annexation of Awadh (Oudh) (1856) caused resentment which fuelled the 1857–8 **Indian Uprising**. He was made a marquis in 1849, and retired through ill health in 1856.

Dalton, (Edward) Hugh (John Neale), Baron (1887–1962)

Labour politician. First elected as an MP in 1924, he held the posts of Minister of Economic Warfare (1940–2) and then President of the Board of Trade (1942–5). In the post-war Labour government he was Chancellor of the Exchequer (1945–7), Chancellor of the Duchy of Lancaster (1948–50), Minister of Town and Country Planning (1950–1), and, briefly, Minister of Local Government (1951). He was elevated to the peerage in 1960. ▷ **Labour Party**

Danegeld

In a narrow sense, the royal tax (Old English *geld*) levied in England between 991 and 1012 according to hidage, but distinct from the ordinary geld, in order to buy peace from Danish invaders. After 1066, the term was used for the general geld, which was effectively abandoned in 1162. ▷ **Danelaw; Ethelred the Unready; Vikings**

Danelaw
That part of England where Danish conquest and colonization in the late 9c left an imprint on not only legal and administrative practices, but on placenames, language, and culture. Danish-derived customs survived even the **Norman Conquest**, and in the 12c all eastern England from the Thames to the Tees was so designated. ▷ **Vikings; Wessex**

Dardanelles or Hellespont
Narrow strait in north-west Turkey, connecting the Aegean Sea and the Sea of Marmara, part of the important waterway linking the Mediterranean and the Black Sea. It was the scene of an unsuccessful Allied campaign in World War I. Intending to overcome the Turks and come to the aid of Russia, the British War Council approved a naval expedition to capture Constantinople by forcing a route up the Dardanelles. Many of the Anglo-French battleships were destroyed during the attempted passage, and efforts were subsequently concentrated on the land attack at **Gallipoli**.

Darnley, Henry Stewart, Lord (1545–67)
English nobleman. He was the second husband of **Mary, Queen of Scots** and father of James VI of Scotland and I of England. He married Mary (his cousin) in 1565, and was made Earl of Ross and Duke of Albany. In Scotland, this debauchery and arrogance made him unpopular, and his part in the murder (1566) of the Queen's secretary, David **Rizzio**, caused his downfall. He became estranged from the Queen, and during an illness was killed at Edinburgh, when Kirk O'Field, the house in which he was sleeping, was destroyed by gunpowder (the result of a plot probably organized by the Earl of **Bothwell**, perhaps with Mary's knowledge). ▷ **James VI and I**

David I (c.1085–1153)
King of Scots (1124/53). He was the youngest son of **Malcolm III** and Queen (later St) **Margaret**. Educated at the court of **Henry I** of England, he became Earl of Huntingdon through his marriage to Maud de Senlis (c.1113). Once King, he emphasized his inde

pendence, systematically strengthened royal power, and firmly secured the foundations of the medieval Kingdom of Scotland. In 1136, as a nominal supporter of the claims of his niece, Empress Matilda, to the English crown, he embarked on wars of territorial conquest against Stephen. He was defeated in 1138 at the Battle of the Standard, near Northallerton, but from 1141 occupied the whole of northern England to the Ribble and the Tees.

David II (1324–71)
King of Scots (1329/71). The only surviving son of Robert **Bruce**, he became King at the age of 5. In 1334, after the victory of **Edward III** of England at the Battle of **Halidon Hill** (1333), he fled to France. He returned in 1341, and later invaded England, but was defeated and captured at Neville's Cross, near Dunbar (1346), and was kept prisoner for 11 years. After his death at Edinburgh he was succeeded by his sister's son, **Robert II**.

Davies, Clement (Edward) (1884–1962)
Welsh politician. Elected MP for Montgomeryshire in 1929, he held his seat until his death. Although offered a post as Education Secretary in Winston **Churchill**'s 1951–5 government, he declined, and thus helped to preserve the independent existence of the **Liberal Party**, which he led from 1945 to 1956.

Davitt, Michael (1846–1906)
Founder of the Irish Land League. Before becoming a journalist, he worked in a cotton mill, where he lost an arm in an accident. In 1866 he joined the Fenian Movement, was arrested in 1870 for sending guns to Ireland, and sentenced to 15 years' penal servitude. Released in 1877, he began an anti-landlord crusade which culminated in the Land League (1879). During a further period of imprisonment, he was elected an MP (1882), but disqualified from taking his seat. A strong Home Ruler but opponent of **Parnell**, he was twice more an MP (1892–3 and 1895–9). ▷ **Fenians; Home Rule**

D-Day (6 June 1944)
The day when the Allies launched the greatest amphibious operation in history (codenamed 'Overlord'), and invaded German-occupied Europe. By the end of D-Day, 130 000 troops had been landed on five beach-heads along a 50 mile stretch of the coast of

Normandy, at a cost of 10 000 casualties. ▷ **Normandy Campaign; World War II**

Declaration of Independence (1776)
The document adopted by the US Continental Congress to proclaim the separation of the 13 colonies from Britain. Drawn up by a committee of John **Adams**, Benjamin Franklin, Thomas Jefferson, Robert R Livingston, and Roger Sherman, it announced the right of revolution, detailing the Americans' reasons for the break, and asserted that American government should be based on a theory of natural law, and should respect the fundamental rights of individuals.

Declaration of Rights (1689)
An English statute which ended the brief interregnum after **James VII and II** quit the throne in Dec 1688, establishing **William III** and Mary II as joint monarchs. The Bill effectively ensured that monarchs must operate with the consent of parliament, and must not suspend or dispense with laws passed by that body. ▷ **bill of rights**

Declaratory Act (1766)
An Act passed by the **Rockingham** government. After much opposition in the US colonies to the introduction of taxes by the preceding George **Grenville** administration, Rockingham repealed the **Stamp Act** (1765); but this legislation reasserted the British parliament's general right to legislate for the colonies 'in all cases whatsoever'.

Defence of the Realm Act ('DORA') (Nov 1914)
An Act introduced to give the government greater controls over the activities of its citizens. The most important control related to restrictions on press reporting and other forms of censorship. The restrictions were increased as **World War I** progressed.

Democratic Unionist Party
The political party formed in Northern Ireland in 1971 under the leadership of Rev Ian **Paisley** after a split in the Unionist Party over Protestant reaction to demands both by Catholics in the Province and from Westminster for greater social and political equality. It has had strong appeal to many working-class Prot-

estants and during the 1980s attracted about one-third of the Unionist vote. Frequently suspicious in the 1970s and early 1980s that the official Unionists were less zealous in their support for Protestantism, the two Unionist parties agreed on concerted opposition to the **Anglo-Irish Agreement** (1985) and agreed in the 1987 general election not to nominate candidates against one another, thus avoiding a split in the Unionist vote.

Derby, Edward Geoffrey Smith Stanley, 14th Earl (1799–1869)

English politician. He entered parliament as a Whig in 1828, and became Chief-Secretary for Ireland (1830) and Colonial Secretary (1833), when he carried the Act for the emancipation of West Indian slaves. In 1834 he withdrew from the party and soon after joined the Conservatives, subsequently becoming party leader, 1846–68. In 1844 he entered the House of Lords as a baronet. He retired from the cabinet in 1845, when **Peel** decided to repeal the **Corn Laws**, and in 1846 headed the Protectionists in the Lords. In 1851 he succeeded his father as Earl of Derby. He led minority governments on three occasions (1852, 1858–9 and 1866–8), and his third administration passed the second Reform Act (1867). ▷ **Conservative Party; Reform Acts; Tories; Whigs**

Desert Rats

Members of the 7th British Armoured Division, which in 1940 took as its badge the jerboa or desert rat, noted for remarkable leaps. The media applied the name generally to all British servicemen in the **North Africa Campaign**, and it was readily adopted by those not entitled to wear the jerboa shoulder flash. ▷ **World War II**

Dettingen, Battle of (27 June 1743)

Fought during the War of the Austrian Succession on the banks of the River Main between British, Hanoverian and Austrian forces, under the nominal command of **George II**, and a French army under Marshal Noailles. The resulting French defeat was not followed up, reducing the battle's strategic importance. This was the last occasion on which a ruling British sovereign took command of troops in battle.

De Valera, Eamon (1882–1975)

Irish politician. Brought up on a farm in County Limerick, he became a teacher in Dublin, and was active in various republican

94

movements. A commandant of the Irish Volunteers in the **Easter Rising** (1916), he was arrested and narrowly escaped the firing squad. He became an MP in 1917 and was Leader of **Sinn Féin** from 1917 to 1926. He was elected President of **Dáil Eireann**, and in 1926 became Leader of **Fianna Fáil**, his newly-formed republican opposition party, which won the 1932 elections. As Prime Minister (1932–48, 1951–4 and 1957–9), he instituted social, industrial and agricultural reforms and was instrumental in framing the constitution of 1937, which established the **Irish Free State** as Eire. He was President of Ireland from 1959 to 1973.

Devonshire, William Cavendish, 4th Duke of (1720–64)

English politician. His family connections enabled him to embark early upon a political career: he became a Whig MP in 1741 and Privy Councillor in 1751. He was appointed Lord Lieutenant and Governor-General of Ireland (1754), succeeding to the dukedom in 1755. He was appointed First Lord of the Treasury by **George II** in 1756 at the beginning of the **Seven Years War**, largely because William **Pitt** 'the Elder', whose inclusion in a war ministry was considered vital, refused to serve under the Duke of Newcastle. He was ineffectual in the post, resigning after six months. He was Lord Chamberlain of the Household from 1757 to 1762.

diarchy

A system where political authority is divided; associated with constitutional reforms introduced by the British into India in 1919. Under the reforms, some departments of provincial government were under Indian control, while others including finance and security remained under British control. The reforms did not extend to central government, and the system is seen by some as a concession to 'moderate' Indian opinion in an attempt to seduce them into cooperation with the British Raj.

Diggers

A radical group in England formed during the **Commonwealth**, led by Gerrard Winstanley (1609–72), preaching and practising agrarian **communism** on common and waste land. From Apr 1649 they established the Digger community at St George's Hill, Surrey, followed by colonies in nine other southern and Midland counties. The movement was suppressed and its communities dispersed by local landowners ▷ **Fifth Monarchists**

Disraeli, Benjamin, 1st Earl of Beaconsfield (1804–81)
British politician and Prime Minister. He made his early reputation as a novelist, publishing his first novel, *Vivian Grey*, in
1826. He is better known for his two political novels, *Coningsby*
(1844) and *Sybil* (1845), which date from his period as a Romantic
Tory, critical of industrial developments. He became leader of the
'Young England' movement which espoused these values, and
came to prominence as a critic of **Peel**'s free-trade policies,
especially the repeal of the **Corn Laws** (1845–6). He became leader
in the Commons of the Conservatives, after the Peelites left the
party, and was Chancellor of the Exchequer in Derby's minority
governments of 1852 and 1858–9. While Chancellor in the government of 1866–8, he piloted the 1867 Reform Bill through the
Commons. He became Prime Minister on **Derby**'s resignation in
1868, but was defeated the same year in the general election. His
second administration (1874–80) was notable both for diplomacy
and social reform, though much of the latter only consolidated
legislation begun under **Gladstone**. During his administration,
Britain became half-owner of the Suez Canal (1875), and the
Queen assumed the title Empress of India (1876). His skilful
diplomacy at the Congress of Berlin (1878) contributed to the
preservation of European peace after conflict between the Russians and the Turks in the Balkans. Defeated in 1880 by Gladstone
and the Liberals, he then effectively retired, dying the following
year. ▷ **Reform Acts; Tories; Victoria**

Disturbances (1935–8)
A series of strikes and riots which took place in the British West
Indies, sometimes known as 'The Troubles'. These had their roots
in post-1918 socio-economic deprivation and this was exacerbated
by the **Great Depression** after 1929 and the lack of political representation in the Crown Colonies. Discontent surfaced first in
Belize and Jamaica (1934), spread to the sugar workers in St
Kitts and Guyana (1935) and culminated in serious disorder in
Trinidad, Jamaica and Barbados (1937–8). In Trinidad **Butler**'s
oratory provoked the oilfield workers, in Barbados Clement
Payne's deportation led to the deaths of 14 people and in Jamaica
the Jamaica Worker's Union of Bustamante brought rioting to
the sugar estates and docks and the arrest of 700 people. Stung
into action by the degree of unrest, the imperial government set
up the **Moyne Commission**.

Divine Right of Kings

The concept of the divinely-ordained authority of monarchs, widely held in the medieval and early modern periods, and often associated with the absolutism of Louis XIV of France and the assertions of the House of **Stuart**.

Domesday Book

The great survey of England south of the Ribble and Tees Rivers (London and Winchester excepted), compiled in 1086 on orders of **William I**; sometimes spelled Doomsday Book. Information is arranged by county and, within each county, according to tenure by major landholders; each manor is described according to value and resources. Domesday is one of the greatest administrative achievements of the **Middle Ages**, yet its central purpose remains unclear. Most probably, it was to assist the royal exploitation of crown lands and feudal rights, and to provide the new nobility with a formal record and confirmation of their lands, thus putting a final seal on the Norman occupation. ▷ **Norman Conquest**

Dominion of Canada

Established on 1 July 1867, by the **British North America Act** of 29 Mar, the Dominion consisted of three provinces, Canada (now divided into Quebec and Ontario), Nova Scotia and New Brunswick, all united by the **Confederation Movement**. Desire for unification had intensified because of the need for improvements in transport and because of the proximity of the USA, which instilled emulation as well as fear. The ending of **reciprocity** in 1866 and the failure of the USA to curb the **Fenians** perhaps accentuated the provinces' link with the British crown, which was a distinguishing feature of the confederation (although the term 'Dominion' was chosen rather than 'Kingdom' in deference to US republican sentiment).

Donald III ('Donald Bane') (c.1033–c.1100)

King of Scots (1093/4 and 1094/7). He was the younger son of **Duncan I**, who seized the throne on **Malcolm III**'s death and killed Malcolm's eldest son, **Duncan II**. Donald's reign was brief and turbulent. He was briefly supplanted by Duncan II and finally overthrown in 1097 by an English army in support of the claim of Edgar, Malcolm's eldest surviving son by his marriage to Mar garet, 'Maid of Norway'. Edgar had him blinded and he was buried on Iona.

Donoughmore Commission

A committee sent by the British government to Ceylon in 1927 to examine the Ceylonese constitution and recommend reforms. These recommendations were reluctantly accepted by Ceylonese political leaders and served as the basis for the new constitution of 1931. The reforms replaced communal electorates by territorial constituencies and extended the franchise to all resident adults. An assembly or state council with legislative and executive powers was also established under the recommendations of the Donoughmore Commission. The new constitution was in effect until 1946.

Douglas

A Scottish family which includes William the Hardy, Crusader, who harried the monks of Melrose and joined **Wallace** in the rising against the English in 1297. His son, Sir James Douglas (c.1286–1330), called also 'the Black Douglas' from his swarthy complexion, effectively shared command with Robert **Bruce** of Scottish forces victorious at the Battle of **Bannockburn** (1314). The hero of 70 fights, he was slain in Andalusia. His son, William, died at the Battle of **Halidon Hill**; and the next Lord of Douglas, Hugh, brother of James, made over the now great domains of the family in 1342 to his nephew, Sir William. ▷ **Scottish War of Independence**

Dover, Treaty of (1670)

A treaty, some of whose terms were kept secret from the British parliament and some of the King's ministers, between **Charles II** of Great Britain and Louis XIV of France. Under its terms, Charles received French subsidies and agreed to maintain amity with France and, at an appropriate time, declare himself a convert to Roman Catholicism. Charles received almost £750 000 during the 1670s, a crucial supplement to inadequate income. Though the secret terms were not revealed until 1682, they were guessed by many in parliament in the later 1670s, doing much to sour relations with the King. ▷ **Exclusion Crisis; Popish Plot**

Dowding, Hugh (Caswell Tremenheere), 1st Baron (1882–1970)
British air chief marshal. He served in the Royal Artillery and the Royal Flying Corps in **World War I**. As Commander-in-Chief of Fighter Command (1936–40), he organized the air defence of Britain during **World War II**, which resulted in the victorious Battle of **Britain** (1940). He retired in 1942 and was created a peer in 1943.

Drake, Sir Francis (c.1540–96)
English seaman and explorer. In 1567 he commanded the *Judith* in his kinsman John Hawkins's ill-fated expedition to the West Indies, and returned there several times to recover the losses sustained from the Spaniards, his exploits gaining him great popularity in England. In 1577 he set out with five ships for the Pacific, through the Straits of Magellan, but after his fleet was battered by storm and fire, he alone continued in the *Golden Hind*. He then struck out across the Pacific, reached Pelew Island, and returned to England via the Cape of Good Hope in 1580 having circumnavigated the globe. The following year, Queen **Elizabeth I** visited his ship and knighted him. In 1585 he sailed with 25 ships against the Spanish Indies, bringing home tobacco, potatoes, and the dispirited Virginian colonists. In the battle against the Spanish **Armada** (1588), which raged for a week in the Channel, his seamanship and courage brought him further distinction. In 1595 he sailed again to the West Indies, but died of dysentery off Porto Bello.

Dunbar, Battle of (27 Apr 1296)
The battle fought between English and Scottish forces after Scottish magnates had deprived King John (**Balliol**) of independent authority and had negotiated alliances with France and Norway. **Edward I** marched north and his victory resulted in Balliol's resignation of the throne. He was taken to England as prisoner. Scotland remained without a King until Robert **Bruce** was crowned in 1306. ▷ **Scottish War of Independence**

Dunbar, Battle of (3 Sep 1650)
Fought between an English army under Oliver **Cromwell** and Scots forces supporting the recognition of **Charles II** after **Charles I**'s execution. Hemmed in by Scottish forces under the Earl of

Leven, Cromwell launched a surprise counter-attack which was entirely successful. ▷ **English Civil Wars**

Duncan I (c.1010–40)
King of Scots (1034/40). He was the grandson of Malcolm II (1005–34) and the son of Bethoc and Crinan, Abbot of Dunkeld. He succeeded to Strathclyde and probably ruled over most of Scotland except the islands and the far north. He attempted southwards expansion and a long and unsuccessful siege of Durham weakened his position. He was killed by **Macbeth** at Pitgaveney, near Elgin.

Duncan II (c.1060–94)
King of Scots (1094). The son of **Malcolm III** and Ingibjorg, he was held hostage by **William I** of England from 1072 but was released and knighted by **William II**. Aided by an English army, he overthrew **Donald III**. Attempting to appease anti-English feeling, he tried to rule without English support but only weakened his position and was killed on 12 Nov 1094 by the mormaer of the Mearns, probably at the instigation of Donald. ▷ **Duncan I**

Dundee, John Graham of Claverhouse, 1st Viscount (c.1649–89)
Scottish soldier, known as 'Bonnie Dundee' or 'Bloody Claverhouse'. In 1672 he entered the Prince of Orange's horseguards, and at the Battle of Seneff saved the future **William III**'s life. He returned to Scotland in 1677, and defeated the **Covenanters** at Bothwell Brig (1679). He was made a Privy Councillor in 1683, and became Viscount Dundee (1688). Joined by the Jacobite clans, he raised the standard for **James VII and II** against William and Mary, but died from a musket wound after his successful battle against Mackay at the Pass of Killiecrankie. ▷ **Jacobites**

Dunkirk, Evacuation of (27 May–3 June 1940)
The evacuation of the **British Expeditionary Force** and other Allied troops from the port of Dunkirk in northern France, isolated after the capitulation of the Belgian army to the north and the advance of German tanks and troops to the south. The evacuation, in which approximately 200 000 British and some 140 000 French troops were safely conveyed to England, was effected with the use of hundreds of naval vessels and small civilian craft, and

aided by cover from British air fighter patrols and an unruffled English Channel.

Dunois, Jean d'Orléans, Count ('The Bastard of Orléans')
(1403–68)
French soldier. The illegitimate son of Louis, Duke of Orléans, he was a general in the **Hundred Years War**. He defeated the English at Montargis (1427), defended Orléans with a small force until its relief by **Joan of Arc** (1429), then inflicted further defeats on the English, forcing them out of Paris, and by 1453 from Normandy and Guyenne.

Durbar
The audience-chamber or body of officials at the Indian royal court. In British India the term was applied to formal assemblies marking important state occasions to which leading Indians were invited, eg the Delhi Durbar of 1911 celebrating the visit of King **George V** and Queen Mary.

Durham, John George Lambton, 1st Earl of (1792–1840)
English politician. He served in the dragoons, and in 1813 became a Whig MP. In 1828 he was created Baron Durham. He became Lord Privy Seal (1830), and was one of those who drew up the Reform Bill. He was made an earl in 1833, and became Ambassador to St Petersburg (1835). As Governor-General of Canada (1838), his measures were statesman-like, but the House of Lords voted disapproval of his amnesty to several of the French-Canadian rebels, and he resigned. His report on Canada (1839) advocated the union of Upper and Lower Canada, which was accepted in 1841. ▷ **Reform Acts; Whigs**

Durham Report
A British government report of 1839 recommending the union of Upper and Lower Canada into a single political structure; produced by Lord Durham, the governor general of Canada, it called for the assimilation of French-Canadian into English-Canadian economic and linguistic culture. It also recommended responsible government.

E

Eastern Question
A complex set of diplomatic problems affecting 18c, 19c and early 20c Europe. It was created by the slowly declining power of the **Ottoman Empire**, the emergence of the Balkan nations and nationalism, and the ambitions in south-east Europe of the Great Powers, especially Russia and Austria (later Austria-Hungary).

Easter Rising (24–9 Apr 1916)
A rebellion of Irish nationalists in Dublin, organized by two revolutionary groups, the Irish Republican Brotherhood led by Patrick Pearse (1879–1916), and **Sinn Féin** under James Connolly (1870–1916). The focal point of the rebellion was the seizing of the General Post Office. The rising was put down and several leaders were executed. The extent of the reprisals increased support for the nationalist cause in Ireland.

East India Company, British
A British trading monopoly, established in India in 1600, which later became involved in politics. Its first 'factory' (trading station) was at Surat (1612), with others at Madras (1639), Bombay (1688) and Calcutta (1690). A rival company was chartered in 1698, but the two companies merged in 1708. During the 18c it received competition from other European countries, in particular France. The company benefited territorially from local Indian disputes and Mughal weakness, gaining control of Bengal (1757), and after the Battle of Baksar receiving the right to collect revenue from the Mughal emperor (1765). Financial indiscipline among company servants led to the 1773 Regulating Act and Pitt's 1784 India Act, which established a Board of Control responsible to Parliament. Thereafter it gradually lost independence. Its monopoly was broken in 1813, and its powers handed over to the British Crown in 1858. It ceased to exist as a legal entity in 1873.

EC (European Community)
A community of 12 states in Western Europe created for the purpose of achieving economic and political integration. It com-

prises three communities. The first of these was the *European Steel and Coal Community*, established in 1952 under the Treaty of Paris by France, West Germany, Italy, Belgium, the Netherlands, and Luxembourg. It created common institutions for regulating the coal and steel industries under a common framework of law and institutions, thereby producing the first breach in the principle of national sovereignty. In the early 1950s, unsuccessful attempts were made to establish a European Defence Community and a European Political Community. In 1958, under the Treaty of Rome, the six states established the *European Economic Community* and the *European Atomic Energy Community*, which provided for collaboration in the civilian sector of nuclear power. Six members have been added to the original six: Denmark, Ireland, and the UK (1973); Greece (1981); and Portugal and Spain (1986). Austria, Cyprus, Malta, Sweden and Turkey are seeking to become members. To develop and oversee the policies of economic and political integration there are a number of supranational community institutions: the Commission, the Council, the European Parliament, and the European Court of Justice. While the Community has grown in the 1970s and 1980s and continues to progress towards economic integration, a political union seems still a distant possibility. ▷ **EEC, EU**

Eden (of Avon), Sir (Robert) Anthony, 1st Earl (1897–1977)

English politician. He became a Conservative MP in 1923, and was Foreign Under-Secretary (1931), Lord Privy Seal (1933), and Foreign Secretary (1935), resigning in 1938 over differences with Neville **Chamberlain**. In **World War II** he was first Dominions Secretary, then Secretary of State for War, and Foreign Secretary (1940–5). Again Foreign Secretary (1951–5), he was involved with the negotiations in Korea and Indo-China, and the 1954 Geneva Summit Conference. He succeeded Winston **Churchill** as Prime Minister (1955–7), and in 1956 ordered British forces (in collaboration with the French and Israelis) to occupy the Suez Canal Zone. His action was condemned by the **UN** and caused a bitter controversy in Britain which did not subside when he ordered a withdrawal. In failing health, he resigned abruptly in 1957. He was created an earl in 1961. ▷ **Conservative Party**

Edgar (943–75)

King of Mercia and Northumbria (957/75) and the King of all England (959/75). He was the younger son of **Edmund I**. He encouraged the reform of the English Church as a means of enhancing his prestige and power, though his lavish support for the monasteries, caused bitterness among an important section of the nobility. He introduced a uniform currency based on new silver pennies c.973. ▷ **Anglo-Saxons**

Edinburgh, Prince Philip, Duke of (1921–)
The husband of Queen Elizabeth II, the son of Prince Andrew of Greece and Princess Alice of Battenberg, born at Corfu. He became a naturalized British subject in 1947, when he was married to the Princess Elizabeth (20 Nov). In 1956 he began the Duke of Edinburgh Award Scheme to foster the leisure activities of young people. ▷ **Elizabeth II**

Edington, Battle of (878)
Decisive victory in Wiltshire for **Alfred, 'the Great'**, King of Wessex against an invading Danish army. The Danes sought peace, left Wessex and their king, **Guthrum**, was baptized a Christian. The peace settled the frontier between Wessex and the Danes, greatly enlarged Alfred's territory and established the West Saxons as the leading English power.

Edmund I (921–46)
King of the English (939/46). He was the half-brother of **Athelstan**. On Edmund's accession, Scandinavian forces from Northumbria, reinforced by levies from Ireland, quickly overran the East Midlands. He re-established his control over the southern **Danelaw** (942) and **Northumbria** (944), and for the remainder of his life ruled a reunited England. He was killed by an outlaw. ▷ **Anglo-Saxons**

Edmund II, 'Ironside' (c.980–1016)
King of the English (1016). The son of **Ethelred the Unready**, he was chosen King by the Londoners on his father's death (Apr 1016), while **Canute** was elected at Southampton by the **witan**. Edmund hastily levied an army, defeated Canute, and attempted to raise the siege of London, but was routed at Ashingdon or possibly Ashdon, Essex (Oct 1016). He agreed to a partition of the country, but died a few weeks later, leaving Canute as sole ruler.

Edward I (1239–1307)

King of England (1272/1307). The elder son of **Henry III** and Eleanor of Provence, he married **Eleanor of Castile** (1254) and later Margaret of France, the sister of Philip IV (1299). In the **Barons War**, he at first supported Simon de **Montfort**, but rejoined his father, and defeated de Montfort at Evesham (1265). He then won renown as a crusader to the Holy Land, and did not return to England until 1274, two years after his father's death. In two devastating campaigns (1276–7 and 1282–3), he annexed north-west Wales, and ensured the permanence of his conquests by building magnificent castles. He reasserted English claims to the overlordship of Scotland when the line of succession failed, and decided in favour of John **Balliol** as King (1292). But Edward's insistence on full rights of suzerainty provoked the Scottish magnates to force Balliol to repudiate Edward and ally with France (1295), thus beginning the Scottish Wars of Independence. Despite prolonged campaigning and victories such as Falkirk (1298), he could not subdue Scotland as he had done Wales. He died while leading his army against Robert **Bruce**. ▷ **Crusades; Scottish War of Independence; Wallace, William; Westminster, Statutes of**

Edward II (1284–1327)

King of England (1307/27). He was the fourth son of **Edward I** and **Eleanor of Castile**. In 1301 he was created Prince of Wales, the first English heir-apparent to bear the title, and in 1308 married **Isabella of France**, the daughter of Philip IV. Throughout his reign, Edward mismanaged the barons, who sought to rid the country of royal favourites and restore their rightful place in government. The Ordinances of 1311 restricted the royal pre-rogative in matters such as appointments to the King's household, and demanded the banishment of Edward's favourite, Piers Gaveston, who was ultimately captured and executed (1312). Edward was humiliated by reverses in Scotland, where he was decisively defeated by Robert **Bruce** at the Battle of **Bannockburn** (1314). The Ordinances were formally annulled (1322), but the King's new favourites, the Despensers, were acquisitive and unpopular, and earned the particular enmity of Queen Isabella. With her lover Roger Mortimer, she toppled the Despensers (1326) and imprisoned Edward in Kenilworth Castle. He renounced the throne in 1327 in favour of his eldest son, **Edward III**, and was then murdered in Berkeley Castle, near Gloucester.

Edward III (1312–77)

King of England (1327/77). The elder son of **Edward II** and **Isabella of France**, he married Philippa of Hainault in 1328, and their eldest child, Edward (later called **Edward, the Black Prince**), was born in 1330. By banishing Queen Isabella from court and executing her lover, Roger Mortimer, he assumed full control of the government (1330), and began to restore the monarchy's authority and prestige. He supported Edward **Balliol**'s attempts to wrest the Scots throne from **David II**, and his victory at the Battle of **Halidon Hill** (1333) forced David to seek refuge in France until 1341. In 1337, after Philip VI had declared **Guyenne** forfeit, he revived his hereditary claim to the French crown through Isabella, the daughter of Philip IV, thus beginning the **Hundred Years War**. He destroyed the French navy at the Battle of Sluys (1340), and won another major victory at the Battle of **Crécy** (1346). David II was captured two months later at the Battle of Neville's Cross, near Durham, and remained a prisoner until 1357. Edward was renowned for his valour and military skill. ▷ **William of Wykeham**

Edward IV (1442–83)

King of England (1461/70 and 1471/83). He was the eldest son of Richard, Duke of York. His father claimed the throne as the lineal descendant of **Edward III**'s third and fifth sons (respectively Lionel, Duke of Clarence, and Edmund, Duke of York), against the Lancastrian King **Henry VI** (the lineal descendant of Edward III's fourth son, **John of Gaunt**). Richard was killed at the Battle of Wakefield (1460), but Edward entered London in 1461, was recognized as King on Henry VI's deposition, and with the support of his cousin Richard Neville, Earl of **Warwick**, decisively defeated the Lancastrians at Towton. He threw off his dependence on Warwick, and secretly married Elizabeth Woodville (1464). Warwick forced him into exile in Holland (Oct 1470), and Henry VI regained the throne. Edward returned to England (Mar 1471), was restored to kingship (11 Apr), then defeated and killed Warwick at the Battle of Barnet (14 Apr), and destroyed the remaining Lancastrian forces at the Battle of **Tewkesbury** (4 May). Henry VI was murdered soon afterwards, and Edward remained secure throughout the rest of his reign. ▷ **Lancaster, House of; Roses, Wars of the**

Edward V (1470–83)
King of England (Apr/June 1483). He was the son of King **Edward IV** and Elizabeth Woodville. Shortly after his accession, he and his younger brother, Richard, Duke of York, were imprisoned in the Tower by their uncle, Richard, Duke of Gloucester, who usurped the throne as **Richard III**. The two princes were never heard of again, and were most likely murdered (Aug 1483) on their uncle's orders. In 1674 a wooden chest containing the bones of two children was discovered in the Tower, and these were interred in Westminster Abbey as their presumed remains.
▷ **Roses, Wars of the**

Edward VI (1537–53)
King of England (1547/53). He was the son of **Henry VIII** by his third queen, Jane **Seymour**. During Edward's reign, power was first in the hands of his uncle, the Duke of Somerset, and after his execution in 1552, of John Dudley, Duke of Northumberland. Edward became a devout Protestant, and under the Protectors the English Reformation flourished. He died of tuberculosis, having agreed to the succession of Lady Jane **Grey** (overthrown after nine days by **Mary I**). ▷ **Reformation** (England)

Edward VII (1841–1910)
King of the UK (1901/10). The eldest son of Queen **Victoria**, in 1863 he married Alexandra, the eldest daughter of Christian IX of Denmark. They had three sons and three daughters: Albert Victor, Duke of Clarence; George; Louise, Princess Royal; Victoria; Maud, who married Haakon VII of Norway; and Alexander. As Prince of Wales, his behaviour led him into several social scandals, and the Queen excluded him from affairs of state. As King, he carried out several visits to Continental capitals which strove to allay international animosities. ▷ **George V**

Edward VIII (1894–1972)
King of the UK (Jan/Dec 1936). He was the eldest son of King **George V**. He joined the navy and, during **World War I**, the army, travelled much, and achieved considerable popularity. He succeeded his father in Jan 1936, but abdicated (11 Dec) in the face of opposition to his proposed marriage to Mrs Ernest Simpson, a commoner who had been twice divorced. He was then given the title of Duke of Windsor, and the marriage took place in France

in 1937. The Duke and Duchess of Windsor lived in Paris, apart from a period in the Bahamas (1940–5), where Edward was Governor.

Edward, 'the Black Prince' (1330–76)

Eldest son of **Edward III**. He was created Earl of Chester (1333), Duke of Cornwall (1337), and Prince of Wales (1343). In 1346, though still a boy, he fought at the Battle of **Crécy**, and is said to have won his popular title (first cited in a 16c work) from his black armour. He won several victories in the **Hundred Years War**, including the Battle of **Poitiers** (1356). He had two sons, Edward (1365–70) and the future **Richard II**. In 1362 he was created Prince of Aquitaine and lived there until 1371, when a revolt forced him to return to England. A great soldier, he was a failure as an administrator.

Edward the Confessor (c.1003–66)

King of England (1042/66). He was the elder son of **Ethelred the Unready** and Emma of Normandy, and the last king of the Old English royal line. After living in exile in Normandy, he joined the household of his half-brother **Hardaknut Knutsson** in 1041, and then succeeded him on the throne. Until 1052 he maintained his position against the ambitious Godwin family by building up Norman favourites, and in 1051 he very probably recognized Duke William of Normandy (later **William I**) as his heir. However, the Godwins regained their ascendancy, and on his deathbed in London, Edward, who remained childless, nominated Harold Godwin (**Harold II**) to succeed, the **Norman Conquest** following soon after. Edward's reputation for holiness began in his lifetime, and he rebuilt Westminster Abbey, where he was buried, in the Romanesque style. His cult grew in popularity, and he was canonized in 1161.

Edward the Elder (c.870–924)

King of **Wessex** (899/924). The elder son of **Alfred, 'the Great'**, he built on his father's successes and established himself as the strongest ruler in Britain. By one of the most decisive military campaigns of the whole Anglo-Saxon period, he conquered and annexed to **Wessex** the southern **Danelaw** (910–18). He also assumed control of **Mercia** (918), and although he exercised no direct power in the north, all the chief rulers beyond the Humber, including the King of Scots, formally recognized his overlordship in 920. ▷ **Anglo-Saxons**

Edward the Martyr (c.962–78)
King of England (975/8). During his reign there was a reaction against the policies in support of monasticism espoused by his father, **Edgar**. He was murdered at Corfe, Dorset, by supporters of his stepmother, Elfrida, and canonized in 1001.

EEC (European Economic Community)
An association within the European Community, established in 1958 after the Treaties of Rome (1957), often referred to as the Common Market. It is essentially a customs union, with a common external tariff and a common market with the removal of barriers to trade among the members. In addition it has a number of common policies, the most important of which is the Common Agricultural Policy, providing for external tariffs to protect domestic agriculture and mechanisms for price support. The cost of support to agriculture takes up about 70 per cent of the European Community's budget and has shown an alarming propensity to grow. Reform of agricultural policy has been on the agenda for a number of years, but many member governments are reluctant to entertain the wrath of the farming vote which remains sizable in their countries. There are common policies for fisheries, regional development, industrial intervention, and economic and social affairs. There is also a European Monetary System, which regulates exchange rate movements among the member states' currencies in an attempt to achieve monetary stability. In 1986 the Single European Act was passed, allowing for the completion of the process of creating a common market within the community by the beginning of 1993. ▷ **EC (European Community), EU**

EFTA (European Free Trade Association)
An association originally of seven Western European states who were not members of the European Economic Community (**EEC**), intended as a counter to the EEC; it was established in 1959 under the Stockholm Convention. The members (Austria, Denmark, Norway, Portugal, Sweden, Switzerland, and the UK) agreed to eliminate over a period of time trade restrictions between them, without having to bring into line individual tariffs and trade policies with other countries. Agriculture was excluded from the agreement, although individual arrangements were permitted.

Both the UK (1973) and Portugal (1986) left to join the EEC, but there has been a free trade agreement between the remaining EFTA countries and the European Community, and considerable trade between the two groupings. Finland joined in 1985. ▷ **EC (European Community)**

Egbert (d.839)

King of **Wessex** (802/39). After his victory in 825 over the Mercians at Ellendun (now Wroughton) in Wiltshire, Essex, Kent, Surrey, and Sussex submitted to him; but his conquest of **Mercia** itself (829) was soon reversed. He extended his control over Cornwall, defeating an alliance between the **Vikings** and Britons at Hingston Down (838). These successes gave him mastery over southern England from Kent to Land's End, and established Wessex as the strongest Anglo-Saxon kingdom. ▷ **Anglo-Saxons**

Eisenhower, Dwight David ('Ike') (1890–1969)

US general and 34th President. In 1942 he commanded Allied forces for the amphibious descent on French North Africa. His ability to coordinate the Allied forces and staff led to his selection as Supreme Commander of the Allied Expeditionary Force which spearheaded the 1944 invasion of Europe. In 1950 he was made Supreme Commander of the NATO forces in Europe and in 1952 he was elected President of the USA (1953–61).

El Alamein, Battle of (23 Oct–4 Nov 1943)

A battle in **World War II**, named after a village on Egypt's Mediterranean coast, which ended in the victory of the British Eighth Army commanded by **Montgomery** over Rommel's Afrika Corps. It proved to be a turning point in the war in the war in Africa. ▷ **North African Campaign**

Eleanor of Castile (c.1245–1290)

Queen consort of **Edward I** of England (1254/90). The daughter of Ferdinand III, she accompanied Edward to the Crusades, and is said to have saved his life by sucking the poison from a wound he had. She died at Harby, Nottinghamshire, and the 'Eleanor Crosses' at Northampton, Geddington, and Waltham Cross are survivors of the 12 erected by Edward at the halting places of her cortège. The last stopping place was Charing Cross, where a replica now stands.

Eliot, Sir John (1592–1632)
English statesman. He entered parliament in 1614, and was knighted in 1618. He became a supporter of **Charles I**'s favourite, the 1st Duke of **Buckingham**, but in 1625 turned against him, and moved his impeachment. His policy of antagonism to the King led to his imprisonment on three occasions. He died in the Tower, thus becoming a martyr to the parliamentary cause.

Elizabeth I (1533–1603)
Queen of England (1558/1603). She was the daughter of **Henry VIII** by his second wife, Anne **Boleyn**. On the death of **Edward VI** (1553), she sided with her Catholic half-sister, Mary, against Lady Jane **Grey** and the Duke of Northumberland, but her identification with Protestantism made Mary suspicious, and she was imprisoned for her alleged part in the rebellion led by Sir Thomas Wyatt (1554). Ascending the throne on **Mary I**'s death, she reduced animosities and promoted stability by engineering a moderate Protestant Church settlement, and it is from this time that a distinctive Anglican Church was effectively established. She made peace with France and Scotland, and strengthened her position by secretly helping Protestants in these countries. **Mary, Queen of Scots**, was thrown into her power (1568) and imprisoned, causing numerous conspiracies among English Catholics. After the most sinister plot was discovered (1586), Elizabeth was reluctantly persuaded to execute Mary (1587); many other Catholics were persecuted in the 1580s and 1590s. Infuriated by this, and by Elizabeth's part in inciting the Netherlands against him, Philip of Spain attacked England with his 'invincible **Armada**' (1588), but England managed to repel the attack, though war continued until 1604. Of all Elizabeth's personal relationships, only one touched her deeply, that with Robert Dudley, Earl of **Leicester**, whom she would probably have married had it not been for her adviser **Cecil**'s remonstrances. A strong and astute, but sometimes cruel and capricious, woman, the 'Virgin Queen' was nevertheless popular with her subjects, becoming later known as 'Good Queen Bess'; and her reign is seen as a period of generally effective government and increased international status.

Elizabeth II (1926–)
Queen of the UK (1952/) and Head of the **Commonwealth of Nations**. The elder daughter of King **George VI**, she was proclaimed Queen on 6 Feb 1952, and crowned on 2 June 1953. Her

husband was created Duke of Edinburgh on the eve of their wedding (20 Nov 1947), and styled Prince Philip in 1957. They have three sons, Prince **Charles**, Prince Andrew, and Prince Edward, and a daughter, Princess Anne.

Ellenborough, Edward Law, 1st Earl of (1790–1871)

English politician. He became a Tory MP in 1813 and held office under several administrations, becoming Governor-General of India (1841). Parliament approved his Afghan policy in 1843, but his subsequent policy led to his early recall (1844). He was then created Viscount Southam and Earl of Ellenborough. He became First Lord of the Admiralty in 1846, and in 1858 was made Minister for India, but the publication of a dispatch in which he rebuked Viscount **Canning** forced him to resign and he held no further office.

Elphinstone, Mountstuart, 11th Lord Elphinstone (1779–1859)

British colonial administrator and historian. He entered the Bengal civil service in 1795, served with distinction on **Wellesley**'s staff (1803) at the Battle of Assaye, and was appointed Resident at Nagpur. In 1808 he was sent as the first British Envoy to Kabul; and as Resident from 1810 at Pune ended the Maratha War of 1817 and organized the newly-acquired territory. He was Governor-General of Bombay (1819–27), where he founded the system of administration, and did much to advance state education in India. He returned to Britain in 1829, and, declining the governor-generalship of India, lived in comparative retirement until his death.

Emancipation Acts

Statutes of imperial legislatures which freed colonial slaves. The bill to emancipate slaves in the **British Empire** was introduced by Buxton and was passed in Aug 1833. It granted financial compensation to the slave owners and freed the slaves under a system of Apprenticeship on 1 Aug 1834. On that date 750 000 slaves became free in the British West Indies and it was reported that the expected trouble had not materialized and that the ex-slaves had spent the weekend in chapels and churches in thanks-giving. France freed its slaves in 1848, the Netherlands in 1863, the USA in 1865 and Spain in 1885.

Emmet, Robert (1778–1803)
Irish patriot. He left Trinity College to join the United Irishmen, and travelled on the Continent for the Irish cause, at one point meeting **Napoleon I**. In 1803, he plotted an insurrection against the English, but it proved a failure. He was captured and hanged in Dublin.

Englandspiel (1942–4)
The codename given to a highly successful German counter-espionage operation in the Netherlands during **World War II**. The occupying German forces obtained the codes used by the Dutch resistance in radio contact with Britain, and by impersonating the resistance the Germans were able to capture 57 agents sent in from England, and to arrest hundreds of resistance personnel. Several English bombers were also brought down by them.

English Civil Wars (1642–8)
The country's greatest internal conflict, between supporters of parliament and supporters of **Charles I**, caused by parliamentary opposition to what it considered growing royal power. Although the King left London in Mar 1642, open hostilities between royalists and parliamentarians did not immediately break out. The prospect of compromise was bleak, but both sides, fearing the consequences of civil strife, moved slowly towards the use of armed force. Charles finally issued commissions of array (June 1642), and raised his standard two months later at Nottingham. The first major engagement took place at Edgehill in Oct. It was inconclusive, but royalist forces then threatened London, the key parliamentary stronghold. Royalist strategy in 1643 centred upon taking the capital by a three-pronged attack from armies in the north, the south-west and the Thames valley. By autumn the north and the west (apart from a garrison in Gloucester) were in their hands, although parliament held back the tide in the (drawn) first Battle of Newbury. The crucial event of 1643 was parliament's alliance with the Scots in the **Solemn League and Covenant**, which strengthened its hand militarily and threatened the King's forces on a new front. In 1644 parliament, assisted by the Scots, became a formidable foe. This was clear in July when its forces, aided by Scottish invaders, inflicted a serious defeat upon the royalists at the Battle of **Marston Moor**. However, the King's forces were swamped in the west. In 1643 they were victorious over the Earl of Essex in the Battle of Lostwithiel, and in the second Battle of

Newbury they were successful against the combined forces of Essex, the Earl of Manchester, and Sir William Waller. In 1645, strengthened by the creation of the **New Model Army**, parliament's cause advanced in the Midlands and the west, with important victories at the Battles of **Naseby** and Langport. The First Civil War ended in 1646 when Charles surrendered to the Scots at Newark in May, and his stronghold of Oxford fell in June. He was taken into parliamentary custody (Jan 1647) when the Scots left for home, and in June was seized by the army. From June 1646 to Apr 1648 there was an uneasy peace and attempts at compromise. Negotiations between the King and parliament had begun as early as 1645, but they achieved little. The main sticking points were religion, particularly parliament's disestablishment of the Church, and the King's prerogative rights, many of which had been abolished by parliament. The climax came (Aug 1647) when the army presented the King with the Heads of Proposals, calling for religious toleration, and parliamentary control of the armed forces. Charles made a secret alliance with the Scots, promising to establish **Presbyterianism** in England which parliament had failed to do; they invaded England (Apr 1648), and were repulsed only after the Battle of Preston (Aug). Bitterly fought, the second war earned Charles the epithet 'that man of blood' and, ultimately, his execution (30 Jan 1649). Possibly 100 000 died in the two wars: 1 in 10 of adult males. ▷ **Cavaliers; Commonwealth; Covenanters; Cromwell, Oliver; Independents; Ireton, Henry**

Entente Cordiale

A term first used in the 1840s to describe a close relationship between the UK and France; then given to a series of agreements in 1904 between the two countries, dealing with a range of issues, in particular establishing the predominant role of the UK in Egypt, and France's interests in Morocco.

Erskine, Thomas, 1st Baron (1750–1823)

Scottish jurist. He sought a career in the navy and army before studying law. Called to the Bar in 1778, his success was immediate and unprecedented, and he became a KC and MP (1783). His sympathy with the French Revolution led him to join the 'Friends of the People', and to undertake the defence in many political prosecutions of 1793–4, notably of Thomas **Paine**. He became a peer in 1806 and for a while acted as Lord Chancellor (1806–7), after which he retired into private life.

Essex, Robert Devereux, 2nd Earl of (1566–1601)
English soldier and courtier. He served in the Netherlands (1585–6), and distinguished himself at Zutphen. At court, he quickly rose in the favour of **Elizabeth I**, despite his clandestine marriage in 1590 with Sir Philip Sidney's widow. In 1591 he commanded the forces sent to help Henry IV of France, and took part in the sacking of Cadiz (1595). He became a Privy Councillor (1593) and Earl Marshal (1597). He alienated the Queen's advisers, and there were constant quarrels with Elizabeth (notably the occasion when he turned his back on her, and she boxed his ears). His six months' lord-lieutenancy of Ireland (1599) proved a failure; he was imprisoned and deprived of his dignities. He attempted to raise the City of London, was found guilty of high treason, and beheaded in the Tower.

Ethelbert (c.552–616)
King of Kent (560/616). In his reign Kent achieved (c.590) control over England south of the Humber, and Christianity was introduced by St **Augustine** (597). To him we owe the first written English laws. ▷ **Anglo-Saxons**

Ethelred I (c.830–71)
King of Wessex (865/71). He was the elder brother of **Alfred, 'the Great'**. It was during Ethelred's reign that the Danes launched their main invasion of England. He died soon after his victory over the invaders. ▷ **Wessex**

Ethelred the Unready (c.968–1016)
King of England (978/1016). The son of **Edgar**, he was aged about 10 when the murder of his half-brother, **Edward the Martyr**, placed him on the throne. In 1002 he confirmed an alliance with **Normandy** by marrying, as his second wife, Duke Richard's daughter Emma — the first dynastic link between the two countries. Renewed attacks by the **Vikings** on England began as raids in the 980s, and in 1013 Sweyn Forkbeard secured mastery over the whole country, and forced Ethelred into exile in Normandy. After Sweyn's death (1014), Ethelred returned to oppose **Canute**, but the unity of English resistance was broken when his son, **Edmund II, 'Ironside'**, rebelled. 'Unready' is a mistranslation of *Unraed*, not recorded as his nickname until after the **Norman**

Conquest, which means 'ill-advised' and is a pun on his given name, Ethelred (literally, 'good counsel').

EU (European Union)

An association of 12 European countries, heralded by the Single European Act (1986) and created by the Treaty of Maastricht Act (in effect from 1 Nov 1993), forming the political and economic infrastructure that enables the free movement of people, goods, and services between member countries. One of its main aims is monetary union, a project handled by the **EC**, which is a component part of the EU. Two other pillars of the Union that require inter-governmental cooperation are the areas of foreign and security policy (handled by the **WEU**) and justice and home affairs. ▷ **EEC**

Exclusion Crisis (1678–81)

The name given to events, beginning with the **Popish Plot**, during a campaign in parliament to exclude **Charles II**'s brother, James, Duke of York (later **James II**), from succession to the throne on grounds of his Catholicism. Showing considerable political skill, the King outmanoeuvred his Whig opponents and undermined their power base. Many were arrested or fled abroad. ▷ **Whigs**

Eyre, Edward John (1815–1901)

British explorer and colonial governor. He emigrated to Australia in 1833, where he drove stock from Sydney to Melbourne and Adelaide. From Adelaide in 1839–40 he made exploratory forays to the north, reaching Lake Eyre, and west across the Eyre Peninsula, but without finding a route out of South Australia. In 1841, with just his overseer, Baxter, and three Aboriginals, he set out to reach Albany in the west. On the way Baxter died and two Aboriginals deserted, but fresh supplies provided by a French whaler enabled Eyre to complete the first crossing from South to Western Australia. In 1841 he was appointed protector of Aboriginals at Moorundie, South Australia, returning to England in 1844. He became Lieutenant-Governor of New Zealand (1846), Lieutenant-Governor of St Vincent (1854), acting Governor (1861) and then Governor of Jamaica (1864). There, his severe repression of a Negro rebellion (1865) created a political storm in England and led to his recall and retirement.

F

Fabian Society

A socialist group established in 1884 which took its name from the Roman general, Fabius Maximus *Cunctator* ('the Delayer'), noted for his cautious military tactics. It adopts a gradualist approach to social reform, and sometimes 'Fabian' is applied to people who are not members of the society but who believe in reformist **socialism**. The society has remained a small select group, but has a close association with the **Labour Party**, and has been a source of socialist ideas and arguments.

Factory Acts

Legislation passed from 1802 onwards to regulate employment in factories. The early Acts were generally concerned to limit the hours of work of women and children in textile factories only. The 1833 Factory Act prohibited children under nine from working in textile mills, and was the first to appoint factory inspectors. A maximum 10-hour working day for women and older children was enacted in 1847.

Fairfax (of Cameron), Thomas, 3rd Baron (1612–71)

English parliamentary general. In the **English Civil Wars**, he distinguished himself at the Battle of **Marston Moor** (1644), and in 1645 was given command of the **New Model Army**, defeating **Charles I** at the Battle of **Naseby**. He was replaced by **Cromwell** in 1650 for refusing to march against the Scots, who had proclaimed **Charles II** king, and withdrew into private life. In 1660 he was head of the commission sent to The Hague to arrange for the King's return.

Falklands War (Apr–June 1982)

A war between Britain and Argentina, precipitated by the Argentine invasion of the Falkland Islands (known to Argentinians as the Malvinas). Britain had ruled the islands continuously since 1833, but Argentina claimed them by inheritance from the Spanish

Empire and through their proximity to her shores. The British had been conducting talks with Argentina on sovereignty over the Falklands, involving either a leaseback arrangement or a joint administration. When these talks broke down, the government of General **Galtieri** issued a warning to the British. The British government announced the withdrawal of HMS *Endurance* from the South Atlantic, and on 19 Mar scrap merchants landed on South Georgia, ostensibly to demolish a whaling station, but they also raised the Argentine flag. On the night of 1–2 Apr the full-scale invasion of the Falklands began. The 70 Royal Marines on the islands were overwhelmed, and the Governor was deported to Uruguay. The British immediately fitted out a task force to retake the islands, and the Foreign Office team, including Lord Carrington, resigned. The task force consisted of almost 70 ships, including some 40 requisitioned merchantmen and some well-known passenger vessels such as the *Queen Elizabeth 2*. A 200-mile maritime exclusion zone was declared around the Falklands, and on 2 May the Argentine cruiser, *General Belgrano*, was sunk by the nuclear submarine, HMS *Conqueror*. This brought to an end peace initiatives conducted by the US Secretary of State, Alexander Haig, and the Peruvian government. South Georgia was retaken (25 Apr); the destroyer HMS *Sheffield* was sunk by an Exocet missile (4 May); 5 000 British troops were landed at Port San Carlos (21 May); and more troops were landed at Bluff Cove (6–8 June), an operation attended by much loss of life when the Argentine air force attacked the *Sir Tristram* and *Sir Galahad*. The British forces took Darwin and Goose Green on 28 May, and after the recapture of the capital, Port Stanley, the Argentinians surrendered (14 June). The war cost the British £700 million; 254 British and 750 Argentine lives were lost; and some political commentators claim that it did much to save the declining fortunes of the government of Margaret **Thatcher**.

fascism

A term applied generically, and often inaccurately, to a variety of extremely nationalistic and authoritarian, populist movements that reached their pinnacle in the inter-war years. The movement originated in Italy, centred on **Mussolini**. It is hard to define the central tenets of fascism even in Italy, where it began as a republican, anti-capitalist, anticlerical movement with a strong syndicalist influence and yet quickly switched to supporting the free market, the monarchy and the Church. However, all fascist movements (Oswald **Mosley**'s **Blackshirts** in Britain, the Iron Guard in Romania, the Croix de Feu in France or any other of its legion manifestations across Europe) shared common features: an aggressive and unquestioning nationalism; a disrespect for democratic and liberal institutions which did not, however, preclude using them to attain power; a profound hatred for socialism; an emphasis on a single charismatic leader; a strong association with militarism. There are many similarities between fascism and Nazism, the latter often being described as simply an extreme manifestation of the former. However, it should be stressed that, although xenophobic, there was nothing intrinsically anti-Semitic about Italian fascism, at least in its early stages. After the end of **World War II**, fascism was largely discredited, although groups such as the Italian Social Movement and the British and French National Fronts show many similarities.

Fashoda Incident (1898)

The settlement of Fashoda (now Kodok) on the upper White Nile, was the scene of a major Anglo-French crisis in this year. French forces under Captain Jean Baptiste Marchand had reached the Nile after an 18-month journey from Brazzaville. The British, who were in the process of retaking the Sudan, issued an ultimatum; France was not prepared to go to war, and Marchand was ordered to withdraw. The incident destroyed French ambitions for a trans-continental African empire, and confirmed British mastery of the Nile region. ▷ **Africa, Partition of; Kitchener, Earl**

Fawcett, Dame Millicent (1847–1929)

English women's rights campaigner. Keenly interested in the higher education of women and the extension of the franchise to her sex, she was made President of the National Union of Women's Suffrage Societies (1897–1919).

Fawkes, Guy (1570–1606)

English conspirator. Born of Protestant parentage, he became a Catholic at an early age, and served in the Spanish Army in the Netherlands (1593–1604). He crossed to England at Robert Catesby's invitation, and became a member of the **Gunpowder Plot** to blow up parliament. Caught red-handed, he was tried and hanged.

Fenians

The short title of the Irish Republican Brotherhood, a nationalist organization founded in New York in 1857. The movement quickly espoused violence as a means of achieving its objective, and is best known for attacks in Manchester and London in 1867 to rescue imprisoned supporters. The fatalities which occurred caused these to be called 'The Fenian Outrages'. ▷ **Sinn Féin**

feudalism

A modern construct from the Latin word *feudum* ('fief'), originally coined in 1839, referring to phenomena associated more or less closely with the **Middle Ages**. In a narrow sense, the word is used to describe the medieval military and political order based on reciprocal ties between lords and vassals, in which the main elements were the giving of homage and the tenure of fiefs. Though normally associated with political fragmentation, feudalism as here defined could serve as the ally of royal power. Polemicists apply it to whatever appears backward or reactionary in the modern world.

Fianna Fáil

Irish political party founded in 1926 by those opposed to the 1921 Anglo-Irish Treaty. It first came to power under **De Valera** in 1932, and has been the governing party for most of the period since. In the 1930s it emphasized separation from the British, and has consistently supported the unification of Ireland. In domestic issues its approach is more pragmatic than ideological.

Field of the Cloth of Gold (June 1520)

The ceremonial meeting in Picardy between **Henry VIII** of England and Francis I of France. Francis was trying (in vain) to woo England away from its alliance with the Emperor Charles V. The lavish finery of the occasion gave the meeting its name, and enhanced the standing of the English monarchy.

Fifteen Rebellion

The name given to the first of the Jacobite rebellions against Hanoverian monarchy to restore the Catholic Stuart Kings to the British throne. The rising began at Braemar (Sep 1715) by the Earl of Mar proclaiming James Edward **Stuart** (the 'Old Pretender') as

King. Jacobite forces were defeated at Preston in Nov, and the rebellion collapsed early in 1716. ▷ **Jacobites; Stuart, House of**

Fifth Monarchists

A millenarian religio-political grouping in England in the 1650s which believed that the second coming of Christ was imminent. The name derived from the Bible (Daniel 2.44), adherents seeking a 'fifth monarchy' to succeed the empires of Assyria, Persia, Greece and Rome. Though radical **Puritans**, Fifth Monarchists did not form a coherent sect. They opposed the new establishment represented by the **Protectorate** of Oliver **Cromwell** supported by the army after the dissolution of **Barebone's Parliament** (1653). Under Thomas Venner, they mounted uprisings against both Cromwell (1657) and the restored monarchy of **Charles II** (1661) after the second of which Venner was executed. ▷ **Restoration**

Fine Gael

Irish political party created out of the pro-Anglo-Irish Treaty (1921) wing of **Sinn Féin**. It was known as *Cumann na nGaedheal* from 1923 until it changed its name in 1933. The first government of the **Irish Free State**, it has largely been in opposition since the 1930s, and has never held power on its own. It supports an Irish confederation, and is largely pragmatic in domestic matters.

Fisher, Andrew (1862–1928)

British-born Australian politician. A coalminer from the age of 12, he emigrated to Queensland in 1885. From mining, he gradually moved into trade-union activity and politics, entering the Queensland state assembly in 1893 and the first federal parliament in 1901. He became Australian Labor Party (ALP) leader in 1907 and then Prime Minister (1908–09, 1910–13 and 1914–15). At the start of **World War I** he made the dramatic promise to support the war effort 'to the last man and the last shilling'. He was Australian High Commissioner in London (1916–21).

Fisher (of Kilverstone), John Arbuthnot, 1st Baron (1841–1920)

British admiral. He joined the navy as a boy in 1854, and rose to be First Sea Lord (1904–10 and 1914–15). His major reforms of the Royal Navy prepared the country for **World War I**, including the introduction of the 'Dreadnought' battleship and 'Invincible' cruiser. He was made a peer in 1909.

121

Flodden, Battle of (9 Sep 1513)

A victory of the English over the Scots, fought in Northumberland. **James IV** of Scotland, allied with France, invaded England in Aug, but was defeated by English forces under Thomas Howard, Earl of Surrey. The Scottish dead included James, 13 earls, and three bishops; the battle ended the Scottish threat for a generation.

Foot, Michael (Mackintosh) (1913–)

English Labour politician. He joined the staff of the *Tribune* in 1937, becoming editor (1948–52 and 1955–60). He was also acting editor of the *Evening Standard* (1942–4) and a political columnist on the *Daily Herald* (1944–64). He became an MP in 1945, serving until 1992, and was Secretary of State for Employment (1974–6), Deputy Leader (1976–80) then Leader (1980–3) of the **Labour Party**, resigning after his party's heavy defeat in the general election. A prominent figure on the party's left and a pacifist, he has long been a supporter of the Campaign for Nuclear Disarmament (**CND**). A prolific writer, his best-known work is his biography of Aneurin **Bevan**.

Formigny, Battle of (1450)

The decisive defeat near Bayeux (Calvados) during the **Hundred Years War** of an army sent by the English government, then bankrupt and bereft of allies, to stem French advances in Normandy. Having lost their previous tactical superiority, the English were bombarded out of their positions by artillery, and routed by infantry. The French reconquest of Normandy was swiftly completed.

Fortescue, Sir John (c.1385–c.1479)

English jurist. He was called to the Bar, and became Lord Chief-Justice of the King's Bench (1442). He sided with the Lancastrians, fled with **Margaret of Anjou** and her son to Scotland, and in 1463 embarked with them for Holland. During exile he wrote his *De Laudibus Legum Angliae* (In Praise of the Laws of England, printed 1537) for the instruction of Prince Edward, a work which came to be of great value to later jurists. After the defeat of the Lancastrians at the Battle of **Tewkesbury**, he submitted to Edward IV. ▷ **Lancaster, House of**

Forty-Five Rebellion (1745–6)

The Jacobite rebellion which aimed to restore the Catholic Stuart kings to the British throne and displace the Hanoverians. It began in July 1745 when Charles Edward **Stuart** (the 'Young Pretender') arrived in Scotland and proclaimed his father King James III. Support came mainly from the Scottish Highland Clans, and there were some early successes. The Jacobite forces reached as far south as Derby, but the rebellion lost support, and was crushingly defeated at the Battle of **Culloden** in 1746. After the '45, the Hanoverian regime brutally suppressed the clan system. ▷ **Jacobites; Stuart, House of**

Four Freedoms (1941)

Four basic human rights proclaimed in an annual message to Congress by President Franklin D Roosevelt as basic human rights. They included freedom of speech and worship, and freedom from want and fear.

Fourteen Points

A peace programme outlined by US President Woodrow Wilson in a message to Congress in 1918, at the end of **World War I**. The programme offered the possibility of an acceptable peace to the Central Powers, and as a result Wilson came to be perceived as a moral leader. It was largely instrumental in bringing about the surrender of Germany and the beginning of peace talks. Several of the points, however, were compromised or defeated in the actual treaty.

Fox, Charles James (1749–1806)

English politician. He became an MP at 19, and two years later was a junior Lord of the Admiralty. He supported Lord **North**, but in 1772 resigned over American policy. Foreign Secretary in 1782 and 1783, he became Secretary of State after North's downfall, and formed a coalition with him, which held office for a short period in 1783. He supported the French Revolution, and strongly opposed the war with France. After **Pitt**, 'the Younger's' death (1806) he was recalled to office as Foreign Secretary, but died soon afterwards.

Frederick (Augustus) (1763–1827)

Duke of York. He was the second son of King **George III**. A soldier by profession, he was unsuccessful both in the field in the

Netherlands (1793–9) and as British commander-in-chief (1798–1809), and earned the nickname of the 'grand old Duke of York' in the nursery rhyme. However, his painstaking reform of the army proved of lasting benefit, especially to **Wellington**. In 1809 he resigned because of the traffic in appointments conducted by his mistress, Mary Anne Clarke, but he was exonerated and reinstated in 1811.

Free French

Frenchmen who answered General de **Gaulle**'s appeal, broadcast from London (18 June 1940), to reject the impending armistice between France and Germany, and join him in fighting on. De Gaulle became leader of the Free French forces, and the 2nd French Armoured Division helped to liberate Paris (25 Aug 1944). ▷ **World War II**

French, John (Denton Pinkstone), Earl of Ypres (1852–1925)

British field marshal. He joined the navy (1866), then the army (1874), and distinguished himself in the Sudan (1884–5) and South Africa (1899–1901). Chief of Imperial General Staff (1911–14), he held supreme command of the British Expeditionary Force in France (1914–15), but was criticized for indecision, and resigned. He was made a viscount (1915) and earl (1921), and was Lord-Lieutenant of Ireland (1918–21). ▷ **World War I**

French and Indian War (1756–63)

The last of the 18c wars between France and Britain for the control of North America. France accepted final defeat at the Treaty of Paris (1763) ▷ **Seven Years War**

French Revolutionary Wars (1792–9)

A series of campaigns between France and neighbouring European states hostile to the Revolution and to French hegemony, merging ultimately into the **Napoleonic Wars** (1799–1815). Starting with France's declaration of war on Emperor Francis II, Prussia, and Sardinia, which precipitated the War of the First Coalition (1792–7), French forces attacked the Rhine, the Netherlands, and Savoy, after checking an initial Austro-Prussian advance at Valmy (1792). France later extended hostilities to Britain, Holland, and Spain (1793); after successfully invading the Netherlands (1794), the French broke the Coalition (1795–6), isolating Britain (1797). A Second Coalition (1798) expelled French forces from Italy and the Rhinelands, before suffering defeat by **Napoleon I** (1799–1800).

Friends, Society of

A Christian sect founded by George Fox and others in mid-17c England, and formally organized in 1667; members are popularly known as Quakers, possibly because of Fox's injunction 'to quake at the word of the Lord'. Persecution led William Penn to establish a Quaker colony (Pennsylvania) in 1682. Belief in the 'inner light', a living contact with the divine Spirit, is the basis of its meetings for worship, where Friends gather in silence until moved by the Spirit to speak. They emphasize simplicity in all things, and are active reformers promoting tolerance, justice, and peace. Today most meetings have programmed orders of worship, though meetings based on silence (unprogrammed) still prevail in the UK and parts of the USA.

fur trade

The history of the fur trade in North America is inextricably linked with the exploration of the continent and the struggle between France and Britain for its control. The trade was first centred along the St Lawrence River and the Atlantic coast around Newfoundland and Acadia during the late 16c and early 17c. The furs were brought to the fishing stations by Indians attracted by the exchange for relatively cheap trinkets and other manufactured goods. In 1608 Samuel Champlain established a base at Quebec and contacts with the Algonkin and Huron tribes, whom he assisted against their traditional enemies the Iroquois. With the advance of settlement and the opening up of trading routes into the interior, it became clear by the late 17c that the French were caught between the British colonies to the south and the **Hudson's Bay Company** (set up in 1670 as the result of information from two disaffected French traders) to the north and west. While the Iroquois acted as middlemen bringing the trade into British hands at Albany, the French re-established a forward position with the chain of forts and trading posts which controlled the Great Lakes region and the upper Mississippi and Ohio valleys until the cession of New France to Britain in 1763. In the late 18c and early 19c the north-western fur trade was bitterly contested between the independents who organized themselves as the North West Company (opening up new routes to the

Pacific seaboard, where they found John Jacob Astor's Pacific Fur Company already established) and the Hudson's Bay Company. After the amalgamation of the two Canadian companies in 1821, the HBC organized the trade on a continental basis, ceding its lands to the Dominion in 1869 but continuing as the most important economic force in the north.

G

Gage, Thomas (1721–87)
British general. In 1760 he became Military Governor of Montreal, in 1763 Commander-in-Chief of the British forces in America, and in 1774 Governor of Massachusetts. In 1775 (18 Apr) he sent a force to seize a quantity of arms at Concord; and next day the skirmish of **Lexington** took place which began the **American Revolution**. After the Battle of Bunker Hill (June 1775) he resigned and returned to England, where he died.

Gaitskell, Hugh (Todd Naylor) (1906–63)
English Labour politician. He became a socialist during the 1926 **General Strike**. He became an MP in 1945, he was Minister of Fuel and Power (1947) and of Economic Affairs (1950), and Chancellor of the Exchequer (1950–1). In 1955 he was elected Leader of the Opposition by a large majority over **Bevan**. He bitterly opposed **Eden**'s Suez action (1956), and refused to accept a narrow conference vote for unilateral disarmament (1960). This caused a crisis of leadership in which he was challenged by Harold **Wilson** (1960) and Arthur Greenwood (1961), but he retained the loyalty of most Labour MPs. ▷ **Butskellism; Labour Party; Suez Crisis**

Gallipoli Campaign (1915–16)
A major campaign of **World War I**. With stalemate on the Western Front, the British War Council advocated operations against the Turks to secure the Dardanelles and aid Russia. The land campaign began with amphibious assaults on the Gallipoli Peninsula (Apr 1915). Australian and New Zealand forces were heavily involved: the beach where they landed is still known as Anzac Cove. Allied casualties were 250 000 out of 480 000 engaged. The operation was abandoned as a costly failure, with successful evacuations of all remaining troops in Jan 1916. ▷ **Dardanelles**

Galtieri, Leopoldo Fortunato (1926–)
Argentine soldier and politician. He became President in 1981. The state of the Argentine economy caused mounting domestic

criticism and to counter this, in Apr 1982, Galtieri ordered the invasion of the long-disputed Malvinas (Falkland) Islands. Their recovery by Britain, after a brief and humiliating war, brought about his downfall. He was court-martialled in 1983 and sentenced to 12 years' imprisonment for negligence in starting and losing the **Falklands War**.

Gandhi, M(ohandas) K(aramchand) (1869–1948)

Indian nationalist leader. He studied law in London, then spent 21 years in South Africa opposing discriminatory legislation against Indians. In 1914 he returned to India, where he supported the Home Rule movement, and became leader of the Indian National Congress, advocating a policy of non-violent non-cooperation to achieve independence. Following his first major non-cooperation and **civil disobedience** campaign (1919–22), he was jailed for conspiracy (1922–4). In 1930 he led a 200-mile march to the sea to collect salt in symbolic defiance of the government monopoly; this marked the beginning of the second major campaign of civil disobedience. On his release from prison (1931), he attended the London Round Table Conference on Indian constitutional reform. In 1946 he negotiated with the Cabinet Mission which recommended the new constitutional structure. After independence (1947), he tried to stop the Hindu/Muslim conflict in Bengal, a policy which led to his assassination in Delhi by Nathuram Godse, a Hindu fanatic. ▷ **Non-Cooperation Movement; Round Table Conferences; Swaraj**

Gaspée

A British customs schooner set afire and destroyed by colonists after it went aground near Providence, Rhode Island (9 June 1772). The schooner had been stationed off the coast to counter the profitable smuggling trade of the region. A subsequent investigation into the incident ended in failure.

Gates, Horatio (1728–1806)

British-born US general. He joined the British Army, served in America in the **Seven Years War** (1756–63), and then settled in Virginia. In the **American Revolution** he sided with his adoptive country and fought for its cause. In 1777 he took command of the Northern department, and forced the British Army to surrender at the Battle of **Saratoga**. In 1780 he commanded the Southern department, but his army was routed by **Cornwallis** at the Battle of **Camden**, and he was superseded. He returned to Virginia, but in 1790 emancipated his slaves and then settled near New York City.

Gaulle, Charles (André Joseph Marie) de (1898–1970)

French general and politician. Only a colonel in 1940, he was known as the author of several books on military and historical topics. He was promoted temporary General of Brigade (1 June 1940), and four days later entered the government as Under-Secretary at the Ministry of National Defence. Refusing to accept the armistice, he fled to England, where (18 June 1940) he appealed to the French people to continue the struggle. As the leader of the **Free French**, he fought many diplomatic battles against President Roosevelt to ensure that France was treated as a co-belligerent, thus emerging in 1944 as head of the Provisional Government. He resigned in 1946, but returned to power in 1958 when the Algerian crisis led to his recall, as the last Prime Minister of the Fourth Republic. He used this position to draw up a new constitution for the Fifth Republic, which embodied the presidential system he had wanted in 1946. He became its first President (1959–69). He concentrated on winning France a leading place in Europe by excluding Britain from the **EC** (European Community) and by signing an historic reconciliation treaty with Germany (both 1963). He developed a French nuclear deterrent, and removed France from its military obligations under **NATO** (1965). His supporters won by a big majority in the elections following the 'events' of 1968, but he lost a referendum on constitutional reform in 1969, and resigned.

General Assembly (politics) ▷ UN

General Strike (4–12 May 1926)

A national strike organized by the Trades Union Congress (TUC) in support of an existing miners' strike to resist wage cuts. The government organized special constables and volunteers to counter the most serious effects of the strike, and issued an anti-strike propaganda journal, *The British Gazette*. The TUC called off the strike, though the miners' strike continued fruitlessly for three more months.

George I (1660–1727)
King of Great Britain and Ireland (1714/27). Born in Hanover, he was the great-grandson of James I of England, and was proclaimed King on the death of Queen **Anne**. Elector of Hanover since 1698, he had commanded the Imperial forces in the **Marlborough** wars. He divorced his wife and cousin, the Princess Dorothea of Zell, imprisoning her in the castle of Ahlde, where she died (1726). He took relatively little part in the government of the country. His affections remained with Hanover, and he lived there as much as possible. ▷ **Jacobites; James VI and I; Walpole, Robert**

George II (1683–1760)
King of Great Britain and Ireland (1727/60) and Elector of Hanover. Born in Hanover, he was the son of **George I**. In 1705 he married Caroline of Anspach (1683–1737). Though he involved himself more in the government of the country than his father had, the policy pursued during the first half of the reign was that of Robert **Walpole**. In the War of the Austrian Succession, he was present at the Battle of **Dettingen** (1743), the last occasion on which a British sovereign commanded an army in the field. His reign also saw the crushing of Jacobite hopes at the Battle of **Culloden** (1746), the foundation of British India after the Battle of Plassey (1757), the beginning of the **Seven Years War**, and the capture of **Quebec** (1759). ▷ **Stuart, Charles**

George III (1738–1820)
King of Great Britain and Ireland (1760/1820), and Elector (1760/1815) and King (1815/20) of Hanover. The eldest son of Frederick Louis, Prince of Wales (1707/51), his father predeceased him, and he thus succeeded his grandfather, **George II**. Eager to govern as well as reign, he did not lack ability but was not politically adept and caused considerable friction. With Lord **North** he shared in the blame for the loss of the American colonies, and popular feeling ran high against him for a time in the 1770s. In 1783 he called **Pitt**, 'the Younger' to office, an important stage in reducing the political influence of a small group of established Whig families. In 1810 he suffered a recurrence of a mental derangement, and the Prince of Wales was made Regent. He died, insane and blind. ▷ **American Revolution**

George IV (1762–1830)
King of the United Kingdom and of Hanover (1820/30). The eldest son of **George III**, he became Prince Regent in 1810, because of his father's insanity. Rebelling against a strict upbringing, he went through a marriage ceremony with Mrs Fitzherbert, a Roman Catholic, in 1785, thus forfeiting his title to the crown. The marriage was later declared invalid, and in 1795 he married Princess Caroline of Brunswick, whom he tried to divorce when he was King. Her death in 1821 ended a scandal in which the people sympathized with the Queen. A frequently vilified and always extravagant monarch, he was responsible for the building of the pavilion at Brighton.

George V (1865–1936)
King of the United Kingdom (1910/36). He was the second son of **Edward VII**. He served in the navy, travelled in many parts of the Empire, and was created Prince of Wales in 1901. His reign saw the creation of the Union of South Africa (1910), **World War I**, the **Irish Free State** settlement (1922), and the **General Strike** (1926). His consort, Mary (1867–1953), married him in 1893; she organized women's war work (1914–18), and continued with many public and philanthropic activities after the death of her husband. They had five sons and one daughter.

George VI (1895–1952)
King of the United Kingdom (1936/52). The second son of **George V**, he served in the Grand Fleet at the Battle of Jutland (1916). In 1920 he was created Duke of York, and married in 1923. He played at Wimbledon in the All-England tennis championships in 1926. He ascended the throne on the abdication of his elder brother, **Edward VIII**. During **World War II** he continued to reside in bomb-damaged Buckingham Palace, visited all theatres of war, and delivered many broadcasts, for which task he mastered a speech impediment. He and his wife, Elizabeth, (*née* Elizabeth Bowes-Lyon), had two children, Princess Elizabeth (later Queen **Elizabeth II**) and Princess Margaret.

Ghent, Treaty of (1814)
The treaty between the USA and Britain which ended the **War of 1812**, without any resolution of the major issues from which

the conflict had grown. These had included maritime rights and military control of the Great Lakes.

Gibraltar

The narrow peninsula rising steeply from the low-lying coast of south-west Spain at the eastern end of the Strait of Gibraltar, which is an important strategic point of control for the western Mediterranean. Settled by the Moors in 711, Gibraltar was taken by Spain in 1462, and ceded to Britain in 1713, becoming a British Crown Colony in 1830. As a Crown Colony, it played a key role in Allied naval operations during both World Wars. A proposal to end British rule was defeated by a referendum in 1967. The frontier with Spain was closed from 1969 until 1985, and Spain continues to claim sovereignty.

Ginkel, Godert de (1630–1703)

Dutch general. He accompanied **William III** to England in 1688, and fought at the Battle of the **Boyne** (1690). As Commander-in-Chief in Ireland, he defeated the remaining rebels, and was created Earl of Athlone (1692). He later led the Dutch troops under the Duke of Marlborough.

Gladstone, W(illiam) E(wart) (1809–98)

English politician and Prime Minister of Britain. He entered parliament in 1832 as a Conservative, working closely with **Peel**. From 1834 he held various junior posts, becoming President of the Board of Trade (1843–5). He was Chancellor of the Exchequer in **Aberdeen**'s coalition (1852–5) and then again under **Palmerston** and **Russell** (1859–66). In 1867 he became leader of the **Liberal Party**, and soon after served his first term as Premier (1868–74). In a ministry notable for administrative reform, he disestablished and disendowed the Irish Church, reformed the Civil Service and established a system of national elementary education (1870). Frequently in office (1880–5, 1886 and 1892–4) until his resignation in 1894, he succeeded in carrying out a scheme of parliamentary reform (1884) which went a long way towards universal male suffrage. In his last two ministries he introduced bills for Irish **Home Rule**, but both were defeated. ▷ **Conservative Party**

Glanvill, Ranulf de (d.1190)
Chief Justiciary of England (1180–9). He was adviser to **Henry II** and reputed author of the earliest treatise on the laws of England. In 1174 he raised a body of knights and captured **William I**, 'the Lion', of Scotland. He joined the third crusade and died during the siege of Acre. ▷ **Crusades**

Glencoe, Massacre of (13 Feb 1692)
The killing of 37 members of the clan of the MacDonalds of Glencoe by soldiers of **William III**, led by Archibald Campbell, 10th earl of Argyll. It has gained notoriety in Scottish history because of the treacherous nature of the attack. Alexander Mac-Donald of Glencoe had delayed his submission to an oath of allegiance until 31 Dec 1691, the day before the deadline imposed by the government, and was then unable to swear until 6 Jan, when a magistrate visited Fort William to receive his oath. The order for punishment was issued, however, and the troops quartered with the MacDonalds suddenly fell upon their hosts. Many escaped, but the chief was slain along with several men, women and children. A long-standing enemy of the MacDonalds, John Campbell, earl of Breadalbane, was suspected of planning the attack.

Glendower, Owen (c.1354–1416)
Welsh chief. He studied law at Westminster, and became esquire to the Earl of Arundel. In 1401 he rebelled against **Henry IV**, proclaimed himself Prince of Wales, established an independent Welsh parliament, and joined the coalition with Harry Percy (Hotspur), who was defeated at the Battle of Shrewsbury (1403). He continued to fight for Welsh independence until his death. ▷ **Percy**

Glorious First of June, Battle of the (1794)
A naval battle fought off the Isle d'Ouessant (near Brest) between British and French navies. The victory for Admiral Richard **Howe** resulted in the capture of a third of the French ships, and confirmation of British naval supremacy. ▷ **French Revolutionary Wars**

Glorious Revolution (Dec 1688–Feb 1689)
The name given to the events during which **James VII and II** fled from England, effectively abdicating the throne, and **William III**

and Mary II were established by parliament as joint monarchs. The title, coined by **Whigs** who in the long term benefited most from it, celebrates the bloodlessness of the event, and the assertion of the constitutional importance of parliament.

Gloucester, Humphrey, Duke of (1391–1447)

Youngest son of **Henry IV**, and protector during the minority of **Henry VI** (1422–9). He greatly increased the difficulties of his brother, Bedford, by his greed, irresponsibility, and factious quarrels with their uncle, Cardinal Henry **Beaufort**. In 1447 he was arrested for high treason at Bury St Edmunds and five days later was found dead in bed (apparently from natural causes). His patronage of literature led to his nickname 'the Good Duke Humphrey'.

Glubb, John Bagot (Glubb Pasha) (1897–1986)

British soldier. Educated in Cheltenham and the Royal Military Academy, Woolwich, he served in **World War I**, and became the first organizer of the native police force in the new state of Iraq (1920). In 1930 he was transferred to British-mandated Transjordan, organizing the Arab Legion's Desert Patrol, and becoming Legion Commandant (1939). He had immense prestige among the Bedouin, but was dismissed from his post in 1956 following Arab criticism. Knighted in 1956, he then became a writer and lecturer.

Goderich, Viscount, Robinson, Frederick John (1st Earl of Ripon) (1782–1859)

English politician and Prime Minister of Britain. He entered parliament as a Tory MP in 1806, becoming President of the Board of Trade (1918–23 and 1841–3) and Chancellor of the Exchequer (1823–7). He was associated with financial reforms to reduce government debt and promote greater freedom of trade. His success earned him the sobriquet 'Prosperity Robinson'. He was Secretary of State for War and the Colonies (1827) under **Canning**, whom he succeeded. His weak leadership was soon exposed and he resigned willingly before meeting parliament as Prime Minister (1827–8), the only Premier to do so. Briefly changing parties, he served in **Grey**'s Whig governments as Secretary for War and the Colonies (1830–3) and Lord Privy Seal (1834–5). His last government office was under **Peel** as President of the Board of Control (1843–6) and he introduced the Bill to repeal the **Corn**

Laws (1846). His extensive governmental career testifies to administrative competence but not to leadership. ▷ **Tories; Whigs**

Godolphin, Sidney Godolphin, 1st Earl of (1645–1712)

English statesman. He entered parliament (1668), visited Holland (1678), and was made head of the Treasury and a baron (1684). He stood by **James VII and II** when William of Orange landed (1688), and voted for a regency; yet in 1689 William reinstated him as First Commissioner of the Treasury. He was ousted in 1696, but made Lord High Treasurer by Queen **Anne** (1702) and created earl (1706). His able management of the finances helped **Marlborough** in the War of the **Spanish Succession** (1700–13); but court intrigues led to his dismissal in 1710. ▷ **William III**

Godwin (d.1053)

Earl of Wessex. He was probably the son of the South Saxon, Wulfnoth. Godwin became powerful under King **Canute**, and in 1042 helped to raise **Edward the Confessor** to the throne, marrying him to his daughter, Edith. He led the struggle against the King's foreign favourites, which Edward revenged by confining Edith in a monastery, and banishing Godwin and his sons (1051). In 1052 Godwin landed in England, received the support of the people, and was reinstated. His son, **Harold II**, was, for a few months, Edward's successor. ▷ **Anglo-Saxons**

Goldie, Sir George Taubman (1846-1925)

British soldier and trader. After service as an army officer, became a trader in West Africa. He foresaw the developing Partition of Africa and believed that British interests must be secured against the French in the Oil Rivers region and along the Niger as a great commercial highway to the interior. By 1884 he had amalgamated all the British companies as the National Africa Company and set out to secure treaties from chiefs throughout the Niger Delta and in northern Nigeria. In 1886 he secured a charter for his renamed Royal Niger Company and effectively ruled the Niger regions until 1898. Frederick Lugard joined his employ and conquered the emirates of Northern Nigeria. ▷ **Africa, Partition of**

Gordon, Charles George (1833–85)

British general. He joined the Royal Engineers in 1852, and in 1855–6 fought in the **Crimean War**. In 1860 he went to China, where he crushed the Taiping Rebellion, for which he became known as 'Chinese Gordon'. In 1877 he was appointed Governor of the Sudan. He resigned in poor health in 1880, but returned in 1884 to relieve Egyptian garrisons which lay in rebel territory. He was besieged at Khartoum for 10 months by the Mahdi's troops, and was killed there two days before a relief force arrived.

Gordon Riots

Anti-Catholic riots in London which caused a breakdown of law and order in parts of the capital for several days in early June 1780. They occurred after Lord George Gordon (1751–93), leader of the Protestant Association, had failed in his attempt to have clauses in the 1778 Catholic Relief Act (removing restrictions on the activities of priests) repealed. ▷ **Catholic Emancipation**

Gorée Island

A small island off the Cape Verde Peninsula, Senegal. Throughout the 18c and early 19c, when Gorée was first a French, and then a British colony, it was a major centre of slave storage before shipping to the Americas. ▷ **slave trade**

Government of India Acts

Measures passed by the British Parliament to regulate the government of India (1883–1935). They included the 1858 Act which transferred British **East India Company** powers to the British Crown, and the 1919 and 1935 Acts which introduced limited constitutional change. Motivated in part by the need for retrenchment and increased taxation in the wake of India's involvement in **World War I**, the 1919 Act attempted to seduce moderate Indian politicians into cooperating with the colonial regime by offering a say in local and provincial government to a small proportion of the population from among the wealthier and more influential sections of society. The 1935 Act went further, although it still fell well short of a universal franchise, and led to the establishment of elected Congress ministries in most of the Indian provinces. Although these provincial governments had no say in matters of security, and the British governors retained a right of veto over both candidates and legislation, they were nonetheless a successful experiment in self-government, persuading some colonial officials that they could perhaps live with democracy. Unfortunately, representatives of minority political parties were largely excluded from the Congress governments, fuelling communal divisions in the country, whilst many officials merely saw provincial government as an undesirable concession, forced upon them by M K Gandhi's civil disobedience movement of 1930–2. The ministries resigned en masse in 1939, following the Viceroy, Linlithgow's, declaration of war with Germany without prior consultation with Indian politicians. ▷ **India Acts; Montagu–Chelmsford Reforms**

Grafton, Augustus Henry Fitzroy, 3rd Duke of (1735–1811)

English politician. He became MP in 1756, succeeding to his peerage in the following year. He was a prominent opponent of **Bute** in 1762–3 and became Secretary of State for the Northern Department (1765–6) under **Rockingham**. He accepted office under the Earl of **Chatham** as First Lord of the Treasury (1766–70) and took over leadership of the administration on his resignation (1768–70). His administration was weak and divided. He wished to pursue a more liberal policy towards the American colonies than his colleagues would allow and he handled **Wilkes**'s expulsion from the Commons ineptly. Soon after his resignation, he resumed office under Lord North as Lord Privy Seal (1771–5) but resigned when war broke out with the colonies. He served in the same office under Rockingham (1782–3) before retirement from politics when he became increasingly sympathetic to evangelicalism. ▷ **George III**

Granby, John Manners, Marquis of (1721–70)

British army officer. He was the eldest son of the Duke of Rutland. His reputation was made in the **Seven Years War**, when he led the British cavalry in a major victory over the French at Warburg (1760). He became a popular hero, and in 1763 was appointed Master-General of the Ordnance.

Grand Alliance, War of the (1805–7)

A phase in the **Napoleonic Wars**. A third coalition of states (Britain, Austria, Russia, Sweden, and Prussia) was formed to attack France by land and sea. Despite Britain's success at the Battle of **Trafalgar** (1805), the coalition was undermined by spectacular French victories at Ulm, Austerlitz (1805), and Jena and Auerstädt (1806). The Treaties of **Pressburg** (1805) and Tilsit (1807) ended hostilities.

Grand Remonstrance

The statement of **Charles I**'s abuses, and of reforms made by the **Long Parliament** in 1640–1; passed by 11 votes in the House of Commons (22 Nov 1641), and thereafter published as an appeal for support. The close vote reflected the formation of roughly equal parties of 'royalists' and 'parliamentarians'.

Great Depression

The worldwide slump in output and prices, and the greatly increased levels of unemployment (2.8 million in Britain in 1932), which developed between 1929 and 1934. It was precipitated by the collapse of the US stock market (the Wall Street crash) in Oct 1929. This ended US loans to Europe and greatly reduced business confidence worldwide. A major Austrian bank also collapsed, producing destabilization in much of Central and Eastern Europe.

Great Plague ▷ Black Death

Great Trek

The movement of parties of Boers (*Voortrekkers*) which made them the masters of large tracts of the interior of southern Africa. Objecting to British suzerainty, they began to leave Cape Colony in 1836 in separate trekking groups. Two parties were wiped out by black African resistance and malaria, when they headed for Delagoa Bay in Mozambique. Some settled in the Transvaal, where they were threatened by the Ndebele. One party in Natal was massacred by the **Zulu**, an event avenged by the Battle of Blood River in 1838. When the British annexed Natal in 1843, the majority of the Boers returned to the interior. The British made several unsuccessful attempts to resolve the divisions in the area, but when the region was reunited it was largely under Boer control. ▷ **Boer Wars**

Greek War of Independence (1821–8)

The struggle of the Greeks to gain independence from the **Ottoman Empire**. The revolt against the Ottoman Turks broke out in the Peloponnese and on several islands in 1821. At first the Turks were unable to retake the areas controlled by the rebels but, with the aid of Egyptian forces, in 1825 they invaded the Peloponnese, capturing Missolonghi (1826), and advanced to take Athens.

Britain, Russia and eventually France came to the aid of the Greek rebels, destroying the Egyptian fleet at **Navarino Bay** (1827). By the Treaty of **Adrianople** (1829), the allies guaranteed Greek independence. The Ottoman Porte formally recognized Greek independence by the Treaty of Constantinople (1832).

Gregory I, 'the Great', St (c.540–604)
Italian Pope (590/604). Appointed Praetor of Rome, he left this office (c.575), distributed his wealth among the poor, and withdrew into a monastery at Rome. It was here that he saw some Anglo-Saxon youths in the slave market, and was seized with a longing to convert their country to Christianity. As Pope, he was a great administrator, reforming all public services and ritual, and systematizing the sacred chants. In his writings the whole dogmatic system of the modern Church is fully developed.

Grenville, George (1712–70)
English politician and Prime Minister of Britain. He practised as a lawyer and was first MP in 1741, becoming Lord of the Admiralty (1744–7), Lord of the Treasury (1747–54) and Treasurer of the Navy (1754–5 and 1756–62). He was briefly Secretary of State for the Northern Department (1762–3) and then became Prime Minister (1763–5). During his period in office, Wilkes was arrested for seditious libel under a general warrant for his attack on the King's speech (1763). The closer supervision of revenue collection (1764–5) and **Stamp Act** (1765) began the process of alienating the American colonies from British rule. His lack of tact and maladroit handling of arrangements to cover a possible regency during **George III**'s first serious illness (1765) led to his dismissal by the King and he remained in opposition for the rest of his life.
▷ **Bute, John; Pelham, Henry; Pelham, Thomas Pelham-Holles**

Grenville, Sir Richard (1542–91)
English naval commander. A cousin of Sir Walter **Raleigh**, he fought in Hungary and Ireland (1566–9) and was knighted c.1577. He commanded, in 1585, the seven ships carrying Raleigh's first colony to Virginia. In 1591, as commander of the *Revenge*, he fought alone against a large Spanish fleet off the Azores, dying of wounds on board a Spanish ship.

Grenville, William Wyndham, 1st Baron (1759–1834)

English politician. The son of George **Grenville**, he studied at Eton and Oxford and entered parliament in 1782. He became Paymaster-General in 1783, Home Secretary in 1790, and Foreign Secretary in 1791. He resigned with **Pitt**, 'the Younger', in 1801 on the refusal of **George III** to agree to **Catholic Emancipation**. In 1806–7 he formed the coalition government of 'All the Talents', which abolished the **slave trade**.

Grey, Charles Grey, 2nd Earl (1764–1845)

British politician. He became a Whig MP in 1786, and was a leading supporter of parliamentary reform in the 1790s. In 1806 he became First Lord of the Admiralty, Foreign Secretary, and Leader of the House of Commons. In 1807 he succeeded his father as 2nd Earl Grey. In 1830 he formed a government promising peace, retrenchment and reform, and after considerable difficulties secured the passage of the 1832 Reform Bill. In the new parliament he carried the Act for the abolition of slavery in the colonies, but was forced to resign in 1834 following disagreement over the Irish question. ▷ **Reform Acts; Whigs**

Grey, Sir George (1812–98)

British colonial governor and Premier of New Zealand. He explored in Western Australia (1837–9), and became successively Governor of South Australia (1841), New Zealand (1845), and Cape Colony (1854). Again Governor of New Zealand (1861–8), he brought the **Maori Wars** to a close. As Premier of New Zealand (1877–9), he had much influence with the Maoris, and wrote on Polynesian culture. He returned to Britain in 1894.

Grey, Lady Jane (1537–54)

Queen of England for nine days in 1553. She was the eldest daughter of Henry Grey, Marquis of Dorset, and great-grand-daughter of **Henry VII**. In 1553 the Duke of Northumberland, foreseeing the death of **Edward VI**, aimed to secure the succession by marrying Jane (against her wish) to his fourth son, Lord Guildford Dudley. Three days after Edward's death (9 July), she was named as his successor, but was forced to abdicate in favour of **Mary I**, who had popular support. She was imprisoned in the Tower of London, and beheaded.

Griffith, Samuel Walker (1845–1920)

Welsh-born Australian judge. Emigrating to Australia in 1854, he studied at Sydney University. From 1867 he practised law in Queensland, entered the state legislature in 1872 and was state Premier (1883–8 and 1890–3). He was an active proponent of federation and as chairman of the Constitutional Committee of the National Australasian Convention in 1891 had a major role in drafting what became, in amended form, in 1900 the Australian Commonwealth Constitution. Chief Justice of Queensland from 1893, he was first Chief Justice of the High Court of Australia (1900–19).

Gulf War (16 Jan–27 Feb 1991)

A war which followed the invasion of Kuwait by Iraq in Aug 1990. A rapid air and land campaign, codenamed 'Desert Storm',was mounted by a US-led United Nations coalition based in Saudi Arabia, with forces from 29 countries including approximately 42 000 troops from Britain. The most severe British losses during the conflict came on 26 Feb, when nine soldiers were killed by 'friendly fire' from a US aircraft after being mistakenly identified. Iraqi forces were expelled from Kuwait and a large part of Iraq's military resources was destroyed.

Gunpowder Plot

A conspiracy by Catholic gentry, led by Robert Catesby, to blow up the English parliament. It failed when Guy **Fawkes**, who placed the explosives, was arrested (5 Nov 1605). The plot failed because one conspirator, Francis Tresham, warned his brother-in-law, Lord Monteagle, not to attend; and Monteagle reported the matter to the government. The scheme reflected Catholic desperation after the failure of previous plots to remove **James VI and I** in 1603; peace with Spain in 1604, which ended the prospect of foreign support; and new sanctions against recusant Catholics, resulting in 5 000 convictions in the spring of 1605.

Gurkhas

An elite infantry unit of the British army recruited from the hill tribes of Nepal. Their characteristic weapon, the Kukri fighting knife with its curved blade, has contributed to their fame, in battles from the North West Frontier of India in the 19c, via the Western Front in **World War I**, to the Burma and Italian campaigns of **World War II**. Gurkha infantry also took part in the **Falklands War** of 1982.

Guthrum (d.890)

Danish King of East Anglia (880/90). The opponent of King **Alfred, 'the Great'**, he led a major Viking invasion of Anglo-Saxon England in 871 (the 'Great Summer Army'), seized East Anglia and conquered Northumbria and Mercia. He attacked Wessex early in 878 and drove Alfred into hiding in Somerset. By May of that year Alfred had recovered sufficiently to defeat the Danes at the crucial Battle of **Edington** in Wiltshire; in the ensuing treaty, Guthrum agreed to leave Wessex and accept baptism as a Christian, and he and his army settled down peacefully in East Anglia.

Guyenne (Guienne)

A medieval duchy, including Gascony, in south-western France, bounded west by the Bay of Biscay. The rump of Aquitaine, it remained a possession of the English crown after **Normandy** and other French territories were lost in 1204–5. The claim of the kings of England to be independent rulers of Guyenne was one of the causes of the **Hundred Years War**. It was finally conquered by the French in 1453. The area is now occupied by the departments of Gironde, Dordogne, Lot, Aveyron, Tarn-et-Garonne, and Lot-et-Garonne. ▷ **Angevins**

H

Hadrian's Wall
The principal northern frontier of the Roman province of Britain. Built AD122–8 on the orders of the Emperor Hadrian and possibly inspired by travellers' accounts of the Great Wall of China, it runs 73 miles (117 kilometres) from the Solway Firth to the River Tyne, the wall itself is 15 feet (4.5 metres) high (probably with a 6 feet (2 metres) timber parapet), its forward defensive ditch c.28 feet (8.5 metres) wide and 10 feet (3 metres) deep. Sixteen forts (the best preserved at Housesteads and Chester) were supplemented by 80 milecastles and numerous signal turrets. Overrun by **Picts** and northern tribes in AD139 and again in 367, the wall was finally abandoned c.400–10. It is now a World Heritage site. ▷ **Antonine Wall; Britain, Roman**

Haganah
The Jewish underground militia in Palestine, founded in the 1920s during the period of the British Mandate in response to nationalist Arab attacks on Jewish settlements. Banned by the British authorities, the *Haganah* ('self-defence') maintained a policy of restraint, opposing the terrorism of the **Irgun** and others. However, this changed when the British sought to limit Jewish immigration after **World War II**. The Haganah comprised a part-time membership, but 1941 saw the creation of a full-time striking force, the *Palmach*. After the War of Independence in 1948, in which it played a central role, the Haganah became the Israel Defence Force, the official Israeli army. ▷ **Jewish Agency; Israel, State of; Stern Gang**

Haig, Douglas, 1st Earl Haig of Bemersyde (1861–1928)
British field marshal. He obtained a commission in the 7th Hussars, and served in Egypt, South Africa and India. In 1914 he led the 1st Army Corps in France, and in 1915 became commander of the **British Expeditionary Force**. He waged a costly and exhausting war of attrition, for which he was much criticized, but led

the final successful offensive in front of Amiens (Aug 1918). In post-war years he devoted himself to the care of ex-servicemen, organizing the Royal British Legion. His earldom was awarded in 1919. ▷ **World War I**

Hailsham, Quintin (McGarel) Hogg, 2nd Viscount (1907–)
English politician. He became a Conservative MP in 1938 and succeeded to his title in 1950. He was First Lord of the Admiralty (1956–7), Minister of Education (1957), Lord President of the Council (1957–9 and 1960–4), Chairman of the **Conservative Party** (1957–9), Minister for Science and Technology (1959–64), and Secretary of State for Education and Science (1964). In 1963 he renounced his peerage and re-entered the House of Commons in an unsuccessful bid to become Leader of the Conservative Party. In 1970 he was created a life peer (Baron Hailsham of Saint Marylebone) and was Lord Chancellor (1970–4), a post he held again from 1979 until his retirement in 1987.

Haldane, Richard Burdon, 1st Viscount (1856–1928)
Scottish politician, philosopher and lawyer. He entered parliament in 1879 as a Liberal. As Secretary of State for War (1905–12), he remodelled the army and founded the Territorials; British mobilization took place in 1914 on the basis of his plans. He was Lord Chancellor (1912–15) and again in 1924 following his move to the **Labour Party**. He also wrote on the philosophical aspects of relativity, and helped to found the London School of Economics (1895). ▷ **Liberal Party**

Halidon Hill, Battle of (19 July 1333)
A battle between England and Scotland during the Scottish Wars of Independence. **Edward III** of England turned from besieging Berwick-upon-Tweed, and inflicted a massive defeat on the Scottish relief army. ▷ **David II; Scottish War of Independence**

Halifax, Charles Montagu, 1st Earl of (1661–1715)
English politician. A Whig, he became MP for Maldon (1688) and a Lord of the Treasury (1692), establishing the National Debt and the Bank of England (1694). As Chancellor of the Exchequer (1694–5), he introduced a new coinage. In 1697 he was First Lord of the Treasury and Leader of the House of Commons, but resigned when the **Tories** came to power in 1699, and became

144

Baron Halifax. On Queen **Anne**'s death he was made a member of the Council of Regency, and on **George I**'s arrival (1714) became an earl and Prime Minister. He was also a patron of letters, and a poet. ▷ **Whigs**

Halifax, Edward Frederick Lindley Wood, 1st Earl of
(2nd creation) (1881–1959)
English politician. He became a Conservative MP (1910–25), and held a range of political posts before becoming (as Baron Irwin, 1925) Viceroy of India (1926–31). He was Foreign Secretary (1938–40) under Neville **Chamberlain**, whose '**appeasement**' policy he implemented, and Ambassador to the USA (1941–6). He was created an earl in 1944. ▷ **Conservative Party**

Halifax, George Savile, 1st Marquis of (1633–95)
English statesman. He was created viscount (1668) for his share in the **Restoration**, and in 1672 was made a marquis and Lord Privy Seal. On the accession of **James II** of England (1685), he became President of the Council, but was dismissed soon after. He was one of the three Commissioners appointed to treat with William of Orange (later **William III**), after he landed in England (1688). He gave allegiance to William and resumed the office of Lord Privy Seal; however, joining the opposition, he resigned his post in 1689.

Hamilton, James, 1st Duke of (1606–49)
Scottish royalist commander during the **English Civil Wars**. He fought during the **Thirty Years War**, leading an army in support of Gustav II Adolf (1631–2), and later played a conspicuous part in the contest between **Charles I** and the **Covenanters**. Created duke in 1643, he led a Scottish army into England (1643), but was defeated by **Cromwell** at the Battle of **Preston**, and beheaded.

Hampden, John (1594–1643)
English parliamentarian and patriot. He became a lawyer, and in 1621 an MP. His opposition to **Charles I**'s financial measures led to his imprisonment (1627–8), and in 1634 he became famous for refusing to pay Charles's imposed levy for outfitting the navy ('ship money'). A member of both the **Short Parliament** and the **Long Parliament**, he was one of the five members whose attempted

seizure by Charles (1642) precipitated the **English Civil Wars**. He fought for the parliamentary army at Edgehill and Reading, but was killed at Thame.

Hanover, House of

A branch of the Guelf Dynasty, more specifically the Brunswick–Lüneburg line which, in 1692, acquired the Electoral dignity for Hanover. On the death of Queen **Anne** in 1714, the Elector Georg Ludwig, who was descended through the female line from Princess Elizabeth, the sister of **Charles I**, became King of Great Britain and Ireland, as **George I**, thus securing the Protestant succession. Monarchs from the House of Hanover ruled their British and German dominions in personal union until the death of **William IV** in 1837. Thereupon, the British crown went to Queen **Victoria** who was, however, disqualified under the Salic Law from succession in Germany. In consequence, her uncle, the Duke of Cumberland, became King of Hanover under the name of Ernest Augustus. While the family name of the British dynasty changed to Saxe-Coburg and Gotha when Victoria married Prince **Albert** in 1840, the Hanoverians continued to rule their native country until 1866 when it was annexed by Prussia for siding with Austria in the preceding war. A descendant of the last King of Hanover succeeded to the Duchy of Brunswick in 1913 after the Brunswick–Wolfenbüttel line had become extinct, but was toppled by the revolution of 1918.

Harald III Sigurdsson, 'Hardraade' (1015–66)

King of Norway (1045/66). The half-brother of **Olaf II** (St Olaf), he was present at the Battle of Stiklestad in 1030 where St Olaf was killed, and sought refuge in Kiev at the court of his kinsman, Prince Yaroslav the Wise, together with his nephew, Magnus I, 'the Good'. He had a lurid career as a Viking mercenary with the Varangian Guard in Constantinople, and returned to Norway in 1045 to demand, and receive, a half-share in the kingdom from his nephew. He became sole king on his nephew's death in 1047, and earned the nickname Hardrada ('Hard-Ruler'). After long and unrelenting wars against King Svein II Ulfsson of Denmark, he invaded England in 1066 to claim the throne after the death of **Edward the Confessor**, but was defeated and killed by **Harold II** at Stamford Bridge.

Hardaknut (1018–42)

King of Denmark (1035/42) and of England (1040/2). He was the son of **Canute** and Emma (the widow of King **Ethelred the Unready**), and was Canute's only legitimate heir. He inherited Denmark on his father's death in 1035, but was unable to come to England immediately to claim the throne there. The English elected his half-brother, **Harold I, 'Harefoot'** regent in his stead, and then confirmed Harold as King in 1037. Hardaknut mounted an expedition to invade England to claim the crown, but Harold died in Mar 1040, before he arrived. Hardaknut was thereupon elected King, and promptly punished the English by imposing a savage fleet-tax to pay for his expedition. His reign was universally disliked; he died (June 1042) of convulsions at a drinking party.

Hardie, (James) Keir (1856–1915)

Scottish politician. He worked in the mines between the ages of seven and 24, and was victimized as the miners' champion. He became a journalist and the first Labour MP, entering parliament for East Ham in 1892. He founded and edited *The Labour Leader*, and was Chairman of the **Independent Labour Party** (founded 1893). Instrumental in the establishment of the Labour Representation Committee, Hardie served as Chairman of the **Labour Party** (1906–8). His strong pacifism led to his becoming isolated within the party, particularly once **World War I** had broken out.

Hardinge (of Lahore), Henry Hardinge, 1st Viscount (1785–1856)

British soldier and colonial administrator. After service in the **Peninsular War**, he became an MP (1820–44) and Secretary of War (1828–30 and 1841–4). In 1844 he was appointed Governor-General of India, and after the first Sikh War was created a viscount (1845). Returning in 1848, he succeeded **Wellington** as Commander-in-Chief of the British Army (1852), but was demoted following the disasters early in the **Crimean War** (1854–6). ▷ **Sikh Wars**

Harley, Robert, 1st Earl of Oxford (1661–1724)

English politician. He became a lawyer, and a Whig MP in 1689. In 1701 he was elected Speaker, and in 1704 became Secretary of State. Shortly after, he became sympathetic to the **Tories**, and from 1708 worked to undermine the power of the **Whigs**. In 1710

Godolphin was dismissed, and Harley made Chancellor of the Exchequer, head of the government, and (1711) Earl of Oxford and Lord High Treasurer. The principal Act of his administration was the Treaty of Utrecht (1713). In 1714 he was dismissed, and after the Hanoverian succession spent two years in prison. He then retired from politics. ▷ **Hanover, House of**

Harold Harefoot (d.1040)
King of England (1037/40). He was the younger son of Canute and his English mistress, Ælfgifu of Northampton. On Canute's death, the English elected Harold regent for his half-brother, **Hardaknut**, King of Denmark, the legitimate heir to the throne, who could not leave Denmark to claim the crown. In 1037 Harold was elected King; he died (Mar 1040) just as Hardaknut was poised to invade England to claim back the throne.

Harold II (c.1022–66)
Last Anglo-Saxon King of England (1066). The second son of Earl Godwin, by 1045 Harold was Earl of East Anglia, and in 1053 succeeded to his father's earldom of **Wessex**, becoming the right hand of **Edward the Confessor**. After Edward's death (Jan 1066), Harold, his nominee, was crowned as King. He defeated his brother **Tostig** and **Harald III Sigurdsson**, King of Norway, at Stamford Bridge, Yorkshire (Sep 1066), but Duke William of Normandy (**William I, 'the Conqueror'**) then invaded England, and defeated him at the Battle of **Hastings** (14 Oct 1066), where he died, shot through the eye with an arrow.

Haselrig (Heselrige), Sir Arthur (d.1661)
English parliamentarian. In 1640 he sat in the **Long Parliament** and **Short Parliament** for his native county, Leicestershire, and he was one of the five members whose attempted seizure by **Charles I** in 1642 precipitated the **English Civil Wars**. He commanded a parliamentary regiment, and in 1647 became Governor of Newcastle. After the **Restoration**, he was imprisoned and died in the Tower of London.

Hastings, Battle of (14 Oct 1066)
The most decisive battle fought on English soil, which led to the successful **Norman Conquest** of England. Norman cavalry overcame the resolute defence of the Anglo-Saxon army fighting

on foot, and **Harold II**'s death in battle cleared the way for Duke William of **Normandy**'s coronation. Not until 1092 (the capture of Carlisle) were the **Normans** masters of all England. ▷ **Anglo-Saxons; William I of England**

Hastings, Warren (1732–1818)
British colonial administrator. Educated at Westminster, he joined the British **East India Company** in 1750, and by 1774 was Governor-General of Bengal. Carrying out several reforms, he made the Company's power paramount in many parts of India. However, wars (1778–84) interfered with trade, and damaged his reputation, and on his return to England in 1884 he was charged with corruption. After a seven-year trial, he was acquitted. The Company made provision for his declining years, which he spent as a country gentleman in Worcestershire, England.

Havelock, Sir Henry (1795–1857)
British soldier. A lawyer by training, he entered the army a month after the Battle of **Waterloo**, and went out to India in 1823. He distinguished himself in the Afghan and Sikh Wars, and in 1856 commanded a division in Persia. On the outbreak of the **Indian Uprising** (1857–8), he organized a column of a 1 000 Higlanders and others at Allahabad with which to relieve Cawnpore and **Lucknow**, engaged and broke the rebels at Fatehpur, and, driving them before him, entered Cawnpore. Next crossing the Ganges, he fought eight victorious battles, but through sickness in his little army had to retire to Cawnpore. In Sep **Outram** arrived with reinforcements, and Havelock again advanced, Outram waiving his superior rank, and serving under Havelock as a volunteer. The relieving force fought their way to the Residency, where they in turn were besieged by the determined rebel forces until Nov, when Sir Colin Campbell forced his way to their rescue. A week after the relief, Havelock died of dysentery. ▷ **Afghan Wars**

Hawke (of Towton), Edward Hawke, 1st Baron (1705–81)
British admiral. As a young commander, he fought against the French and Spanish, for which he was knighted (1747). His major victory was against the French at Quiberon Bay (1759), which caused the collapse of their invasion plans. He also became an MP (1747), First Lord of the Admiralty (1766–71), and a baron (1776).

Hawkyns, Sir John (1532–95)
English sailor. He was the first Englishman to traffic in slaves (1562) between West Africa and the West Indies, but on his third expedition his fleet was destroyed by the Spanish (1567). He became navy treasurer (1573), and was knighted for his services against the Spanish **Armada** in 1588. In 1595, with his kinsman **Drake**, he commanded an expedition to the Spanish Main, but died at Puerto Rico.

Heath, Edward (Richard George), ('Ted') (1916–)
English politician and Prime Minister of Britain. He served in **World War II**, and became a Conservative MP in 1950. Following a career in the Whips' office (1951–9), he was Minister of Labour (1959–60), then Lord Privy Seal (1960–3) and the chief negotiator for Britain's entry into the European Common Market (**EEC**). He became the **Conservative Party**'s first elected leader in 1965, and remained Leader of the Opposition until the 1970 election, when he became Prime Minister (1970–4). After a confrontation with the miners' union in 1973, he narrowly lost the two elections of 1974, and in 1975 was replaced as leader by Margaret **Thatcher**. He has continued to play an active part in politics, being particularly critical of his successor's policies.

Henderson, Arthur (1863–1935)
Sottish politician. Several times Chairman of the **Labour Party** (1908–10, 1914–17 and 1931–2), he was elected an MP in 1903, served in the coalition cabinets (1915–17), and became Home Secretary (1924) and Foreign Secretary (1929–31) in the first Labour governments. He was President of the World Disarmament Conference in 1932, won the Nobel Peace Prize in 1934, and also helped to establish the **League of Nations**. ▷ **MacDonald, Ramsay**

Henry I (1068–1135)
King of England (1100/35) and Duke of Normandy (1106/35). He was the youngest son of **William I, the Conqueror**. Under Henry, the Norman empire attained the height of its power. He conquered Normandy from his brother, Robert Curthose, at the Battle of Tinchebrai (1106), maintained his position on the Continent, and exercised varying degrees of authority over the King of Scots, the Welsh princes, the Duke of Brittany, and also the Counts of Flanders, Boulogne, and Ponthieu. His government

of England and **Normandy** became increasingly centralized and interventionist, with the overriding aim of financing warfare and alliances, and consolidating the unity of the two countries as a single cross-Channel state. His only legitimate son, William Adelin, was drowned in 1120, and in 1127 he nominated his daughter Empress Matilda, widow of Emperor Henry V of Germany, as his heir for both England and Normandy. But Matilda and her second husband, Geoffrey of Anjou, proved unacceptable to the King's leading subjects. After Henry's death, the crown was seized by **Stephen**, son of his sister, Adela. ▷ **Angevins**

Henry II (1133–89)

King of England (1154/89). He was the son of Empress Matilda, **Henry I**'s daughter and acknowledged heir, by her second husband, Geoffrey of Anjou. Already established as Duke of Normandy (1150) and Count of Anjou (1151), and as Duke of Aquitaine by marriage to **Eleanor of Aquitaine** (1152), Henry invaded England in 1153, and was recognized (Treaty of Wellingford) as the lawful successor of **Stephen**. He founded the Angevin or Plantagenet Dynasty of English kings, and ruled England as part of a wider Angevin empire. Henry restored and transformed English governance after the disorders of Stephen's reign. His efforts to restrict clerical independence caused conflict with his former Chancellor, Thomas **Becket**, Archbishop of Canterbury, which was ended only with Becket's murder (1170). Henry led a major expedition to Ireland (1171), which resulted in its annexation. The most serious challenge to his power came in 1173–4 when his son, the young Henry, encouraged by Queen Eleanor, rebelled in alliance with Louis VII of France, **William I** of Scotland, and Count Philip of Flanders. All parts of the King's dominions were threatened, but his enemies were defeated. In 1189 he faced further disloyalty from his family when his sons, **John** and **Richard I**, allied with Philip II of France, who overran Maine and Touraine. Henry agreed a peace which recognized Richard as his sole heir for the Angevin empire, and he died shortly afterwards at Chinon. ▷ **Angevins; Clarendon, Constitutions of; Plantagenets**

Henry III (1207–72)

King of England (1216/72). He was the elder son and successor, at the age of nine, of **John**. He declared an end to his minority in 1227, and in 1232 stripped the justiciar, Hubert de **Burgh**, of

151

power. His arbitrary assertion of royal rights conflicted with the principles of **Magna Carta**, and antagonized many nobles. Although he failed to recover Poitou (northern Aquitaine) in 1242, he accepted the Kingdom of Sicily (1254). This forced him to seek the support of the barons, who under the leadership of the King's brother-in-law, Simon de **Montfort**, imposed far-reaching reforms by the Provisions of **Oxford** (1258), which gave them a definite role in government. When Henry sought to restore royal power, the barons rebelled and captured him at Lewes (1264), but were defeated at Evesham (1265). The Dictum of Kenilworth (1266), though favourable to Henry, urged him to observe Magna Carta. Organized resistance ended in 1267, and the rest of the reign was stable. Henry was succeeded by his elder son, **Edward I**. ▷ **Barons Wars**

Henry IV (1366–1413)

King of England (1399/1413). The first king of the House of **Lancaster**, he was the son of **John of Gaunt** (who was the fourth son of **Edward III**). In 1397 he supported **Richard II** against the Duke of **Gloucester**, and was created Duke of Hereford, but was banished in 1398. After landing at Ravenspur, Yorkshire, Henry induced Richard, now deserted, to abdicate in his favour. During his reign, rebellion and lawlessness were rife, and he was constantly hampered by lack of money. Under Owen **Glendower** the Welsh maintained their independence, and Henry's attack on Scotland in 1400 ended in his retreat with no victories won. The Scots were, however, defeated by a force led by the Percies at Homildon Hill (1402), and it was partly annoyance at the King's apparent ingratitude which led the Percies to support the Scots and Welsh against Henry, which in turn led to the King's victory against them at Shrewsbury (1403). Henry was a chronic invalid in later years, and only rarely asserted himself in power struggles between the Prince of Wales and Archbishop Arundel, who was supported by Henry's second son, Thomas. ▷ **Percy**

Henry V (1387–1422)

King of England (1413/22). The eldest son of **Henry IV**, he fought against **Glendower** and the Welsh rebels (1402–8), and became Constable of Dover (1409) and Captain of Calais (1410). To this time belong the exaggerated stories of his wild youth. The main effort of his reign was his claim, through his great-grandfather, **Edward III**, to the French crown. In 1415 he invaded France, and won the Battle of **Agincourt** against great odds. By 1419 Normandy was again under English control, and in 1420 was concluded the 'perpetual peace' of Troyes, under which Henry was recognized as heir to the French throne and Regent of France, and married Charles VI's daughter, Catherine of Valois. ▷ **Hundred Years War**

Henry VI (1421–71)

King of England (1422/61 and 1470/1). He was the only child of **Henry V** and Catherine of Valois. During Henry's minority, his uncle John, Duke of **Bedford**, was Regent in France, and another uncle, Humphrey, Duke of **Gloucester**, was Lord Protector of England. Henry was crowned King of France at Paris in 1431, two years after his coronation in England. But once the Burgundians had made a separate peace with Charles VII (1435), Henry V's French conquests were progressively eroded, and by 1453 the English retained only Calais. Henry had few kingly qualities, and from 1453 suffered from periodic bouts of insanity. Richard, Duke of York, seized power as Lord Protector in 1454, and defeated the King's army at St Albans (1455), the first battle of the Wars of the **Roses**. Fighting resumed in 1459, and although York himself was killed at Wakefield (1460), his heir was proclaimed King as **Edward IV** after Henry's deposition (1461). In 1464 Henry returned from exile in Scotland to lead the Lancastrian cause, but was captured and imprisoned (1465–70). Richard Neville, Earl of **Warwick**, restored him to the throne (Oct 1470), his nominal rule ending when Edward IV returned to London (Apr 1471). After the Yorkist victory at the Battle of **Tewkesbury** (May 1471), where his only son was killed, Henry was murdered in the Tower. ▷ **Hundred Years War**

Henry VII (1457–1509)

King of England (1485/1509). The founder of the Tudor Dynasty, he was the grandson of Owen Tudor, who married Queen Catherine of Valois, the widow of **Henry V**. After the Lancastrian defeat at the Battle of **Tewkesbury** (1471), Henry was taken to Brittany, where several Yorkist attempts on his life and liberty were frustrated. In 1485 he landed unopposed at Milford Haven, and defeated **Richard III** at the Battle of **Bosworth Field**. As King, he restored peace and prosperity to the country, which was helped by his marriage of reconciliation with Elizabeth of York. He was also noted for the efficiency of his financial and administrative policies. He dealt efficiently with Yorkist plots, such as those surrounding Lambert Simmel and Perkin Warbeck, who impersonated the Yorkist 'Princes in the Tower', Edward of Warwick and Richard of York respectively. Peace was concluded with France (1492), and the marriage of his heir Arthur to **Catherine of Aragon** cemented an alliance with Spain. He was succeeded by his son, as **Henry VIII**. ▷ **Tudor, House of**

Henry VIII (1491–1547)
King of England (1509/47). The second son of **Henry VII**, soon after his accession he married **Catherine of Aragon**, his brother Arthur's widow. As a member of the **Holy League**, he invaded France (1512), winning the Battle of the **Spurs** (1513); and while abroad, the Scots were defeated at the Battle of **Flodden**. In 1521 he published a book defending the Catholic Sacraments in reply to Luther, receiving from the Pope the title 'Defender of the Faith'. From 1527 he determined to divorce Catherine, whose children, except for Mary (later **Mary I**), had died in infancy. This policy directly precipitated the Reformation in England. He tried to put pressure on the Pope by humbling the clergy, and in defiance of Rome was privately married to Anne **Boleyn** (1533). Using parliamentary statute to strengthen his actions against the Catholic Church, it was enacted in 1534 that his marriage to Catherine was invalid, and that the King was the sole head of the Church of England. The policy of suppressing the monasteries followed (1536–9). In 1536 Catherine died, and Anne Boleyn was executed for infidelity. Henry then married Jane **Seymour** (c.1509–37), who died leaving a son, afterwards **Edward VI**. In 1540 **Anne of Cleves** became his fourth wife, in the hope of attaching the Protestant interest of Germany; but dislike of her appearance caused him to divorce her speedily. He then married Catherine **Howard** (1540), who two years later was executed on grounds of infidelity (1542). In 1543 his last marriage was to Catherine **Parr**, who survived him. His later years saw further war with France and Scotland, before peace was concluded with France in 1546. He was succeeded by his son, Edward VI. ▷ **Cromwell, Thomas; More, Thomas; Reformation** (England)**; Wolsey, Thomas**

Hereward, 'the Wake' (d.c.1080)
Anglo-Saxon thegn. He returned from exile to lead in East Anglia the last organized English resistance against the Norman invaders. He held the Isle of Ely against **William I, 'the Conqueror'** for

nearly a year (1070–1), then disappeared from history, and entered medieval outlaw legend as a celebrated opponent of the forces of injustice. ▷ **Anglo-Saxons; Norman Conquest**

Heseltine, Michael (Ray Dibdin) (1933–   )
English politician. He built up a publishing business before becoming a Conservative MP in 1966. After holding junior posts in Transport (1970), Environment (1970–2), and Aerospace and Shipping (1972–4), he was appointed Secretary of State for the Environment (1979–83), and then Defence Secretary (1983–6). He resigned from the government in dramatic fashion by walking out of a cabinet meeting over the issue of the takeover of Westland helicopters. His challenge to Margaret **Thatcher**'s leadership of the **Conservative Party** directly led to her resignation (Nov 1990) but he was defeated by John **Major** in the election to succeed her.

Hitler, Adolf (1889–1945)
German dictator and leader of the Nazi Party. In 1914 he served in a Bavarian regiment, became a corporal, was decorated, and was wounded in the last stages of **World War I**. In 1919 he joined a small political party which in 1920 he renamed as the National Socialist German Workers' Party. He expanded his party greatly in the late 1920s, won important parliamentary election victories in 1930 and 1932 and though he was unsuccessful in the presidential elections of 1932 against Hindenburg, he was made Chancellor in 1933. He then suspended the constitution, silenced all opposition, exploited successfully the burning of the Reichstag building, and brought the Nazi Party to power, having dozens of his opponents within his own party and the SA murdered by his bodyguard, the SS, in the Night of the Long Knives (1934). He openly rearmed the country (1935), established the Rome–Berlin 'axis' with Mussolini (1936) and pursued an aggressive foreign policy which culminated in **World War II** (3 Sep 1939). With his early war successes, he increasingly ignored the advice of military experts. After the British withdrawal from France and the evacuation from **Dunkirk**, he failed to press his advantage, and did not invade Britain. Instead, he wantonly extended the war with his long-desired invasion of the USSR in 1941. The tide turned in 1942 after the defeats at **El Alamein** and Stalingrad. He miraculously survived the explosion of the bomb placed at his feet by Colonel Stauffenberg (July 1944), and purged the army of all suspects.

When Germany was invaded, he retired to his *Bunker*, an air-raid shelter under the Chancellory building in Berlin. All available evidence suggests that Hitler and his wife committed suicide and had their bodies cremated (30 Apr 1945).

Hoare–Laval Pact

An agreement concluded in 1935 by the British Foreign Secretary Samuel Hoare and the French Prime Minister Pierre Laval aimed at the settlement of a dispute between Italy and Abyssinia. By this pact, large parts of Abyssinia were ceded to Italy. A public outcry against the pact led to its repudiation by Britain and to Hoare's resignation.

Holy Alliance (20 Nov 1815)

The alliance concluded on this day after the final defeat of **Napoleon I** between Austria, Britain, Prussia and Russia, which was designed to ensure the exclusion of the House of Bonaparte from power in France and to guarantee the monarchist order in Europe. Each power made specific military commitments in the event of war with France; however royalist France itself joined the alliance at the Congress of Aachen (Aix-la-Chapelle) in 1818.

Holy League (1510)

An alliance of the papacy under Julius II with Venice, Aragon and England against France.

Home Guard

A home defence militia, raised during the summer of 1940, when the German armies seemed poised to complete the conquest of Western Europe by invading Great Britain. At first called the Local Defence Volunteers, the name was changed at Prime Minister Winston **Churchill**'s urging to the more evocative title of 'Home Guard'. The force was finally stood down in 1945.
▷ **World War II**

Home of the Hirsel, Baron (formerly, Sir Alec Douglas-Home) (1903–)

Scottish politician. He became a Conservative MP in 1931 and was Neville **Chamberlain**'s Secretary during the negotiations with **Hitler** and beyond (1937–40). He became Minister of State at the Scottish Office (1951–5), succeeded to the peerage as 14th Earl of

Home (1951), was Commonwealth Relations Secretary (1955–60), and Foreign Secretary (1960–3). After **Macmillan**'s resignation, he surprisingly emerged from the process of consultation as Leader of the **Conservative Party** and, thus, Premier (1963–4). He made history by renouncing his peerage and fighting a by-election, during which, although Premier, he was technically a member of neither House. After the 1964 defeat by the **Labour Party**, he was Leader of the Opposition until replaced in 1965 by Edward **Heath**, in whose 1970–4 government he was Foreign Secretary. In 1974 he was made a life peer.

Home Rule

The handing down of certain legislative powers and administrative functions, previously exercised by a higher authority, to an elected body within a geographically defined area; usually put forward as an alternative to separatism. In British history, it has usually been applied to policies for Ireland, as with **Gladstone** in the 1880s and 1890s. It was also illustrated by the government of Northern Ireland (1922–72) when **Stormont**, the Northern Ireland parliament, was abolished. Since the early 1970s in the UK, for political movements such as the **Scottish National Party** and Irish republicans, home rule has tended to become synonymous with separatism. ▷ **IRA; Plaid Cymru**

Hong Kong, Cession of (1842)

One of the terms of the Treaty of **Nanjing** signed by Britain and China following the end of the first of the **Opium Wars**. China was compelled to cede the island of Hong Kong 'in perpetuity' to Britain. Under British rule, Hong Kong became a free-trade entrepot. The Kowloon Peninsula was added to Britain's colony of Hong Kong in 1860, following the second of the Opium Wars, and in 1898 the New Territories were leased to Britain until 1997. On the expiry of the lease, Hong Kong will be restored to China (under the Sino-British Declaration initialled in 1984).

Hood (of Whitley), Samuel, 1st Viscount (1724–1816)

British admiral. He joined the navy in 1741, and fought during the **American Revolution**, when he defeated the French in the West Indies (1782), for which he was made a baron in the Irish peerage. In 1784 he became an MP, and in 1788 a Lord of the Admiralty. In 1793, he directed the occupation of Toulon and the operations in the Gulf of Lyons. He was made viscount in 1796. ▷ **American Revolution**

Hore-Belisha (of Devonport), (Isaac) Leslie Hore-Belisha, 1st Baron (1893–1957)

English barrister and politician. He became a London journalist, and a Liberal MP (1923). In 1934, as Minister of Transport, he gave his name to the 'Belisha' beacons, drafted a new highway code, and inaugurated driving tests for motorists. As Secretary of State for War (1937–40) he carried out several army reforms, and introduced conscription in 1939. He received a peerage in 1954. ▷ **Liberal Party**

Horrocks, Sir Brian (Gwynne) (1895–1985)

British general. He joined the army in 1914, and served in France and Russia. In 1942 he commanded the 9th Armoured Division and then the 13th and 10th Corps in North Africa, where he helped to defeat Rommel. Wounded at Tunis, he headed the 30th Corps during the Allied invasion (1944). Horrocks was well known as a military journalist and broadcaster. ▷ **North African Campaign; World War II**

Howard, Catherine (c.1520–42)

Queen of England. She was the fifth wife of **Henry VIII**, and was a granddaughter of the 2nd Duke of Norfolk. She became Queen in the same month as **Anne of Cleves** was divorced (July 1540). A year later she was charged by **Cranmer** with intercourse before her marriage with a musician and a kinsman, and was beheaded for treason.

Howard, Charles, 1st Earl of Nottingham (1536–1624)

English admiral. A cousin of Queen **Elizabeth I**, he commanded the English fleet against the Spanish **Armada** (1588). He succeeded to his father's title in 1573, and became Lord High Admiral in 1585. For his role in the Cadiz expedition (1596) he was created an earl, and in 1601 he quelled **Essex**'s rising.

Howard, Thomas, 3rd Duke of Norfolk (1473–1554)

English statesman. The brother-in-law of **Henry VII**, he held several high offices under **Henry VIII**. He was the uncle of Anne **Boleyn** and Catherine **Howard**, after whose execution (1542) he lost power. The father of the Earl of Surrey, who was executed for treason by Henry VIII, he would himself have been executed as an accessory, but for Henry's own death. He remained in prison during the reign of **Edward VI**, but was released by the Catholic **Mary I**.

Howe, Richard, 1st Earl (1726–99)

British admiral. The brother of William, 5th Viscount **Howe**, he entered the navy at 13, and distinguished himself in the **Seven Years War**. He became a Lord of the Admiralty (1763), Treasurer of the Navy (1765), First Lord of the Admiralty (1783), and earl (1788). In 1776 he was appointed commander of the British fleet during the American War of Independence and, in 1778, defended the American coast against a superior French force. On the outbreak of war with France (1793), he took command of the Channel Fleet, defeating the French off Ushant at the Battle of the **Glorious First of June** (1794). ▷ **French Revolutionary Wars**

Howe, Sir (Richard Edward) Geoffrey (1926–)

English politician. He became a Conservative MP in 1964. Knighted in 1970, he became Solicitor-General (1970–2), Minister for Trade and Consumer Affairs (1972–4), Chancellor of the Exchequer (1979–83), and then Foreign Secretary (1983–9). A loyal supporter of Margaret **Thatcher**, in 1989 he was made Deputy Prime Minister, Lord President of the Council, and Leader of the House of Commons, but resigned from the government (Nov 1990) because of Thatcher's hostility towards European Monetary Union. His resignation speech set in train the events which led to the Premier's resignation. ▷ **Conservative Party**

Howe, William, 5th Viscount Howe (1729–1814)

English soldier. The brother of Richard, 1st Earl **Howe**, he joined the British army in 1746 and served under General James **Wolfe** at Louisbourg (1758) and **Quebec** (1759), where he led the famous advance to the Heights of **Abraham** (1759). He became an MP in 1758. He was a commander in North America during the **American Revolution**, and in the American War of Independence his victories included Bunker Hill (1775), the capture of New York City (1776, with naval support provided by his brother) and Brandywine Creek (1777). After his failure at Valley Forge (1778), he was superseded by Sir Henry Clinton. He returned to England and was made a viscount in 1799.

Hudson's Bay Company

A London-based corporation which was granted a Royal Charter to trade (principally in furs) in most of north and west Canada (Rupert's Land) in 1670. It annexed its main competitors, the North West Company, in 1821, and developed extensive sea-based trade in otter pelts along the coast of British Columbia. Rupert's Land was purchased by the Canadian Government in 1870.

Hughes, William M(orris) (1864–1952)

British-born Australian politician and Prime Minister (1915–23). Hughes emigrated to Australia in 1884. He entered the New South Wales Legislature in 1894 and federal politics in 1901. He was Attorney-General (1908–9, 1910–13 and 1914–15), succeeding Fisher as Labor Leader and Prime Minister in 1915. A long-standing supporter of compulsory military service, he returned from a visit to Britain in 1916 to campaign for conscription. The referendum was lost, but Hughes and his followers were expelled from the Australian Labor Party. He formed the Nationalist Party in 1917, retained office and represented Australia at the **Paris Peace Conference** of 1919. After the election of 1922, the Country Party held the balance of power and forced his retirement in favour of S M Bruce (1923). He engineered the overthrow of the Bruce–Page government in 1929 for which he was expelled from the Nationalist Party. Involved in the foundation of the United Australia Party, he held various offices during the 1930s and was briefly party leader in 1941. He remained in parliament until his death in 1952.

Hume, Allan Octavian (1829–1912)

British colonialist and naturalist. After studying medicine, Hume joined the Bengal Civil Service in 1849. He became Commissioner of Customs for the North West Provinces, and Director-General of Agriculture. Having served in the **Indian Uprising** of 1857–8, he carried with him a morbid fear of the repetition of these events. In order to provide an outlet for educated opinion, therefore, he organized the first National Congress in India, in Bombay in 1885, remaining the Secretary of this organization until 1908.

Hume, Joseph (1777–1855)

Scottish radical politician. He studied medicine at Edinburgh, and then in 1797 became assistant surgeon under the East India

Company. After returning to England (1808), he sat in parliament (1812 and 1819–55), where his reform campaigns included the legalizing of trade unions, freedom of trade with India, and the abolition of army flogging, naval impressment, and imprisonment for debt. ▷ **East India Company, British**

Hundred Years War

A series of wars between England and France dated by convention 1337–1453. They formed part of a longer contest which began when England was linked with **Normandy** (1066), then with Anjou and Aquitaine (1154). In the 13c, the Capetians redoubled their efforts to rule all France. But when **Edward III** claimed the French throne, from 1340 styling himself 'King of England and France', traditional rivalries exploded into a dynastic struggle. Under **Henry V** (1415/22) the English turned from raiding to territorial conquest, a task ultimately beyond their resources. Eviction from Guyenne (1453) reduced England's French territories to Calais (lost in 1558) and the Channel Islands, but the title of King of France was abandoned only in 1801. ▷ **Agincourt, Battle of; Angevins**

Hunt, Henry ('Orator Hunt') (1773–1835)

English radical agitator. He was a well-to-do farmer who in 1800 became a staunch radical, and spent the rest of his life advocating the repeal of the **Corn Laws**, democracy, and parliamentary reform. In 1819, on the occasion of the **Peterloo Massacre**, he delivered a speech which cost him three years' imprisonment. He became an MP in 1831.

Hurd, Douglas (Richard) (1930–)

English politician. He followed a career in the Diplomatic Corps (1952–66) before moving to work in the Conservative Research Department (1966–70). A Conservative MP from 1974, he was Northern Ireland Secretary (1984–5), Home Secretary (1985–9), and Foreign Secretary from 1989. He was an unsuccessful candidate for the **Conservative Party** leadership (Nov 1990). ▷ **Thatcher, Margaret**

Hus, Jan (c.1372–1415)

Bohemian religious reformer. He was born at Husinec, from which his name derives. At the relatively new and intellectually

161

lively University of Prague he became a bachelor of arts in 1393, master of arts in 1396 and was elected dean of the faculty in 1401. He was influenced by the writings of Wycliffe among others. His preaching won him both royal and popular Czech support but in 1410 he was excommunicated by the Archbishop of Prague. He continued to preach even when, in 1412, the Pope issued a papal bull against him and put Prague under an interdict. He was, therefore, called before a General Council at Constance and, despite a guarantee of safe conduct from Emperor Sigismund, he was burned after refusing to recant. The anger of his followers in the Czech lands led to the **Hussite Wars**, which lasted almost until the mid-15c and for a time guaranteed Czech independence. Hus's ideas exerted an important influence on the Protestant reformers in the 16c.

Husayn ibn 'Ali (1856–1931)

Sharif of Mecca (1908/16) and King of the Hijaz (1916/24). The founder of the modern Arab Hashimite Dynasty, when **World War I** began and the British tried to persuade him to rise up against the Turks, he negotiated with Sir Henry McMahon, British High Commissioner in Egypt, and proposed that Britain should accept as independent an area that included the present states of Syria, Lebanon, Iraq, Jordan and the Arabian Peninsula, except for Aden. McMahon accepted most of his demands but the British were making other agreements which conflicted with the promises made to Husayn, such as the **Sykes–Picot Agreement** with France (May 1916). Husayn began his revolt in June 1916, soon captured Mecca and in 1917 moved out of the Hijaz and supported Allenby as he advanced into Palestine. At the end of the war, he was frustrated and bitter, as the Allies recognized him only as King of the Hijaz and he was driven from there after a conflict (1919–24) with 'Abd al-'Aziz ibn Sa'ud. His sons, Faysal and Abdullah, became respectively King of Iraq and of Transjordan, but Husayn felt betrayed by Britain and France, who had left only Arabia as a truly independent Arab area. ▷ **Arab Revolt; Husayn–McMahon Correspondence**

Husayn–McMahon Correspondence

The notorious correspondence between Sharif **Husayn ibn 'Ali** of Mecca and Sir Henry McMahon, the British High Commissioner in Egypt, initiated in 1915. It resulted in Husayn's becoming convinced that Britain supported the emancipation of the Arabs from Ottoman rule and the establishment of a Greater Arab Kingdom in the Arabian Peninsula and parts of the Fertile Crescent. This conviction derived from an assurance dispatched by McMahon in Oct 1915 that Britain was 'prepared to recognize and support the independence of the Arabs' in accordance with Husayn's demands, subject to three reservations. Despite these reservations (which concerned those parts of the Levant 'west of the districts of Damascus, Homs, Hama and Aleppo' as not being wholly Arab, an exclusion with regard to British interests in lower Iraq, and an allusion to the 'interests of her (Britain's) ally France'), this correspondence has been a major source of irritation amongst the Arabs where their relations with Britain are concerned. It undoubtedly played a decisive part in encouraging the 1916 **Arab Revolt**, and the conflict between the tenor of the correspondence with the **Sykes–Picot Agreement**, coupled with the absence of any specific mention in the correspondence of the status of Palestine (despite McMahon's much later avowal that he had always thought of Palestine as being excluded from the territories promised to the Arabs), has done nothing to promote cordial relations between Britain and the Arabs.

Hussite Wars (1419–36)

The burning at the stake of Jan **Hus** aroused enormous religious and national unrest in Bohemia and led to the formation of a Hussite League. The movement spread rapidly under King Wenceslas IV and open war broke out under Sigismund, whom the Bohemians held responsible for Hus's death. In 1420 the pope called for a crusade against the Hussites. The Emperor suffered serious defeats, and raids into Silesia, Austria and as far as Danzig spread fear of the Hussites. For the first time, an imperial tax was levied to fund the war against them. Continued Hussite successes led to a diplomatic solution being reached in the pacts of Prague (1433) and Iglau (1436).

I

Ibbetson, Denzil (1847–1948)
British Lieutenant-Governor of Punjab. Educated at Cambridge, Ibbetson entered the Indian Civil Service in 1870 and was posted to Punjab. During his career, he held various posts among which were the posts of the Superintendent of Census, Financial Commissioner, and Secretary to the Government of India in the Department of Revenue and Agriculture. He was also a retired member of the Viceroy's Executive Council, India. Ibbetson published the census Report of Punjab in 1883 and the Gazetteer of Punjab in 1883–5.

Iceni
An ancient British tribe occupying what is now Norfolk and north-west Suffolk. They rebelled in AD47 and again in 60, when their queen, **Boudicca**, led them and other tribes in a major revolt that briefly threatened the collapse of the Roman administration in Britain.

Ilbert Bill
The bill, introduced in 1883 by Courtney Ilbert, according to which the privilege enjoyed by every British subject in India to be tried only by a magistrate of his own race was to be withdrawn. However in deference to strong expressions of European public opinion, this privilege was withdrawn merely to the extent of conferring jurisdiction in such cases on all magistrates of whatever race as well as on justices of the peace, who were European British subjects and also the highest magistrates. This stirred up resentment amongst Indians, including early nationalist politicians, who felt that a racial privilege was being perpetuated, and that a slur was being cast upon Indian magistrates.

Image-breaking Riots (1566)
Generally, the violent destruction of high-church statues and valuables, such as that carried out in England by the soldiers of Oliver

Cromwell; however, the most famous outburst was in the Low Countries almost a century before. The riots of 1566 began in Aug in Steenvoorde in Flanders, where a mob smashed the decorations of a Catholic convent church; within a month the destruction had spread right through the Netherlands northwards to Groningen. The leadership was unidentified and much of the popular support was spontaneous; however Calvinist preachers were usually the immediate instigators. Besides the obvious anti-Catholicism, the movement was motivated by economic crisis and frustration that the Dutch Revolt against Spain seemed to be achieving little. The result of the riots was a hardening of Spanish attitudes: **Philip II** decided to send the Duke of Alva to restore order, and his harsh conduct signalled the start of the Eighty Years War (1568).

impeachment

A legal process for removing public officials from office. Originating in medieval England, the process was revived in that country in the 17c, when the Rump Parliament voted to bring Charles I to trial, resulting in his conviction and beheading. In the USA, the Constitution provides that the House of Representatives may move to impeach for 'high crimes and misdemeanors'. The case is then tried by the Senate, where a two-thirds majority is required for conviction. It is generally agreed that impeachment is a cumbersome method because of the problem of defining unacceptable behaviour and crimes. The move to impeach President Richard **Nixon** in 1974 did, however, have the effect of forcing his resignation. Earlier, the impeachment proceedings against President Andrew Johnson in 1867, which were politically inspired, resulted in his acquittal by the Senate.

Imperial British East Africa Company

A British company founded and chartered to rule a large area of East Africa in 1888. It was designed to ward off the German and French threats to the area and maintain British access to Lake Victoria, Uganda, and the upper Nile. However, it was seriously undercapitalized, and could not find the resources to develop the region, create an infrastructure, or withstand African resistance. It was wound up in 1894, and its territories became the protectorates (later Crown Colonies) of Kenya and Uganda.

Imperial Conferences

The consultative arrangements devised in 1907 by which the British and Dominion governments met on a regular basis. A permanent secretariat was established and meetings at four-year intervals were organized. The Canadian Prime Minister, Sir Wilfred Laurier, was suspicious of both the title and its implications, but he wished to challenge the London government's right to decide the foreign policy of the empire as a whole and thereby commit Canada without proper consultation. The 1911 conference provided the first occasion for at least some briefing by the imperial government when Sir Edward Grey gave the Prime Ministers a cagey description of the European situation. By 1926 the conference at last accepted the principle that the dominions were independent nations. The **Balfour Declaration** recommended a new constitutional framework for the Empire in which the dominions became 'autonomous communities within the **British Empire**, equal in status' but still 'united by a common allegiance to the crown', and this was embodied in the Statute of **Westminster**. However, there were limits to the British government's readiness to see the dominions as equal partners. At the 1930 conference it refused to consider the Canadian Prime Minister R B Bennett's plea for imperial preferential tariffs. By 1944, however, the Imperial Conference had become a genuine means by which the Prime Ministers discussed problems and suggested mutually acceptable solutions.

Imperial Federation League (1884–94)

A British pressure group, with branches in Canada, working towards federation for the British Empire. Its members saw this as answer to the challenge of industrial powers such as Germany and the USA, to Britain's isolation within Europe, and to the rivalry with other imperial powers that emerged after 1880. The British league split over the tariff in 1893 and was succeeded by the British Empire League; but this, with its Canadian counterpart, dwindled away in the early 1900s.

imperialism

The extension of the power of the state through the acquisition, normally by force, of other territories, which are then subject to rule by the imperial power. Many suggest that the motivation behind imperialism is economic, through the exploitation of cheap labour and resources, and the opening up of new markets. Others

166

suggest that non-economic factors are involved, including nationalism, racism and the pursuit of international power. The main era of imperialism was the 1880s to 1914, when many European powers sought to gain territories in Africa and Asia. Imperialism of the form associated with the establishment of European empires has in large measure disappeared, but the term is now often applied to any attempts by developed countries to interfere in underdeveloped countries. There is also increasing interest in the idea of *neo-colonialism*, where certain countries are subjugated by the economic power of developed countries, rather than through direct rule. ▷ **indirect rule**

Indentured Servants
The name given to Europeans who were contracted to serve as field labourers mainly in St Kitts and Barbados prior to the **Sugar Revolution**. In those colonies the native population was hostile or non-existent and a source of labour was found in the 'rejects' of England and France: common criminals, beggars and rebels, although some penurious gentlemen also served. The contract provided passage, board and lodging and the promise of land or a passage home after the 3–7 year period of indenture was completed. The civil unrest in England and Ireland between 1640 and 1660 resulted in many deportations and Barbados alone received 23 000 servants in the period 1645–60. As conditions were very harsh and mortality high, many indentured servants took to buccaneering, the most notable being Henry **Morgan**.
▷ **buccaneers**

Independent Labour Party (ILP)
A political party formed in 1893 with the objective of sending working men to parliament. It was socialist in aim, but wished to gain the support of working people whether they were socialist or not. One of its leading figures was Keir **Hardie**. Many of its leaders played a major part in founding the Labour Representation Committee (1900), which became the **Labour Party** in 1906. It was affiliated to the Labour Party but put up its own candidates, and was disaffiliated in 1932. It continued to have a few members of parliament up to 1950. ▷ **socialism**

Independents
The name given to those Puritans in favour of religious toleration who rejected a Presbyterian establishment in England during the

1640s and who founded their own independent congregations. From these developed Congregationalism. The term is also used to distinguish those parliamentarians who favoured an all-out war against **Charles I** involving, if necessary, his deposition from 'Presbyterians' who wanted a defensive war and accommodation with the King. The leadership of the **New Model Army** from 1645 reflected 'independent' objectives. ▷ **Cromwell, Oliver; English Civil Wars; Puritanism**

India Acts

Passed by the British parliament, the Regulating Act of 1773 and India Act of 1784 attempted to reform the corrupt and inefficient administration of the British **East India Company** over the developing Indian empire, whilst avoiding the necessity for Parliament to have to take direct responsibility for governing the newly-acquired territories. The 1773 Act set up the post of Governor-General and a Governing Council in India and that of 1784 established a Board of Control in London, made up of members of the cabinet, to decide on strategic questions concerning the government of India. The Acts were intended to meet criticism amongst the English establishment of the all too evident speculation of Company funds, seen in the growing number of 'Nabobs' (merchants and Company employees returning from India with vast fortunes who then bribed their way into positions of influence), as well as the maladministration of Bengal (which resulted in the death of one third of the population in the famine of 1770) and the warmongering of Warren **Hastings** (Governor-General, 1773–85). Subsequent Acts in 1813 and and 1830 deprived the East India Company of its monopoly of the East Indies trade and then of its trading functions altogether, allowing it to concentrate entirely on the business of administration. During this later period, the so-called 'era of reform', zealous attempts were made to improve the Company's administration along utilitarian lines, as well as to impress the mark of British rule on the Indian population. the result was the **Indian Uprising** of 1857 and the abolition of the Company the following year. ▷ **Government of India Acts**

India, Partition of (1947)

Under the Indian Independence Act of July 1947, the formerly British-ruled Indian sub-continent was partitioned on 14–15 Aug into two independent countries, a predominantly Hindu India and a predominantly Muslim Pakistan. The subsequent migration of Muslims from India to Pakistan and Hindus from Pakistan to India resulted in massive refugee populations, and in places there was a total collapse of law and order, before, during and after the partition. The violence which accompanied the migration resulted in what is believed to have been near to a million deaths — although the official total was 180 000. All princely states in the Indian subcontinent were left to choose their own fate but were advised to integrate with either India or Pakistan according to the religious affiliations of their peoples and their geographical positions. The state of Kashmir, however, remains in dispute.

Indian Civil Service (ICS)

Formerly known as the Covenanted Civil Service because its nominated members entered into covenants originally with the British **East India Company**, and afterwards with the Secretary of State in council, ICS members filled the higher posts in the government secretariats in various departments. Under a decree dating 1853, the ICS was opened to all natural-born British subjects, regardless of race, who would be appointed as civil servants subject to their performance in a competitive examination held in England. The first Indian, the poet Tagore's brother, Satyendranath Tagore, entered the ICS in 1864. At Independence, the ICS was renamed as the Indian Administrative Service (IAS).

Indian Uprising (1857–8)

A serious rebellion against British rule, triggered off partly by the belief among Indian troops in British service that new cartridges had been greased with animal fat — something which would have been abhorrent to both Hindus and Muslims. At the same time, there was resentment among the old governing class over the reduction in their power, and Western innovations. The uprising at Meerut (10 May 1857) spread throughout northern India, with both urban and rural populations rising in revolt. Delhi quickly fell, and Kanpur and Lucknow garrisons were besieged. The British finally regained full control in mid-1858. The immediate result was the transfer of government from the British **East India Company** to the British Crown (1858), but the long-term result was a legacy of bitterness on both sides. The element of national consciousness present made the episode a source of inspiration for later Indian nationalists. The uprising is also known as the **Indian Mutiny** or the 1st National War of Independence.

indirect rule

A form of colonial rule especially characteristic of British rule in Africa during the inter-war years. In general terms it involved the use of existing political structures, leaders, and local organs of authority. Thus local political elites enjoyed considerable autonomy, although they still had to keep in accord with the interests of the colonial power. It was adopted on grounds of its cheapness and to allow for independent cultural development, but was increasingly criticized for its failure to introduce a modernizing role into colonial administration, and was gradually given up after 1945.

Industrial Revolution

A term usually associated with the accelerated pace of economic change, the associated technical and mechanical innovations, and the emergence of mass markets for manufactured goods, beginning in Britain in the last quarter of the 18c with the mechanization of the cotton and woollen industries of Lancashire, Central Scotland, and the West Riding of Yorkshire. After the harnessing of steam power, cotton and woollen factories were increasingly concentrated in towns, and there were hugely increased rates of urbanization. A rapid population increase, stimulated by greater economic opportunities for early marriage, is also associated with this type of economic growth. The mechanization of heavier industries (iron and steel) was slower, but sustained the Industrial Revolution in its second phase from c.1830.

Innocent XIII (Michelangelo dei Conti) (1655–1724)

Italian Pope (1721/4). A former papal ambassador to Switzerland and Portugal and a Cardinal from 1706, it was Innocent XIII who in 1721 invested the Holy Roman Emperor Charles VI with sovereignty over Naples. He recognized James Francis Edward **Stuart** ('the Old Pretender') as King of England and promised him subsidies if he returned England to Roman Catholicism. Although he was hostile towards the Jansenists — he confirmed the Bull *Unigenitus* in 1722 — he was also distrustful of the Jesuits, taking particular issue with the modified 'Chinese rites' which they employed with some success to attract converts in Asia.

interregnum

A period between rulers; normally, in British history, the period between **Charles I**'s execution (30 Jan 1649) and the **Restoration** of **Charles II** (5 May 1660); also, the period between the departure of **James VII and II** (22 Dec 1688) and the accession of **William III** and Mary II (23 Feb 1689; in Scotland until 20 Apr 1689).

Intolerable Acts (1774)

The American name for laws passed by parliament in London to punish Massachusetts for the **Boston Tea Party** (1773). They were called the Boston Port Act, the Massachusetts Government Act, the Administration of Justice Act, and a Quartering Act. The **Quebec Act**, though addressing a different problem, was also taken by colonists to add insult to the injury of the Intolerable Acts.

IRA (Irish Republican Army)

An anti-British paramilitary guerrilla force established in 1919 by Irish nationalists to combat British forces in Ireland. It opposed the Anglo-Irish Treaty of 1921 because Ireland was a dominion and the six counties of the North of Ireland were part of the UK, but it was suppressed by the Irish government in the 1922 rising, banned by Eamon **De Valera** in 1936 and remained largely inactive until the late 1960s. In 1969, a major split in its ranks led to the formation of the Provisional IRA alongside the Official IRA, and a serious schism between the two sides in the early 1970s. The Official IRA has been virtually inactive since 1972, and generally supports political action to achieve Irish unity. The Provisionals have become the dominant republican force, responsible for shootings and bombings in Northern Ireland, Britain, and Western Europe. Targets have mainly been security and military personnel and establishments, although there have been many sectarian killings and attempts to disrupt civilian life. ▷ **Sinn Féin**

Iran, Anglo-Soviet Invasion of (Aug 1941)

Suspicions that Reza Shah was sympathetic to the Germans in **World War II** resulted in the Anglo-Soviet invasion of Iran in Aug 1941, although it is possible that a desire to protect oil supplies among other things was as much of a motive for the invasion on the British side as any inklings of pro-German leanings in the Shah. The invasion and subsequent occupation forced

171

the abdication of Reza Shah in favour of his son, Muhammad Reza, and the presence of the Soviets allowed a brief reappearance of the Tudeh Party. The country was subjected to Anglo-Soviet military occupation until 1946.

Ireton, Henry (1611–51)

English soldier. At the outbreak of the **English Civil Wars** he fought for parliament, and served at Edgehill, **Naseby**, and the Siege of Bristol. **Cromwell**'s son-in-law from 1646, he was one of the most implacable enemies of the King (**Charles I**), and signed the warrant for his execution. He accompanied Cromwell to Ireland, and in 1650 became Lord Deputy. He died of the plague during the Siege of Limerick.

Irgun (Zvai Leumi)

The terrorist organization operating in Palestine during the British Mandate and seeking the establishment of a Jewish state. Formed in 1931 after disagreement with the **Haganah** and reconstituted in 1937, it accepted **Jabotinsky**'s ideology and engaged in armed conflict with Arabs and the British. Led by Menachem Begin from 1943, Irgun bombed Jerusalem's **King David Hotel** in 1946, hanged two British sergeants in 1947 in response to the execution of its members, and attacked the Arab village of Deir Yassin in 1948. Condemned for this by the Jewish Agency, the Irgun became the nucleus of the right-wing Herut Party in Israel after 1948.

Irish Free State

A form of **Home Rule**, established by the Anglo-Irish Treaty (Dec 1921). Accordingly, 26 counties (excluding the six of Northern Ireland) became a Dominion under the British crown. The treaty was ratified by a small majority in the **Dáil** and power was transferred from Westminster (Mar 1922). Republicans, led by **De Valera**, refused to accept the authority of the crown and civil war (1922–3) ensued. The name 'Irish Free State' was retained until Dominion status was dismantled with the new constitution of 1937. ▷ **Collins, Michael**

Irish Republic

The name given to the republic declared in Dec 1948 which came into effect in 1949 (Republic of Ireland Act). It changed the relationship between Ireland and Britain. The republic retained special citizenship arrangements and trade preference with Britain, but left the **Commonwealth of Nations**. The Westminster parliament passed the Ireland Act (1949) which confirmed a special relationship of Irish citizens in the UK, but declared that Northern Ireland would remain part of the UK until its citizens declared otherwise. ▷ **Irish Free State**

Ironside, William Edmund, 1st Baron (1880–1959)

British field marshal. He served as a secret agent disguised as a railwayman in the **Boer Wars**, held several staff appointments in **World War I**, and commanded the Archangel expedition against the Bolsheviks (1918). He was Chief of the Imperial General Staff at the outbreak of **World War II**, and placed in command of the Home Defence Forces (1940). The 'Ironsides', fast light-armoured vehicles, were named after him. He was made a peer in 1941.

Isabella of France (1292–1358)

Queen consort of **Edward II** of England. The daughter of Philip IV of France, in 1308 at Boulogne she married Edward. She became the mistress of Roger Mortimer, with whom she overthrew and murdered the King (1327). Her son, **Edward III**, had Mortimer executed in 1330, and Isabella was sent into retirement, eventually to join an order of nuns.

Isandlhwana, Battle of (1879)

A notorious reverse for the British in the Zulu War of 1879. Through mismanagement, an entire British regiment, its ammunition in boxes which could not be opened, was virtually destroyed by the Zulu using their traditional tactics. It caused considerable public alarm in Britain, allayed only by the victory at Ulundi later in the same year. ▷ **Zulu Wars**

Israel, State of

Democratic republic in the Middle East, with Jerusalem as its capital, bordered by Lebanon, Syria, Jordan, Egypt and the Mediterranean Sea. Since the 1967 Six-Day War, Israel has controlled the so-called 'occupied territories': the Golan Heights, West Bank, East Jerusalem and Gaza Strip. Excluding these, the population, mostly Jewish but with a sizable Arab minority, exceeds 4 500 000. Ultimate authority lay with the Knesset (parliament), consisting of 120 members elected for a four year term. Zionists settled in

Palestine in the 1880s under Ottoman rule, while the British declared support for a Jewish state there in 1917. However, this never materialized under the British Mandate (1918–47), although Jewish immigration in the 1930s and 1940s increased greatly due to Nazi persecution. Resultant tension between Arabs and Jews led the UN in 1947 to support the formation of two states in Palestine, one Jewish and the other Arab. When the Arab side rejected this, David **Ben-Gurion** announced the creation of the state of Israel on 14 May 1948. Military conflict with surrounding countries ensued in which Israeli forces were victorious. Further wars took place in 1958, 1967, 1973 and 1982. In contrast, a peace agreement between Israel and Egypt's President, Anwar Sadat, was reached in 1979. ▷ **Balfour Declaration; Irgun**

J

Jabotinsky, Vladimir (1880–1940)
Jewish writer and Zionist, born in Odessa. Realizing that **World War I** would spell the end of the **Ottoman Empire**, Jabotinsky and others persuaded the British government to allow Jewish involvement in the fight for Palestine. The result was a Jewish transport unit which fought in the **Gallipoli Campaign** but was disbanded in 1916. However, Jabotinsky was instrumental in convincing the British to sanction the more substantial Jewish Legion which took recruits from Britain, North America and, towards the end of the war, Jews from Palestine. Thereafter, the Legion became the basis for the **Haganah**. Unlike that of others, Jabotinsky's **Zionism** was right-wing and hostile to socialism. This led him to found in 1925 the Zionist Revisionist Movement, later renamed the New Zionist Organization. With growing resistance to Jewish immigration to Palestine under the British Mandate, Jabotinsky supported terrorist activities by the **Irgun**.

Jacobites
Those who supported the claim of the Catholic **James VII and II** of England, and his successors, to the British throne. The Jacobites launched two major rebellions, in 1715 (the **Fifteen Rebellion**) and 1745 (the **Forty-Five Rebellion**), against the Protestant Hanoverian succession, and in the period 1714–60 some British Tory politicians had Jacobite sympathies. ▷ **Tories**

James I (1394–1437)
King of Scots (1406/37). His father, Robert III, sent him for safety to France, but he was captured at sea (1406), held prisoner in England for 18 years, and did not begin to rule until his release in 1424. An accomplished poet, he wrote *The Kingis Quair* to celebrate his romance with Joan Beaufort, a cousin of **Henry V** of England, whom he married in 1424. He was acquisitive and vindictive, and his ruthlessness towards the House of **Stuart** led to his murder at Perth.

James I of England ▷ **James VI and I**

James II (1430–60)
King of Scots (1437/60). The son of **James I** of Scotland, he came to the throne at the age of six, and took control of the government in 1449. The early years of his personal rule were dominated by his efforts to curb the power of the mighty Black Douglases, whom he eventually defeated in 1455. He later attempted to recover Roxburgh Castle from the English, and was killed during the siege. ▷ **Douglas**

James II of England ▷ **James VII and II**

James III (1452–88)
King of Scots (1460/88). The eldest son of **James II** of Scotland, he came to the throne at the age of eight, and took control of the government in 1469. His marriage in that year to Margaret of Denmark led to the incorporation of Orkney and Shetland within the Scottish realm (1472). He was defeated and killed by rebel nobles at the Battle of Sauchieburn, near Stirling.

James IV (1473–1513)
King of Scots (1488/1513). The eldest son of **James III** of Scotland, he became active in government at his accession, at the age of 15, and gradually exerted his authority over the nobility. In 1503 he married **Margaret Tudor**, the eldest daughter of **Henry VII**: an alliance which led ultimately to the union of the crowns. However, he adhered to the French alliance when **Henry VIII** joined the **Holy League** against France, and was induced to invade England by the French. He was defeated and killed, along with the flower of his nobility, at the Battle of **Flodden**.

James V (1512–42)
King of Scots (1513/42). The son of **James IV** of Scotland, and an infant at his father's death, he grew up amid the struggle between the pro-French and pro-English factions in his country. In 1536 he visited France, marrying Magdeleine, the daughter of Francis I (1537), and after her death, Mary of Guise (1538). War with England followed from the French alliance (1542), and after an attempt to invade England, he was routed at Solway Moss. He

retired to Falkland Palace, Fife, where he died soon after the birth of his daughter, Mary (later, **Mary, Queen of Scots**).

James VI and I (1566–1625)

King of Scotland (1567/1625) as James VI and, as James I, the first Stuart King of England and Ireland (1603/25). He was the son of **Mary, Queen of Scots**, and Henry, Lord **Darnley**. On his mother's forced abdication, he was proclaimed King, and brought up by several regents. When he began to govern for himself, he ruled through his favourites, which caused a rebellion, and a period of imprisonment. In 1589 he married Princess Anne from Kristiania. Hating Puritanism, he managed in 1600 to establish bishops in Scotland. On **Elizabeth I**'s death, he ascended the English throne as great-grandson of **James IV** of Scotland's English wife, **Margaret Tudor**. At first well received, his favouritism again brought him unpopularity. ▷ **Addled Parliament**

James VII and II (1633–1701)

King of Scotland, as James VII, and of England and Ireland, as James II (1685/8). The second son of **Charles I** of England, he escaped to Holland nine months before his father's execution. At the Restoration (1660) he was made Lord High Admiral of England, and commanded the fleet in the Dutch Wars; but after converting to Catholicism he was forced to resign his post. The national ferment caused by the **Popish Plot** (1678) became so formidable that he had to retire to the Continent, and several unsuccessful attempts were made to exclude him from the succession. During his reign his actions in favour of Catholicism raised general indignation, and William, Prince of Orange, his son-in-law and nephew, was finally asked by leading clerics and landowners to invade. Deserted by ministers and troops, James escaped to France, where he was warmly received by Louis XIV. He made an ineffectual attempt to regain his throne in Ireland, which ended in the Battle of the **Boyne** (1690), and remained at St Germain until his death. ▷ **Anglo-Dutch Wars**

Jameson, Sir Leander Starr, 1st Baronet (1853–1917)

South African politician. After studying medicine, he set up in practice in Kimberley (1878). Through Cecil **Rhodes**, 'Dr Jim' engaged in pioneer work, was in 1891 made administrator for the South Africa Company at Fort Salisbury, and won popularity among the whites for his lack of administrative scruple. In 1895 he withdrew the British South African Police from Mashonaland to Bechuanaland (Botswana) to support a supposed uprising of Uitlanders in Johannesburg. He invaded the Transvaal (the **Jameson Raid**) on 29 Dec 1895, but the expected rising failed to materialize. At Krugersdorp Jameson and his men were overpowered by a force of Boers, and after a sharp fight were compelled to surrender (2 Jan 1896). Handed over to the British authorities in July, Jameson was condemned in London to 15 months' imprisonment, but was released in Dec. In 1900 he was elected to the Cape Legislative Assembly, and in 1904–8 was (Progressive) Premier of Cape Colony. Made a baronet in 1911, he retired from politics the following year.

Jameson Raid (Dec 1895–Jan 1896)

An expedition against the South African Republic, which was supposed to link up with a revolt by White workers on the Rand and topple the government of President **Kruger**. Leander Starr **Jameson**, administrator for the South Africa Company at Fort Salisbury, led a detachment of British South Africa Police into the Transvaal, but they were easily defeated and arrested. The German Emperor, William II, sent a telegram of congratulation to Kruger, and the incident caused a major government crisis in Britain as well as contributing to the tensions that led to the Boer War. ▷ **Boer Wars**

Jarrow March (Oct 1936)

A march to London by unemployed workers in the Durham shipbuilding and mining town, to put the unemployed case. Jarrow was among the towns worst affected by the Depression, and the march took place at a time when the economy was recovering in much of the rest of the country. It alerted the more prosperous South and Midlands to the intractable problems of depressed areas.

Jay's Treaty (1794)

An agreement between the USA and Britain to end the British occupation of military posts in the northwestern parts of US territory, and for altering the terms of US commerce with Britain and its colonies. Negotiated by John Jay, it was very unpopular with the US public, largely because of the restrictions it imposed on US trade with the West Indies.

Jeffreys (of Wem), George, 1st Baron (1648–89)

English judge. Called to the Bar in 1668, he rose rapidly, was knighted (1677), and became Recorder of London (1678). He was active in the **Popish Plot** prosecutions, became Chief Justice of Chester (1680), baronet (1681), and Chief Justice of the King's Bench (1683). In every state trial he proved a willing tool of the crown, and was raised to the peerage by **James II** (1685). His journey to the West country to try the followers of **Monmouth** earned the name of the 'bloody assizes' for its severity. He was Lord Chancellor (1685–8), but on James's flight was imprisoned in the Tower of London, where he died.

Jellicoe, John Rushworth, 1st Earl (1859–1935)

British admiral. He became Third Sea Lord (1908), and was Commander-in-Chief, Grand Fleet at the outbreak of **World War I**. His main engagement was the inconclusive Battle of **Jutland** (1916), for which at the time he was much criticized. Promoted First Sea Lord, he organized the defences against German submarines, and was made Admiral of the Fleet (1919). He later became Governor of New Zealand (1920–4). He was created an earl in 1925.

Jenkins, Roy (Harris), Baron (1920–)

Welsh politician. He became a Labour MP in 1948, and was Minister of Aviation (1964–5), Home Secretary (1965–7), Chancellor of the Exchequer (1967–70), Deputy Leader of the **Labour Party** in opposition (1970–2) and again Home Secretary (1974–6). He resigned as an MP in 1976 to take up the presidency of the European Commission (1977–81). Upon his return to Britain, he co-founded the **Social Democratic Party** (1981), and became its first leader, standing down after the 1983 election in favour of David **Owen**. Defeated in the 1987 election, he was given a life peerage and also became Chancellor of Oxford University. ▷ **Liberal Party**

Jenkins' Ear, War of

A war between Britain and Spain which started in 1739, and soon merged into the wider War of the Austrian Succession (1740–8). Some of the violent anti-Spanish indignation in Britain that provoked the war was due to Captain Robert Jenkins, who claimed to have had an ear cut off by Spanish coastguards in the Caribbean.

Joan of Arc, St (The Maid of Orléans) (c.1412–31)

French patriot and martyr. She halted the English ascendancy in France during the **Hundred Years War**. Born into a peasant family, at the age of 13 she heard the voices of Saints Michael, Catherine, and Margaret bidding her rescue France from English domination. She was taken to the Dauphin, and eventually allowed to lead the army assembled for the relief of Orléans. Clad in a suit of white armour and flying her own standard, she entered Orléans (1429), forced the English to retire, and took the Dauphin to be crowned Charles VII at Rheims. She then set out to relieve Compiègne, but was captured and sold to the English by John of Luxembourg. Put on trial (1431) for heresy and sorcery, she was found guilty by an English-dominated court, and burnt. She was canonized in 1920.

John ('John Lackland') (1167–1216)

King of England (1199/1216). The youngest son of **Henry II** of England, he was one of the least popular monarchs in English history. He tried to seize the crown during **Richard I**'s captivity in Germany (1193–4), but was forgiven and nominated successor by Richard, who thus set aside the rights of Prince **Arthur**, the son of John's elder brother Geoffrey. Arthur's claims were supported by Philip II of France, and after Arthur was murdered on John's orders (1203), Philip marched against him with superior forces, and conquered all but a portion of Aquitaine (1204–5). In 1206 John refused to receive Stephen Langton as Archbishop of Canterbury, and in 1208 his kingdom was placed under papal interdict. He was then excommunicated (1209), and finally conceded (1213). His oppressive government, and failure to recover **Normandy**, provoked baronial opposition, which led to demands for constitutional reform. The barons met the King at Runnymede, and forced him to seal the Great Charter (**Magna Carta**) (June 1215), the basis of the English constitution. His repudiation of the Charter precipitated the first **Barons War** (1215–17).

John Lackland ▷ **John** of England

John of Gaunt (1340–99)

Duke of Lancaster. He was the fourth son of King **Edward III** of England, and ancestor of Kings **Henry IV, V** and **VI** of England. In 1359 he married his cousin, Blanche of Lancaster, and through her succeeded to the dukedom in 1362. After her death (1369), he married Constance, daughter of Pedro, the Cruel of Castile, and assumed the title of King of Castile, though he failed by his expeditions to oust his rival, Henry of Trestamare. In England he became highly influential as a peacemaker during the troubled reign of **Richard II**. He was made Duke of Aquitaine by Richard (1390), and sent on several embassies to France. On his second wife's death (1394) he married his mistress, Catherine Swynford, by whom he had three sons; from the eldest descended **Henry VII**.

Johnston, Sir Harry H (1858–1927)

British administrator, explorer and artist. He played a significant part in the Partition of Africa. Trained as an artist, he also developed scientific and linguistic interests and in 1879 he went to Tunis to paint and explore. Later he travelled in Angola, the Congo and (in 1884) the Kilimanjaro region of East Africa, where he collected treaties with local chiefs. He subsequently served the Foreign Office in West Africa (1885–9), Lisbon in 1889, Mozambique (1889–91), British Central Africa (Malawi, 1891–6), Tunis (1897–9) and Uganda (1899–1901). He is generally credited with inventing the phrase 'Cape to Cairo'. ▷ **Africa, Partition of**

Jones, (John) Paul (1747–92)

Scottish-born American naval commander. Originally named John Paul, he was apprenticed as a cabin boy, made several voyages to America, and in 1773 inherited property in Virginia. He joined the navy at the outbreak of the **American Revolution**, and performed a number of daring exploits off the British coast, capturing and sinking several ships. Outmanned and outgunned in the famous battle against the Serapis, he refused to surrender, declaring 'I have not yet begun to fight' and through sheer grit emerged victorious.

Joyce, William ('Lord Haw-Haw') (1906–46)

British traitor. As a child, he lived in Ireland and in 1922 his family emigrated to England. In 1937, he founded the fanatical

British National Socialist Party, and fled to Germany before war broke out. Throughout **World War II**, he broadcast from Radio Hamburg propaganda against Britain, gaining his byname from his upper-class drawl. He was captured by the British at Flensburg, and was tried and executed in London.

Jutes

A Germanic people whose original homeland was the northern part of the Danish peninsula (Jutland). The tradition preserved by **Bede**, that Jutes participated in the 5c Germanic invasions of Britain and settled in Kent and the Isle of Wight, is confirmed by archaeological evidence. ▷ **Anglo-Saxons**

Jutland, Battle of (31 May–1 June 1916)

A sea battle of **World War I** (and the first major challenge to British naval supremacy since the Battle of **Trafalgar** in 1805), in which Admiral **Jellicoe** led the British Grand Fleet from Scapa Flow and intercepted the German High Seas Fleet of the west coast of Jutland, Denmark. Though the battle itself was inconclusive, German naval chiefs withdrew their fleet to port, and turned to unrestricted submarine warfare as a means of challenging British command of the sea.

K

Kanpur, Massacre of (1857)
The native cavalry of the garrison of Kanpur (Cawnpore), based in Uttar Pradesh in northern India, rebelled against their British masters on 4 June 1857 and the garrison, led by Sir Hugh Wheeler, was besieged for three weeks. On 27 June, members of the garrison were offered a safe passage to Allahabad on thatched barges. However, as they were leaving, the barges came under gunfire and were set ablaze. The survivors, including women and children, were later transferred to a small house called the Bibighar where they were killed on 15 July by the Nana Sahib's men.

Kimberley, Siege of (1899–1900)
One of the three sieges of the second Boer War, in which Boer forces attempted to pen up their British opponents and secure control of vital lines of communication. The siege lasted from the middle of Oct 1899 until Feb 1900, when the town was relieved by General French. ▷ **Boer Wars**

King David Hotel, Bombing of the (22 July 1946)
The attack by the **Irgun** on a wing of the King David Hotel in Jerusalem, the headquarters of British rule in Palestine. It took place as part of a wider campaign by the Irgun and others in response to opposition from the British Labour government to Jewish immigration into Palestine. ▷ **Zionism**

King William's War (1689–97)
The first of the great wars between France and England for the control of North America. Known in Europe as the War of the League of **Augsburg**, it was settled by the Treaty of Ryswick (1697). ▷ **William III**

Kinnock, Neil (Gordon) (1942–)
Welsh politician. He became a Labour MP in 1970, joined the **Labour Party**'s National Executive Committee (1978), and was

chief opposition spokesman on education (1979–83). He was elected Party Leader in 1983, following Michael **Foot**. During the 1980s he reorganized the party and led successsful attacks on its left-wing influence and on **Militant Tendency**. He resigned the Labour Party leadership in 1992, following his defeat by John **Major** in the general election of Apr 1992, and was succeeded by John **Smith**.

Kitchener (of Khartoum and of Broome), (Horatio) Herbert, 1st Earl (1850–1916)

British field marshal and statesman. He joined the Royal Engineers in 1871, and served in Palestine (1874), Cyprus (1878), and the Sudan (1883). By the final rout of the Khalifa at **Omdurman** (1898), he won back the Sudan for Egypt, and was made a peer. Successively Chief-of-Staff and Commander-in-Chief in South Africa (1900–2), he brought the Boer War to an end, and was made viscount. He then became Commander-in-Chief in India (1902–9), Consul-General in Egypt (1911), and Secretary for War (1914), for which he organized manpower on a vast scale ('Kitchener armies'). He was lost with HMS *Hampshire*, mined off the Orkney Islands. ▷ **Boer Wars; World War I**

Knox, John (c.1513–72)

Scottish Protestant reformer. A Catholic priest, he acted as notary in Haddington from 1540 to 1543, and in 1544 came under the influence of George Wishart, the Lutheran reformer. After Wishart's burning in 1546, Knox joined the reformers defending the castle of St Andrews, and became a minister. When the castle surrendered to the French, he became a prisoner on French galleys until 1549, then became a chaplain to Edward VI. Although he refused the bishopric of Rochester in 1552, he was consulted by Cranmer over the forty-two articles of faith for the church. On Mary's accession (1553), he fled to the continent, finding a congregation in Geneva, where he was much influenced by Calvin. He made a preaching trip to Scotland in 1555, and again in 1559, and gained many supporters of reform there. His party drew up a *Confession of Faith*, the basis of the Church of Scotland (1560). After the return of the Catholic **Mary, Queen of Scots** he maintained an attitude of uncompromising antagonism towards her. He died in Edinburgh, leaving behind his most famous and individual work, the *History of the Reformation in Scotland*. ▷ **Presbyterianism; Reformation** (Scotland)

Kruger, Stephanus Johannes Paulus (Paul) (Oom ('Uncle') Paul)
(1825–1904)
Afrikaner politician. He took part in the Great Trek of the 1930s, becoming leader of the independence movement when Britain annexed Transvaal (1877). In the first Boer War (1881), he was head of the Provisional Government, and subsequently became President of the South African Republic (1883–1902). During the second Boer War (1899–1902), he came to Europe to seek (in vain) alliances against Britain, making his headquarters at Utrecht. He died at Clarens, Switzerland. ▷ **Boer Wars; Great Trek**

Kut al-Amara, Battles of (28 Sep 1915 and 29 Apr 1916) and
Siege of (1915–16)
Kut al-Amara, on the west bank of the Tigris, some 100 miles from Baghdad, was taken first by the British under Major-General Charles Townshend in Sep 1915. Townshend later over-reached himself and was forced to fall back on Kut al-Amara, having suffered a reverse near the site of the ancient Ctesiphon. The Turks laid siege to Kut in Dec 1915 and, despite attempts to relieve Kut by British forces in Iraq, Townshend was forced to ask for terms. Townshend's proposals for terms were refused by the Turks and he surrendered, having first obtained a guarantee for his troops, in 1916.

L

Labourers' Statute (1351)

A law passed in an endeavour to stabilize the English economy in the wake of the Black Death, it represented the first ever attempt to control wages and prices by freezing wages and the prices of manufactured articles, and by restricting the movement of labour. Like most subsequent attempts, it failed abysmally to achieve its aims and contributed largely to the 1381 **Peasants Revolt**.

Labour Party

A socialist/social democratic political party, originally formed in 1900 as the Labour Representation Committee to represent trade unions and socialist societies as a distinct group in parliament. In 1906, 26 MPs were elected, and the name changed to the **Labour Party**. In 1922 it overtook the Liberals as the main opposition party, and the first minority Labour government was elected in 1924, lasting 11 months. The first majority Labour government under Clement **Attlee** (1945–51) established the welfare state and carried out a significant nationalization programme. Since then Labour have been in office 1964–70 and 1974–9. The breakaway **Social Democratic Party** of the 1980s hurt the party's electoral chances throughout that decade. Outside parliament, the annual conference and the National Executive Committee share policymaking, though their influence is greater in opposition. The leader and deputy leader are elected annually when in opposition by an electoral college composed of trade unions, constituency parties, and the parliamentary Labour Party. The British Labour Party has been little influenced by **Marxism**, unlike the corresponding parties in Europe. ▷ **socialism**

Ladysmith, Siege of (1899–1900)

One of the three sieges of the second Boer War in which Boer forces attempted to pen up their British opponents, and around which many of the actions of the war took place. An attempt to relieve the town was frustrated at the Battle of **Spion Kop** (Jan

1900), but General Sir Redvers Buller (1839–1908) succeeded in raising the siege on 28 Feb 1900. ▷ **Boer Wars; Kimberley, Siege of; Mafeking, Siege of**

La Hogue, Battle of (13–17 May 1692)
A naval victory in the Channel, won by an Anglo-Dutch force after a five-day running battle over a numerically inferior French fleet. The defeat seriously reduced Colbert's navy, ended French hopes of invading England, and gave the Allies control of the seas for the duration of the Nine Years War (1689–97).

laissez-faire
An economic doctrine (in French literally 'leave alone') advocating that commerce and trade should be permitted to operate free of government controls. It was a popular view in the mid-19c and is still part of modern-day conservative political thinking. The phrase originated with the French 18c free trade economists.

Lambert, John (1619–84)
English general. He studied law, then joined the parliamentary army in the **English Civil Wars**, commanding the cavalry at the Battle of **Marston Moor** (1644), and participating in several victories. He headed the army group which overthrew Richard Cromwell (1659), and virtually governed the country with his officers as the 'Committee of Safety'. After the **Restoration** (1661) he was tried, and imprisoned on Drake's Island, Plymouth, until his death.

Lancaster, House of
The younger branch of the Plantagenet Dynasty, founded by Edmund 'Crouchback', the younger son of **Henry III** and 1st Earl of Lancaster (1267–96), whence came three kings of England: **Henry IV**; **Henry V**; and **Henry VI**. ▷ **Edward IV; Roses, Wars of the; York, House of**

Lancaster House
The London venue for various conferences preparing the way for independence in several parts of the British empire. It is most noted for the 1961 conference, which paved the way to Kenyan independence and the 1989 conference in which the British

Foreign Secretary, Lord Carrington, managed to forge agreement for an independence constitution for Zimbabwe and procedures to end the civil war in that country.

Land Acts, Irish

A succession of British Acts passed in 1870, 1881, 1903, and 1909 with the objective first of giving tenants greater security and compensation for improvements, and later of enabling tenants to buy the estates they farmed. The Acts also aimed at reducing nationalist grievances and agitation. ▷ **Land League**

Land League

An association formed in Ireland in 1879 by Michael **Davitt** to agitate for greater tenant rights, in particular the '3 Fs': *fair rents*, to be fixed by arbitration if necessary; *fixity of tenure* while rents were paid; and *freedom* for tenants to sell rights of occupancy. **Gladstone** conceded the essence of these demands in the 1881 Land Act. ▷ **Land Acts, Irish**

Lansbury, George (1859–1940)

English politician. Active as a radical since boyhood, he became a convinced socialist in 1890 and a Labour MP in 1910, resigning in 1912 to stand in support of women's suffrage. He was defeated and not re-elected until 1922. He founded and edited the *Daily Herald* (1912–22), and became Commissioner of Works (1929) and Leader of the **Labour Party** (1931–5). ▷ **MacDonald, Ramsay; socialism**

Latimer, Hugh (c.1485–1555)

English Protestant reformer and martyr. He was appointed a university preacher in 1522. Converted to Protestantism, he was one of the divines who examined the lawfulness of **Henry VIII**'s marriage, and declared on the King's side. In 1535 he was made Bishop of Worcester, but opposed the Six Articles of Henry VIII, for which he was imprisoned in 1536, 1546, and 1553. He became known as a preacher under **Edward VI**, but under **Mary I** was tried for heresy and was burnt. ▷ **Reformation** (England)

Laud, William (1573–1645)

Archbishop of Canterbury. He was ordained in 1601. His learning and industry brought him many patrons, and he rapidly received preferment, becoming King's Chaplain (1611), Bishop of St David's (1621), Bishop of Bath and Wells and a Privy Councillor (1626), Bishop of London (1628), and Archbishop of Canterbury (1633). With **Strafford** and **Charles I**, he worked for absolutism in Church and state. In Scotland, his attempt (1635–7) to Anglicize the Church led to the **Bishops Wars**. In 1640 the **Long Parliament** impeached him. He was found guilty, and executed on Tower Hill.

Lauderdale, John Maitland, Duke of (1616–82)

Scottish statesman. He was an ardent supporter of the **Covenanters** (1638), and in 1643 became a Scottish Commissioner at Westminster. Made earl in 1645, he was captured at Worcester (1651) and imprisoned. At the **Restoration** (1660) he became Scottish Secretary of State. A Privy Councillor, he was a member of the **Cabal** advisers to **Charles II**, and was created duke in 1672.
▷ **English Civil Wars**

Law, (Andrew) Bonar (1858–1923)

Canadian-born Scottish politician. He was an iron merchant in Glasgow, became a Unionist MP in 1900, and in 1911 succeeded **Balfour** as Unionist leader. He acted as Colonial Secretary (1915–16), a member of the war cabinet, Chancellor of the Exchequer (1916–18), Lord Privy Seal (1919), and from 1916 Leader of the House of Commons. He retired in 1921 through ill health, but returned to serve as Premier for several months in 1922–3.

Lawrence, Sir Henry Montgomery (1806–57)

English soldier and colonial administrator. In 1823 he joined the Bengal Artillery and took part in the first Burmese War (1828), the first of the **Afghan Wars** (1838), and the Sikh Wars (1845 and 1848). In 1856 he pointed out the danger of reducing the British army, and the latent germs of rebellion. The following year he was appointed to Lucknow, and did all he could to restore contentment there, but the **Indian Uprising** broke out in May. It was owing to his foresight that it was made possible for 1 000 Europeans and 800 Indians to defend the Residency for nearly four months against 7 000 rebels. He was mortally injured during this defence.

Lawrence, T(homas) E(dward) ('Lawrence of Arabia') (1888–1935)
Anglo-Irish soldier and author. Before **World War I** he travelled
in the Middle East, studying Crusader castles and participating
in the excavation of Carchemish. In 1914 he joined military intelligence and was sent to Cairo, where he became a member of the
Arab Bureau. In 1916 he was appointed the British liaison officer
to the **Arab Revolt**, led by Faysal, the son of Sharif **Husayn ibn
'Ali** of Mecca, and was present at the taking of Aqaba (1917) and
of Damascus (1918). He was an adviser to Faisal at the **Paris
Peace Conference** and a member of the Middle East Department
at the Colonial Office (1921). His account of the Arab Revolt,
Seven Pillars of Wisdom, abridged by himself as *Revolt in the
Desert*, became one of the classics of war literature. His exploits
received so much publicity that he became a legendary figure, and
so he attempted to escape his fame by enlisting in the ranks of the
RAF (1922) as J H Ross, in the Royal Tank Corps (1923) as T E
Shaw, and again in the RAF in 1925. He retired in 1935 and was
killed in a motorcycling accident the same year.

**Lawrence (of the Punjab and of Grately), John Laird Mair,
1st Baron** (1811–79)
British colonial administrator. He joined the Indian Civil Service
in Delhi, and became Commissioner, then Lieutenant-Governor,
of the Punjab. He carried out many economic and social reforms,
for which he was nicknamed 'the Saviour of the Punjab'. After
helping to put down the **Indian Uprising** of 1857–8, he was made
a baronet, and in 1863 became Governor-General of India. He
returned to England in 1869, was made a baron, and died in
London.

Lawson, Nigel (1932–)
English Conservative politician. He spent some time working for
various newspapers and also for television (1956–72), and during
this time edited the *Spectator* (1966–70). Elected to parliament
in 1974, when the Conservatives returned to office he became
Financial Secretary to the Treasury (1979–81), Energy Secretary
(1981–3), and Chancellor of the Exchequer (1983–9). During his
time at the Exchequer, Britain saw lower direct taxes, but high
interest rates and record trade deficits. ▷ **Conservative Party**

League of Nations

A former international organization whose constitution was drafted at the **Paris Peace Conference** in 1919 and incorporated into the Treaty of **Versailles**. The main aims were to preserve international peace and security by the prevention or speedy settlement of disputes and the promotion of disarmament. With its headquarters in Geneva, the League operated through a Council, which met several times a year, and an annual Assembly. Its original members included the victorious Allies of **World War I**, except for the USA, which refused to join, and most of the neutral nations. Germany joined in 1926, and the USSR in 1934, but Germany and Japan withdrew in 1933, and Italy in 1936. Although the League succeeded in settling some minor disputes, it became increasingly ineffective in the later 1930s, when it failed to stop major acts of aggression by Japan, Italy, and Germany. In 1946 it transferred its functions to the **UN**.

Lee (of Asheridge), Jennie, Baroness (1904–88)

Scottish Labour politician. The daughter of a Scottish miner, she made her own way in socialist politics, becoming the youngest elected woman MP (1929–31). She married Aneurin **Bevan** in 1934. Re-elected to parliament in 1945, she became Minister for the Arts (1967–70), and was given the task of establishing the Open University. She retired from the House of Commons in 1970 to be made a life peer. ▷ **Labour Party; socialism**

Leeds, Thomas Osborne, 1st Duke of (1631–1712)

English politician. He became MP for York in 1665. After opposition to **Clarendon**, he was appointed Treasurer of the Navy (1668) and Privy Councillor (1673). He became Lord Treasurer in 1673, succeeding Clifford as King **Charles II**'s Chief Minister until his fall during the **Exclusion Crisis** (1679). He was successively Viscount Osborne of Dunblane, Baron Osborne of Kiveton and Viscount Latimer (1673), Earl of Danby (1674), Marquis of Carmarthen (1689) and Duke of Leeds (1694). Under Charles, he increased the yield from taxes and thus the King's financial independence. He also worked for the marriage of Mary, daughter of James, Duke of York, to **William III** (1677). He was impeached on charges of secret financial dealings with Louis XIV of France on Charles's behalf, and imprisoned in the Tower (1684). During **James VII and II**'s reign, he opposed the King's Catholic policies. His negotiations with the Dutch were part of a process which culminated in William of Orange's arrival in England (1688) and assumption of the crown. He was rewarded with the Presidency of the Council (1689–99) but further impeachment proceedings, for taking a bribe to secure a charter for the new East India Company (1695), ended his career as Chief Minister. In semi-retirement during Queen **Anne**'s reign, he supported the **Tories**, especially defending the Church of England. ▷ **East India Company, British; Popish Plot**

Leicester, Robert Dudley, Earl of (c.1532–88)

English nobleman. The favourite of **Elizabeth I**, he became Master of the Horse, Knight of the Garter, a privy councillor, baron, and finally Earl of Leicester (1564). He continued to receive favour in spite of his unpopularity at court and a secret marriage in 1573 to the Dowager Lady Sheffield. In 1578 he bigamously married the widow of Walter, Earl of Essex; yet Elizabeth was only temporarily offended. In 1585 he commanded the expedition to the Low Countries, but was recalled for incompetence in 1587. He was nonetheless appointed in 1588 to command the forces against the Spanish **Armada**, and died later that year.

Lend-Lease Agreement (1941)

The arrangement by which the USA lent or leased war supplies and arms to Britain and other Allies during **World War II**. It was a measure in which President Roosevelt took a close personal interest. The Lend–Lease Act was passed by Congress in Mar 1941, when British reserves were almost exhausted. By the time the agreement terminated in 1945, the allies had received about £5 000 million worth of materials.

Levellers

A radical political movement during the **English Civil Wars** and the **Commonwealth**. It called for the extension of manhood franchise to all but the poorest, religious toleration, and the abolition of the monarchy and the House of Lords. Led by John Lilburne (c.1614–57), Richard Overton (c.1631–64) and William Walwyn (1600–80), it was supported by 'agitators' in the parliamentary army 1647–9, and was defeated at Burford (May 1649).

Leven, Alexander Leslie, 1st Earl of (c.1580–1661)

Scottish general. He became Field Marshal of Sweden under Gustav II Adolf. Recalled to Scotland in 1639, he took command of the Covenanting army in the **Bishops Wars** against **Charles I**, who made him an earl in 1641 in the hope of winning his allegiance. He fought for the parliamentary army in the **English Civil Wars**, and received Charles's surrender at Newark. After the execution of the King, he supported **Charles II**, was captured in 1651, and imprisoned until 1654. ▷ **Dunbar, Battle of** (1650)

Lexington and Concord, Battles of (19 Apr 1775)

The first battles of the **American Revolution**, fought in Massachusetts after British troops tried to seize supplies stored at the village of Concord, and were confronted by colonial militia. ▷ **Gage, Thomas**

Liberal Party

One of the two major political parties in the UK in the 19c and early 20c. It developed from the aristocratic Whig Party in the middle years of the 19c when, especially under **Gladstone**'s leadership, it appealed to the rapidly growing urban middle classes, to skilled working men and to religious nonconformists. Many of its landowning supporters and also radical imperialists were alienated by Gladstone's Irish **Home Rule** policy from the mid-1880s. Based on values of economic freedom and, from the late 19c, social justice, the last Liberal government enacted in the decade before **World War I** many important social reforms which anticipated the Welfare State. Internal splits and the challenge of a reorganized **Labour Party** weakened it from 1918 onwards and by the end of the 1920s the Liberals were clearly a minority third party on the centre-left of British politics, a position they have not been able to escape despite revivals in the 1970s and alliance with the **Social Democratic Party** in the 1980s. The party became known as the Liberal Democrats after the decision to merge with the Social Democrats in 1987. ▷ **Conservative Party; Tories; Whigs**

Lilburne, John (c.1614–57)

English revolutionary. Imprisoned by the **Star Chamber** in 1638 for importing Puritan literature, he rose in the parliamentary army, but resigned from it in 1645 over the Covenant. He became an indefatigable agitator for the **Levellers** during the **English Civil Wars**, thought Cromwell's republic too aristocratic, and demanded greater liberty of conscience and numerous reforms. He was repeatedly imprisoned for his treasonable pamphlets.

Linlithgow, Victor Alexander John Hope, 2nd Marquess of
(1887–1952)
Scottish politician. He served during **World War I** on the Western Front. He was Chairman of the Royal Commission on Agriculture in India (1926–8) and was also a member of the Select Committee on Indian Constitutional Reform. In 1936 he became Viceroy of India, in succession to Lord Willingdon, and held the post until 1943, thus becoming the longest holder of that office. In 1939, he declared war against Germany before consulting the Indian political parties; the Congress Party was offended by this step, and provincial Congress ministries resigned in protest. Although he suppressed opposition to British rule in India during **World War II**, under him provincial autonomy functioned smoothly. He was responsible for jailing the Congress leaders of the **Quit India Movement** in 1942–3.

Liverpool, Robert Banks Jenkinson, 2nd Earl of (1770–1828)
English politician. He entered parliament in 1790, and was a member of the India Board (1793–6), Master of the Royal Mint (1799–1801), Foreign Secretary (1801–4), Home Secretary (1804–6 and 1807–9) and Secretary for War and the Colonies (1809–12). He succeeded his father as Earl of Liverpool in 1807. As Tory Premier (1812–27), he oversaw the final years of the **Napoleonic Wars**, the war of 1812–14 with the USA, and a difficult and lengthy process of readjustment to peace. His administrations adopted trade liberalization policies in the 1820s. He resigned after suffering a stroke early in 1827. ▷ **Tories**

Livingstone, David (1813–73)
Scottish missionary and traveller. As a youth he worked in a cotton factory in his native Lanarkshire, but became fired with the desire to entry missionary work. After training to become a doctor he was ordained under the London Missionary Society in 1840. He worked for several years in Bechuanaland before travelling northwards (1852–6), discovering Lake Ngami and the Victoria Falls. On his return to Britain he wrote *Missionary Travels* (1857). He was chosen to lead an expedition to the Zambezi (1858–64), and discovered Lake Shirwa and Lake Nyasa. The government expedition was recalled in 1863, but Livingstone, convinced that the area around Lake Nyasa was ideal for commercial and missionary operations, funded his journey 100 miles

westwards and sailed to Bombay himself, then returned to Britain to write *The Zambesi and its Tributaries* (1865), in which he exposed the activities of Portuguese slave-traders. In 1866 he returned to Africa to settle the vexed question of the Nile sources, but the river he finally reached proved later to be the Congo. Returning to Ujiji after severe illness, he was found there in 1871 by Henry Morton Stanley, sent to look for him by the *New York Herald*. He again set out to find the Nile, but died in Old Chitambo (now in Zambia). He is buried in Westminster Abbey. ▷ **Zambezi Expedition**

Lloyd-George (of Dwyfor), David, 1st Earl (1863–1945)

Welsh politician. He became a solicitor and in 1890, as a strong supporter of **Home Rule**, began his political career as Liberal MP for Caernarvon Boroughs (a seat he was to hold for 55 years). He was President of the Board of Trade (1905–8) and Chancellor of the Exchequer (1905–15). His 'people's budget' of 1909–10 was rejected by the House of Lords, and led to a constitutional crisis and the Parliament Act of 1911, which removed the Lords' power of veto. He became Minister of Munitions (1915), Secretary for War (1916), and superseded **Asquith** as coalition Prime Minister (1916–22), carrying on a forceful war policy. After **World War I** he continued as head of a coalition government dominated by Conservatives. He negotiated with **Sinn Féin**, and conceded the **Irish Free State** (1921) — a measure which precipitated his downfall. His energies could not sufficiently revive the fortunes of a divided **Liberal Party** and, following the 1931 general election, he led a 'family' group of Independent Liberal MPs. He was made an earl in 1945. ▷ **Boer Wars**

Llywelyn

The name of two Welsh princes. **Llywelyn ap Iorwerth** or **Llywelyn the Great** (d.1240) successfully maintained his independence against King **John** and **Henry III**, and gained recognition of Welsh rights in the **Magna Carta** (1215). **Llywelyn ap Gruffydd** (d.1282) helped the English barons against Henry III, and opposed **Edward I**, who forced his submission. He was slain near Builth, at which point Wales lost her political independence.

Lollards

A derisive term applied to the followers of the English theologian John **Wycliffe**. The movement, responsible for the translation of the Bible into the vernacular, was suppressed; however, it continued among the enthusiastic but less literate of society, generally anticlerical in attitude, and in some ways anticipated the **Reformation** in England.

London, Treaties of (1827, 1830, 1913 and 1915)

By the 1827 treaty, Britain, France and Russia agreed to work for Greek autonomy and to mediate between the rebels and the Ottoman Porte. By the 1830 treaty, the Great Powers agreed to Greek independence and established the boundaries of the new Greek kingdom. By the 1913 treaty at the end of the Balkan Wars, it reduced Ottoman possessions in Europe to the area around Constantinople, while Crete was ceded to Greece and Bulgaria gained Adrianople. The 1915 treaty secured Italian entry into **World War I** on the side of the Allies and promised the Italians the South Tyrol, Trentino, Gorizia, Gradisca, **Trieste**, Istria, part of Dalmatia, Saseno and Vlorë in Albania, as well as continued possession of the Dodecanese Islands and a share in the Turkish and German colonies.

London Convention (1884)

A convention agreed between President Paul Kruger and the British Government which revised the Pretoria Convention of 1881. The British secured the definition of the western border of the Transvaal which laid the way open to their annexation of Bechuanaland and the maintenance of the 'road to the north', while in exchange Kruger persuaded the British to reduce the republic's debt, remove the British resident from Pretoria, recognize the name 'South African Republic' and abolish the Queen's suzerainty except in respect of specific powers.

Long Parliament

An English parliament called (Nov 1640) by **Charles I** after his defeat by the Scots in the second of the **Bishops Wars**. It was legally in being 1640–60, but did not meet continuously. It attacked prerogative rights and alleged abuses of power by the King and his ministers, and abolished the Court of **Star Chamber**, the Councils of the North and for Wales, and the Ecclesiastical Court of High Commission (1641), the bishops and the Court of Wards (1646), and the monarchy and the House of Lords (1649). Moderates were eliminated in **Pride**'s Purge (Dec 1648), and the remaining **Rump Parliament** was dismissed by **Cromwell** in 1653.

The Rump was recalled in the death-throes of the **Protectorate** (May 1659), and all members in Dec 1659.

Lords, House of
The non-elected house of the UK legislature. Its membership, currently c.1 200, includes hereditary peers and life peers (including judicial members — the *Lords of Appeal in Ordinary*); also the two archbishops and certain bishops of the Church of England. The House can no longer veto, though it can delay, bills passed by the House of Commons, with the exception of a bill to prolong the duration of a parliament. Its functions are mainly deliberative, its authority based on the expertise of its membership. The House of Lords also constitutes the most senior court in the UK. Appeals heard by the House are confined to matters of law.

Loyalists
Colonial Americans who remained loyal to Britain during the **American Revolution**. Britain defined the term carefully, since loyalists were eligible for compensation. It was not enough to have been born or been living in the American colonies at the onset of revolution; it was necessary to have served the British cause in some substantial manner and to have left the USA before or soon after the termination of hostilities. During the revolution special corps were established for over 19 000 loyalist troops. Half of the 80 000–100 000 refugees went to Canada, especially to the Maritime Provinces, and their presence contributed to the creation of Upper Canada in 1791. Their influence was not insubstantial in the establishment of governmental, social, educational and religious institutions. In 1789 Lord Dorchester (Sir Guy **Carleton**) ordained that both they and their children were entitled to add the letters 'UE' after their names, indicating their belief in the Unity of Empire. They then became known as the United Empire Loyalists.

Lucknow, Siege of (1857–8)
The siege of the Lucknow garrison began on 1 July 1857. On 25 Sep, Henry Havelock's forces broke through the siege and reinforced the garrison. Additional British forces under Sir Colin Campbell broke through on 18 Nov and women, children, the sick and the wounded were removed to safety. Two days later Havelock died and Campbell left for Kanpur. During Campbell's absence, Tantia Tope attacked the garrison forcing Campbell to

return to Lucknow. Campbell defeated Tantia on 6 Dec and went to Kanpur from where he returned with a large army on 28 Feb 1858 and succeeded in repossessing Lucknow for the British on 21 Mar.

Luddites

The name given to the group of workers who destroyed newly-introduced textile machinery in Nottingham, Yorkshire and Lancashire (1811–12). Their fear was that the output of the equipment was so much faster than the output of a hand-loom operator that many jobs would be lost. Known as 'the Luds', after their leader, Ned Ludd, when the movement ended with a mass trial in York in 1813 many were hanged or transported to Australia. The term has since been used to describe any resistance to technological innovation.

Luftwaffe

The correct name for the German Air Force, re-established in 1935 under Goering, in contravention of the Treaty of **Versailles**. Dominant in the early years of German victory in **World War II**, the *Luftwaffe* suffered production shortfalls and poor central leadership which led to defeat in the Battle of Britain. It had all but ceased to exist by 1945, having lost some 100 000 aircraft. The Federal Republic of Germany's air force, also known as the *Luftwaffe*, was re-established in 1956, and today is a critical element in **NATO**, operating over 600 combat aircraft. ▷ **Britain, Battle of**

Lugard, Frederick John Dealtry, Baron (1858–1945)

British soldier and colonial administrator, born in Madras. In 1878 he was commissioned as an army officer, serving in the Sudan against Mohammed Ahmed, the Mahdi (1885), and in Burma after the fall of King Thibaw (1886), and commanded an expedition against slavers in Nyasaland (1888). His activities in rough-and-ready Uganda peacekeeping led to its being made a British protectorate in 1894. Appointed Commissioner in the Nigerian hinterland by Joseph **Chamberlain** (1897), he kept a French challenge at bay and kept the peace. Britain having declared a protectorate over Northern and Southern Nigeria, Lugard was high commissioner for the North (1900–7), and established administrative paternalistic control with minimal force. He was Governor of Hong Kong from 1907, helping to establish its University in 1911. He returned to Nigeria as Governor of the two protectorates, becoming Governor-General (1914–19) on their amalgamation. His principle was one of use of existing tribal institutions as the infrastructure for British rule.

Lusitania, Sinking of the (May 1915)

A Cunard passenger liner torpedoed by a German submarine off the Irish Coast while in transit from New York to Liverpool, with 128 Americans among those lost. The German government had announced (Feb 1915) that any passenger ship caught within a designated war zone around the British Isles would be sunk without warning. President Woodrow Wilson declared he would hold Germany accountable for such deaths in the future. Although the German authorities argued that the *Lusitania* was carrying war munitions for the Allies, they did eventually make **reparations**. However, any US sympathy toward Germany up to this point disappeared, and many called for a declaration of war.

M

Macbeth (c.1005–57)
King of Scots (1040/57). He was probably a grandson of Kenneth
II (971/95), son of Findleach, Mormaer of Moray, and nephew
of Malcolm II. Macbeth overthrew and killed **Duncan I** in 1040
and defeated a challenge to his kingship from Crinan, father of
Duncan I, in 1045. Despite his malign Shakespearean image, he
seems to have ruled wisely, avoiding expensive and debilitating
raids on England; he was a benefactor of the Church and went
on pilgrimage to Rome (1050). He was defeated and killed by
Malcolm III, 'Canmore', son of Duncan I, at Lumphanan on 15
Aug 1057 after an invasion from England aided by Earl Siward
of Northumbria.

Macdonald, Flora (1722–90)
Scottish heroine. After the **Forty-five Rebellion**, she conducted the
Young Pretender, Charles Edward Stuart, disguised as 'Betty
Burke', to safety in Skye. For this she was imprisoned in the
Tower of London, but released in 1747. She married in 1750, and
in 1774 emigrated to North Carolina, where her husband fought
in the **American Revolution**. When he was captured (1779), Flora
returned to Scotland, to be rejoined there in 1781 by her husband.
They settled at Kingsburgh, Skye.

MacDonald, (James) Ramsay (1866–1937)
British politician. He had little formal education, worked as a
clerk, then joined the **Independent Labour Party** in 1894, eventually becoming its leader (1911–14 and 1922–31). He became an
MP in 1906, and was Prime Minister and Foreign Secretary of
the first British Labour government (1924). Prime Minister again
(1929–31 and 1931–5), he met the financial crisis of 1931 by
forming a largely Conservative 'National' government, most of
his party opposing, and reconstructed it the same year after a
general election. Defeated by Shinwell in the 1935 general election,

he returned to parliament in 1936, and became Lord President. He died on his way to South America. ▷ **Labour Party**

Mackinnon, William (1823–93)
Scottish merchant and shipowner. A significant late-19c imperialist figure, he went to India in 1847 and founded a prosperous general mercantile company in Calcutta with his partner, Robert Mackenzie. In 1856 he formed the Calcutta and Rangoon Steam Navigation Company (later renamed the British India Steam Navigation Company), which became one of the largest shipping companies in the world. Mackinnon developed an interest in East Africa and secured (1877) a concession from Barghash, Sultan of Zanzibar, to develop the mainland territories of Zanzibar. The British government refused to support Mackinnon, but once German competition had become a real threat in the area a charter was granted to Mackinnon's Imperial British East Africa Company (1888). The chartered company ruled Kenya and Uganda for only a few years but failed through lack of capital and the costs of suppressing African resistance. The territories were taken over by the British government in 1893.

Maclean, Donald (Duart) (1913–83)
British double agent. He studied at Cambridge at the same time as **Burgess** and **Philby**, and was similarly influenced by **communism**. He joined the diplomatic service in 1935, serving in Paris, Washington (1944–8), and Cairo (1948–50), and from 1944 acted as a Soviet agent. He became head of the American Department of the Foreign Office, but by 1951 was a suspected traitor, and in May of that year, after Philby's warning, disappeared with Burgess to the USSR. He died in Moscow.

Macmillan, (Maurice) Harold, 1st Earl of Stockton (1894–1986)
English politician. He became a Conservative MP in 1924. He was Minister of Housing (1951–4) and Defence (1954–5), Foreign Secretary (1955), Chancellor of the Exchequer (1955–7), and succeeded **Eden** as Premier (1957–63). He became popular and respected during a period of economic boom, earning the sobriquet 'Supermac'. He was re-elected in 1959. After several political setbacks, and a major scandal (the **Profumo** Affair), he resigned through ill health in 1963, and left the House of Commons in 1964. He became Chancellor of Oxford University in 1960, an earl in 1984. ▷ **Conservative Party**

Macquarie, Lachlan (1761–1824)

Scottish soldier and colonial administrator, known as the 'Father of Australia'. He became Governor of New South Wales in 1810 after the deposition of **Bligh**. He raised the colony to a state of lawfulness and prosperity, but his liberal policies towards ex-convicts united his opponents, and caused his resignation. He returned to Britain in 1822.

Mafeking, Siege of (Oct 1899–May 1900)

The most celebrated siege of the second Boer War, during which Colonel Robert **Baden-Powell** and a detachment of British troops were besieged by the Boers. The news of their relief aroused public hysteria in Britain, the celebrations being known as 'mafficking'. The truth about the siege was rather different from the heroic action depicted by the British press. It is now known that the White garrison survived in reasonable comfort as the result of appropriating the rations of the Blacks, who were faced either with starvation or with running the gauntlet of the Boers by escaping from the town. ▷ **Boer Wars; Kimberley, Siege of; Ladysmith, Siege of**

Magersfontein, Battle of (1899)

An engagement of the second Boer War in which British forces were defeated by the Boers. It followed on the defeat of the British at **Modder River** several days previously, both actions taking place a few miles from Kimberley as part of the British attempts to relieve that town. ▷ **Boer Wars; Kimberley, Siege of**

Magna Carta

The 'Great Charter', imposed (June 1215) by rebellious barons on King **John** of England, it was designed to prohibit arbitrary royal acts by declaring a body of defined law and custom which the King must respect in dealing with all his free subjects. The principle that kings should rule justly was of long standing, but in Magna Carta the first systematic attempt was made to distinguish between kingship and tyranny. While failing to resolve all the problems raised by the nature of the English crown's relations with the community, it endured as a symbol of the sovereignty of the rule of law, and was of fundamental importance to the constitutional development of England and other countries whose legal and governmental systems were modelled on English conventions. ▷ **Barons War**

Major, John (1943–)
English politician. He had a career in banking before becoming a Conservative MP in 1976. He rose to become Chief Secretary to the Treasury, was unexpectedly made Foreign Secretary in Margaret **Thatcher**'s cabinet reshuffle in 1989, and soon after replaced Nigel **Lawson** as Chancellor of the Exchequer. He won the leadership contest following Thatcher's resignation, and became Prime Minister (1990–). ▷ **Conservative Party**

Majuba Hill, Battle of (1881)
An engagement which ended the first Boer War. In 1877 the British had attempted to federate the British and Boer territories of South Africa by invading and annexing the Transvaal. The latter was successfully accomplished, but the plan was destroyed by the British victory at Ulundi in the Zulu War of 1879. With the **Zulu** threat removed, the Boers resolved to re-establish their independence. The British suffered several small reverses, culminating in their defeat at Majuba Hill. **Gladstone**'s government restored a limited independence to the Orange Free State and the Transvaal under the Pretoria Convention, subsequently modified by the London Convention of 1884. Disagreements about the interpretation of these Conventions were to increase tensions later in the 19c. ▷ **Boer Wars; Jameson Raid**

Malayan Emergency (1948)
The name given to the insurrection led by the Malayan Communist Party (MCP) against British rule, and the campaign to crush that insurrection, in post-war Malaya. Following growing MCP violence, including the murder of European estate managers, on 18 June 1948 the British administration declared a state of emergency throughout Malaya. In the early years of the insurrection, the MCP achieved a number of notable successes, including the assassination of the High Commissioner, Sir Henry Gurney, in Oct 1951. However, by the mid-1950s, through a combination of fierce military measures, substantial resettlement of the Chinese rural population (which had provided much of the MCP's support) and the introduction of political initiatives that clearly would soon take Malaya to independence, the insurrection was broken, although, officially, it did not end until 31 July 1960.

Malcolm III, 'Canmore' ('large-headed') (c.1031–93)
King of Scots (1058/93). He was the son of **Duncan I**, who was slain by **Macbeth** in 1040. He returned from exile in 1054, and conquered southern Scotland; but he did not become king until he had defeated and killed Macbeth (1057), and disposed of Macbeth's stepson, Lulach (1058). He first married Ingibjorg, daughter of the Earl of Orkney, by whom he had a son, **Duncan II**, briefly King of Scots (1094). His second marriage was to the English Princess Margaret (later St **Margaret**), sister of Edgar the Atheling. He launched five invasions of England between 1061 and died in a skirmish near Alnwick, Northumberland. ▷ **Northumbria**

Malcolm IV, 'the Maiden' (c.1141–65)
King of Scots (1153/65). He was the grandson and successor of **David I**. Compelled to restore the northern English counties to **Henry II** in return for the earldom and honour of Huntingdon (1157), he served on Henry's expedition to Toulouse (1159), and was then knighted. Malcolm continued to implement David I's Normanizing policies, despite native opposition. He defeated Fergus, Lord of Galloway, in 1161, and in 1164 Somerled, Lord of Argyll, was vanquished and slain at Renfrew. His byname was coined in the 15c, in recognition of his well-attested reputation for chastity.

mandates
A system under which former territories of the German and Ottoman empires were to be administered by the victorious powers of **World War I** under international supervision. The mandates were granted by the **League of Nations**, and annual reports had to be submitted to its Permanent Mandates Commission. Britain and France acquired mandates in the Middle East (Palestine, Iraq, Transjordan, Syria, Lebanon) and Africa (Tanganyika, Togo, Cameroon) while Belgium acquired Rwanda-Urundi, South Africa acquired South-West Africa, and Australia and New Zealand acquired New Guinea and Western Samoa. The functions of the Commission were later taken over by the Trusteeship Council of the **UN**.

Mansfield (of Caen Wood), William Murray, 1st Earl (1705–93)
English judge. He became Solicitor-General (1742), an MP, Attorney-General (1754), Chief Justice of the King's Bench

(1756), a member of the cabinet, and baron. He was impartial as a judge, but his opinions were unpopular, and during the **Gordon Riots** of 1780 his house was burnt. Made earl in 1776, he resigned office in 1788.

Mansfield Judgement (1772)
The name given to the ruling by Lord Justice **Mansfield** in a case involving a runaway black slave that slavery was neither allowed nor approved under English law, and which effectively abolished slavery in England and Wales. ▷ **slave trade**

Maori Wars
A succession of conflicts (1843–7 and 1860–72) in which the Maori people attempted, unsuccessfully, to resist the occupation of New Zealand by British settlers. The wars, both in the 1840s and the 1860s, concerned the settlers' demands for land and the growing opposition of a section of Maori opinion to land sales, with the colonial government caught between them, but in practice favouring the settlers. The fighting involved the contrasting slow, methodical sieges of efficiently defended Maori strongholds and widespread guerrilla conflict as Maori resistance was often local-ized and tribal. Nevertheless, time and numbers were on the side of the Europeans; Maori resistance was worn down, and they were forced to surrender or retreat to the wilder central North Island where pursuit was both difficult and unnecessary. An uneasy stand-off was reached by the early 1870s but peace was not formalized until 1881.

Margaret ('Maid of Norway') (1283–90)
Infant Queen of Scotland (1286/90). The grand-daughter of **Alexander III** of Scotland, she was the only child of Alexander's daugh-ter, Margaret (who died in childbirth) and King Erik II of Norway. When Alexander III died in 1286, Margaret was the only direct survivor of the Scottish royal line. In 1289 she was betrothed to the infant Prince Edward (the future **Edward II** of England), son of **Edward I**; but she died at sea the following year on her way from Norway to the Orkneys.

Margaret, St (c.1045–93)
Scottish Queen. Born in Hungary, she came to England, but after the **Norman Conquest** fled to Scotland with her boy brother,

Edgar the Atheling. She married the Scottish king, **Malcolm III, 'Canmore'**, and did much to civilize the realm, and to assimilate the old Celtic Church into the rest of Christendom. She was canonized in 1250.

Margaret of Anjou (1429–82)

Queen Consort of **Henry VI** of England (1445/82). She was the daughter of René of Anjou. Because of Henry's madness, she became deeply involved in political life, and during the Wars of the **Roses**, was a leading Lancastrian. Defeated at the Battle of **Tewkesbury** (1471), she was imprisoned in the Tower for four years, until ransomed by Louis XI of France. She then retired to France, where she died. ▷ **Lancaster, House of**

Margaret Tudor (1489–1541)

Queen of Scotland. The eldest daughter of **Henry VII** of England, she became the wife of **James IV** of Scotland (1503) and the mother of **James V**, for whom she acted as Regent. After James IV's death in 1513 she married twice again, to the Earl of Angus (1514) and Lord Methven (1527). She was much involved in the political intrigues between the pro-French and pro-English factions in Scotland, but lacking Tudor shrewdness, she was discredited (1534). Her great-grandson was **James VI and I**. ▷ **Tudor, House of**

Markievicz, Constance (Georgine), Countess (1868–1927)

Irish nationalist. The daughter of Sir Henry Gore-Booth of County Sligo, she married the Polish count, Casimir Markievicz. She fought in the **Easter Rising** (1916), and was sentenced to death but reprieved. Elected the first British woman MP in 1918, she did not take her seat, but was a member of the **Dáil Eireann** from 1923.

Marlborough, John Churchill, 1st Duke of (1650–1722)

English general. Commissioned as an ensign in the Guards (1667), he fought in the Low Countries. In 1678 he married Sarah Jennings, a close friend and attendant of Princess Anne, and was further promoted. On **James VII and II**'s accession (1685), he was elevated to an English barony and given the rank of general. He took a leading part in quelling **Monmouth**'s rebellion at Sedgemoor but, concerned for the integrity of the Anglican Church under James, in 1688 he deserted to the Prince of Orange (later **William III**), and served the Protestant cause in campaigns in Ireland and Flanders. Under Queen **Anne**, he was appointed Supreme Commander of the British forces in the War of the **Spanish Succession**, and he became Captain-General of the Allied armies. His military flair and organization skills resulted in several great victories — Donauwörth and Blenheim (1704), Ramillies (1706), Oudenarde and the capture of Lille (1708) — for which he was richly rewarded with Blenheim Palace and a dukedom. Forced by political interests to align himself with the Whig war party (1708), his influence waned with theirs after 1710. When his wife fell from royal favour, the **Tories** pressed for his downfall. Dismissed on charges of embezzling, he left England for continental Europe (1712), returning after **George I**'s accession (1714), when he was restored to his former offices. ▷ **Whigs**

Marne, Battle of the (1914)
A battle early in **World War I**, in which General Joffre's French armies and the **British Expeditionary Force** halted German forces which had crossed the Marne and were approaching Paris, thus ending German hopes of a swift victory. The German line withdrew across the River Aisne, dug in, and occupied much the same positions until 1918.

Marprelate Tracts
Seven pamphlets covertly published in London in 1587–9. The pseudonymous author, 'Martin Marprelate', satirized the Elizabethan Church and bishops, and favoured a Presbyterian system. One alleged author, John Penry, was executed; another, John Udall, died in prison; a third, Job Throckmorton, successfully refuted the accusations. The Tracts led to statutes against dissenting sects and sedition (1593).

Marston Moor, Battle of (2 July 1644)
A major conflict in the first of the **English Civil Wars**, in which a force of 27 000 parliamentary and Scottish troops defeated 18 000 royalists near York. The royalist cavalry was led by Prince **Rupert**; the parliamentary horse by Oliver **Cromwell**. The defeat led to the fall of the royalist stronghold of York, and the virtual collapse of **Charles I**'s cause in the north.

Mary I (1516–58)

Queen of England and Ireland (1553/8). She was the daughter of **Henry VIII** of England by his first wife, **Catherine of Aragon**. A devout Catholic, during the reign of her half-brother, **Edward VI**, she lived in retirement, refusing to conform to the new religion. Despite Northumberland's conspiracy to prevent her succession on Edward's death (1553), she relied on the support of the country, entered London and ousted Lady Jane **Grey**. Thereafter she proceeded cautiously, repealing anti-Catholic legislation and reviving Catholic practices, but her intention was to restore papal supremacy with the assistance of Cardinal **Pole**, and to cement a Catholic union with **Philip II** of Spain. These aspirations provoked a rebellion led by the Protestant Sir Thomas Wyatt (1554), followed by the execution of Lady Jane **Grey** and the imprisonment of Mary's half-sister, Elizabeth (later **Elizabeth I**), on suspicion of complicity. Mary's unpopular marriage to Philip (1554) was followed by the persecution of some 300 Protestants, which earned her the name of 'Bloody Mary' in Protestant hagiography, though her direct responsibility is unproven. Broken by childlessness, sickness, grief at her husband's departure from England, and the loss of Calais to the French, she died in London. ▷ **Cranmer, Thomas; Latimer, Hugh; Reformation** (England)**; Ridley, Nicholas**

Mary, Queen of Scots (1542–87)

Queen Consort of France (1559/60). She was the daughter of **James V** of Scotland by his second wife, Mary of Guise. Queen of Scotland at a week old, her betrothal to Prince Edward (later **Edward VI**) of England was annulled by the Scottish parliament, precipitating war with England. After the Scots' defeat at **Pinkie** (1547), she was sent to the French court and married (1558) the Dauphin (later Francis II), but was widowed at 18 (1560) and returned to Scotland (1561). A Catholic with a clear dynastic claim, she was ambitious for the English throne, and in 1565 she married her cousin, Henry Stuart, Lord **Darnley**, a grandson of **Margaret Tudor**, but disgusted by his debauchery, was soon alienated from him. The vicious murder of **Rizzio**, her Italian secretary, by Darnley and a group of Protestant nobles in her presence (1566) confirmed her insecurity. The birth of a son (the future **James VI and I**) failed to bring a reconciliation. When Darnley was found, strangled, after an explosion at his residence (1567), the chief suspect was the Earl of **Bothwell**, who underwent a mock trial and was acquitted. Mary's involvement is unclear, but she consented to marry Bothwell, a divorcee with whom she had become infatuated. The Protestant nobles under Morton rose against her; she surrendered at Carberry Hill, was imprisoned at Loch Leven, and compelled to abdicate. After escaping, she raised an army, but was defeated again by the confederate lords at Langside (1568). Placing herself under the protection of Queen **Elizabeth I**, she found herself instead a prisoner for life. Her presence in England stimulated numerous plots to depose Elizabeth. Finally, after the **Babington** conspiracy (1586) she was brought to trial for treason, and executed in Fotheringay Castle, Northamptonshire. ▷ **Moray, James; Morton, James**

Massachusetts Bay Company

A joint stock company established in 1629 by royal charter to promote trade and colonization along the Merrimack and Charles rivers in New England. Its Puritan stockholders won the right to acquire all of the company's stocks. The company became self-governing, and it elected John Winthrop its first governor. Puritan settlers began what would become the Great Puritan Migration. The first group arrived in Salem in 1630, and later established a settlement in Boston. The company and the Massachusetts Bay Colony were one in the same, but in 1684 the company lost its charter, two years later the colony became part of the Dominion of New England.

Mayflower Compact (1620)

An agreement to establish a 'civil body politic', signed aboard the ship *Mayflower* by members of the Pilgrim party about to settle in the Cape Cod region.

May Thirtieth Movement (1925)

The large-scale anti-imperialist demonstrations in China which resulted in increased membership for both the Chinese Communist Party and the Guomindang. On this day, a crowd of workers and students in Shanghai protesting against the earlier killing of a Chinese worker in a Japanese textile mill was fired upon by the British-led International settlement police force. The incident, during which 13 died and many more were injured, led to nationwide strikes and boycotts. The most significant of these was the 15-month boycott against the British colony of Hong Kong following the killing of 52 demonstrators by British and French troops in Canton (23 June 1925). The movement clearly revealed the strength of opposition to foreign privilege in China. The powers, adapting to the new situation, began discussions in 1925 on the return to China of tariff autonomy.

Melbourne, William Lamb, 2nd Viscount (1779–1848)

English politician. He became a Whig MP in 1805, and Chief Secretary for Ireland (1827–8). Succeeding as second viscount (1828), he became Home Secretary (1830–4) under **Grey**. Prime Minister in 1834 and 1835–41, he formed a close, almost avuncular, relationship with the young Queen **Victoria**. Defeated in the election of 1841, he resigned and thereafter took little part in public affairs. His wife (1785–1828) wrote novels as Lady Caroline Lamb, and was notorious for her nine months' devotion (1812–13) to Lord Byron. ▷ **Whigs**

Mercia

A kingdom of the Anglo-Saxon heptarchy, with its main centres at Tamworth, Lichfield and Repton. Mercian supremacy over the other Anglo-Saxon kingdoms reached its height under **Offa**, whom Charlemagne treated as an equal, but by the early 10c Mercia had been brought under the direct rule of **Wessex**.
▷ **Anglo-Saxons**

Merriman, John Xavier (1841–1926)

English-born South African politician. He went early to South Africa, where his father was Bishop of Grahamstown. He was a member of various Cape ministries from 1875, and Premier (South African Party) from 1908 to 1910.

Mesopotamia Campaign

This campaign in **World War I** represented an effort by the British to safeguard both the route to India and the newly discovered oilfields of Persia. The Ottomans had declared for the German interest in the war and it was thus essential, for the realization of the above two aims, that British arms prevail in Iraq. After the catastrophe of **Kut al-Amara** earlier in the war, a regrouped British offensive under General Maude took Kut early in 1917 and entered Baghdad in Mar of the same year. Further operations on the River Euphrates and the River Tigris as far as Mosul resulted in a complete British occupation of Mesopotamia.

Metcalfe, Charles Theophilus Metcalfe, Baron (1785–1846)
British colonial official. He went in 1808 as an envoy of Lord
Minto to the Sikh ruler Ranjit Singh of Lahore, in order to cement
the cracks in the East India Company's north-western front. After
heading the Delhi Residency (1811–18), he was Resident in Hyderabad (1820–5), where he exposed irregularities in the Nizam's
financial relations with the House of Palmer and Co, in whose
Hyderabad branch Lord **Hastings**, the then Governor-General,
was personally interested. Serving continously in India from 1800,
he was Lord Bentinck's right-hand man during most of his government and, following his retirement (1835), acted as Governor-
General until the arrival of his permanent successor. He resigned
from the service in 1837 and became Governor-General of
Jamaica (1839) and Governor-General of Canada (1843). Having
succeeded Sir Charles Bagot in 1843, he attempted to reverse the
trend towards responsible government and reassert his independence of ministers. On his pressing the crown's right to make
all appointments, the ministry, including Robert Baldwin and La
Fontaine, resigned, and the assembly showed their support for
them in a vote of no confidence. Metcalfe then dismissed the
government and, in the following bitterly-fought election
campaign, appealed to the country for support; he won, but with
a dangerously narrow margin. His ministers were weak and
unpopular, although they managed to remain in power for two
years. With the end of the mercantile system and repeal of the
Corn Laws, the need to maintain the colonies in political dependence was diminished and in 1845 Metcalfe resigned, to allow for
the introduction of responsible government.

Middle Ages
The period of European history between the collapse of the
Roman Empire in the West and the Renaissance (c.500–c.1500);
sometimes, however, the term is restricted in its use to the four or
five centuries after the year 1000. By the early 16c, humanists
regarded the civilization that followed the fall of Rome as distinctly different from the classical culture that preceded it and the
classical revival of their own day. The notion of a separate but
inferior medieval civilization has since been transformed into a
more positive appreciation of the age and its achievements,
notably the emergence of national states, the vigour of cultural
life, and the spiritual attainments of the Church in what was above
all an age of faith. Though quite a well defined period between

ancient and modern times, it has no obvious beginning, still less an obvious end.

Militant Tendency

A political group which came to prominence in the 1980s. Ostensibly, *Militant* is a newspaper published by **Labour Party** members espousing Marxist positions. In practice, critics have argued, the newspaper is a front for a 'party within a party', a separate organization of revolutionary Trotskyists who have entered the Labour Party (*entryism*) to use its organizational base for its own political ends. They claim that Militant is a cover for the Revolutionary Socialist League, the original British section of the Fourth International. In the 1980s, its supporters infiltrated a number of local Labour parties and the Young Socialists (its youth wing). Fearing the adverse electoral publicity resulting from Militant activities, the Labour Party moved to expel members of Militant on the grounds that they were members of a separate political party, which is against the party's constitution. Many of those expelled took the party to court, but their cases were not upheld. Since then, Militant's influence has declined.

Milner (of St James's and Cape Town), Alfred, 1st Viscount
(1854–1925)

English politician and colonial administrator. He established his reputation in Egypt and was appointed Governor of the Cape and High Commissioner in South Africa (1897). There he became convinced that the British position was endangered by the South African Republic (Transvaal), and set about the political rationalization of the region through the **Boer Wars**. He hoped to encourage sufficient English-speaking immigration to outnumber the Boers in a South African dominion. He additionally became Governor of the Transvaal and Orange River Colony in 1901, but was forced to resign in 1905 as a result of irregularities over Chinese labour he had introduced for the Rand gold mines. He was Secretary for War (1916–19) and Colonial Secretary (1919–21), and died in Kent, England.

Minto, Gilbert John Elliot-Murray-Kynynmound, 4th Earl of
(1845–1914)

British colonial administrator. After service in the Scots Guards (1867–70) and work as a journalist in Spain and Turkey (1874–7), he fought in the second Afghan War (1879) before going to Canada. As Governor-General (1898–1905) he was an intermediary between the Prime Minister, Wilfrid Laurier, and Joseph Chamberlain, the British Colonial Secretary. As Viceroy of India (1905–10), in succession to Lord Curzon, he found an associate in John Morley, the radical Secretary of State. Both were convinced that something must be done to associate articulate Indian opinion more closely with the government. The two men, though different in their origins and natures, made an effective team. Among the problems tackled by Minto and Morley were the securing of better representation of important Indian interests and the enlargement of the powers of the existing legislative councils. The Indian Councils Act, the core of what is generally known as the Morley–Minto Reforms, became law in 1909. As a result of a campaign by a Muslim delegation for representation of Muslim interests through special constituencies this law introduced the principle of communal representation. Six special Muslim constituencies of land-holders were created for the Imperial Legislative Council, and others in some other provinces. This measure is considered as the official germ of Pakistan.

Modder River, Battle of (1899)

One of the engagements of the second Boer War through which the British hoped to relieve the Siege of **Kimberley**. The Boers had command of a hilltop, a traditional Boer tactic; but as this made them vulnerable to modern artillery, they gave up the hilltop and dug trenches by the river. The British failed to take the positions, and were defeated two weeks later at Magersfontein, putting back the relief of Kimberley by three months. ▷ **Boer Wars**

Monck, George (1608–70)

English general. He fought in the Low Countries, and with the royalists in Scotland, then joined the **Commonwealth** cause and served successfully in Ireland, Scotland, and (1652–4) in the first of the **Anglo-Dutch Wars**. He feared a return to civil war during and after Richard Cromwell's regime (1658–9), and was instrumental (as commander of the army in Scotland) in bringing about the **Restoration** of **Charles II**, for which he was created Duke of Albermarle. ▷ **English Civil Wars**

Monmouth, James, Duke of (1649–85)
Illegitimate son of **Charles II** of England. He was created Duke
of Monmouth in 1663, and became Captain-General in 1670. He
had substantial popular support, and as a Protestant became a
focus of opposition to Charles II. After the discovery of the **Rye
House Plot** (1683), he fled to the Low Countries. In 1685 he landed
at Lyme Regis, and asserted his right to the crown. He was
defeated at the Battle of **Sedgemoor**, captured, and beheaded.
▷ **James VII and II**

Mons Graupius, Battle of (AD83)
The battle fought at an unidentified site (possibly near Mount
Bennachie, Aberdeenshire) between Roman forces under Gnaeus
Julius **Agricola** and Caledonians under Galgacus. The Roman
victory enabled them to establish extensive, though temporary,
settlement in north-eastern Scotland. Agricola's ambition to conquer the whole of Britain was not realized; fortifications were
abandoned and legions withdrawn from northern Scotland later
in the same decade. ▷ **Britain, Roman**

Montagu–Chelmsford Reforms
After a report (Apr 1918) by the Secretary of State for India, E S
Montagu, and the Viceroy, Lord Chelmsford, the British agreed
the 1919 Government of India Act. Promising progressive moves
towards Indian self-government within the British Empire, it provided as a first step enlarged electorates, and partial provincial
autonomy whereby responsibility for certain aspects of government was transferred to elected Indian ministers; at the centre a
bicameral legislature comprising a Council of State and a Legislative Assembly with increased powers. The number of Indians
on the central executive council was also enlarged; the Indian
government gained a larger degree of independence from the
control of Whitehall. It was rejected by many Indians, and its
promise of future progress was resisted by some British Conservatives, but a further step was taken, with full provincial autonomy under Indian control, in 1935. ▷ **Government of India Acts**

Montfort, Simon de, Earl of Leicester (c.1208–65)
English politician and soldier. In 1238 he married **Henry III** of
England's youngest sister, Eleanor, and as the king's deputy in
Gascony (1248) put down disaffection with a heavy hand. He

returned to England in 1253, became the leader of the barons in their opposition to the king, and defeated him at Lewes (1264). He then became virtual ruler of England, calling a parliament in 1265; but the barons soon grew dissatisfied with his rule, and the ing's army defeated him at Evesham, where he was killed.
▷ **Barons Wars**

Montgomery (of Alamein), Bernard Law, 1st Viscount (1887–1976) British field marshal. Commissioned into the Royal Warwickshire Regiment (1908), in **World War II** he gained renown as arguably the best British field commander since **Wellington**. A controversial and outspoken figure, he was nevertheless a 'soldier's general', able to establish a remarkable rapport with his troops. He commanded the 8th Army in North Africa, and defeated Rommel at the Battle of **El Alamein** (1942). He played a key role in the invasion of Sicily and Italy (1943), and was appointed Commander-in-Chief, Ground Forces, for the Allied **Normandy Campaign** (1944). On his insistence, the invasion frontage was widened, and more troops were committed to the initial assault. Criticized for slow progress after **D-Day**, he uncharacteristically agreed to the badly-planned airborne landings at Arnhem (Sep 1944), which resulted in the only defeat of his military career. In 1945, German forces in north-western Germany, Holland, and Denmark surrendered to him on Lüneberg Heath. Appointed field marshal (1944) and viscount (1946), he served successively as Chief of the Imperial General Staff (1946–8) and Deputy Supreme Commander of **NATO** forces in Europe (1951–8). ▷ **North African Campaign**

Montrose, James Graham, 1st Marquis of (1612–50)
Scottish general. He helped to draw up the Covenant in support of **Presbyterianism**. He served in the Covenanter army in 1640, but transferred his allegiance to **Charles I**, and led the royalist army to victory at Tippermuir (1644). After the royalist defeat at the Battle of **Naseby** (1645), his army became disaffected, and his remaining force was defeated at Philiphaugh. He fled to Europe, returning to Scotland after Charles's execution to avenge his death; but his army was largely lost by shipwreck, and the remnant defeated at Invercharron (1650). He was taken prisoner, and hanged in Edinburgh. ▷ **Covenanters; English Civil Wars**

Moore, John (1761–1809)
British general. From 1794 he served in many countries in Europe, and in the West Indies, but is remembered for his command of the English Army in Spain (1808–9), where he was forced to retreat to Corunâ. There he defeated a French attack, but was mortally wounded. ▷ **Peninsular War**

Moray, James Stuart, 1st Earl of (1531–70)
Regent of Scotland (1567/70). He was the illegitimate son of **James V** of Scotland, and half-brother of **Mary, Queen of Scots**. He acted as Mary's chief adviser (1560), but supported John **Knox** and opposed Mary's marriage to **Darnley**. After an attempted coup, he was outlawed and took refuge in England (1565). Pardoned the following year, he became regent for Mary's baby son when she abdicated (1567), and defeated her army at Langside (1568). His Protestant and pro-English policies alienated some Scots nobles, and he was killed at Linlithgow by one of Mary's supporters.

More, Sir Thomas (St Thomas More) (1478–1535)
English statesman. He became a lawyer, then spent four years in a Carthusian monastery to test his vocation for the priesthood. He did not take holy orders, and under **Henry VIII** of England became Master of Requests (1514), Treasurer of the Exchequer (1521), and Chancellor of the Duchy of Lancaster (1525). On the fall of **Wolsey** (1529), he was appointed Lord Chancellor, but resigned in 1532 following his opposition to Henry's break with Rome. On refusing to recognize Henry as head of the English Church, he was imprisoned and beheaded. A leading humanist scholar, as revealed in his Latin *Utopia* (1516) and many other works, he was canonized in 1935. ▷ **Reformation** (England)

Morgan, Henry (c.1635–88)
British buccaneer. Morgan's 'Brethren of the Cross' terrorized Spanish settlements in the Caribbean between 1655 and 1671. Welsh-born, Morgan went to Barbados as an indentured servant but later joined the cosmopolitan **buccaneers** in St Domingue. In 1655 he took part in the capture of Jamaica and Mansfield's raid on Cuba. Provided with letters of marque by the Governor of Jamaica, Thomas Modyford, Morgan made daring, brutal and profitable attacks on Puerto Bello (1668), Maracaibo (1669) and

Rio de la Hacha and Panama (1670–1). When buccaneering was outlawed by the Treaty of Madrid (1670), Morgan returned to Port Royal and was twice made Deputy Governor of Jamaica. ▷ **Indentured Servants**

Morrison (of Lambeth), Herbert Stanley, 1st Baron (1888–1965)
English politician. Largely self-educated, he helped to found the London **Labour Party** of which he became Secretary (1915). First elected an MP in 1923, he was Minister of Transport (1929–31), Minister of Supply (1940), and Home Secretary (1940–5). He served in the war cabinet from 1942, and became a powerful post-war figure, acting as Deputy Prime Minister (1945–51), but was defeated by **Gaitskell** for the leadership of the Labour Party in 1955. He was made a life peer in 1959.

Morton, James Douglas, 4th Earl of (c.1525–81)
Regent of Scotland (1572/8). Although a Protestant, he was made Lord High Chancellor by **Mary, Queen of Scots** (1563); yet he was involved in the murders of **Rizzio** (1566) and **Darnley** (1567), and played an important part in the overthrow of the Queen. He joined the hostile noble confederacy, leading its forces at Carberry Hill and Langside, and succeeded **Moray** as regent for **James VI and I**. However, his high-handed treatment of the nobles and Presbyterian clergy caused his downfall (1581). He was arraigned for his part in Darnley's murder, and executed at Edinburgh.

Morton, John (c.1420–1500)
English statesman and cardinal. He practised as a lawyer, and adhered with great fidelity to **Henry VI**, but after the Battle of **Tewkesbury** made his peace with **Edward IV**, and became Master of the Rolls (1473) and Bishop of Ely (1479). **Richard III** imprisoned him (1483), but he escaped, and after the accession of **Henry VII** was made Archbishop of Canterbury (1486), Chancellor (1487), and cardinal (1493). ▷ **Roses, Wars of the**

Mosley, Sir Oswald (Ernald), 6th Baronet (1896–1980)
English politician. He was successively a Conservative, Independent and Labour MP, and a member of the 1929 Labour government. He resigned from the **Labour Party**, and founded, first, the New Party (1931), and then, following a visit to Italy, the British Union of Fascists, of which he became leader, and

which is remembered for its anti-Semitic violence in the East End of London and its support for **Hitler**. Detained under the Defence Regulations during **World War II**, he founded another racialist party, the **Union Movement**, in 1948. He died in Orsay, near Paris, where he mainly lived after the war. ▷ **Blackshirts**

Mountbatten (of Burma), Louis (Francis Albert Victor Nicholas), 1st Earl (1900–79)

British Admiral of the Fleet and statesman. He was the younger son of Prince Louis of Battenberg (later Louis Mountbatten, Marquess of Milford Haven) and Princess Victoria of Hesse, the granddaughter of Queen **Victoria**. Having joined the Royal Navy in 1916, in **World War II** he became chief of **Combined Operations Command** (1942), and played a key role in preparations for **D-Day**. In 1943 he was appointed Supreme Commander, South-East Asia, where he defeated the Japanese offensive into India (1944), and worked closely with **Slim** to reconquer Burma (1945). He received the Japanese surrender at Singapore, and in 1947 was sworn in as last Viceroy of India prior to independence. Created an earl in 1947, he returned to the Admiralty, and became First Sea Lord (1954) and Chief of the Defence Staff (1959). Retiring in 1965, he remained in the public eye, and was assassinated by Irish terrorists while fishing near his summer home in the Irish Republic.

Moyne Commission (1940)

A royal government commission set up after the **Disturbances** to investigate the social and economic conditions prevailing in the British West Indies. Headed by the Lord Moyne, its members toured the British Caribbean colonies (1938–9) and its recommendations were made public in 1940, although because of its critical nature, the full report was not published until 1945. It attributed social discontent to the current appalling socio-economic conditions and recommended the creation of an imperially-financed Colonial Development and Welfare Fund to encourage spending on health, education and housing projects. The Commission also supported the growth of trade unions, but was ambivalent towards constitutional progress.

Mudros Armistice (30 Oct 1918)

The armistice which took the Ottomans out of **World War I**, signed at Mudros, a harbour on the Aegean island of Lemnos.

The principal participants were Huseyn Rauf Bey, the Ottoman Navy Minister, and Vice-Admiral Calthorpe, commander of the British forces in the Aegean, representing the Entente. The armistice provided for an immediate end to hostilities, demobilization of the Ottoman land forces, surrender of the Ottoman fleet, the withdrawal of Ottoman troops from certain specified territories, and the breaking of all contact with the Austro-Hungarian and German empires. This break in relations was to be accompanied by the expulsion of all nationals of the two Powers' name. The agreement also covered the opening of the Dardanelles and Bosphorus, the stationing of appropriate personnel in strategic positions and access to all Ottoman naval and military facilities. Despite the theoretically provisional nature of the armistice, the British handling of it left suspicions of British intent in the minds of both the French and the Turks. Calthorpe had been ordered by the British government to exclude the French from the talks, and the British approach to enforcing the terms of the armistice, particularly regarding demobilization and the surrender of important positions, led the Turks to suspect that the British intention was no less than a piecemeal dismemberment of what remained of the **Ottoman Empire** in Thrace and Anatolia. Although the Nationalists were able successfully to oppose some of the armistice provisions, the British handling of the matter did little for future relations between the two countries.

Munich Agreement (29 Sep 1938)

One of the more infamous acts in history that has come to stand for a betrayal for the worst of reasons and with the worst of consequences. After a long period of pressurizing Czechoslovakia to make whatever concessions its Sudeten German subjects demanded, the Prime Ministers of Britain and France, **Chamberlain** and Daladier, sat down with the two fascist dictators of Italy and Germany, **Mussolini** and **Hitler**, and, in the absence of Benes, they agreed to its virtual dismemberment, allegedly in the interest of European peace. But the peace Chamberlain and Daladier bought at the price of Czechoslovakia only encouraged Hitler and Mussolini and, a year later, they had to go to war in worse circumstances for the sake of Poland.

Munro, Sir Thomas (1761–1827)

British colonial administrator. A British **East India Company** official, of humble Scottish origins, he contributed significantly to early British knowledge of, and authority over, its subject population in India. He was associated with the introduction, in the early 19c, of the Ryotwari system of land revenue collection, which advocated settlement direct with the cultivator. As with many of his other innovations, Ryotwari grew out of Munro's understanding of Indian traditions and problems acquired through many years of service both as a soldier and administrator. During his governorship of Madras, the Ryotwari system became a rule, although it only acquired its modern methodical form after 1885.

Murray, General Sir James (1721–94)

Scottish soldier and administrator. Military commander after the death of General James **Wolfe**, he was responsible for the application of the 1763 Proclamation which excluded Catholics from holding public office. It was impossible for the very few Protestants to supply an Assembly, and it was also dangerous to retain the judiciary within the control of such a small number. Murray, therefore, had to make adjustments in order to establish a stable government. Already on bad terms with the English-speaking merchants (he thought them subversive, while they disliked military rule), Murray modified the proclamation to allow Catholics to sit on juries and to practise law, and introduced French legal customs into the judicial system. These concessions, as well as the lack of *habeas corpus*, angered the English-speaking merchants, who petitioned London for his replacement. In 1766 he was recalled, although the **Quebec Act** later adopted many of his administrative arrangements, and was one of the factors which prevented the colony from joining the **American Revolution**.

Muscovy Company

An English trading company granted a charter in 1554 allowing it to monopolize trade between England and Russia. In 1568 Tsar Ivan IV, 'the Terrible' allowed the company to conduct trade with the Orient via the River Volga. Political intrigues led to the expulsion of the company's agents from Russia in 1649, after which it ceased to exist.

Mussolini, Benito (1883–1945)

Italian politician. He established the fascist movement in 1919, borrowing ideas from Gabriele D'Annunzio and the 'futurists'; in Oct 1921 he converted this into the Fascist Party. In Oct 1922 he was asked by Victor Emmanuel III to form a government and the following month assumed dictatorial powers. In 1935 he launched the Conquest of Abyssinia which was followed by large-scale intervention in the **Spanish Civil War** on the side of Franco. During this period he moved increasingly towards cooperation with **Hitler**, which culminated in the Pact of Steel and eventually in the invasion of France in 1940. In 1939 Mussolini annexed Albania but (Oct 1940) failed to seize Greece. The arrival of German troops to assist in the conquest of Greece signalled the beginning of his dependence on Hitler, and henceforth his actions were dictated largely by the needs of Berlin. In Sep 1943 he was established at the head of the puppet Republic of Salò in German-occupied northern Italy but was no more than an impotent quisling. On 28 Apr 1945 he was captured by partisans and shot while trying to flee Italy.

N

Nanjing, Treaty of (29 Aug 1842)

Signed at the conclusion of the **Opium War** between China and Britain, it was to be the first of a series of unequal treaties that gave extensive privileges to the foreign powers in China. Five **treaty ports** were opened for British residence and trade; British consuls were to be stationed permanently in these ports; the Cohong monopoly system was abolished; a huge indemnity was imposed on the Chinese government to compensate for the opium confiscated in 1839 and to cover the expenses of the British military expedition; and the island of Hong Kong was ceded to Britain 'in perpetuity'. A supplementary treaty (1843) fixed tariff rates, thus infringing on China's tariff autonomy, and stipulated a 'most-favoured nation' clause: any privileges or immunities granted to the nationals of other foreign countries were to be automatically extended to those of Britain. The USA and France concluded similar treaties with China in 1844; additional privileges granted included the enjoyment of extraterritoriality (foreigners in the treaty ports to be subject to the jurisdiction of their own consuls) and the right of missionaries to build churches and proselytize in the treaty ports. While the Qing Dynasty regarded such concessions as minor irritants, by the turn of the century Chinese nationalists were to view the Nanjing Treaty as the opening move in a full-scale imperialist onslaught on China.

Napier, Sir Charles James (1782–1853)

British general and colonial administrator. He fought in the **Peninsular War** from 1808 to 1811, against the USA (1812), and in 1842 was sent to India to take command of the war in Sind. He defeated the amirs at Miani (1843), and was made Governor of the province. In 1847 he returned to England, but went back to India before the end of the second of the **Sikh Wars** to command the army. He left India in 1851.

Napier (of Magdala), Robert (Cornelis), 1st Baron (1810–90)

British field marshal. Born in Ceylon, he joined the army in 1826 and distinguished himself at the Siege of **Lucknow** (1857–8). He carried out successful expeditions during the Chinese War (1860) and in Abyssinia (1868), and became Commander-in-Chief in India (1870), Governor of Gibraltar (1876–82), and Constable of the Tower of London (1887). Created a baron in 1868, he died in London. ▷ **Indian Uprising**

Napoleon I (Napoleon Bonaparte) (1769–1821)
French general and Emperor (1804/15). He entered the military schools at Brienne (1779) and Paris (1784), commanded the artillery at the Siege of Toulon (1793), and was promoted Brigadier-General. In 1796 he married Josephine, widow of the Viscount of Beauharnais, and soon after left for Italy, where he skilfully defeated the Piedmontese and Austrians, and made several gains through the Treaty of Campo Formio (1797). Intending to break British trade by conquering Egypt, he captured Malta (1798), and entered Cairo, defeating the Turks; but after the French fleet was destroyed by Nelson at the Battle of the Nile, he returned to France (1799), having learnt of French reverses in Europe. The coup d'état of 18th Brumaire followed (9 Nov 1799) in which Napoleon assumed power as First Consul, instituting a military dictatorship. He then routed the Austrians at Marengo (1800), made further gains at the Treaty of Luneville (1801), and consolidated French domination by the Concordat (1801) with Rome and the Peace of Amiens with England (1802). Elected consul for life, he crowned himself Emperor in 1804. His administrative, military, educational, and legal reforms (notably the Code Napoléon) made a lasting impact on French society. War with England was renewed, and extended to Russia and Austria. Forced by England's naval victory at **Trafalgar** (1805) to abandon the notion of invasion, he attacked the Austrians and Russians, gaining victories at Ulm and Austerlitz (1805). Prussia was defeated at Jena and Auerstädt (1806), and Russia at Friedland (1807). After the Peace of Tilsit, he became the arbiter of Europe. He then tried to cripple England with the Continental System, ordering the European states under his control to boycott British goods. He sent armies into Portugal and Spain, which resulted in the bitter and ultimately unsuccessful Peninsular War (1808–14). In 1809, wanting an heir, he divorced Josephine, who was childless, and married the Archduchess Marie Louise of Austria, a son being born in 1811. Believing that Russia was planning an alliance with England, he invaded, defeating the Russians at Borodino, before entering Moscow, but he was forced to retreat, his army broken

by hunger and the Russian winter. In 1813 his victories over the allied armies continued at Lützen, Bautzen and Dresden, but he was routed at the Battle of Leipzig, and France was invaded. Forced to abdicate, he was given the sovereignty of Elba (1814). The unpopularity which followed the return of the Bourbons motivated him to return to France in 1815. He regained power for a period known as the Hundred Days, but was defeated by the combination of **Wellington**'s and **Blücher**'s forces at **Waterloo**. He fled to Paris, abdicated, surrendered to the British, and was banished to St Helena, where he died. ▷ **Amiens, Treaty of; Napoleonic Wars; Nelson, Horatio; Peninsular War**

Napoleonic Wars (1800–15)
The continuation of the **French Revolutionary Wars**, fought to preserve French hegemony in Europe. They increasingly became a manifestation of **Napoleon I**'s personal ambitions. The wars began with Napoleon's destruction of the Second Coalition (1800); after a peaceful interlude (1802–3) Britain resumed hostilities, prompting Napoleon to prepare for invasion, and encouraging the formation of a Third Coalition (1805–7). While Britain retained naval superiority (1805), Napoleon established territorial domination, sustained by economic warfare, resulting in the invasions of Spain (1808) and Russia (1812). Gradually the French were overwhelmed by the Fourth Coalition (1813–14); the Hundred Days' epilogue ended with the Battle of **Waterloo** (1815). ▷ **Copenhagen, Battle of; Grand Alliance, War of the; Paris, Treaties of; Peninsular Wars; Trafalgar, Battle of**

Naseby, Battle of (14 June 1645)
A major conflict of the **English Civil Wars** in Northamptonshire. The royalist forces of **Charles I**, outnumbered by two to one, were defeated by parliament's **New Model Army** led by **Fairfax**, with **Cromwell** commanding the cavalry. Royalist cavalry, led by Prince **Rupert**, left the main battle, fatally weakening Charles's forces.

Nash, Sir Walter (1882–1968)
English-born New Zealand politician. Nash went to New Zealand in 1909. From 1919 to 1960 he served on the national executive of the New Zealand Labour Party, encouraging the adoption of a moderate reform programme in the Christian socialist tradition. A member of parliament from 1929, he held numerous ministerial appointments from 1935 onwards and in **World War II** was

Deputy Prime Minister to Peter Fraser, although from 1942 to 1944 he headed a special mission to the USA. He was Prime Minister (1957–60), retiring from the party leadership in 1963.

National Front (NF)

A strongly nationalist political party which centres its political programme on opposition to immigration, and calls for the repatriation of ethnic minorities even if they were born in the UK. The party was created in 1960 by the merger of the White Defence League and the National Labour Party, and in its early years was a small neo-Nazi grouping. In the mid- and late 1970s it had some minor impact in elections and its membership grew. It tried to develop a more respectable face and recruited some members from the right of the **Conservative Party** to widen its base beyond hardline neo-fascists. Its political appeal declined with the election of a Conservative government in 1979.

NATO (North Atlantic Treaty Organization)

An organization established by a treaty signed in 1949 by Belgium, Canada, Denmark, France, Iceland, Italy, Luxembourg, the Netherlands, Norway, Portugal, the UK and the USA; Greece and Turkey acceded in 1952, West Germany in 1955 and Spain in 1982. NATO is a permanent military alliance established to defend Western Europe against Soviet aggression. The treaty commits the members to treat an armed attack on one of them as an attack on all of them, and for all to assist the country attacked by such actions as are deemed necessary. The alliance forces are based on contributions from the member countries' armed services and operate under a multi-national command. The remit includes the deployment of nuclear, as well as conventional, weapons. Its institutions include a Council, an International Secretariat, the Supreme Headquarters Allied Powers, Europe (SHAPE) and various committees to formulate common policies. In the 1970s and 1980s, NATO policy of a first-strike nuclear attack to fend off a Soviet conventional attack became controversial in Western Europe, where many thought it increased the possibility of nuclear war. In 1966 France under Charles de **Gaulle** withdrew all its forces from NATO command, but it remains a member. After the 1989 changes in E Europe, a NATO summit in London (July 1990) began the process of redefining NATO's military and political goals. ▷ **nuclear weapons**

Navarino Bay, Battle of (1827)

A battle fought when the British and French (with the agreement of the Russians) destroyed the Turkish and Egyptian fleets off south-west Greece. The outcome was an important factor in the achievement of Greek independence from the **Ottoman Empire**, which was formally recognized in 1828.

Navigation Acts (1650–96)

Protective legislation designed to increase England's share of overseas carrying trade. The laws stated that all imports to England had to be in English ships or in those of the country of origin. The laws were frequently contentious in the 18c, adding to the 13 American colonies' sense of grievance against the mother country. These Acts were not repealed until 1849. ▷ **American Revolution**

Nelson, Horatio, Viscount (1758–1805)

British admiral. He joined the navy in 1770, and was sent to the West Indies (1784) to enforce the Navigation Act against the newly independent USA. There he married Frances Nisbet, and in 1787 retired with her to Burnham Thorpe. In 1794 he commanded the naval brigade at the reduction of Bastia and Calvi where he lost the sight of his right eye, and in an action at Santa Cruz had his right arm amputated. In 1798 he followed the French fleet to Egypt, destroying it at the Battle of **Aboukir Bay**. On his return to Naples, he fell in love with Emma, Lady Hamilton, and began a liaison with her which lasted until his death. In 1801 he was made rear-admiral, and led the attack on Copenhagen. Previously created a baron, he then became a viscount, and Commander-in-Chief. In 1805 he gained his greatest victory, against the combined French and Spanish fleet at the Battle of **Trafalgar**. During the battle he was mortally wounded on his flagship, HMS *Victory*. His body was brought home and buried in St Paul's Cathedral, London. ▷ **Hood, Samuel; Napoleonic Wars**

New Model Army

An English army established by Parliament (15 Feb 1645) to strengthen its forces in the first civil war against royalists. The county and regional armies of Essex, Manchester, and Waller were merged into a successful national force. The cavalry and artillery were augmented; the battle tactics of Gustav II Adolf adopted; discipline and pay improved; and religious toleration introduced. ▷ **English Civil Wars; Naseby, Battle of**

New Right

A wide-ranging ideological movement associated with the revival of conservatism in the 1970s and 1980s, particularly in the UK and USA. Its ideas are most prominently connected with classical liberal economic theory from the 19c. It is strongly in favour of state withdrawal from ownership, and intervention in the economy in favour of a free-enterprise system. There is also a strong moral conservatism — an emphasis on respect for authority, combined with a strong expression of patriotism and support for the idea of the family. Politically, the New Right adopts an aggressive style which places weight on pursuing convictions rather than on generating a consensus. In the USA in the 1980s it has been associated with the emergence of Christian fundamentalism.

Nithsdale, William Maxwell, 5th Earl of (1676–1744)

Scottish Jacobite. In 1699 he married Lady Winifred Herbert, the youngest daughter of the Marquis of Powis. A Catholic in 1715, he joined the English **Jacobites** and was taken prisoner at Preston, tried for treason, and sentenced to death. The night before his execution he escaped from the Tower in woman's clothes, through the heroism of his countess. They settled at Rome, where he died.

Non-Cooperation Movement

A nationalist campaign (1919–22) led by M K **Gandhi** and Congress in protest against the **Amritsar Massacre** and the Montagu-Chelmsford Reforms, and to force the British to grant Indian independence. Locally, it took up many issues, and was linked, especially by Gandhi, with the Khilafat Movement. The movement marked M K **Gandhi**'s rise to pre-eminence in the Congress. It involved the boycott of Government institutions and foreign goods, and was abandoned when the protest became violent.

non-violent resistance

The use of non-violent means to resist occupation by a foreign power or other political purposes. It can involve an appeal to wider world opinion, as well as various forms of peaceful political resistance, such as general strikes and **civil disobedience**. Damage to property is not necessarily ruled out. Non-violent resistance is most famously associated with **M K Gandhi**'s resistance to British rule in India, and was popular with the civil rights movements of the 1960s.

Norman Conquest

A fundamental watershed in English political and social history, though some of its consequences are much debated. It not only began the rule of a dynasty of Norman kings (1066–1154), but entailed the virtual replacement of the Anglo-Saxon nobility by **Normans**, Bretons, and Flemings, many of whom retained lands in northern France. Moreover, between 1066 and 1144 England and **Normandy** were normally united under one king-duke, and the result was the formation of a single cross-Channel state. The Angevin conquest of Normandy (1144–5) and takeover of England (1154) ensured that England's fortunes would continue to be linked with France, even after the French annexation of Normandy in 1204. ▷ **Angevins; Domesday Book; Hastings, Battle of; Henry I of England; Hundred Years War; William I, 'the Conqueror'; William II, 'Rufus'**

Normandy

Former duchy and province in north-western France, along the littoral of the English Channel between Brittany and French Flanders; now occupying the regions of Haute-Normandie and Basse-Normandie. A leading state in the **Middle Ages**, **William I, 'the Conqueror'**, as Duke of Normandy, conquered England in 1066. Captured by France in 1204, the ownership of Normandy was disputed between France and England in the **Hundred Years War** until it became part of France in 1449. In 1944 it was the scene of the Allied invasion of occupied France. ▷ **Normandy Campaign**

Normandy Campaign (1944)

A **World War II** campaign which began on **D-Day** (6 June 1944). Allied forces under the command of General **Eisenhower** began the liberation of Western Europe from Germany by landing on the **Normandy** coast between the Orne River and St Marcouf. Artificial harbours were constructed along a strip of beach so that armoured vehicles and heavy guns could be unloaded. Heavy fighting ensued for three weeks, before Allied troops captured

Cherbourg (27 June). Tanks broke through the German defences, and Paris was liberated (25 Aug), followed by the liberation of Brussels (2 Sep), and the crossing of the German frontier (12 Sep).

Normans
By the early 11c, a label (derived from 'Northmen', ie **Vikings**) applied to all the people inhabiting **Normandy**, a duchy (and later province) in northern France, though probably only a small element was actually of Scandinavian descent. During the second half of the 11c and the first decade of the 12c, their achievements, especially as conquerors, were remarkable. They completed the conquest and aristocratic colonization of England and a large part of Wales, established a kingdom in southern Italy and Sicily, and founded the Norman principality of Antioch. They also fought against the Muslims in Spain and settled peacefully in Scotland.

North, Frederick, 8th Lord North (1732–92)
English politician. He became a Lord of the Treasury (1759) and Chancellor of the Exchequer (1767), and as Prime Minister (1770–82) brought **George III** a period of political stability. He was widely criticized both for failing to avert the **Declaration of Independence** by the North American colonies (1776) and for failing to defeat them in the subsequent war (1776–83). He annoyed the King by resigning in 1782, then formed a coalition with his former Whig opponent, **Fox** (1783), but it did not survive royal hostility. After this coalition was dismissed (1783), he remained an opposition politician until his death. ▷ **American Revolution**

North African Campaign (1940–3)
A campaign fought during **World War II** between Allied and Axis troops. After an initial Italian invasion of Egypt, Italian forces were driven back deep into Libya, and Rommel was sent to North Africa with the specially trained Afrika Corps to stem a further Italian retreat. The British were driven back to the Egyptian border, though they defended Tobruk. They counter-attacked late in 1941, and fighting continued the following year, with Rommel once more gaining the initiative. In Oct, British troops under **Montgomery** defeated Rommel at the Battle of **El Alamein**, and drove the German troops W once more. In Feb 1943, the Germans attacked US troops in Tunisia, were driven back, and finally

250 000 Axis troops, half of them German, were caught in a pincer movement by Allied forces advancing from the east and west.
▷ **Axis Powers**

Northumbria
The largest kingdom of the Anglo-Saxon heptarchy. In the 7c it established a broad dominance in Britain both north and south of the Humber, while in the 8c the Northumbrian monasteries gained a European-wide reputation for sanctity and learning. The kingdom came to an end in 876, and by the 12c Northumbria was equivalent to the earldom or county of Northumberland.
▷ **Anglo-Saxons**

Notting Hill Riots (1958)
A series of violent demonstrations in north-west London. Directed at non-white immigrants living there, they brought immigration into the British political arena for the first time.

Nuclear Non-Proliferation Treaty (NPT)
A treaty signed in 1968 by the USA, the USSR, the UK and an open-ended list of over 100 other countries. It sought to limit the spread of **nuclear weapons**, those possessing them agreeing not to transfer the capability to produce them, and those not possessing them agreeing not to acquire the capability. Recent reductions in US and Russian nuclear stockpiles appear to have reinforced the Treaty, but a number of other states are thought to be close to producing their own nuclear arms.

nuclear weapons
Bomb, missile or other weapon of mass destruction deriving its destructive force from the energy released during nuclear fission or nuclear fusion. According to their size and the means of delivery, they may be classified as tactical short-range weapons (for use on the battlefield), theatre medium-range weapons (for use against deep military targets), or strategic long-range weapons (for use against enemy cities and command centres). ▷ **CND; Nuclear Non-Proliferation Treaty**

Nuremberg Trials
Proceedings held by the Allies at Nuremberg after **World War II** to try Nazi war criminals, following a decision made in 1943. An

International Military Tribunal was set up in Aug 1945, and sat from Nov 1945 until Oct 1946. Twenty-one Nazis were tried in person, including Goering and Ribbentrop (who were sentenced to death), and Hess (who was given life imprisonment).

O

Oastler, Richard (1789–1861)

English social reformer. A Tory humanitarian, he attacked the employment of children in factories and advocated a shorter working day, in campaigns resulting in the Factory Act (1833) and Ten Hours Act (1847). He was a strong opponent of **laissez-faire** political economy, and campaigned against the implementation of the Poor Law Amendment Act (1834), which he believed reduced paupers to the status of slaves. His *Fleet Papers*, attacking the Poor Law and criticizing the government, were edited from prison, where he had been placed for debts owing to his former employer. ▷ **Poor Laws; Tories**

O'Brien, William (1852–1928)

Irish journalist and nationalist. He became editor of the weekly *United Ireland*, and sat in parliament as a Nationalist (1883–95). Several times prosecuted, and imprisoned for two years, he later returned to parliament (1900–18), and founded the United Irish League (1898) and the All-for-Ireland League (1910).

O'Brien, William Smith (1803–64)

Irish nationalist. He entered parliament in 1826, joining Daniel **O'Connell**'s Repeal Association (1843), but withdrew in 1846 after disputes over the use of force. Leader of the **Young Ireland** movement, he organized an unsuccessful rebellion in 1848, and was given a death sentence, commuted to transportation for life. In 1854 he was released, on condition of his not returning to Ireland, and in 1856 he received a free pardon.

O'Connell, Daniel (1775–1847)

Irish political leader. He became a lawyer, and in 1823 formed the Catholic Association, which successfully fought elections against the landlords. His election as MP for County Clare precipitated a crisis in **Wellington**'s government, which eventually granted **Catholic Emancipation** in 1829, enabling him to take his seat in the Commons. In 1840 he founded the Repeal Association, and agitation to end the union with Britain increased. In 1844 he was imprisoned for 14 weeks on a charge of sedition. In conflict with the **Young Ireland** movement (1846), and failing in health, 'the Liberator' left Ireland in 1847, and died in Genoa.

O'Connor, Feargus Edward (1794–1855)
Irish Chartist leader. He studied at Dublin, became a lawyer, and entered parliament in 1832. Estranged from **O'Connell**, he devoted himself to the cause of the working classes in England. His Leeds *Northern Star* (1837) became the most influential Chartist newspaper. He attempted, without great success, to unify the Chartist movement via the National Charter Association (1840), and presented himself as leader of the Chartist cause. Elected MP for Nottingham in 1847, in 1852 he became insane. ▷ **Chartists**

Offa (d.796)
King of Mercia (757/96). He was the greatest Anglo-Saxon ruler in the 8c, treated as an equal by Charlemagne. Styling himself 'King of the English', he asserted his authority over all the kingdoms south of the Humber, and treated their rulers as subordinate provincial governors. He was responsible for constructing Offa's Dyke, and established a new currency based on the silver penny which, with numerous changes of design, remained the standard coin of England for many centuries. His reign represents an important but flawed attempt to unify England, with the Mercian supremacy collapsing soon after his death. ▷ **Anglo-Saxons; Mercia**

Oldcastle, Sir John (c.1378–1417)
English Lollard leader and knight. After serving in the Scottish and Welsh wars, and becoming an intimate of **Henry V** when Prince of Wales, he was tried and convicted on charges of heresy in 1413. He escaped from the Tower, and conspired with other **Lollards** to capture Henry V at Eltham Palace, Kent, and take control of London. The rising was abortive. Oldcastle remained free until caught near Welshpool in 1417, and was hanged and burnt. Shakespeare's character Falstaff is based partly on him.

Omdurman, Battle of (1898)
An engagement outside Khartoum, across the Nile, which confirmed the British reconquest of the Sudan. The British campaign

under **Kitchener** had been authorized in 1895, and instituted with powerful Anglo-Egyptian forces in 1896. The overwhelming defeat of the massed forces of the Khalifa (the successor of the Mahdi), with many casualties, illustrated the power of modern weapons. ▷ **Fashoda Incident**

O'Neill (of the Maine), Terence (Marne), Baron (1914–90)

Ulster politician. He served in the Irish Guards during **World War II**. A member of the Northern Ireland parliament (1946–70), he held junior posts before becoming Minister for Home Affairs (1956), Finance (1956–63), and then Prime Minister (1963–9). A supporter of closer cross-border links with the Irish Republic, he angered many Unionists. Following a general election in 1969, dissension in the Unionist Party increased, and he resigned the premiership soon after. Made a life peer in 1970, he continued to speak out on Northern Ireland issues. ▷ **Democratic Unionist Party**

Opium Wars

Two wars (1839–42 and 1856–60) between Britain and China, fought over the question of commercial rights in China, specifically relating to the opium trade. The British were victorious on each occasion, and gained increased access to China through the Treaties of **Nanjing** (Nanking) (1842) and **Tianjin** (Tientsin) (1858). ▷ **Arrow War; treaty ports**

Orange Order

An association that developed from the Orange Society, which had been formed in 1795 to counteract growing Catholic influence in Ireland and 'to maintain the laws and peace of the country and the Protestant constitution'. The name was taken from the Protestant Dutch dynasty represented by **William III**. Organized in 'Lodges', it provided the backbone of resistance to **Home Rule** proposals from the mid-1880s, and has operated as organized Protestantism in Northern Ireland since partition.

Oregon Boundary Dispute

A disagreement between the British and US governments over the frontier between respective possessions on the west coast of North America. Britain claimed the north-west basin of the Columbia River to its mouth at Fort Vancouver, while the USA sought a boundary farther north. The Oregon Treaty (1846) settled the US–Canadian boundary on the 49th parallel, dipping south at Juan de Fuca Strait to maintain British claims to Vancouver Island. Residual disputes over the disposition of the Gulf/San Juan Islands in the strait were settled by arbitration in 1872.

Orléans, Siege of (Oct 1428–May 1429)

The English blockade of the main stronghold still loyal to Charles VII of France, during the **Hundred Years War**. Orléans was relieved by troops inspired by **Joan of Arc**. Anglo-Burgundian forces, who already controlled most of northern France, were prevented from pressing south; but the event was less of a turning point in the war than the Franco-Burgundian rapprochement of 1435.

Ormonde, James Butler, 1st Duke of (1610–88)

Anglo-Irish general. In the **English Civil Wars** he commanded the royalist army in Ireland (1641–50), and was compelled to retire to France. At the **Restoration** he was rewarded by the ducal title of Ormonde, and twice became Lord-Lieutenant of Ireland.

Osman I (1259–1326)

Founder of the **Ottoman Empire**. Born in Bithynia, the son of a border chief, he founded a small Turkish state in Asia Minor called Osmanli (or Ottoman). On the overthrow of the Seljuk sultanate of Iconium in 1299 by the Mongols, he gradually subdued a great part of Asia Minor.

Ottawa Conferences (1894, 1932)

British **Imperial Conferences**. The main topic in 1894 was the development of communications between the individual units of the **British Empire**. Underlying the conference was a realization that the nature of imperial relationships had altered and that a new way of dealing with them had to be found. A major evolution was evident by 1932 in the agreements at the Ottawa economic conference held between Britain and its dominions at the height of the world depression. The conference negotiated a limited amount of imperial preference following the adoption of a new protective tariff by the British government earlier that year.

Ottoman Empire

A Muslim empire founded c.1300 by Sultan **Osman I**, and originating in Asia Minor. Ottoman forces entered Europe in 1345, conquered Constantinople in 1453, and by 1520 controlled most of south-eastern Europe, including part of Hungary, the Middle East, and North Africa. Following the 'golden age' of Suleyman I, 'the Magnificent', the empire began a protracted decline. During the 19c and early 20c, Ottoman power was eroded by the ambitions of Russia and Austria in south-east Europe, the ambitions of France, Britain, and Italy in North Africa, the emergence of the Balkan nations, and internal loss of authority. It joined the Central Powers in 1914, and collapsed with their defeat in 1918.

Outram, James (1803–63)

British general and political officer. He joined the Bombay native infantry in 1819, and became political agent in Gujarat (1835–8). He fought in the first of the **Afghan Wars** (1838–42), and took part in the relief of Lucknow (1857–8). Known as 'the Bayard of India' because of his reputation for chivalry, he was made a baronet in 1858. ▷ **Indian Uprising**

Owen, David (Anthony Llewellyn) (1938–   )

English politician. He trained in medicine, then became an MP (1966) and Under-Secretary to the Navy (1968). He was Secretary for Health (1974–6) and Foreign Secretary (1977–9). One of the so-called 'Gang of Four' who formed the **Social Democratic Party** (SDP) in 1981, he succeeded Roy **Jenkins** as its leader in 1983. Following the Alliance's disappointing result in the 1987 general election, he opposed Liberal leader David **Steel** over the question of the merger of the two parties. In 1988, after the SDP voted to accept merger, Owen led the smaller section of the party to a brief independent existence. He retired from parliament in 1992 and went on to become, along with Cyrus Vance, a peace-broker in the troubles that erupted after the disintegration of Yugoslavia.

Oxford, Provisions of (1258)

A baronial programme imposing constitutional limitations on the English crown. **Henry III** of England had to share power with a permanent council of barons, parliaments meeting three times a year, and independent executive officers (chancellor, justiciar, treasurer). In 1261 the Pope absolved Henry from his oath to observe the Provisions. ▷ **Barons Wars**

P

Paardeberg, Battle of (1900)
The first major British victory of the second Boer War, following the relief of the Siege of **Kimberley**. The Boers abandoned the position they had held at **Magersfontein**, and moved east to defend Bloemfontein. Their defeat at Paardeberg opened the way for the full-scale attack on the Orange Free State and the Transvaal, and the taking of the Boer cities. ▷ **Boer Wars**

Paine, Thomas (1737–1809)
British-American political writer. In 1774 he sailed for Philadelphia, where his pamphlet *Common Sense* (1776) argued for complete independence from Britain. He served with the American Army, and was made Secretary to the Committee of Foreign Affairs. In 1787 he returned to England, where he wrote *The Rights of Man* (1791–2) in support of the French Revolution. Indicted for treason, he fled to Paris in 1792, where he was elected a Deputy to the National Convention, but imprisoned for his proposal to offer the King asylum in the USA. At this time (1794–5) he wrote *The Age of Reason*, in favour of deism. Released in 1796, he returned to the USA in 1802.

Paisley, Rev Ian (Richard Kyle) (1926–)
Northern Irish militant Protestant clergyman and politician. An ordained minister since 1946, he formed his own Church (the Free Presbyterian Church of Ulster) in 1951, and from the 1960s became deeply involved in Ulster politics. He founded the Protestant **Democratic Unionist Party** and stood as its MP for four years until 1974, since when he has been the Democratic Unionist MP for North Antrim. He has been a member of the European Parliament since 1979. A rousing orator, he is strongly in favour of maintaining the Union with Britain, and fiercely opposed to the **IRA**, Roman Catholicism, and the unification of Ireland.

Palmerston (of Palmerston), Henry John Temple, 3rd Viscount (1784–1865)
English politician. He became a Tory MP in 1807, served as Secretary of War (1809–28), joined the **Whigs** (1830), and was three times Foreign Secretary (1830–4, 1835–41 and 1846–51). His brusque speech, assertive manner, and robust defences of what he considered to be British interests abroad made him a controversial figure and secured him the name of 'Firebrand Palmerston'. He was unpopular with Queen **Victoria** and many of his political colleagues but cultivated public opinion. Home Secretary in **Aberdeen**'s coalition (1852), he became Premier in 1855, when he vigorously prosecuted the **Crimean War** with Russia. He remained in office until 1858, and was Prime Minister again in 1859–65.
▷ **Liberal Party; Tories; Wellington, Duke of**

Pankhurst, Emmeline (1858–1928)
English suffragette. In 1905 she organized the Women's Social and Political Union, and fought for women's suffrage by violent means, on several occasions being arrested and going on hunger strike. After the outbreak of **World War I**, she worked instead for the industrial mobilization of women. Of her daughters and fellow workers, Dame Christabel turned later to preaching Christ's Second Coming; and Sylvia diverged to pacificism, internationalism, and Labour politics. ▷ **suffragettes**

Paris, Treaties of (1814–15)
Successive peace settlements involving France and the victorious coalition of Britain, Austria, Prussia, Russia, Sweden and Portugal, restoring the Bourbon monarchy to France in place of the Napoleonic Empire, before and after the Hundred Days (1815). In 1815 a large indemnity and army of occupation replaced the generous terms of 1814. ▷ **Napoleonic Wars**

Paris, Treaty of (1763)
The peace settlement ending the **Seven Years War** (1756–63), signed by Britain, France and Spain. Spain surrendered Florida to the British, but received the Louisiana Territory and New Orleans from France, and Havana and Manila from Britain. In exchange for minor concessions, France ceded Canada, America east of the Mississippi, Cape Breton and the St Lawrence islands, Dominica, Tobago, the Grenadines, and Senegal to Britain. In

the short term, Britain was isolated by the French determination for revenge, but the final consequence was British colonial supremacy.

Paris, Treaty of (30 Mar 1856)

The treaty bringing to an end the **Crimean War** and enshrining the defeat of Russia by Britain and France. Russia had to cede southern Bessarabia to Moldavia, had to give up its virtual protectorate over Moldavia and Wallachia, and had to accept the neutrality of the Black Sea, including the dismantling of its own coastal fortresses. The **Ottoman Empire** was admitted to the so-called Concert of European Powers, but did not keep its promise to respect the rights of its subjects. Russia was driven back in on itself and under Alexander II embarked upon its first serious programme of domestic reform.

Paris Peace Conference (1946–7)

Meetings of the five members of the Council of Foreign Ministers, representing the main **World War II** Allies (USA, Russia, UK, France and China), and delegates from 16 other nations involved against the **Axis Powers**. It drew up peace treaties with Bulgaria, Finland, Hungary, Romania and Italy. Despite repeated divisions, agreement was finally reached and the treaties signed in the spring of 1947.

Parnell, Charles Stewart (1846–91)

Irish politician. He studied at Cambridge, and in 1875 became an MP, supporting **Home Rule**, and gaining great popularity in Ireland by his audacity in the use of obstructive parliamentary tactics. In 1878 he was elected President of the Irish National Land League, and in 1886 allied with the Liberals in support of **Gladstone**'s **Home Rule** Bill. He remained an influential figure until 1890, when he was cited as co-respondent in a divorce case, and was forced to retire as leader of the Irish nationalists. ▷ **Liberal Party**

Parr, Catherine (1512–48)

Queen of England (1543/7). The daughter of Sir Thomas Parr of Kendal, she married first Edward Borough, then Lord Latimer, before becoming Queen of England (1543), as the sixth wife of **Henry VIII**. A learned, tolerant and tactful woman, she persuaded

Henry to restore the succession to his daughters, and showed her stepchildren much kindness. Very soon after Henry's death (1547), she married a former suitor, Lord Thomas Seymour of Sudeley, and died in childbirth the following year.

Passchendaele, Battle of (31 July–10 Nov 1917)
The third battle of Ypres during **World War I**; a British offensive which was continued despite no hope of a breakthrough to the Belgian ports, the original objective. It was notable for appallingly muddy conditions, minimal gains, and British casualties of at least 300 000. In the final action, Canadians captured the village of Passchendaele, six miles north-east of Ypres.

Paul III (Alessandro Farnese) (1468–1549)
Italian Pope (1534/49). The first of the popes of the Counter-Reformation, in 1538 he issued the bull of excommunication and deposition against **Henry VIII** of England, and also the bull instituting the Order of the Jesuits in 1540. He also summoned the Council of Trent (1545).

Peasants Revolt (June 1381)
An English popular rising, among townsmen as well as peasants, based in Essex, Kent, and London, with associated insurrections elsewhere. It was precipitated by the three oppressive poll taxes of 1377–81, the underlying causes being misgovernment, the desire for personal freedom, and an assortment of local grievances. It was quickly suppressed.

Peel, Sir Robert (1788–1850)
English politician. He became a Tory MP in 1809. He was made Secretary for Ireland (1812–18), where he displayed a strong anti-Catholic spirit, and was fiercely attacked by **O'Connell**, earning the nickname 'Orange Peel'. As Home Secretary (1822–7 and 1828–30), he carried through the **Catholic Emancipation** Act (1829) and reorganized the London police force ('Peelers' or 'Bobbies'). As Prime Minister (1834–5 and 1841–6), his second ministry concentrated upon economic reforms, but his decision to phase out agricultural protection by repealing the **Corn Laws** (1846) split his party and precipitated his resignation. He remained in parliament as leader of the 'Peelites' (1846–50). ▷ **Tories; Whigs**

Peel Commission

The report of this commission (issued 7 July 1937) is famous (or notorious) for being the first formal recommendation of the partition of Palestine into separate states, Arab and Jewish, with the retention by the British of a corridor to the Mediterranean. Serious rioting by the Arabs, directed against the Jews, had led Stanley **Baldwin**, the British Prime Minister, to appoint a royal commission to enquire into the working of the British mandate under the leadership of Earl Peel. Despite the commission's evident recognition that there was an intractable problem in Palestine (a situation which had been foreseen by Henry King and Charles Crane nearly two decades before) and their earnest endeavour to find a solution of some sort, the commission's recommendations found favour with only some Arabs and Zionists, and was rejected by the British House of Lords.

Pelham, Henry (c.1695–1754)

English politician. He became a Whig MP in 1717 and regularly supported **Walpole** and **Townshend**, his relatives by marriage. His political advance was steady; he became Lord of the Treasury (1721–4), Secretary for War (1724–30) and Paymaster-General (1730–42). After Walpole's fall, he refused to serve under Wilmington, but replaced him as First Lord of Treasury in Aug 1743, a post he held until his death, acting also as Chancellor of the Exchequer. He admitted several **Tories** to his ministry (1744), which became colloquially known as the 'Broad Bottom', and defeated a challenge to his leadership by Carteret and the Prince of Wales (1746). His ministry presided over the peace negotiations ending the War of the Austrian Succession (1748). Buttressed by a secure parliamentary majority largely achieved through deployment of patronage considered by his opponents as corrupt, Pelham provided **George II** with secure, if unimaginative, government until his death in London while still in office. ▷ **Seven Years War**

Pelham, Thomas Pelham-Holles, 1st Duke of Newcastle (1693–1768)

English politician. He became Earl of Clare in 1714 and Duke of Newcastle in 1715. A Whig and a supporter of **Walpole**, in 1724 he became Secretary of State, and held the office for 30 years. He succeeded his brother, Henry **Pelham** as Premier (1754–6), and was extremely influential during the reigns of **George I** and **II**. In 1757 he was in coalition with **Pitt the Elder** during the **Seven Years War**, but resigned in 1762 after hostility from the new King, **George III**. ▷ **Whigs**

Penal Laws

Collectively, statutes passed in the 16–17c against the practice of Roman Catholicism in Britain and Ireland, when Catholic nations were perceived as a threat. They prevented Catholics from voting and holding public office. Fines and imprisonment were prescribed for participation in Catholic services, while officiating priests could be executed. The laws were repealed in stages, from the late 18c, the last not until 1926. ▷ **Catholic Emancipation**

penal settlements

Places of secondary punishment in Australia where convicts found guilty of serious offences were sent; also used for colonial criminals sentenced to **transportation**, and (after 1842) for British convicts transported for life. About 10 per cent of the 162 000 convicts transported to Australia spent some time in these settlements, which were mainly at Newcastle (1801–24), Port Macquarie (1821–30), Moreton Bay (1824–39), Macquarie Harbour (1822–33), Port Arthur (after 1830) and Norfolk Island (after 1825). Life in these settlements varied from hard to savage, with hard labour and frequent and severe floggings; the last three named had deservedly fearsome reputations.

Penda (c.575–655)

King of Mercia (c.632/55). He established mastery over the English Midlands, and was frequently at war with the kings of **Northumbria**. His forces defeated and killed Edwin, King of Northumbria, at Hatfield, Yorkshire (633), and also Edwin's successor, Oswald, when he invaded Penda's territories (642). Penda was himself slain in battle near Leeds while campaigning against Oswald's successor, Oswiu. ▷ **Anglo-Saxons**

Peniakoff, Vladimir ('Popski') (1897–1951)

Belgian soldier and author. Born in Belgium of Russian parentage, he was educated in England. He joined the British army and from 1940 to 1942 served with the Long Range Desert Group and the Libyan Arab Force. In Oct 1942, with the sanction of the army, he formed his own force, Popski's Private Army, which carried out spectacular raids behind the German lines. He rose to the rank of lieutenant-colonel and was decorated for bravery by Britain, France and Belgium.

Peninsular War (1808–14)

The prolonged struggle for the Iberian Peninsula between the occupying French and a British army under **Wellington** (formerly Wellesley), supported by Portuguese and Spanish forces. Known in Spain as the 'War of Independence' and to Napoleonic France as 'the Spanish ulcer', it started as a Spanish revolt against the imposition of **Napoleon I**'s brother Joseph Bonaparte as King of Spain, but developed into a bitter conflict, as British troops repulsed Masséna's Lisbon offensive (1810–11) and advanced from their base behind the Torres Vedras to liberate Spain. Following Napoleon's Moscow campaign (1812), French resources were over-extended, enabling Wellington's army to invade southwest France (1813–14). ▷ **Napoleonic Wars**

Penn, William (1644–1718)

English Quaker leader and founder of Pennsylvania. Expelled from Oxford for his Puritan leanings, he joined the Quakers in 1666, was imprisoned for his writings (1668), and while in the Tower of London wrote the most popular of his books, *No Cross, no Crown*. In 1681 he obtained a grant of land in North America, which was called Pennsylvania in honour of his father. In 1682 he was granted land that later became Delaware. He referred to Pennsylvania as a 'Holy Experiment', where religious and political freedom could flourish.

Pequot War (1637)

Colonial North American War between English settlers and the Pequot tribe of Connecticut. After the Pequots murdered an English trader, the settlers retaliated with the aid of their allies, the Mohegans and the Narrangansetts. They attacked the main Pequot town on the Mystic River and slaughtered hundreds of men, women and children, effectively destroying the tribe.

Perceval, Spencer (1762–1812)

English politician. He became an MP in 1796 and went on to become Solicitor-General (1801), Attorney-General (1802) and

Chancellor of the Exchequer (1807). He was Premier from 1809 until 1812, when he was shot dead while entering the lobby of the House of Commons by a bankrupt Liverpool broker, John Bellingham. An efficient administrator, he had succeeded in establishing a firm Tory government. ▷ **Tories**

Percy

A noble family from the north of England, whose founder, William de Percy (c.1030–96), went to England with **William I, 'the Conqueror'**. The best-known member of the family was Henry (1364–1403), the famous 'Hotspur', who fell fighting against **Henry IV** at Shrewsbury. His father, who had helped Henry of Lancaster to the throne, was dissatisfied with the King's gratitude, and plotted the insurrection with his son.

Peterloo Massacre (1819)

The name given to the forcible breakup of a mass meeting about parliamentary reform held at St Peter's Fields, Manchester. The Manchester Yeomanry charged into the crowd, killing 11 people. The incident strengthened the campaign for reform. 'Peterloo' was a sardonic pun on the **Waterloo** victory of 1815. ▷ **Reform Acts**

Petition of Right

Legal mechanism for asserting a right or appealing against the English monarch. The most famous use of the petition in English history was that of 1628, in which Parliament complained to Charles I of a series of misdemeanours against the law. ▷ **Coke, Sir Edward**

Philby, Kim (Harold Adrian Russell) (1912–88)

British double agent. He was educated at Cambridge, where, like **Burgess**, **Maclean** and **Blunt**, he became a communist. Already recruited as a Soviet agent, he was employed by the British Secret Intelligence Service (MI6), from 1944 to 1946 as head of anti-communist counter-espionage. He was First Secretary of the British Embassy in Washington, working in liaison with the CIA (1949–51), and from 1956 worked in Beirut as a journalist. In 1963 he disappeared to the USSR, where he was granted citizenship.

Philip II (1527–98)

King of Spain (1556/98) and (as Philip I) King of Portugal (1580/98). He was the only son of Emperor Charles V and Isabella of Portugal. Following the death of his first wife, Maria of Portugal, in childbirth (1545), he married **Mary I** (1554), becoming joint sovereign of England. Before Mary's death (1558) he had inherited the Habsburg possessions in Italy, the Netherlands, Spain, and the New World. To seal the end of Valois–Habsburg conflict, he married Elizabeth of France (1559), who bore him two daughters. His brief fourth marriage to his cousin, Anna of Austria (1570), produced another son, the future Philip III of Spain. As the champion of the Counter-Reformation, he tried to destroy infidels and heretics alike. He sought to crush Protestantism, first in the Low Countries (from 1568), then in England and France. The destruction of the **Armada** (1588) and the continuing revolt of the Netherlands, along with domestic economic problems and internal unrest, suggest a reign marked by failure. However, among his political achievements were the curbing of Ottoman seapower after the Battle of Lepanto (1571) and the conquest of Portugal (1580).

Phoenix Park Murders (6 May 1882)

The murder in Dublin of the recently appointed Chief Secretary for Ireland, Lord Frederick Cavendish, brother of Spencer Compton **Cavendish**, 8th Duke of Devonshire, and his Under-Secretary, Thomas Henry Burke, by a terrorist nationalist group called 'The Invincibles'. More murders followed during the summer. The British government responded with a fierce Coercion Act, which permitted trials for treason and murder to take place before a judicial tribunal and without a jury, and gave police extensive additional search powers. Five of the Phoenix Park murderers were arrested and hanged.

Picts

A general term coined by the Romans in the 3c for their barbarian enemies in Britain north of the **Antonine Wall**, and then used to describe the subjects of kings ruling north and south of the East Grampians. The name derives from the local custom of body tattooing. They disappear from history soon after being united with the Scots under Kenneth I. Traces of their language and art (notably the enigmatic Pictish symbol stones) survive.

Pilgrimage of Grace (Oct 1536–Jan 1537)
A major Tudor rebellion in England, a series of armed demonstrations in six northern counties. It was directed against the policies and ministers of **Henry VIII**, and combined upper-class and popular discontent over religious and secular issues, especially the Dissolution of the Monasteries. It was led by Lord Thomas Darcy, Robert Aske, and 'pilgrims' carrying banners of the Five Wounds of Christ. Darcy and Aske were subsequently executed for treason.

Pilgrim Fathers
The English religious dissenters who established Plymouth Colony in America in 1620, after crossing the Atlantic on the *Mayflower*. The men, women and children included Puritan separatists and non-separatists. Before disembarking the adult males aboard signed the **Mayflower Compact**.

Pinkie, Battle of (10 Sep 1547)
A battle fought between the English and the Scots at Musselburgh, east of Edinburgh. The English forces under Protector Somerset were victorious, but the aim of the war, of 'rough wooing' (to secure **Mary, Queen of Scots** as a bride for **Edward VI**) was frustrated. Mary and Scotland formed an alliance with the French; and England was forced to evacuate by the Treaty of Boulogne (1550).

Pitt, William, 1st Earl of Chatham, 'the Elder' (1708–78)
English politician and orator. He joined the army (1731) and then entered parliament for the family borough, Old Sarum (1735). He led the young 'Patriot' **Whigs**, and in 1756 became nominally Secretary of State, but virtually Premier. The enmity of **George II** led him to resign in 1757, but public demand caused his recall. Again compelled to resign when his cabinet refused to declare war with Spain (1761), he vigorously attacked the peace terms of the Treaty of Paris (1763) as too generous to France. He formed a new ministry in 1766, but ill health contributed to his resignation in 1768. He died in the House of Lords. His eldest son, John, 2nd Earl of Chatham (1756–1835), commanded the luckless Walcheren Expedition (1809). ▷ **Pitt, William, 'the Younger'; Seven Years War**

Pitt, William, 'the Younger' (1759–1806)

English politician. The second son of William **Pitt**, 'the Elder', he studied law, but then became an MP (1781), his first post being Chancellor of the Exchequer under **Shelburne** (1782). He became First Lord of the Treasury (1783), and was confirmed as Prime Minister at the election of 1784. During his long first ministry (1783–1801), he carried through important administrative and financial reforms, his policy being influenced by the political economy of Adam Smith. He negotiated coalitions against France (1793 and 1798), but these had little success. After the Irish rebellion of 1798, he proposed a legislative union which would be followed by Catholic emancipation. The union was effected in 1800, but Pitt resigned office in 1801 rather than contest **George III**'s hostility to emancipation. He resumed office in 1804. He drank very heavily, and this contributed to his early death while still in office. ▷ **Napoleonic Wars**

Plaid Cymru

The Welsh National Party, founded in 1925, with the aim of achieving independence for Wales. It stands for election throughout Wales, but finds support mainly in the north of the country. It had one MP following the 1987 general election, and has never had more than three.

Plantagenet Dynasty

The name given by historians to the royal dynasty in England from **Henry II** to **Richard II** (1154–1399), then continued by two rival houses of younger lines, Lancaster and York, until 1485. The dynasty was so called because, allegedly, Henry II's father Geoffrey of Anjou, sported a sprig of broom (Old French, *plante genêt*) in his cap. ▷ **Angevins; Edward I; Edward II; Edward III; Henry III; John; Lancaster, House of; Richard I; York, House of**

Plantation of Ireland

The colonization and conquest of Ireland, begun in 1556 and continued to 1660; at first mainly English, but Scottish settlers came to Ulster (1608–11). The policy led to rebellions by the native Irish and Anglo-Irish aristocracy (1563–9, 1580–3, 1598–1603 and 1641) and the eventual conquest of Ireland under **Cromwell**, in which possibly two-thirds of the Irish died.

Plassey, Battle of (1757)
The decisive victory of Robert **Clive of Plassey** over **Siraj ud-Daula**, Nawab of Bengal, India. Clive's success was aided by the treachery of the Nawab's general, Mir Jafar, whom the British subsequently placed on the throne. The victory was an important step in the British acquisition of Bengal. ▷ **East India Company, British**

Poitiers, Battle of (19 Sep 1356)
A battle between England and France during the **Hundred Years War**. The English forces, under **Edward the Black Prince** (son of **Edward III**), were victorious and King John II of France was captured. The battle had important consequences, the French King agreeing to return all possessions in France which had been held by **Henry II** of England. When the French nobility resisted these terms, Edward III invaded France and laid siege to Paris. The Treaty of Bretigny (1360), which ceded much territory in France to Edward III together with a large ransom for King John, represented one of the high-water marks of English success during the war.

Pole, Reginald (1500–58)
English Roman Catholic churchman and Archbishop of Canterbury. He received several Church posts, and was at first high in **Henry VIII**'s favour; but after opposing the King on divorce, he left for Italy, and lost all his preferments. In 1536 the Pope made him a cardinal, and in 1554, in the reign of the Catholic Queen **Mary I**, he returned to England as papal legate. He became one of her most powerful advisers, returned the country to Rome, and became Archbishop of Canterbury. ▷ **Reformation** (England)

Pollock, Sir George (1786–1872)
English soldier. Entering the British **East India Company**'s army in 1803, he was engaged at the siege of Bhartpur (1805) and in other operations. Pollock saw service in the Nepal (Gurkha) campaigns of 1814–16, and was promoted colonel in the first Burmese War (1824–6). In 1838 he was made major-general. After the massacre of General **Elphinstone** in Afghanistan, the Indian government sent him to the relief of Sir Robert Sale in Jelalabad. In Apr 1842 he forced his way through the Khyber Pass and reached Sale, pushed on to Kabul, defeated the Afghan army,

and recovered 135 British prisoners. He conducted the united armies back to India, and was rewarded with a political appointment at Lucknow. He returned to England in 1846, was Director of the East India Company from 1854 to 1856 and was created a field marshal in 1870.

Poor Laws

Legislation originally formulated in 1598 and 1601, whereby relief of poverty was the responsibility of individual parishes under the supervision of Justices of the Peace and the administration of Overseers. Funds were provided by local property rates. As the population grew and rates rose at the end of the 18c, the Poor Laws were increasingly criticized. The Poor Law Amendment Act of 1834 radically changed the system, aiming to make application for poor relief less attractive and instituting a centralized poor law commission. The laws continued to operate in the 20c.

Popish Plot

An apocryphal Jesuit conspiracy in 1678 to assassinate **Charles II** of England, burn London, slaughter Protestants, and place James, Duke of York (later James VII of Scotland and II of England), on the throne. Created by opportunist rogues, Titus Oates and Israel Tonge, it resulted in 35 executions, bills in three parliaments for the exclusion of James from the succession, and the fall of the Danby government. ▷ **James VII and II**

Portland, William Henry Cavendish Bentinck, 3rd Duke of

(1738–1809)

English politician and Prime Minister of Britain. He became an MP in 1761, succeeding to the dukedom in 1762. His first cabinet post was as Lord Chamberlain of the Household under **Rockingham** (1765–6). Along with other aristocratic **Whigs**, he maintained connection with Rockingham which kept him in opposition until 1782, when he was Lord Lieutenant of Ireland. Portland was nominal head of the ministry (Apr–Dec 1783) usually known as the **Fox–North** coalition which **George III** hated and rapidly dismissed. He led the Whigs in opposition to **Pitt 'the Younger'** until 1794 when he agreed to join him in a coalition government to provide order and stability and to meet the challenge of the **French Revolutionary Wars**. Some have seen the Pitt–Portland coalition as the foundation of the modern Tory (later Conservative) Party. He served as Home Secretary (1794–1801) during a period of considerable radical disturbance in England and rebellion in Ireland (1798) and as Lord President of the Council under Addington (1801–3). In Pitt's last ministry he was successively Lord President (1804–5) and Minister without Portfolio (1805–6). He was summoned by **George III** in 1807 to head an administration of Pittites after the fall of the 'Ministry of all the Talents'; by now old, frail and gouty, he was little more than titular leader until his death in office. ▷ **Tories**

Potsdam Conference (17 July–2 Aug 1945)
The last of the great **World War II** strategic conferences, following the **Tehran Conference** and **Yalta Conference**. During this period Winston **Churchill** (and later Clement **Attlee**), Stalin and Truman met to discuss the post-war settlement in Europe. Soviet power in Eastern Europe was recognized *de facto*, and it was agreed that Poland's western frontier should run along the Oder–Neisse Line. The decision was also made to divide Germany into four occupation zones. The political differences which began to emerge between the USA and the USSR could be said to have marked the start of the **Cold War**.

Powell, (John) Enoch (1912–)
English politician. Professor of Greek at Sydney (1937–9), he became a Conservative MP in 1950. He held several junior posts before he became Minister of Health (1960–3). His outspoken attitude on the issues of non-white immigration and racial integration came to national attention in 1968, and as a consequence of this he was dismissed from the shadow cabinet. He was elected as an Ulster Unionist MP in Oct 1974, losing his seat in 1987. ▷ **Conservative Party**

Poynings' Law (1495)
Statutes enacted by the Irish parliament at the direction of Sir Edward Poynings, English Lord Deputy, in 1494, removing its right to meet without the English government's agreement and to pass laws without prior approval. The immediate object was to crush Yorkist support, but over the long term it bolstered English claims to sovereignty and conquest. It was effectively repealed in 1782. ▷ **Roses, Wars of the**

Presbyterianism

The form of government of the Reformed Churches, deriving from the 16c Reformation spearheaded by John Calvin in Geneva and John **Knox** in Scotland. In this biblically based system, the basis of the Church of Scotland, the Church is seen as a body of equal members under the headship of Christ, and hence office is held only by election, providing just representation of the whole congregation. Government is administered at local (eg kirk session), regional (presbytery), and national (General Assembly) levels, and ordained laymen, elders,participate in all courts along with ministers. Through emigration and mission work from Scotland, Ireland and England, Presbyterianism has diffused across world. The World Presbyterian Alliance, formed in 1878, was succeeded in 1970 by the World Alliance of Reformed Churches.
▷ **Reformation** (Scotland)

Preston, Battle of (17–19 Aug 1648)

A series of engagements between the English Parliamentary Army under **Cromwell** and **Lambert** and a numerically superior Scottish force in support of **Charles I** under the Duke of **Hamilton**. Hamilton's inability to concentrate his forces enabled them to be picked off piecemeal. The defeat ended the Second Civil War. Hamilton was captured and executed (1649). ▷ **English Civil Wars**

Pretoria Convention (1881)

The agreement which brought to an end the first Boer War, establishing limited independence for the Boers in the Transvaal. In 1877 the Secretary of State for the Colonies, Lord Carnarvon, and the High Commissioner in South Africa, Sir Bartle Frere, resolved to attempt to reunite the two British colonies and two Boer states in southern Africa. The Transvaal was invaded and annexed by Sir Theophilus Shepstone in an attempt to place its bankrupt finances on a sound footing, but after the British suffered reverses in the Zulu war in 1879, the Boers set about re-establishing their independence. The British were defeated at a number of small engagements in the eastern Transvaal, notably **Majuba Hill** where the British commander, General Sir George Colley, was killed. **Gladstone**'s Cabinet resolved to abandon imperial responsibilities in return for a vague declaration of suzerainty, under which the British would control Boer foreign policy. The interpretation of the extent of such 'suzerainty' beggared relations between British and Boer up to the Boer War of 1899–1902. ▷ **Boer Wars**

Pride, Sir Thomas (d.1658)
English army officer during the **English Civil Wars**. Little is known of his early life. He commanded a regiment at the Battle of **Naseby** (1645), and served in Scotland. When the House of Commons betrayed a disposition to effect a settlement with **Charles I**, he was appointed by the army (1648) to expel its Presbyterian royalist members ('Pride's Purge'). He sat among the King's judges, and signed the death warrant. He was knighted by **Cromwell** in 1656.
▷ **Long Parliament**

Princely States, Indian
Before the colonial period, India was composed of various independent kingdoms, with only the north of the country being dominated by the Mughal Empire. With the slow collapse of this empire, many of its constituent parts broke off to become effectively independent states (such as Hyderabad). With the rise of British colonial rule, many of these newly emergent successor states, as well as others with much longer histories, succeeded in maintaining their independence by entering into treaties with the British. Those which resisted, such as Mysore, were often crushed, but even those which were defeated, such as Gwalior and Holkar, having been deprived of much of their territory, continued as nominally independent rulers. This meant that, although the British dominated the subcontinent by the 19c, they never directly administered more than two-thirds of the country. Under Lord **Dalhousie**'s notorious policy of lapse, some independent states (such as Jhansi) were taken over in the 1850s; others, such as Awadh (Oudh), were too wealthy a prize to be resisted and were annexed without a pretext. Such high-handedness, however, caused resentment which was a factor in the **Indian Uprising** of 1857–8. Subsequently, the British propped up the Indian aristocracy wherever possible, provided they were willing to serve as loyal collaborators. The rewards for this loyalty were sumptuous, giving many rulers fabulous wealth which, combined with a lack of real power, earned them a reputation for decadence. On independence in 1947, the government of Independent India and Pakistan saw the Indian princes as a relic of colonial rule and had little use for them. Some, such as Hyderabad, Kashmir and Junagadh, made a bid for independence, but all were sooner or later annexed

Some ex-rulers went on to enjoy successful political careers but, following the abolition of aristocracy and all its privileges by Indira Gandhi in 1971, the majority sank into obscurity.

Profumo, John (Dennis) (1915–)
English politician. He became a Conservative MP in 1940, and held several government posts before becoming Secretary of State for War in 1960. He resigned in 1963 after admitting that he had been guilty of a grave misdemeanour in deceiving the House of Commons about the nature of his relationship with Christine Keeler, who was at the time also involved with a Soviet diplomat. He later sought anonymity in social and charitable services.
▷ **Conservative Party**

Protectorate
A regime established by the Instrument of Government (1653), the work of army conservatives, England's only written constitution. The Lord Protectors, Oliver **Cromwell** (1653/8) and his son Richard (ruled 1658/9), issued ordinances and controlled the armed forces, subject to the advice of a Council of State and with parliament as legislative partner. It failed to maintain support, and its collapse led to the **Restoration**. ▷ **Commonwealth**

Prynne, William (1600–69)
English Puritan pamphleteer. In 1633 his *Histrio-Mastix: the Players Scourge* appeared, which contained an apparent attack on Queen Henrietta Maria, wife of **Charles I**; for this he was tortured, fined and imprisoned. Released in 1640 by the **Long Parliament**, he prosecuted **Laud** (1644), and became an MP (1648). Purged from the House in 1650, he was again imprisoned (1650–2). After **Cromwell**'s death he returned to parliament as a royalist, for which he was made Keeper of the Tower Records. ▷ **Protectorate; Puritanism**

Puritanism
The belief that further reformation was required in the Church of England under **Elizabeth I** and the Stuarts. It arose in the 1560s out of dissatisfaction with the 'popish elements', such as surplices, which had been retained by the Elizabethan religious settlement. It was not always a coherent, organized movement; rather, a diverse body of opinions and personalities, which occasionally

came together. It included the anti-episcopal Presbyterian move-ment of John Field and Thomas Cartwright in the 1570s and 1580s; the separatist churches that left England for Holland and America from 1590 to 1640; the 'presbyterian', 'independent', and more radical groups which emerged during the **English Civil Wars** and **interregnum**; and the nonconformist sects persecuted by the **Cavalier Parliament**'s '**Clarendon Code**' under **Charles II**.
▷ **Restoration; Stuart, House of**

Pym, John (1584–1643)
English politician. He left Oxford without taking a degree, studied law, and entered parliament (1614). In 1641 he took a leading part in the impeachment of **Strafford**, helped to draw up the **Grand Remonstrance**, and in 1642 was one of the five members whom **Charles I** singled out by name. He stayed in London during the **English Civil Wars**, and died soon after, being appointed Lieutenant of the Ordnance.

Q

Quadruple Alliance (1718)
A treaty signed by Britain, France and the Habsburg Emperor, Charles VI, to which the Dutch were expected to accede, to ensure the principle of collective security in Western Europe. It provided for mutual guarantees of titles, possessions and rights of succession, despite Spain's hostility to Italian territorial provisions, and secured peace for a generation (1718–33).

Quakers ▷ Friends, Society of

Quebec, Battle of (13 Sep 1759)
A battle fought during the **Seven Years War** between British forces under General James **Wolfe** and French forces defending Quebec under the Marquis of Montcalm. It followed an audacious plan by Wolfe to transport British troops from the St Lawrence River up steep, wooded cliffs. British victory led to speedy capture of Quebec and the subsequent collapse of French power in Canada. Both Wolfe and Montcalm were killed in the battle.

Quebec Act (1774)
British statute enacted to remedy the anomalous situation of Quebec within the empire. In 1769 the Board of Trade advised the extension of British institutions to the new colony and suggested that the French should participate in the government of the colony. Sir Guy **Carleton** took a different view of the problem, believing that the French seigniorial system should be maintained and that responsible government should be withheld. The Board of Trade report was suppressed and the Quebec Act, which reversed the established principle of colonial rule through British institutions, was passed. The governor was to rule with the assistance of a council which included the French seigniors; the seigniorial system of tenure continued and the position of the Catholic Church was maintained. The Act showed generosity to a conquered people but omitted to consider the expectations of either

the *habitants* or the English-speaking settlers who were unhappy at the retention of the civil law embodied in the Custom of Paris and the absence of *habeas corpus*. The Act was superseded by the Constitutional Act of 1791.

Queen Anne's War (1702–13)
The second of the four intercolonial wars waged by Britain and France for control of colonial North America, known in Europe as the War of the **Spanish Succession**. Both sides made considerable use of Indian allies. Settled by the Treaty of **Utrecht** (1713), the war resulted in British control of Newfoundland, Acadia and Hudson's Bay. Britain also gained the Asiento, allowing trade with Spanish America.

Queenston Heights, Battle of (1812)
Military engagement in the **War of 1812**. A victory for the British regular army, it reassured Canadians who doubted Britain's commitment to their defence, while pro-Americans were forced to reconsider their loyalties. A monument was erected as a memorial to Isaac Brock, the commanding officer who charged somewhat injudiciously up the face of the Heights.

Quit India Movement
A campaign launched (Aug 1942) by the Indian National Congress calling for immediate independence from Britain, and threatening mass non-violent struggle if its demands were not met. **M K Gandhi** and other Congress leaders were arrested, and the movement was suppressed, though not without difficulty. It was described by the Viceroy, Lord Linlithgow, as 'by far the most serious rebellion since that of 1857': 57 army battalions had to be used to help restore order and there were more than 1 000 deaths. It contributed significantly to the eventual decision by Britain to withdraw from India soon after the end of **World War II**.
▷ **Indian Uprising**

R

radicalism

Any set of ideas, normally of the left but not exclusively so, which argues for more substantial social and political change than is supported in the political mainstream. What is radical is a matter of judgement, and so the term is very widely applied. In a number of countries, including Britain, there are radical parties which are left of centre.

Raffles, Sir (Thomas) Stamford (1781–1826)

British colonial administrator. He became the Lieutenant-Governor of Java (1811–16), where he reformed the administration during that British **interregnum**. In 1816 ill health brought him home to England, where he was knighted. As Lieutenant-Governor of Benkoelen (1818–23), he established a British settlement at Singapore, which rapidly grew into one of the more important trading centres in the East. He was closely involved in the establishment of the Zoological Society of London in the early 1820s.
▷ **East India Company, British**

Raglan (of Raglan), Fitzroy James Henry Somerset, 1st Baron (1788–1855)

British general. He joined the army in 1804, fought at the Battle of **Waterloo** (1815), became an MP, and was made a baron in 1852. In 1854 he led an ill-prepared force against the Russians in the **Crimean War**, but though victorious at Alma he did not follow up his advantage. His ambiguous order led to the **Charge of the Light Brigade** (1854) at Balaclava. He died at **Sevastopol**. His name was given to the raglan sleeve, which came into use in the 1850s.

Raleigh (Ralegh), Sir Walter (1552–1618)

English courtier, navigator and author. He became prime favourite of Queen **Elizabeth I**. He was knighted in 1584, and that year sent the first of three expeditions to America. After the arrival of the Earl of **Essex** at court, he lost influence, and spent some years in Ireland. On his return, Elizabeth discovered his intrigue with Bessy Throckmorton, one of her maids-of-honour, and he was committed to the Tower of London. On his release, he married Bessy, and lived at Sherborne. He took little part in the intrigues at the close of Elizabeth's reign, but his enemies turned **James VI and I** against him, and he was imprisoned (1603), his death sentence being commuted to life imprisonment. While in the Tower, he wrote his *History of the World* (1614), and several other works. Released in 1616, he made an expedition to the Orinoco in search of a goldmine, which was a failure. His death sentence was invoked, and he was executed.

Rebellions of 1837

(1) A rebellion in Quebec in Lower Canada generated by a stalemate between the legislative council and the appointed executive council over control of provincial revenues. Led by Papineau and his *Parti Patriote*, it sought to dissolve the unsatisfactory imperial tie with Britain. It was crushed by British government troops after several brief confrontations. (2) Later in 1837, a rebellion in Ontario in Upper Canada, which opposed the oligarchical control exercised by the Family Compact, and the position of preferment enjoyed by the Church of England. Armed radicals led by Mackenzie marched on Toronto to seize the government, but were repulsed by pro-government troops and volunteers. Mackenzie and Papineau both fled to the USA.

Redmond, John Edward (1856–1918)

Irish politician. He entered parliament in 1881. A champion of **Home Rule**, he was Chairman of the Nationalist Party in 1900. He declined a seat in **Asquith**'s coalition ministry (1915), but supported **World War II**, deplored the Irish rebellion, and opposed **Sinn Féin**.

Reform Acts

Legislation in Britain which altered parliamentary constituencies and increased the size of the electorate. The main Acts were: 1832, which gave the vote to almost all members of the middle classes, and introduced a uniform 10 franchise in the boroughs; 1867, which gave the vote to all settled tenants in the boroughs, thus creating a substantial working-class franchise for the first time; 1884, which extended a similar franchise to rural and mining areas; 1885, which aimed to create parliamentary constituencies of broadly equal size; 1918, which created a universal male suffrage and gave the vote to women of 30 years and over; 1928, which gave the vote to all adult women; and 1969, which lowered the minimum voting age from 21 years to 18. The 1832 Reform Act was the subject of furious controversy, and was preceded by widespread agitation.

Reformation (England)

The process by which the English Church rejected the authority of the Roman Catholic Church and established its own doctrine and liturgy. The English Reformation, unlike that of most European countries, was not predominantly doctrinal in origin. It was precipitated by **Henry VIII** after the Church refused to permit his divorce from **Catherine of Aragon** in order to marry Anne **Boleyn** with the intention of producing a male heir. Henry's response was to use parliament to pass statutes distancing the English Church from Rome. The English clergy were permitted to recognize Henry, rather than the Pope, as Supreme Head of the Church in 1531 and the Act of Supremacy (1534) ended the Pope's formal authority in England. Monasteries were dissolved during the later 1530s and their treasures forfeit to the Crown. Catholic doctrine was upheld by the 'Six Articles' (1539) but, during the reign of **Edward VI**, Protestant usages were promoted in two Acts of Uniformity (1549 and 1552). During the reign of **Mary I**, England was formally reunited with Rome but the succession of **Elizabeth I** (1558) confirmed England as a non-Catholic country. The Act of Uniformity (1559) and the 39 Articles of Religion (1563) were recognizably Protestant although Elizabeth's Church Settlement rejected extreme Protestantism. Elizabeth's control over the Church as 'Supreme Governor' was established by the Act of Supremacy (1559). ▷ **Cranmer, Thomas; Cromwell, Thomas; Pilgrimage of Grace; Reformation** (Scotland)

Reformation (Scotland)

The term used to describe the religious changes whereby the authority of the Pope was repudiated and Protestant forms of doctrine and worship established. Following a period of toleration for Protestants under the Regent, Mary of Guise, in the 1550s, 'Lords of the Congregation' asserted their intention to overthrow Catholicism (1557). The Regent's attempts to suppress Protestantism (1558–9) failed but **Elizabeth I**'s intervention in Scotland was decisive. The Protestant party, aided by John **Knox**, gained control. Catholicism was repudiated at a meeting of the Estates in 1560 ('Reformation Parliament') and celebration of Mass proscribed. One third of ecclesiastical revenues were appropriated to pay Ministers of the Reformed Church and to augment royal finances (1562). **Mary, Queen of Scots**, did not ratify the religious changes which were finally confirmed by **Moray**, Regent for James VI, in 1567. Controversy between Presbyterians (led by Andrew Melville), who insisted on equality of ministers, and Episcopalians, who upheld the hierarchy of bishops, continued within the Church in the late 16c and 17c. ▷ **James VI and I; Reformation** (England)

Reform League (1863)
An organization of middle-class radicals and skilled trade unionists by working-class radicals to extend male suffrage, whose 1866 demonstrations against the fall of the Liberal Reform Bill was a factor in persuading the subsequent Conservative administrations of Lord **Derby** and Benjamin **Disraeli** to introduce their own reform proposals. It won the support of the Liberals in their 1868 election campaign, but was dissolved soon afterwards. ▷ **Reform Acts**

reparations
Payments imposed on the powers defeated in war to cover the costs incurred by the victors. For example, they were levied by the Allies on Germany at the end of **World War I**, though the final sum of £6 000 million plus interest was not fixed until Apr 1921. The Dawes (1924) and Young (1929) Plans revised the payment schedule and reduced the scale of the payments, which were finally abandoned after 1932, because of the Depression.

Restoration
The return of **Charles II** to England (May 1660) at the request of the Convention Parliament, following the collapse of the **Protectorate** regime; but many royal prerogative powers and institutions were not restored. The bishops and the Church of England returned, but parliament took the lead in passing the **Clarendon Code** (1661–5) outlawing dissent from the Book of Common Prayer (1662).

Reynolds, Albert (1932–)
Irish politician. His early career was as an entrepreneur in the entertainment and food-manufacturing industries. He became **Fianna Fáil** MP for Longford-West Meath (1977) and was Minister for Industry and Commerce (1987–9) and Finance (1989–91). Dismissed after an unsuccessful challenge to Charles Haughey (1991), he nevertheless won the party leadership by a large majority after Haughey's resignation (Feb 1992), becoming Prime Minister the same year.

Rhodes, Cecil (John) (1853–1902)
South African politician. After studying in Oxford, he entered the Cape House of Assembly, securing Bechuanaland as a protectorate (1885) and the charter for the British South Africa Company (1889), whose territory was later to be named after him, as Rhodesia. In 1890 he became Prime Minister of Cape Colony, but was forced to resign in 1896 because of complications arising from the **Jameson Raid**. He was a conspicuous figure during the Boer War of 1899–1902, when he organized the defences during the Siege of **Kimberley**. He died at Muizenberg, Cape Colony, and in his will founded scholarships at Oxford for Americans, Germans and colonials ('Rhodes scholars'). ▷ **Boer Wars**

Rhodesia Crisis
The series of events that began with the declaration by Prime Minister Ian Smith of a Unilateral Declaration of Independence (11 Nov 1965), following the Rhodesian Government's failure to agree with successive British Administrations on a constitutional independence settlement that ensured the continuance of white supremacy. The British Government was successful in gaining **UN** support for sanctions while ruling out the use of force and, in 1966 and 1968, Smith engaged with Prime Minister Harold **Wilson** in (ultimately unsuccessful) attempts to resolve the crisis. An agreement was reached with Edward **Heath**'s Conservative Government in 1971, but was ruled out after an independent fact-finding mission determined that it would be unacceptable to the black majority. The growing influence of the ANC (African National Congress), and the withdrawal of the Portuguese from Angola and Mozambique, served to remind Smith of his isolationism, and in 1977 he announced that he was willing to enter into new talks on a one-man, one-vote basis, and released nationalist leaders Ndabaningi Sithole and Joshua Nkomo as a sign of good

faith. However, they initially refused to participate in negotiations, and the escalation of terrorist activities continued
unabated despite Smith having attained in 1978 an internal settlement, thus providing for multiracial government, with the moderate Sithole and Bishop Abel Muzorewa. The return of a Conservative Government in 1979 provided the springboard for fresh
talks and a new settlement, leading to elections in 1980 that were
won by the former Marxist guerrilla leader, Robert Mugabe.

Richard I, 'the Lionheart' (1157–99)

King of England (1189/99). Known also as Richard, Cœur de
Lion, he was the third son of **Henry II** and **Eleanor of Aquitaine**. Of
his 10-year reign, he spent only five months in England, devoting
himself to crusading, and defending the Angevin lands in France.
Already recognized as an outstanding soldier, he took Messina
(1190), Cyprus, and Acre (1191) during the Third Crusade, and
advanced to within sight of Jerusalem. On the return journey, he
was arrested at Vienna (1192), and remained a prisoner of the
German Emperor **Henry VI** until he agreed to be ransomed (1194).
The rest of his reign was occupied in warfare against Philip II of
France, while the government of England was conducted by the
justiciar, Hubert **Walter**. Richard was mortally wounded while
besieging the castle of Châlus, Aquitaine. ▷ **Angevins; Crusades**

Richard II (1367–1400)

King of England (1377/99). He was the younger son of **Edward,
'the Black Prince'**, and succeeded his grandfather, **Edward III** of
England, at the age of 10. He displayed great bravery in con-
fronting the rebels in London during the **Peasants Revolt** (1381);
but already parliament was concerned about his favourites, and
the reign was dominated by the struggle between Richard's desire
to act independently, and the magnates' concern to curb his
power. He quarrelled with his uncle, **John of Gaunt**, and his
main supporters were found guilty of treason in the 'Merciless
Parliament' of 1388. After Richard had declared an end to his
minority in 1389, he built up a stronger following, and in 1397–8
took his revenge by having the Earl of Arundel executed, the
Duke of Gloucester murdered, and several lords banished, the
exiles including Gaunt's son, Henry Bolingbroke (later **Henry IV**
of England). His final act of oppression was to confiscate the
Lancastrian estates after Gaunt's death (1399). Having failed to
restrain the King by constitutional means, the magnates resolved

to unseat him from the throne. Bolingbroke invaded England unopposed, and Richard was deposed in his favour (Sep 1399). He died in Pontefract Castle, Yorkshire, possibly of starvation.
▷ **Lancaster, House of**

Richard III (1452–85)

King of England (1483/5). He was the youngest son of Richard, Duke of York. Created Duke of Gloucester by his brother, **Edward IV**, in 1461, he accompanied him into exile (1470), and played a key role in his restoration (1471). Rewarded with part of the Neville inheritance, he exercised viceregal powers in northern England, and in 1482 recaptured Berwick-upon-Tweed from the Scots. When Edward died (1483) and was succeeded by his under-age son, **Edward V**, Richard acted first as protector; but within three months, he had overthrown the Woodvilles (relations of Edward IV's Queen, Elizabeth Woodville), seen to the execution of Lord Hastings, and had himself proclaimed and crowned as the rightful King. Young Edward and his brother Richard were probably murdered in the Tower on Richard's orders. He tried to stabilize his position, but failed to win broad-based support. His rival, Henry Tudor (later **Henry VII**), confronted him in battle at **Bosworth Field**, and Richard died fighting bravely against heavy odds. Though ruthless, he was not the absolute monster Tudor historians portrayed him to be. Nor is there proof he was a hunchback.

Ridley, Nicholas (c.1500–55)

English Protestant martyr. He was ordained c.1524, and studied in Paris and Louvain (1527–30). He then held a variety of posts, including chaplain to Thomas **Cranmer** and **Henry VIII**, and Bishop of Rochester (1547). An ardent reformer, he became Bishop of London (1550), and helped Cranmer prepare the Thirty-Nine Articles. On the death of **Edward VI** he espoused the cause of Lady Jane **Grey**, was imprisoned, and executed at Oxford.
▷ **Reformation** (England)

Rijswijk, Treaty of (1697)

A settlement ending the Nine Years War or the War of the League of **Augsburg** (1688–97), mediated by Sweden, between pleni-potentiaries of Louis XIV of France on the one hand, and on the other Charles II of Spain, **William III** of Britain (also representing the Netherlands), and the Emperor Leopold I. Although the treaty ostensibly checked French expansionism, peace was short-lived; it freed Louis XIV to concentrate on the War of the **Spanish Succession**.

Riot Act

Legislation aimed at preserving public order, first passed at the beginning of the Hanoverian era in 1714. When 12 or more people were unlawfully assembled and refused to disperse, they were, after the reading of a section of this Act by a person in authority, immediately considered felons having committed a serious crime.

Rising in the North (1569–70)

A rebellion (sometimes known as 'The Rebellion of the Northern Earls') against **Elizabeth I** by the Earls of Northumberland and Westmoreland. It was motivated by strong support for Catholicism in the north of England and precipitated by the arrival of **Mary, Queen of Scots** in England (1568). A general rising was aborted when the Duke of Norfolk refused to lead it and the northern rising, beginning in Nov 1569 and centering on Durham, was confused and aimless, collapsing by Feb 1570. Westmoreland fled to the Netherlands but Northumberland was captured in Scotland and executed (1572). Despite its outcome, the rising demonstrated the limited impact of the Reformation in northern England. ▷ **Reformation** (England)

Rizzio, David (c.1533–66)

Italian courtier and musician. He entered the service of **Mary, Queen of Scots** in 1561, and rapidly becoming her favourite, was appointed Private Foreign Secretary in 1564. He negotiated Mary's marriage (1565) with **Darnley**, with whom he was at first on friendliest terms, but the Queen's husband soon became jealous of his influence over Mary and of his strong political power, and entered with other nobles into a plot to kill him. Rizzio was dragged from the Queen's presence and brutally murdered at the palace of Holyrood.

Robert II (1316–90)

King of Scots (1371/90). He was the son of Walter, hereditary Steward of Scotland. Robert acted as sole regent during the exile and captivity of **David II**; on the latter's death, he became King in right of his descent from his maternal grandfather, Robert **Bruce**, and founded the Stuart royal dynasty. ▷ **Stuart, House of**

Roberts (of Kandahar, Pretoria, and Waterford), Frederick Sleigh Roberts, 1st Earl (1832–1914)

British field marshal. He took an active part in the **Indian Uprising** of 1857–8, for which he was decorated with the Victoria Cross in 1858. He became Commander-in-Chief in India (1885–93), and served as Supreme Commander in South Africa during the Boer War, relieving the Siege of **Kimberley** (1900). He was created earl in 1901, and died while visiting troops in the field in France. ▷ **Afghan Wars; Boer Wars**

Robinson, Mary (1944–)

Irish politician. She trained as a lawyer and was Professor of Law at Trinity College, Dublin, from 1969. She was a member of the Irish Senate (1969–89) and participated in numerous legal associations in the European Community (**EC**). She became an activist on many social issues, including women's and single-parents' rights and the decriminalization of homosexuality. Nominated by the Labour Party, from which she had resigned in 1985 over the **Anglo-Irish Agreement**, she unexpectedly defeated the Fine Fáil candidate Brian Lenihan in the presidential elections of Nov 1990.

Roca–Runciman Pact (May 1933)

A commercial treaty between Britain and Argentina, referred to by the names of the chief negotiators, Vice-President Julio Argentino Roca (Argentina) and Walter Runciman (Britain). The pact guaranteed Argentina a share of the British meat market in return for various economic concessions. Nevertheless, the debates over the pact weakened the *Concordancia* or 'coalition' government of General Augustin Justo, which was faced with a vigorous nationalist campaign.

Rockingham, Charles Watson Wentworth, 2nd Marquess of (1730–82)

English politician. He was created Earl of Malton in 1750 and served as gentleman of the bedchamber to both **George II** and

George III. As leader of a prominent Whig opposition group, he was called upon to form a ministry in 1765. He repealed the **Stamp Act**, affecting the American colonies, then court intrigues caused his resignation (1766). He opposed Britain's war against the colonists. His was the most consistent opposition Whig group to George III's government in the 1760s and 1770s, and leading spokesmen, such as **Fox** and **Burke**, were adherents. He became Prime Minister again in 1782, the year he died. ▷ **American Revolution**

Rodney (of Stoke-Rodney), George Brydges Rodney, 1st Baron (1719–92)

British admiral. He joined the navy in 1732, became Governor of Newfoundland (1748–52), and won several victories during the **Seven Years War** and after the **American Revolution**, when he defeated French fleets in the West Indies, notably off Dominica in 1782. He was made a baron after his return to England.

Rogers, John (c.1500–55)

English Protestant reformer and martyr. He was a London rector who converted to Protestantism at Antwerp, and helped to prepare the new translation called 'Matthew's Bible' in 1537. He returned to England in 1548, preached an anti-Catholic sermon at St Paul's Cross in 1553, just after the accession of **Mary I**, and was burnt. ▷ **Reformation** (England)

Rosebery, Archibald Philip Primrose, 5th Earl of (1847–1929)

Scottish Liberal politician. He succeeded to the earldom in 1868, and after holding various educational and political posts, became Foreign Secretary (1886 and 1892–4) under **Gladstone**, whom he briefly (1894–5) succeeded as Premier before the Liberals lost the election of 1895. He was noted for his racehorse stables, and in his later years as a biographer of British statesmen. ▷ **Liberal Party**

Roses, Wars of the (1455–85)

A series of civil wars in England, which started during the weak monarchy of King **Henry VI**; named from the emblems of the two rival branches of the House of Plantagenet, York (white rose) and Lancaster (red rose) — a symbolism which was propagated by the Tudor Dynasty (1485–1603), which united the two roses. The

wars began when Richard, Duke of York, claimed protectorship of the crown after the King's mental breakdown (1453–4), and effectively ended with Henry Tudor's defeat of **Richard III** at Bosworth (1485). The armies were small, and the warfare intermittent, although marked by brutal executions. The wars were not purely dynastic in origin, and were exacerbated by the gentry and by aristocratic feuds, notably between the Neville and the **Percy** Family, and by the unstable 'bastard feudal' system, in which relations among landed élites were increasingly based upon self-interest — a system that the **Tudors** sought to control.
▷ **Henry VII; Lancaster, House of; Plantagenet Dynasty; York, House of**

Round Table Conferences (1930–2)

A series of meetings in London between British government and Indian representatives to discuss the future constitution of India. It was prompted by the Simon Commission Report (1930) on the working of the 1919 Government of India Act. It helped in the formulation of the 1935 Government of India Act. ▷ **Government of India Acts; Montagu–Chelmsford Report**

Rowlatt Act (1919)

Passed by the British colonial government, the Anarchical and Revolutionary Crimes Act, popularly known by the name of its author, Sir Sidney Rowlatt, made the suspension of civil liberties during wartime by the Defence of India Act of 1915 a permanent feature of India's peacetime constitution. The Act aroused opposition amongst Indian nationalist politicians and caused **M K Gandhi** to organize the first all-India Satyagraha, an initially peaceful protest involving strikes, demonstrations and the deliberate courting of arrest, in opposition to the measure. Popular support was widespread, partly because of economic distress but also due to anger amongst the Muslim community at the proposed post-war division of the empire of the Ottoman Sultan, Khalifa, the protector of Islam's holy places in the Middle East and the organization and involvement of India's Sikh community as part of a general movement of religious revivalism in India at this time. Unfortunately, the Satyagraha was accompanied by violent incidents, some of them committed by Ghadrites, which led to the imposition of martial law in the Punjab and the infamous Amritsar Massacre. Shocked at this outcome, Gandhi called the Satyagraha a 'Himalayan blunder', but the real blunder was committed by the British, as clumsy attempts to cover up the massacre and to absolve those involved from responsibility convinced many moderate and reformist Indian politicians (including Gandhi himself) of the impossibility of Indians ever securing justice under colonial rule.

Royal Niger Company

A company founded to secure the Niger regions for the British against French competition. British traders on the River Niger had been amalgamated into the National African Company, which in 1886 obtained a royal charter to rule a large part of what later became Nigeria. They secured the navigable portions of the Niger, frustrated the French, and destroyed the power of African middlemen. The charter was wound up in 1898, and the various parts of Nigeria were later amalgamated as a British colony, which achieved independence in 1960.

Rump Parliament

The members of the English **Long Parliament** who were left after **Pride**'s Purge of conservative and moderate 'presbyterian' elements (Dec 1648). It numbered about 60, but by-elections brought it up to 125 by 1652. It abolished the monarchy and the House of Lords. When it fell out with the army, **Cromwell** dismissed it (Apr 1653). It was recalled in 1659 with the fall of the **Protectorate**, and dissolved itself in 1660. ▷ **Presbyterianism**

Rum Rebellion (1808)

An uprising in Sydney which deposed the Governor of New South Wales, Captain William **Bligh**. Led by John Macarthur, a former army officer turned pastoralist, Major George Johnston and officers of the New South Wales Corps, the rebellion occurred because of personal antagonisms, and Bligh's attempt to end the use of rum as a currency. Bligh returned to England but was not reinstated as governor; Johnston was court-martialled and dismissed from the army; and Macarthur, on going to Britain, was forbidden to return to Australia until 1817.

Rupert (1619–82)

Prince and royalist commander in the **English Civil Wars**. He was the third son of the Elector Palatine Frederick V and Elizabeth, daughter of **James VI and I**. A notable cavalry leader, he won several victories in the major battles of the war, but was defeated at **Marston Moor** (1644), and after his surrender of Bristol, was dismissed by **Charles I**. Banished by parliament, he led the small royalist fleet until it was routed by Robert **Blake** (1650). He escaped to the West Indies, returning to Europe in 1653, and living in Germany until the **Restoration**.

Rush–Bagot Convention(1817)

An agreement between the USA and Britain to demilitarize the Great Lakes by limiting the number, tonnage, and armament of ships on each side. The convention ended the threat of a Great Lakes arms race, but complete disarmament on the US/Canada border did not follow until decades later. The parties involved were acting US Secretary of State Richard Rush, and British Minister to the USA, Charles Bagot.

Rushdie, (Ahmad) Salman (1947–)

British writer. Born in Bombay in India of Muslim parents, he was educated there and in England, at Rugby and Cambridge. He became widely known after the publication of his second novel, *Midnight's Children* (1981). *The Satanic Verses* (1988) caused worldwide controversy because of its treatment of Islam from a secular point of view, and in Feb 1989 he was forced to go into hiding because of a sentence of death passed on him by Ayatollah Khomeini of Iran.

Russell (of Kingston Russell), John, 1st Earl (1792–1878)

English politician. He became an MP in 1813. He was Home Secretary (1835–9) and Secretary for War (1839–41), and became Whig–Liberal Prime Minister (1846–52) after the **Conservative Party** split over the repeal of the **Corn Laws**. In **Aberdeen**'s coalition of 1852 he was Foreign Secretary and leader in the Commons. He lost popularity over alleged incompetent management of the **Crimean War**, and in 1855 he retired; but he became Foreign Secretary again in the second **Palmerston** administration (1859), and was made an earl in 1861. On Palmerston's death (1865), he again became Premier, but resigned the following year. ▷ **Liberal Party; Whigs**

Russell, Lord William (1639–83)

English politician. He travelled in Europe, and at the **Restoration** became an MP. A supporter of the 1st Earl of **Shaftesbury**, he was a leading member of the movement to exclude James VII of Scotland and II of England from the succession. He was arrested with others for participation in the **Rye House Plot** (1683), found guilty by a packed jury, and beheaded in London. ▷ **James VII and II; Whigs**

Rye House Plot (Apr 1683)

An alleged plot by **Whigs** to murder **Charles II** of England and James, Duke of York, at Rye House near Hoddesdon, Hertfordshire. A counterpart to the alleged **Popish Plot** of 1678, it was foiled by the early departure of the royal pair from Newmarket. The conspirators were betrayed and captured; two of them, Algernon **Sidney** and William, Lord **Russell**, were executed. ▷ **James VII and II**

S

Saintes, Battle of the (12 Apr 1782)
A major Caribbean Anglo-French naval action during the **American Revolution**. In that war, France and Spain sided with Britain's rebellious North American colonists and used the British preoccupation with the Americans to obtain naval supremacy and capture British colonies in the Caribbean. In 1782 the British admiral George **Rodney** (who had taken St Lucia in 1778) returned from Europe to shadow the French commander, the Count de Grasse, who was planning to attack Jamaica with 35 warships. Battle was joined off the Saintes (the small rocky islets between Dominica and Guadeloupe) on 12 Apr and, after a day of heavy fighting, de Grasse, his flagship, the *Ville de Paris*, and six other ships were captured by the British. Rodney was hailed as the saviour of Jamaica.

Samuel, Herbert (Louis), 1st Viscount (1870–1963)
English politician and philosopher. Educated at Oxford, he became an MP in 1902, and held various offices, including Postmaster-General (1910–14 and 1915–16), Home Secretary (1916 and 1931–2), and High Commissioner for Palestine (1920–5), where he pursued a policy of trying to establish a multi-national commonwealth to include the Jews. He was Leader of the **Liberal Party** in the Commons (1931–5), and later Liberal Leader in the Lords (1944–55). He was created a viscount in 1937.

Sand River Convention (1852)
An agreement whereby the British acknowledged the independence of the Boers beyond the Vaal River. After the Great Trek, the Boers had established a number of communities in the interior of southern Africa north of the Orange and the Vaal Rivers. In 1848 Governor Sir Harry Smith of the Cape proclaimed the authority of Queen Victoria over these territories. Further frontier problems and Boer resistance under Andries Pretorius caused the British to reconsider their responsibilities beyond the

272

borders of the Cape colony. The Sand River Convention was followed within two years by the Bloemfontein Convention, under which the British relinquished authority over the Orange River Sovereignty. The British re-established imperial power over these territories between 1877 and 1881, and 1902 and 1906–7.

San Remo, Conference of (Apr 1920)
This conference, attended by representatives of Britain, France and Italy, reached agreement on the Middle East settlement after **World War I**. The agreement covered the peace treaty with Turkey (eventually signed in Sèvres, Aug 1920), and the eventual independence of the Middle Eastern states. However, it also granted interim mandates to Britain over Iraq and Palestine, and to France over Syria and Lebanon (as had earlier been formulated in principle by the **Sykes–Picot Agreement**). Japan, Greece and Belgium were also party to the Conference, but not the USA or USSR.

Saratoga, Battle of (Oct 1777)
One of the most important engagements of the American Revolution. Actually fought near modern Schuylerville, New York, the battle brought the defeat of a large British army under John Burgoyne by American continental troops and militia under Horatio Gates. The outcome ended British plans to cut New England off from the rest of the states, and encouraged French intervention on the American side.

Saxe-Coburg-Gotha
The name of the British royal family, 1901–17. King **Edward VII** inherited it from his father, Prince **Albert**, the second son of the Duke of Saxe-Coburg-Gotha. The obviously Germanic name was abandoned during **World War I** as a means of asserting the 'Englishness' of royalty and playing down the extent of its German blood. ▷ **Windsor, House of**

Saxons
A Germanic people from the north German plain. With the Angles, they formed the bulk of the invaders who in the two centuries following the Roman withdrawal from Britain (409) conquered and colonized most of what became England. They were especially prominent in Essex, Sussex and **Wessex**. ▷ **Anglo-Saxons; Britain, Roman**

273

Scottish National Party (SNP)

A political party formed in 1928 as the National Party of Scotland, which merged with the Scottish Party in 1933. It first won a seat at a by-election in 1945. Its greatest success was in the 1974 general election, when it took nearly a third of Scottish votes and won 11 seats. Since then its support has declined, although in 1988 it achieved a surprise victory in the Govan by-election. Its principal policy aim is independence for Scotland from the UK. ▷ **Home Rule**

Scottish War of Independence

The conflict between the Scots and English in the late 13c and early 14c. After heavy defeats by **Edward I** at the Battle of **Dunbar** (1296) and Falkirk (1298), the Scots regrouped first under William **Wallace** and then Robert **Bruce**. The fall of Stirling Castle (1304) led to the capture and execution of Wallace but Bruce was crowned (1306) and, after Edward I's death (1307), increasingly asserted his authority. His victory at the Battle of **Bannockburn** (1314) secured Scotland from English rule and the Scottish barons declared their allegiance to Bruce in the face of papal opposition to his kingship (Declaration of **Arbroath**, 1320). A truce between England and Scotland (1323) was broken when the Scots crossed into Northumberland and ravaged it (1327–8). Queen **Isabella of France** and her lover Roger Mortimer sued for peace. The English renounced all claims to feudal superiority over Scotland (1328) and recognized Bruce as its king. In 1329 Pope John XXII issued a Bull authorizing Robert to be crowned and anointed.
▷ **Edward II**

Sedgemoor, Battle of (5 July 1685)

A battle near Bridgwater, Somerset, which ended the Duke of **Monmouth**'s rebellion against James VII of Scotland and II of England. The rebel army received popular support and outnumbered the royal army by 4 000 to 2 500, but desertions provoked an abortive night attack. Monmouth was executed, and his supporters suffered under Judge **Jeffreys**' 'Bloody Assize'.
▷ **James VII and II**

Septennial Act (1716)

Legislation repealing the Triennial Act (1694) which extended the maximum life of parliament from three years to seven. Remaining in force until the Parliament Act (1911) restricted parliaments to five years, it was important in easing the transition to political stability and to Whig supremacy in the early years of the Hanoverian monarchy. ▷ **Hanover, House of; Triennial Acts; Whigs**

Settlement, Act of

An important statute of 1701 which determined the succession of the English throne after the death of Queen **Anne** and her heirs, if any. It excluded the Catholic Stuarts from the succession, which was to pass to the Electress Sophia of Hanover, descendant through the female line of James VI of Scotland and I of England. Future monarchs were to be communicant members of the Church of England, and were not permitted to leave the country without the consent of parliament. ▷ **James VI and I; Stuart, House of**

Sevastopol, Siege of (1854–5)

The centre-piece of the **Crimean War**. Britain, France and Turkey chose to attack Russia's main naval base in the Black Sea in order to reduce its alleged threat to the status quo in the **Ottoman Empire** and the Mediterranean. Time was lost through opting to surround it, and initial successes were not followed up. The result was that General Totleben was able to build formidable defences which Admiral Nakhimov used to good effect. In the event it took 12 months and many casualties to capture Sevastopol. Although Russia therefore lost the war, the battle honours were shared. The Russian surgeon, Nikolai Pirogov, played a similar role inside the fortifications to Florence Nightingale outside.

Seven Years War (1756–63)

A major European conflict rooted in the rivalry between Austria and Prussia and the imminent colonial struggle between Britain and France in the New World and the Far East. Hostilities in North America (1754) pre-dated the Diplomatic Revolution in Europe (1756), which created two opposing power blocs: Austria, France, Russia, Sweden and Saxony against Prussia, Britain and Portugal. British maritime superiority countered Franco-Spanish naval power, and prevented a French invasion. The European war, precipitated by Prussia's seizure of Saxony, was marked by many notable pitched land battles. Saved from total defeat when Russia switched sides, **Frederick II, 'the Great'** of Prussia retained Silesia in 1763. ▷ **George II; Granby; Paris, Treaty of**

Seymour, Jane (c.1509–37)
Queen of England. She was the third wife of **Henry VIII**, the mother of **Edward VI**, and the sister of Protector Somerset. She was a lady-in-waiting to Henry's first two wives, and married him 11 days after the execution of Anne **Boleyn**. She died soon after the birth of her son.

Shaftesbury, Anthony Ashley Cooper, 1st Earl of (1621–83)
English statesman. He became a member of the **Short Parliament** (1640) and of the **Barebone's Parliament** (1653), and was made one of **Cromwell**'s Council of State, but from 1655 was in opposition. At the **Restoration** he became a baron and Chancellor of the Exchequer (1661–72), a member of the **Cabal** (1667), an earl (1672), and Lord Chancellor (1672–3). He was dismissed in 1673, and led the opposition to the succession of James, Duke of York (later **James II**). Charged with treason in 1681, he was acquitted, but fled to Holland in 1682, and died soon after in Amsterdam.
▷ **English Civil Wars**

Shaftesbury, Anthony Ashley Cooper, 7th Earl of (1801–85)
British factory reformer and philanthropist. He entered parliament in 1826, and become the main spokesman of the factory reform movement. He piloted successive **Factory Acts** (1847 and 1859) through parliament, regulated conditions in the coalmines (1842), and provided lodging houses for the poor (1851). A leader of the evangelical movement within the Church of England, he succeeded to his earldom in 1851.

Sheffield Disturbances (1866–7)
The name given to an outbreak of violence against non-unionized labour in the cutlery trade which prompted the government to establish the first ever Royal Commission on trade unionism.

Shelburne, William Petty Fitzmaurice, 2nd Earl of (1737–1805)
English politician and Prime Minister. He entered parliament, succeeded to his earldom in 1761, became President of the Board of Trade (1763) and Secretary of State (1766). Made Premier on the death of **Rockingham** (1782), he resigned in 1783 when out-voted by the coalition between **Fox** and **North**. In 1784 he was made Marquis of Lansdowne.

Sherbrooke, Sir John Coape (1764–1830)
British general and Lieutenant-Governor of Nova Scotia (1811–16). His reputation was made during the Peninsular War and in the **War of 1812** he conducted a vigorous defence, which included the capture of Castine (Maine). He served as Governor-in-Chief at Quebec from 1816 until he suffered a stroke in 1818.

Short Parliament (Apr–May 1640)
The brief parliament summoned by **Charles I** of England to vote supplies for his campaigns against the Scots. It refused to do so, however, whereupon the King dissolved it after only three weeks, adding to parliament's sense of grievance.

Sidmouth (of Sidmouth), Henry Addington, 1st Viscount
(1757–1844)
English politician. He left law for politics, and became an MP in 1783. He was Speaker of the House (1789–1801) when, upon the resignation of **Pitt**, 'the Younger', he was invited to form a ministry. His Tory administration negotiated the Treaty of Amiens (1802), which held for barely a year. His government ended in 1804, when he was created a viscount. He later became Home Secretary under **Liverpool** (1812–21), and was unpopular for coercive measures such as the Six Acts (1819), which restricted newspaper publication and the holding of political meetings. It was during his period of office that the **Peterloo Massacre** took place in Manchester. ▷ **Napoleonic Wars**

Sidney, Algernon (1622–83)
English politician. He became a cavalry officer in the **English Civil Wars** on the parliamentary side, and was wounded at the Battle of **Marston Moor** (1644). In 1645 he entered parliament, and served as governor in several cities. An extreme republican, he resented **Cromwell**'s usurpation of power, and retired from public life (1653–9). After the **Restoration** he lived on the Continent, but in 1677 was pardoned and returned to England. However, in 1683, he was implicated on very little evidence in the **Rye House Plot**, and beheaded in London. ▷ **Whigs**

Sikh Wars (1845–6 and 1848–9)
Two campaigns between the British and the Sikhs which led to the British conquest and annexation of the Punjab, north-west India (Mar 1849).

Simcoe, Sir John Graves (1752–1806)

British colonial administrator. As Lieutenant-Governor of Upper Canada (1792–94), his intention was to re-create British social and political patterns in the colony, but his disagreements with both London and Canadian administrators caused his recall in 1796. His most positive accomplishment was the use of the army in a huge road-building programme.

Simon (of Stackpole Elidor), John (Allsebrook), 1st Viscount (1873–1954)

English politician and lawyer. A Liberal, he entered parliament in 1906, and was knighted in 1910. He was Attorney-General (1913–15) and Home Secretary (1915–16), before resigning from the cabinet for his opposition to conscription. Deserting the Liberals to form the Liberal National Party, he supported Ramsay **MacDonald**'s coalition governments and became Foreign Secretary (1931–5), Home Secretary in the Conservative government (1935–7), Chancellor of the Exchequer (1937–40), and Lord Chancellor in Winston **Churchill**'s war-time coalition (1940–5). He was created viscount in 1940. ▷ **Liberal Party**

Sinn Féin

Irish political party (literally, 'Ourselves Alone') which developed during the period 1905–8 under the direction of Arthur Griffith in support of Irish independence from Britain. By the end of **World War I** it had become the main Irish nationalist party. It formed a separate assembly from the UK parliament, and succeeded in creating the **Irish Free State** (1922). Following the Anglo-Irish Treaty (1921), it split to form the two main Irish parties, and in 1970 it split again into official and provisional wings. It has remained active in Northern Ireland, and has close contacts with the **IRA**. ▷ **Adams, Gerry; Fine Gael**

Siraj ud-Daula (Mirza Muhammad) (c.1732–57)

Nawab (Ruler) of Bengal under the nominal suzerainty of the Mughal Empire (1756/7). He came into conflict with the British over their fortification of Calcutta, and marched on the city in 1756. The British surrender led to the infamous **Black Hole of Calcutta**, for which he was held responsible. Following the recapture of Calcutta, the British under **Clive of Plassey** joined forces with Siraj ud-Daula's general, Mir Jafar, and defeated him at the

Battle of **Plassey** in 1757. He fled to Murshidabad, but was captured and executed.

slave trade

A trade in Africa which started in ancient times. Slaves were sent across the Sahara and were traded in the Mediterranean by Phoenicians; Graeco-Roman traders in the Red Sea and beyond traded slaves from East Africa to Egypt and the Middle East. These trades continued in medieval times, but the scale of the trade built up with the arrival of the Portuguese in Africa and the development of the labour-intensive plantation system in the West African islands of São Tomé and Principe, Brazil, the Caribbean, the southern American colonies, and later the Indian Ocean islands and South and East Africa. The Portuguese dominated the trade in the 16c, the Dutch in the early 17c, while the late 17c was a period of intense competition with the French, British, Danes and Swedes joining the early practitioners. The trade reached its peak in the second half of the 18c, and from this period the East African slave trade became more significant, particularly during the period of Omani power up to the 1860s. The British abolished the slave trade in 1807, and the institution of slavery in 1833. They then instituted Royal Naval anti-slavery squadrons on the coasts of western and eastern Africa. There have been various estimates of the number of slaves removed from Africa, the most reliable figure being c.12.5 million between 1650 and 1850. Many other people must have lost their lives in the wars stimulated by the trade, and the total drain meant that at the very least the African population remained static for over two centuries. ▷ **Williams Thesis**

Slave Trade, Abolition of the

Effected in the **British Empire** by an Act of parliament of 1807. The Society for Effecting the Abolition of the Slave Trade was founded in 1787 and was spearheaded by the 'Clapham Sect' or 'Saints', whose membership included Ramsay, Clarkson, Stephen and Fowell Buxton and which found a political voice in William **Wilberforce**, the MP for Yorkshire. Although Wilberforce's abolition bill had lacked government support during the **Pitt** administration, in 1806 the **Tories** were replaced by the **Whigs** of Charles James **Fox**, the bill became law a year later and the last British slave trader, the *Kitty Amelia* left Liverpool in May 1808.

Denmark had abolished its trade in 1804, the USA in 1808, France in 1818 and Spain in 1820.

Slim (of Yarralumia and of Bishopston), William (Joseph), 1st Viscount (1891–1970)

British field marshal. He served during **World War I** in the **Gallipoli Campaign** and in Mesopotamia. In **World War II**, his greatest achievement was to lead his reorganized forces, the famous 14th 'forgotten' army, to victory over the Japanese in Burma. He was Chief of the Imperial General Staff (1948–52) and a highly successful Governor-General of Australia (1953–60). Knighted in 1944, he became a viscount in 1960.

Sluys, Battle of (1340)

A naval battle fought in the Zwyn estuary in Flanders, the first major English victory in the **Hundred Years War**. **Edward III**, King of England, personally commanded the English fleet, which wiped out or captured all but 24 of 200 French ships. However, he failed to follow up his victory, either on land or sea.

Smith, John (1580–1631)

English colonist and explorer. He fought in Transylvania and Hungary, where he was captured by the Turks, and sold as a slave. After escaping to Russia, he joined an expedition to colonize Virginia (1607), and helped found Jamestown. He was saved from death by the native princess Pocahontas. His energy and tact in dealing with the Indians led to his being elected president of the colony (1608–9). He wrote valuable accounts of his travels, and died in London.

Smith, John (1938–94)

Scottish politician. He was called to the Scottish bar in 1967 and made a QC in 1983. He entered the House of Commons, representing Lanarkshire North, in 1970 and from 1983 Monklands East. He served in the administrations of Harold **Wilson** and James **Callaghan**, becoming trade secretary in 1978. From 1979 to 1992 he was front bench opposition spokesman on trade, energy, employment and economic affairs, one of Labour's most respected politicians. After the Labour election defeat of 1992 and the subsequent resignation of Neil **Kinnock**, he emerged as the leader of the party. His political career had been threatened by a heart attack in 1988, and although he appeared to have made a complete recovery and returned to the front bench in 1989, a second heart attack proved fatal. His death was a great and unexpected blow to his party.

Smuts, Jan (Christian) (1870–1950)

South African general and politician. Educated at the University of Cambridge, England, he became a lawyer, fought in the second Boer War (1899–1902), and entered the House of Assembly in 1907. He held several Cabinet posts, led campaigns against the Germans in south-west Africa and Tanganyika, was a member of the Imperial War Cabinet in **World War I**, and succeeded Louis Botha as Prime Minister (1919–24). He was a significant figure at Versailles, and was instrumental in the founding of the **League of Nations**. As Minister of Justice under Hertzog, his coalition with the Nationalists in 1934 produced the United Party; he was Premier again from 1939 to 1948. ▷ **Boer Wars**

Social Democratic Party (SDP)

Political party formed in 1981 by a 'gang of four', comprising David **Owen**, Shirley Williams, Roy **Jenkins**, and Bill Rogers. They broke away from the **Labour Party** primarily over disagreements on policy and the degree of influence exerted on party policy by the trade unions. Although espousing socialist principles, the party was a moderate centrist one. The SDP formed an electoral pact with the Liberals in 1981, but despite some early electoral successes failed to break the two-party 'mould' of British politics. It merged with the **Liberal Party** in 1988 becoming the **Social and Liberal Democratic Party**, although a rump, led by David Owen, continued in existence as the SDP until 1990.

socialism

A wide-ranging political doctrine which first emerged in Europe during industrialization in the 18c. Most socialists would agree that social and economic relationships play a major part in determining human possibilities, and that the unequal ownership of property under capitalism creates an unequal and conflictive society. The removal of private property or some means of counterbalancing its power, it is held, will produce a more equal society where individuals enjoy greater freedom and are able to realize their potential more fully. A socialist society will thus be more co-operative and fraternal. Possibly the major division within socialism is between those who believe that to bring it about revolution is necessary, and those who believe change can be achieved through reforms within the confines of democratic politics. There are also differences as to how far capitalist production needs to be eradicated to bring about a socialist society. In Britain, promoters of socialism have included the **Fabian Society**, the **Independent Labour Party** and the **Labour Party**.

Solemn League and Covenant (Sep 1643)
An alliance between the English parliament and the Scottish rebels against King **Charles I**. Parliament promised £30 000 a month to the Scots and the introduction of full **Presbyterianism** in England; the Scots agreed to provide an army to the hard-pressed parliamentarians to fight Charles. The pact facilitated parliamentary victory in the first of the **English Civil Wars**, but Presbyterianism was never fully implemented. ▷ **Covenanters**

Somers (of Evesham), John, 1st Baron (1651–1716)
English politician. A Whig, he became a lawyer (1676) and an MP (1689). He helped to draft the **Declaration of Rights** (1689), and after the **Glorious Revolution** (1688) held several posts under **William III**, culminating as Lord Chancellor (1697). William's most trusted minister, he was the object of frequent attacks, which led to his impeachment (and acquittal) in 1701. He was President of the Privy Council under Queen **Anne** (1708–14) ▷ **Whigs**

Somme, Battle of the (1 July–19 Nov 1916)
A major **World War I** British offensive against German troops in north-western France which developed into the bloodiest battle in world history, with more than a million casualties. It was launched by British Commander-in-Chief, Douglas **Haig**. When the attack was abandoned, the Allies had advanced 10 miles from previous positions. The battle formed part of the war of attrition on the Western Front.

South Africa Act (1909)
The act of the British parliament which created the Union of South Africa, with dominion status, in 1910. After the Boer War, the Liberal government which came to power in 1905 moved rapidly to restore responsible self-government to the Transvaal (1906) and the Orange Free State (1907). A series of constitutional

conventions then set about federating the two Boer territories with the British colonies of the Cape and Natal. In the event, a union constitution was agreed upon, with the parliamentary capital in Cape Town, the administrative capital in Pretoria and the major law courts in Bloemfontein. The Union constitution ensured that the Afrikaners would remain the dominant political force in South Africa. It was hailed as a colonial triumph for **Asquith**'s government in keeping South Africa within the British Empire and ultimately ensuring its participation in two world wars. However, the British failed to establish black political rights or protect the franchise enjoyed by limited numbers of Africans at the Cape. It led not to a liberalizing of the South African system, as the British had hoped, but to white supremacist rule and apartheid. ▷ **Boer Wars**

South Sea Bubble
A financial crisis in Britain (1720) arising out of speculation mania generated by parliament's approval of the South Sea Company proposal to take over three-fifths of the National Debt. Many investors were ruined in the aftermath, but Robert **Walpole**'s plan for stock transfer retrieved the situation and made his reputation.

Spanish Civil War (1936–9)
The conflict between supporters and opponents of the Spanish Second Republic (1931–6). The 'Republicans' included moderates, socialists, communists and Catalan and Basque regionalists and anarchists. The 'Nationalist' insurgents included monarchists, Carlists, conservative Catholics and fascist Falangists. The armed forces were divided. Both sides attracted foreign assistance: the Republic from the USSR and the International Brigades; the Nationalists from fascist Italy and Nazi Germany. The Nationalist victory was due to the balance of foreign aid; to 'non-intervention' on the part of the Western democracies; and to greater internal unity, achieved under the leadership of General Franco. The war took the course of a slow Nationalist advance. The Nationalists initially (July 1936) seized much of north-west Spain and part of the south-west, then (autumn 1936) advanced upon but failed to capture Madrid. They captured Malaga (Mar 1937) and the north coast (Mar–Oct 1937); advanced to the Mediterranean, cutting Republican Spain in two (Apr 1938); overran Catalonia (Dec 1938–Feb 1939); and finally occupied Madrid and south-east Spain (Mar 1939). ▷ **fascism**

Spanish Succession, War of the (1702–13)

The war fought nominally over the throne of Spain, but which involved worldwide interests in trade and the colonies. The succession, in dispute for a generation because of the lack of an heir to Charles II, the last Habsburg ruler of Spain, had initially been resolved by partition treaties between the major European powers. Charles II's will aimed to avoid any carve-up of the monarchy by settling the throne on Louis XIV of France's grandson, Philip, Duke of Anjou; in 1700, the latter became King of Spain, thereby provoking a declaration of war by the other disappointed powers. The Grand Alliance of the Hague (1701) united England, the Holy Roman Empire and the United Provinces of the Netherlands against France and Spain. The main centre of land operations was in the Netherlands, where the Duke of Marlborough inflicted major defeats on the French at Blenheim (1704) and Ramillies (1706), but there were also crucial spheres of conflict in Italy and the Iberian Peninsula. In Italy the successful Imperial forces, commanded by Eugene of Savoy, defeated the French at Turin (1706) and subsequently drove the Spanish out of the greater part of Italy. In the Iberian Peninsula, the Allies were supported by the Portuguese and the Catalans, enabling their armies to capture all the major cities of the peninsula by 1706. Gibraltar fell into Allied hands in 1704. Strong Franco-Spanish forces under the Marshal Duke of **Berwick**, however, won a decisive victory at Almansa (1707), and the Bourbon forces laid siege to Barcelona, which fell in 1714. The general European war was settled by the Peace of **Utrecht** (1713), which confirmed the Bourbon succession in Spain, and by the Peace of Rastatt (1714).

Special Operations Executive (SOE)

An organization set up with British war cabinet approval in July 1940 in response to Winston **Churchill**'s directive to 'set Europe ablaze'; it later also operated in the Far East. It promoted and coordinated resistance activity in enemy-occupied territory until the end of **World War II**. ▷ **Free French**

Speenhamland system

The most famous of many local expedients to improve the operation of the old **Poor Laws** at a time of crisis. The name was taken from the Berkshire parish whose magistrates in 1795 introduced scales of relief for labourers dependent both on the prevailing price of bread and the size of labourers' families. The principles spread to many southern and eastern parishes in the early 19c. It was much criticized by political economists for encouraging the poor to breed!

Spion Kop, Battle of (1900)

A battle of the second Boer War which was part of the British attempt to relieve the Siege of **Ladysmith**, a town in Natal besieged by the Boers since Oct 1899. British forces attempted to take a hill a few miles from the town, and although they were close to success at one stage, the Boers succeeded in beating them off. There were 1 500 British casualties, and together with the reverse at Vaal Krantz in the same week, it continued the succession of defeats which the British suffered during the early months of the war. ▷ **Boer Wars**

Spurs, Battle of the (16 Aug 1513)

A battle between France and England, who had joined the **Holy League** of the Pope, Spain, and Venice against the French. **Henry VIII** laid siege to Thérouanne, near St Omer (Pas-de-Calais), and beat off the French relieving force in this battle, which was so called because of the precipitate French retreat. Thérouanne and Tournai were taken, but these successes had no lasting significance.

Stack, Lee (d.1924)

British soldier. He was Sirdar (British Commander-in-Chief of the Egyptian Army) in 1924, at a time when a combination of the first Wafdist government in Egypt and the first Labour government in Britain was resulting in a certain amount of British sympathy being shown for Egyptian nationalist aspirations. Unfortunately for both sides, when Sa'd Zaghlul came to London for negotiations his demands were well beyond what the British government was prepared to concede. The upshot was increased hostility to the British in Egypt and particularly to the rank and status of the Sirdar. Stack was murdered in Cairo in late 1924 to some extent as a result of this. The subsequent ultimatum presented to Egypt by the British, although certainly not strong enough for the British expatriates in Egypt, was sufficient to jolt the Egyptian government. This, coupled with the complicity in a number of political murders with which certain Wafdists were charged, was enough to bring down the Wafdist government.

St Alban's Raid (1865)
A Confederate attack made from Canada, on the town of St Albans, Vermont, during the American Civil War. Such raids heightened tension between Great Britain and the USA during the Civil War, and fears of retaliation were one of the factors leading Canadians to Confederation.

Stamp Act (1765)
A British Act passed by the administration of George **Grenville**, which levied a direct tax on all papers required in discharging official business in the American colonies. It was the first direct tax levied without the consent of the colonial assemblies, and it caused much discontent in the colonies, six of which petitioned against it. (The measure provoked the colonists' famous slogan, 'No taxation without representation'.) The Act was withdrawn by the **Rockingham** government in 1766. ▷ **American Revolution**

Stanhope, Charles, 3rd Earl (1753–1816)
English scientist and politician. He became an MP and married the daughter of **Pitt, 'the Elder'**. A strong enthusiast for the French Revolution, he advocated peace with **Napoleon I** (1800). As a scientist, he invented a new microscope lens, two types of calculating machine, the first iron hand-printing press, and several other devices.

Stanhope, James, 1st Earl (1675–1721)
English soldier and politician. He entered parliament as a Whig in 1701, and commanded in Spain during the War of the **Spanish Succession** (1702–13). He was Secretary of State for Foreign Affairs under **George I**, and became his Chief Minister in 1717. ▷ **Whigs**

Star Chamber, Court of
The royal prerogative court for hearing subjects' petitions and grievances, of uncertain date but increasingly prominent under the Tudors and early Stuarts. It consisted of privy councillors and two chief justices, who dealt swiftly and efficiently with cases, particularly those involving public order. **Charles I** used it against government opponents. It was abolished by the **Long Parliament** in 1641. ▷ **Stuart, House of; Tudor, House of**

Steel, Sir David (Martin Scott) (1938–   )
Scottish politician. He became an MP in 1965, sponsored a controversial Bill to reform the laws on abortion (1966–7), and was active in the anti-apartheid movement. He became Liberal Chief Whip (1970–5), before succeeding Jeremy Thorpe as Liberal Party leader (1976–88). In 1981 he led the party into an alliance with the **Social Democratic Party**. Following successful merger negotiations between the two parties (1987–8), he was the last leader of the Liberal Party. He remained active in politics both as an MP and party spokesman.

Stephen (c.1090–1154)
Last Norman King of England (1135/54). He was the son of Stephen, Count of Blois, and Adela, the daughter of **William I, 'the Conqueror'**. He had sworn to accept **Henry I**'s daughter, Empress Matilda, as Queen, but seized the English crown and was recognized as Duke of Normandy on Henry's death in 1135. Though defeated and captured at the Battle of Lincoln (Feb 1141), he was released nine months later, after Matilda's supporters had been routed at Winchester. However, Matilda strengthened her grip on the West Country; **David I** of Scotland annexed the northern English counties by 1141; and Matilda's husband, Count Geoffrey of Anjou, conquered Normandy by 1144–5. Stephen was also repeatedly challenged by baronial rebellions, and after 18 years of virtually continuous warfare, he was forced in 1153 to accept Matilda's son, the future **Henry II**, as his lawful successor. His reputation as the classic incompetent king of English medieval history is nevertheless undeserved. He was remarkably tenacious in seeking to uphold royal rights, and his war strategy was basically sound. His inability to defend the Norman Empire was due largely to the sheer weight of his military burdens, especially the major offensives of the Scots in the north and the **Angevins** in the south.

Stern Gang
Palestinian covert organization formed under Avraham Stern in 1940 after disagreement with the **Irgun** over a cease-fire with the British during **World War II**. Conflict between the Stern Gang and the British climaxed in 1942, when British forces sought and killed members of the group, including Stern himself. Thereafter, his followers adopted the name *Lohamei Herut Yisrael* ('Fighters for Israel's Freedom'), but others dubbed them the Stern Gang/

Group. Their aim was to attack British installations and personnel in Palestine in the struggle for a Jewish state. Although collaborating with the **Haganah** and Irgun during 1945, many found the Stern Gang unnecessarily brutal. After 1948 the group was disbanded.

Stirling, William Alexander, 1st Earl of (1567–1640)
Scottish statesman, poet and scholar. Having gained the patronage of King **James VI and I** through his poetry and his kinship to the Earl of Argyll, he gained the King's support for his aim of acquiring a colony for Scotland, along the lines of New France and New England. He was granted (1621) the proprietorship of Nova Scotia ('New Scotland'), the three Atlantic provinces and the Gaspé Peninsula. The last was also claimed by the French, and the renewal of their claim eventually led to the failure of his ambitions. Alexander's major problem was to find Scots willing to settle in the colony, and James sought to help him by the promise of hereditary baronetcies and territory in the colony to Scots who would support a number of settlers. However, this measure failed under both James and his son, **Charles I**. In 1631 Alexander was commanded to yield Port-Royal to the French, after a challenge from Richelieu's Company of One Hundred Associates. He died with his dream unfulfilled, surrounded by creditors.

Stormberg, Battle of (1899)
One of the battles of the 'black week' when the British suffered several reverses during the Boer War. They were defeated while attempting to take an important railway junction to the south of the Orange River, one of the keys to Bloemfontein. ▷ **Boer Wars**

Stormont
A suburb of east Belfast and site of a castle which housed the seat of government in Northern Ireland from 1921 to 1972. The Northern Ireland parliament, created by the Government of Ireland Act 1920, comprised a Senate and a House of Commons, both dominated by Protestants. It had jurisdiction over domestic affairs in the province until suspended by the Northern Ireland (Temporary Provisions) Act, 1972 which established direct rule from Westminster. ▷ **Bloody Sunday** (1972); **Ulster 'Troubles'**

Strafford, Thomas Wentworth, 1st Earl of (1593–1641)
English statesman. He was knighted in 1611, and in 1614 succeeded to his baronetcy, and entered parliament. He acted with the Opposition (1625–8), but after being appointed President of the North and Baron Wentworth (1628), he supported **Charles I**. In 1632 he became Lord Deputy of Ireland, where he imposed firm rule. In 1639 he became the King's principal adviser, and Earl of Strafford. His suppression of the rebellion in Scotland failed, and he was impeached by the **Long Parliament**. Despite a famous defence at Westminster, he was executed on Tower Hill.
▷ **Bishops Wars**

Straits Convention (1841)
By this treaty, the Straits, the passage from the Bosphorus to the Dardanelles which links the Black Sea to the Mediterranean, was placed under international control. The treaty between the Great Powers closed the Straits to foreign warships during peacetime, a provision intended to reconcile Russian and British shipping interests since neither country would be able to menace the other's fleet on the Black Sea or the Mediterranean.

Stresa, Conference of (11–14 Apr 1935)
Following **Hitler**'s declaration of German rearmament (16 Mar 1935), the Italian, French and British governments condemned the move at a meeting in Stresa. They guaranteed Austria's independence and agreed on future cooperation (Stresa Front). The Front was quickly undermined by the Anglo-German Naval Treaty (18 June 1935) and Italy's invasion of Abyssinia and intervention in the **Spanish Civil War**.

Stuart, Charles Edward (Louis Philip Casimir), 'the Young Pretender' (1720–88)
Claimant to the British crown. The son of James Francis Edward **Stuart**, he became the focus of Jacobite hopes. In 1744 he went to France to head the planned invasion of England, but after the defeat of the French fleet he was unable to leave for over a year. He landed with seven followers at Eriskay in the Hebrides (July 1745) and in Aug raised his father's standard at Glenfinnan. The clansmen flocked to him, Edinburgh surrendered, and he kept court at Holyrood. Victorious at Prestonpans, he invaded England, but turned back at Derby for lack of evident English

support, and was routed by the Duke of **Cumberland** at the Battle of **Culloden** (1746). The rising was ruthlessly suppressed, and he was hunted for five months. With the help of Flora **Macdonald** he crossed from Benbecula to Portree, disguised as her maid. He landed in Brittany, then lived in France and Italy, where (after his father's death in 1766) he assumed the title of Charles III of Great Britain. ▷ **Forty-Five Rebellion; Jacobites; Stuart, House of**

Stuart, House of

The Scottish royal family, commencing with **Robert II** (1371/90), which succeeded to the English throne in 1603 with the accession of **James VI and I**, the cousin of **Elizabeth I**, and the great-grandson of **Henry VIII**'s sister, Margaret. As English monarchs the family's fortunes were mixed. James VI and I and **Charles II** were both successful politicians (although the second spent his first 11 years as king in exile). But **Charles I** and **James VII and II** were not, and both lost their thrones. The Stuart monarchy ended in 1714 with the death of Queen **Anne**, although pretenders laid claim to the throne and invaded Britain in support of their claims as late as 1745. ▷ **Stuart, Charles Edward; Stuart, James Francis Edward**

Stuart, James Francis Edward, 'the Old Pretender' (1688–1766)

Claimant to the British throne. He was the only son of James VII of Scotland and II of England and his second wife, Mary of Modena. As a baby he was conveyed to St Germain, and proclaimed successor on his father's death (1701). After failing to land in Scotland in 1708, he served with the French in the Low Countries. In 1715 he landed at Peterhead during the Jacobite rising, but left Scotland some weeks later. Thereafter he lived mainly in Rome, where he died. ▷ **Fifteen Rebellion; Jacobites; James VII and II; Stuart, Charles Edward; Stuart, House of**

Suez Crisis (1956)

A political crisis focused on the Suez Canal. Intensive rearmament by Egypt, the Egyptian nationalization of the Suez Canal, and the establishment of a unified command with Jordan and Syria aimed at surrounding and eliminating Israel, led in Oct to a pre-emptive strike by Israel in Sinai. Following this attack, the UK and France asked both sides to withdraw from the Canal Zone and agree to temporary occupation. When this was rejected by Egypt, the British and French invaded, but had to withdraw

following diplomatic action by the USA and USSR. Israel was also forced to relinquish the Sinai Peninsula. There have been many allegations of collusion between Israel, France and the UK.
▷ **Eden, Anthony**

suffragettes

Those women who identified with and were members of the late 19c movement to secure voting rights for women. The vote was 'won' after the end of **World War I** (1918), though it was limited to those women of 30 years of age or over. There were many men and women opponents of female suffrage, and in England it was not until 1928 that women over 21 achieved the right to vote.
▷ **Pankhurst, Emmeline**

Sugar Act (1764)

British statute that attempted for the first time to raise colonial revenue without reference to the colonial assemblies. Its main aim was to impose and collect customs duties and to prevent illegal trade.The colonials responded with protest, but not outright resistance, and the Act was sporadically enforced until the complete breakdown of British-American relations. ▷ **American Revolution; Boston Tea Party; Stamp Act; Townshend Acts**

Sunderland, Robert Spencer, 2nd Earl of (1641–1702)

English statesman. He became an influential adviser, successively, of **Charles II**, **James VII and II** and **William III**. He was dismissed as Secretary of State in 1681 for voting to exclude James from the succession, but reinstated in 1683, becoming Chief Minister under James in 1685, and a Catholic (1688). On William's accession, he fled to Europe, but after renouncing his Catholicism was allowed to return in 1691. He was Lord Chancellor for a while in 1697.

Surat

A coastal town in present-day Gujarat, which was subordinated by the British in 1709. Surat was a big trading and export centre under the Mughals and its value as a fort and as a strategic point between the Deccan and Gujarat was very high. In its heyday, ships from Surat traded with East Africa, the Middle East and throughout the Indian Ocean, and fortunes were made from the sale of textiles, precious metals and spices. In 1664 Surat was sacked by the Maratha leader, Shivaji. Although it subsequently recovered from this, in the declining years of the Mughal Empire the port became increasingly vulnerable. After the death of Muhammad Ali, the last great merchant of Surat, at the hands of the Mughal governor in 1733, a British blockade in 1734 and an attack on the merchant fleet in 1735, the majority of merchants fled to the relative safety of the British-controlled port of Bombay. After the establishment of British paramountcy in western India in 1803, the fortunes of the port then slowly recovered. Surat became important to the Indian national movement when a famous session of the Indian National Congress was held there in 1907. This session witnessed a clash between so-called 'moderates' and 'extremists'. The meeting broke up in disorder because of extremist attempts at coercion, but the episode ended with the assertion of the supremacy of the 'moderate' faction under Gokhale Banerjee, Sinha and Mehta.

Svein I Haraldsson, 'Fork-Beard' (d.1014)
King of Denmark (985/1014) and, for five winter weeks, of England (1014). He was the son of Harald Bluetooth, but rebelled against his father and deposed him in 985. His reign was notable for a series of military campaigns against England from 994 onwards. On each occasion, King **Ethelred the Unready** paid escalating amounts of *Danegeld* to buy off the Danish invaders but each time they returned for more. In 1013 Svein Fork-Beard launched another expedition with imperial intent, taking with him his son, **Canute**. By the end of the year, King Ethelred had fled to safety in Normandy, leaving Svein to take up the crown; but five weeks later, on 3 Feb 1014, Svein died, and Canute returned for a time to Denmark.

Swadeshi
A Hindi term meaning 'of one's own country', this was a slogan used as part of an Indian campaign of boycotting foreign-made goods, initiated in protest against the partition of Bengal into two separate administrative divisions by the British in 1905, in defiance of Indian public opinion. The policy was viewed as an attempt to perpetuate British rule by dividing the Indian population, particularly the Muslims of East Bengal from the Hindus of West Bengal. Advocates of *Swadeshi* urged the Indian people to wear *khadi* or home-made country-cloth, amongst other things. The first example of mass opposition to British rule, the campaign led eventually to the abandonment of the partition of Bengal in 1911.

Swaraj

A Hindi term meaning 'self-government' or 'home rule'. It was used by Indian nationalists to describe independence from British rule.

Swing Riots (1830–1)

A movement of agricultural workers, especially in the south and east of England, consisting of a series of arson attacks and the destruction of threshing machines. The uprising was put down by the Whig government, resulting in 19 executions and nearly 500 transportations, but the labourers won some wage concessions and delayed the introduction of mechanization. ▷ **Luddites**

Sykes–Picot Agreement (1916)

A secret agreement concluded in this year by diplomat Sir Mark Sykes (for Britain) and Georges Picot (for France) partitioning the **Ottoman Empire** after the war. France was to be the dominant power in Syria and Lebanon, and Britain in Transjordan, Iraq, and northern Palestine. The rest of Palestine was to be under international control, and an Arab state was to be established.

T

Tehran Conference (28 Nov–1 Dec 1943)

The first inter-allied conference of **World War II**, attended by Stalin, Roosevelt and Winston **Churchill**. The subjects discussed were the coordination of Allied landings in France with the Soviet offensive against Germany, Russian entry in the war against Japan, and the establishment of a post-war international organization. Failure to agree on the future government of Poland foreshadowed the start of the **Cold War**.

Tel el-Kebir, Battle of (1882)

An engagement between British and Egyptian forces which resulted in the British becoming the effective rulers of Egypt. It followed a period of increasing Egyptian ambition to extend her power, which had led to a financial crisis. In 1875 the Egyptian Khedive Ismail sold his Suez Canal shares to the British government, and in 1880 an international debt commission was established. These inroads on Egyptian independence stirred the nationalism of young army officers. In 1881 an army faction under Colonel 'Urabi Pasha forced the Khedive to appoint a new ministry with 'Urabi as Minister for War. The British regarded this as a dangerous destabilization of the country; the Royal Navy bombarded Alexandria and landed a British army under Sir Garnet **Wolseley**, who defeated 'Urabi at Tel el-Kebir.

temperance movement

An organized response to the social disruption caused by the alcoholism so widespread in the 18c and 19c. Temperance societies were started first in the USA, then in Britain and Scandinavia. The original aim was to moderate drinking, but prohibition became the goal. Federal prohibition became a reality in the USA in 1919, but was impossible to enforce and was repealed in 1933.

Test Act (1673)

A British Act passed by a parliament anxious to curb Catholic influence at **Charles II**'s court. Every office holder had to take

294

Oaths of Supremacy and Allegiance, and to take communion according to the rites of the Church of England. A declaration against transubstantiation also had to be made. The passage of the Act necessitated the resignation of the King's brother, James, Duke of York, as Lord High Admiral. The Act remained in force until 1828. ▷ **Catholic Emancipation**

Tewkesbury, Battle of (4 May 1471)

A decisive battle in the Wars of the **Roses** at which **Edward IV** defeated Lancastrian forces hastily assembled by Queen Margaret, wife of **Henry VI**. Their son, Prince Edward, was killed as were many other leading Lancastrian supporters. Soon afterwards, Edward IV was able to re-enter London, order the death of Henry VI in the Tower of London and resume his reign, which was not thereafter seriously challenged.

Thatcher, Margaret (Hilda) (1925–)

English politician. Elected to parliament in 1959, after holding junior office, she became Minister of Education (1970–4). In 1975 she replaced Edward **Heath** as Leader of the **Conservative Party** to become the first woman party leader in British politics. Under her leadership, the Conservative Party moved towards a more 'right-wing' position, and British politics and society became more polarized than at any other time since **World War II**. Her government (1979–90) privatized several nationalized industries and utilities, made professional services, such as healthcare and education, more responsive to market forces, and reduced the role of local government as a provider of services. Her election for a third term of office in 1987 was aided, as in 1983, by divisions in the **Labour Party** and a more equal division of votes between the opposition parties than had hitherto been usual. She became the longest serving 20c Prime Minister in 1988 but her popularity waned and her anti-European statements caused damaging division within the Conservative Party. She resigned soon after failing to win a sufficiently large majority in the Conservative leadership contest of Nov 1990, and retired from her parliamentary seat of Finchley in 1992.

Thirty Years War (1618–48)

A complex phase, specifically German in origin, of a long and intermittent power struggle between the kings of France and the Habsburg rulers of the Holy Roman Empire and Spain (1491–

1715). The background was complicated by the developing confrontation between militant Calvinism and reinvigorated, post-Tridentine Catholicism; also by the underlying constitutional conflict between the Holy Roman Emperor and the German princes, illustrated in the Bohemian Revolt (1618). With the Elector Frederick V's defeat (1620) and intervention by other powers (eg Sweden, Transylvania, Denmark and France), the conflict intensified, spreading to other theatres. Isolated as Spain collapsed, the Emperor opened negotiations (1643–8) which ended the German war, at the Peace of Westphalia. ▷ **Trent, Council of**

Throckmorton, Sir Nicholas (1515–71)
English diplomat. He fought at the Battle of **Pinkie** (1547), was knighted in 1547, and became Ambassador to France and Scotland. In 1569 he was imprisoned for promoting the scheme to marry **Mary, Queen of Scots**, to the Duke of Norfolk, but soon released. His daughter, Elizabeth, married Sir Walter **Raleigh**; his nephew, Francis (1554–84) was executed for planning a conspiracy to overthrow **Elizabeth I**.

Tianjin, Treaty of (1858)
The second unequal treaty imposed on China by the Western powers following the invasion of an Anglo-French expeditionary force in 1856 to enforce revision of the Treaty of **Nanjing** (1842) to allow for an expansion of foreign trade. Under the terms of the treaty, China was compelled to open 10 new **treaty ports** and to allow permanent foreign legations in the capital. Furthermore, foreigners could travel in the interior (where they would continue to enjoy the privilege of extraterritoriality), while the Yangzi River was opened to foreign navigation. When the Qing court refused to ratify the treaty, a second Anglo-French offensive was launched, which led to the occupation of the Chinese capital in 1860. The Beijing Convention (1860) confirmed the terms of this treaty, although additional concessions were wrung from the Qing: Britain acquired the Kowloon peninsula (which became part of the colony of Hong Kong), while missionaries gained the right to travel and own property in the interior.

Tobruk, Battles of (1941–2)
A key city in Libya, Tobruk was taken from the Italians in Jan 1941 by Wavell, then in command of the Eighth Army. The arrival, however, in Libya of Rommel with his Afrika Korps in

Mar of the same year saw the British withdrawing eastward. The subsequent siege of Tobruk, which was garrisoned largely by Australian troops, lasted for some eight months until the garrison was able to break out. Auchinleck, who was now in command of the Eighth Army and whom they managed to join, mounted a major offensive which was to extend British control over Cyrenaica as far as Benghazi bringing back Tobruk with it. However, Rommel's counter-offensive towards Egypt meant that Tobruk was again placed under siege, this time falling in June 1942. In the event, Auchinleck was able to check Rommel's advance at the first Battle of **El Alamein** and it was the successful western drive of Montgomery which finally recaptured Tobruk in Nov 1942.

Tolpuddle Martyrs
Agricultural labourers at Tolpuddle, Dorset, in England, who were organized in 1833 into a trade union by a Methodist local preacher, George Loveless (1796–1874), convicted of taking illegal oaths, and transported. The action provoked substantial protests, and the labourers were eventually pardoned.

Tone, (Theobald) Wolfe (1763–98)
Irish nationalist. He acted as Secretary of the Catholic Committee, helped to organize the Society of **United Irishmen** (1791), and had to flee to the USA and to France (1795). He induced France to invade Ireland on two occasions, and was captured during the second expedition. He was condemned to be hanged, but committed suicide in Dublin.

Tooke, John Horne (1736–1812)
English politician. Born John Horne, he became a lawyer and in 1760 a vicar. A radical, in 1771 he formed the Constitutional Society, supporting the American colonists and parliamentary reform. His spirited opposition to an enclosure bill procured him the favour of the rich Mr Tooke of Purley in Surrey, which led to his new surname and *The Diversions of Purley* (1786), written while in prison for supporting the American cause. He was tried for high treason in 1794, acquitted, and became an MP in 1801.
▷ **American Revolution; Wilkes, John**

Tories
The political party that emerged in 1679–80 as the group opposed to the exclusion of James, Duke of York, from succession to the

throne. The name was taken from 17c Irish outlaws who plundered and killed English settlers. The party developed after the **Glorious Revolution** (1688) as the supporters of the divine right of monarchy, and had especial support from the country squire-archy and most sections of the Anglican Church. It opposed religious toleration for Catholics and Dissenters. The Tories enjoyed periods of power in the reign of Queen **Anne**, but the party went into decline after the Hanoverian succession, when some of its supporters became **Jacobites**. It is generally agreed to have revived under **Pitt**, 'the Younger' as the leading opposition to French revolutionary ideology in the 1790s, and Lord **Liverpool** became the first Prime Minister to acknowledge the title 'Tory' in the early 19c. Toryism developed into Conservatism under **Peel**, but survived as a nickname for the Conservatives. ▷ **Conservative Party; James VII and II; Whigs**

Tostig (d.1066)
Earl of Northumbria. He was the son of Godwin and brother of **Harold II**. After return from banishment in 1052, **Edward the Confessor** created him Earl of Northumbria (1055) over which he ruled both violently and as a frequent absentee. He was supplanted by Morcar, whose title was confirmed by Edward and Harold. Tostig was banished and, upon Harold's succession (1066), plotted to overthrow him. He aided **Harald Hardraade**'s invasion from Norway in Sep and was killed at the Battle of Stamford Bridge (25 Sep 1066).

Townshend (of Rainham), Charles, 2nd Viscount (1674–1738)
English politician. He succeeded his father as viscount (1687), was made Secretary of State by **George I** (1714–16 and 1721–30), and became a leading figure in the Whig ministry with his brother-in-law, Robert **Walpole**. After a resignation engineered by Walpole, he became known as 'turnip Townshend' for his interest in agricultural improvement, and his proposal to use turnips in crop rotation. ▷ **Whigs**

Townshend Acts (1767)
British statutes imposing taxes on five categories of goods imported into the American colonies, after successful colonial resistance to the **Stamp Act** (1765). The Townshend Taxes likewise met resistance from the colonists, and four categories were repealed in 1770. The fifth, on tea, stayed in effect until the **Boston**

Tea Party. The Acts are named after British Chancellor of the Exchequer, Charles Townshend (1725–67), who sponsored them.
▷ **American Revolution**

Trafalgar, Battle of (21 Oct 1805)
The most famous naval engagement of the **Napoleonic Wars**, which destroyed **Napoleon I**'s hopes of invading England and established British naval supremacy for a century. Fought off Cape Trafalgar, Spain, between the British and Franco-Spanish fleets, the British triumph was marred by the death of **Nelson** at the moment of victory.

transportation
Sentence of banishment from England for those convicted of certain offences, introduced in 1597. Increasingly large numbers of English convicts were shipped to North America in the 17c and 18c, but the practice was ended by the **American Revolution**. As a result, the British government turned their attention to Australia. 162 000 convicts (137 000 males and 25 000 females) were transported to Australia from 1788 to 1868, mainly to New South Wales (1788–1840), Van Diemen's Land (1803–52) and Western Australia (1850–68). Most of the convicts were young, poorly-educated urban-dwellers convicted of some form of theft. In the early years of settlement, convict labour was used on public works; subsequently the typical fate of most convicts was assignment to private service. ▷ **penal settlements**

treaty ports
The ports opened by China during the 19c as a result of unequal treaties with the West. The first five (Canton, Amoy (Xiamen), Fuzhou, Ningbo and Shanghai) were opened by the Treaty of **Nanjing** (1842) and by the end of the 19c there were over 50 treaty ports. Situated along China's coast and inland on major rivers, the treaty ports were places in which foreigners could reside, trade, and (after 1895) establish manufacturing enterprises whose goods were not subject to Chinese taxation. Foreigners enjoyed the privilege of extraterritoriality. In a number of treaty ports (eg Shanghai) foreign powers also leased land (known as concession areas) where they exercised legal jurisdiction and collected taxes. Condemned as bastions of foreign privilege by a growing Chinese anti-imperialist movement from the 1920s on, the treaty ports

came to an end when the unequal treaties were formally abolished in 1943.

Trenchard (of Wolfeton), Hugh Montague, 1st Viscount
(1873–1956)
English service chief, marshal of the RAF. He joined the army in 1893, served in India, South Africa, and West Africa, and developed an interest in aviation. He commanded the Royal Flying Corps in **World War I**, helped to establish the RAF (1918), and became the first Chief of Air Staff (1918–29). As Commissioner of the London Metropolitan Police (1931–5), he founded the police college at Hendon. He became a peer in 1930.

Trent Affair (1861)
An incident between the USA and Britain during the American Civil War, in which the USS *San Jacinto* forcibly removed two officials of the Confederate States from the British ship *Trent* while in international waters. The issue provoked considerable British anger until the Confederate officials were released by the American Secretary of State.

Triennial Acts (1641, 1664 and 1694)
The collective name given to legislation passed requiring Parliament to assemble at least once every three years, as a reaction to the personal rule of **Charles I**. The 1694 Act also limited the life of each parliament to three years. ▷ **Septennial Act**

Tripartite Declaration (May 1950)
This represented an attempt by Britain, France and the USA to limit arms supplies to Israel and the Arab states in the wake of the emergence of the state of Israel, in the hope that this would ensure some stability for the area. Arms supplies were to be conditional on non-aggression, and the signatories to the Declaration undertook to take action both within and outside the framework of the **UN** in cases of frontier violation. Closer French relations with Israel subjected the Declaration to some strain, and with the Soviet arms deal with Gamal Abd al-Nasser's Egypt in 1955 it became a dead letter.

Triple Entente

A series of agreements between Britain and France (1904) and Britain and Russia (1907) initially to resolve outstanding colonial differences. It aligned Britain to France and Russia, who had concluded a military alliance in 1893–4. In 1914, the Triple Entente became a military alliance.

Tudor, House of

A North Wales gentry family, one of whose scions married a Plantagenet in the early 15c. Elevated to the peerage in the mid-15c, they ruled England from 1485 to 1603. The dynasty began when Henry (later **Henry VII**), 2nd Earl of Richmond and son of Margaret Beaufort (a Lancastrian claimant to the crown), overthrew **Richard III** in 1485. It ended with the death of **Elizabeth I** in 1603. ▷ **Edward VI; Henry VIII; Mary I; Plantagenet Dynasty**

Tyler, Wat (d.1381)

English leader of the **Peasants Revolt** (1381). The rebels of Kent, after taking Rochester Castle, chose him as captain, and marched to Canterbury and London. At the Smithfield conference with **Richard II** blows were exchanged, and Tyler was wounded by the Mayor of London, William Walworth. He was taken to St Bartholomew's Hospital, where Walworth had him dragged out and beheaded.

U

Ulster 'Troubles'

The name conventionally given to violence in Northern Ireland
from 1968. They originated in conflict between Catholics and
Protestants over civil rights and perceived discrimation against
the Catholic minority in the Province. The promise of reforms by
the Ulster Premier Terence O'Neill lost him the confidence of
loyalists in his Unionist Party and he resigned in 1969. Reforms
implemented by his successor, James Chichester-Clark, provoked
rioting between Protestants and Catholics and an increase in the
specific acts of sectarian violence. The British Army was sent to
maintain peace in 1969 but continuing violence resulted in the
imposition of internment without trial for Catholics only under
Brian Faulkner's administration. Anti-British Army feeling
among the Catholics and mainland **IRA** attacks increased mark-
edly after the **Bloody Sunday** demonstrations (30 Jan 1972) and
direct rule was imposed in Mar. In Dec 1973, the British, Ulster
and Irish governments signed the power-sharing Sunningdale
Agreement, providing for representation in the Province's government of both the Catholic and Protestant populations, but continued Protestant Unionist resistance to the agreement led to the
collapse of the **Stormont** executive in May 1974. Since then Ulster
has been ruled directly from Westminster and sectarian killings
have continued. The IRA has from time to time concentrated
its attention on England with bombings and assassinations of
prominent Conservative politicians, such as Airey Neave in 1979
and Ian Gow in 1990. Political initiatives to find a solution to an
apparently intractable problem have been frustrated.

UN (United Nations Organisation)

An organization formed to maintain world peace and foster international cooperation, formally established on 24 Oct 1945 with
51 founder countries. The UN Charter, which was drafted during
the war by the USA, UK and USSR, remains virtually unaltered
despite the growth in membership and activities. There are six

'principal organs'. The General Assembly is the plenary body which controls much of the UN's work, supervises the subsidiary organs, sets priorities, and debates major issues of international affairs. The 15-member Security Council is dominated by the five permanent members (China, France, UK, USSR and USA) who each have the power of veto over any resolutions; the remaining 10 are elected for two-year periods. The primary role of the Council is to maintain international peace and security; its decisions, unlike those of the General Assembly, are binding on all other members. It is empowered to order mandatory sanctions, call for ceasefires, and establish peacekeeping forces (these forces were awarded the Nobel Peace Prize in 1988). The use of the veto has prevented it from intervening in a number of disputes, such as Vietnam. The Secretariat, under the Secretary-General, employs some 16 000 at the UN's headquarters in New York City and 50 000 worldwide. The staff are answerable only to the UN, not national governments, and are engaged in considerable diplomatic work. The Secretary-General is often a significant person in international diplomacy and is able to take independent initiatives. The International Court of Justice consists of 15 judges appointed by the Council and the Assembly. As only states can bring issues before it, its jurisdiction depends on the consent of the states who are a party to a dispute. It also offers advisory opinions to various organs of the UN. The Economic and Social Council is elected by the General Assembly; it supervises the work of various committees, commissions, and expert bodies in the economic and social area, and co-ordinates the work of UN specialized agencies. The Trusteeship Council oversees the transition of Trust territories to self-government. In addition to the organs established under the Charter, there is a range of subsidiary agencies, many with their own constitutions and membership, and some predating the UN. The main agencies are the Food and Agriculture Organization, the Intergovernmental Maritime Consultative Organization, the International Atomic Energy Authority, the International Bank for Reconstruction and Development ('World Bank'), the International Civil Aviation Organization, the International Development Association, the International Finance Corporation, the International Fund for Agricultural Development, the International Labour Organization, the International Monetary Fund, the United Nations Educational, Scientific and Cultural Organization, the Universal Postal Union, the International Telecommunication Union, the World Meteorological

Organization, and the World Health Organization. The UN has presently 160 members. It is generally seen as a forum where states pursue their national interest, rather than as an institution of world government, but it is not without considerable impact.

Uniformity, Acts of (1549, 1552, 1559 and 1662)
A series of acts passed by English parliaments which sought to impose religious uniformity by requiring the use of the Church of England liturgy as contained in the Book of Common Prayer (various editions, 1549–1662). The act of 1552 penalized Catholic recusants; that of 1662 excluded dissenting Protestant clergy.

Union, Acts of (1707 and 1800)
The Acts which joined England in legislative union with Scotland (1707) and Ireland (1800). The 1707 Act brought 45 Scottish MPs to join the new House of Commons of Great Britain, and 16 peers became members of the House of Lords; the Scottish legal system, however, remained separate. The 1800 Act created the United Kingdom of Great Britain and Ireland, which came into effect in 1801, and lasted until 1922. Union was brought about after the collapse of the Irish rebellion (1798) in order to increase British security during the French wars. The Irish parliament was abolished; 100 Irish MPs were added to the UK House of Commons, and 32 Peers to the Lords. The Churches of England and Ireland were united.

Union Movement
A party formed by Sir Oswald **Mosley** in 1948 as a successor to his New Party (1931) and the British Union of Fascists (1932). It put up a handful of candidates during the period 1959–66, but failed to secure a significant number of votes. The party's main platform was opposition to immigration, but it also included a call to unite Europe into a vast market to buy from and sell to Africa. Mosley gave up the leadership in 1966, and the movement went into decline, dying out by the end of the 1960s. ▷ **Blackshirts**

United Irishmen, Society of
A society formed in Belfast in 1791 by Protestant lawyer Wolfe **Tone**, which supported the French Revolution and espoused both religious equality and parliamentary reform. Its early support was primarily located in Ulster. As agitation increased, so United

Irishmen became increasingly associated with support for Catholicism. The society was instrumental in organizing French support for the unsuccessful Irish rebellion of 1798, and afterwards went into decline.

Utrecht, Peace of (11 Apr 1713)

The treaty which ended the War of the **Spanish Succession**, signed between England, the Dutch Republic, Spain and France, with the other powers agreeing in due course. By its terms Philip of Anjou became King Philip V of Spain, but the southern Netherlands went to the Austrian Habsburgs, along with Spanish parts of Italy. England obtained Gibraltar, and parts of Canada (from France). The Dutch contained France, obtained some possessions in Gelderland, and gained English support for the **Barrier Treaties**.

V

Vaal Kraantz Reverse (5–8 Feb 1900)

An incident in the Boer War in which the British general Sir Redvers Buller attacked Boers on a ridge of kopjes a few miles east of Spion Kop in an attempt to relieve Ladysmith. He was forced to withdraw and the British commander-in-chief, Roberts, was given authority to dismiss Sir 'Reverses' Buller.

Vane, Sir Henry (1613–62)

English statesman. He travelled in Europe, became a Puritan, and sailed for New England in 1635, where he was Governor of Massachusetts; but his advocacy of religious toleration lost him popularity, and he returned in 1637. He entered parliament, became joint Treasurer of the Navy, and was knighted (1640). He helped to impeach **Strafford**, promoted the **Solemn League and Covenant** (1643), and was a strong supporter of the parliamentary cause in the **English Civil Wars**. During the **Commonwealth** he was appointed one of the Council of State (1649–53), but he opposed **Cromwell**'s becoming Lord Protector in 1653, and retired from politics. On Cromwell's death he returned to public life (1659), opposed the **Restoration**, and was imprisoned and executed. ▷ **Protectorate**

Venezuelan Boundary Dispute

A dispute between Britain and Venezuela over the boundary of British Guiana (now Guyana). In 1895 this provoked a brief but acute crisis in Anglo-American relations, the USA forcing Britain to accept arbitration. The dispute was settled in 1899.

Vereeniging, Peace of (1902)

The peace treaty which ended the Boer War, signed at Pretoria. The Boers won three important concessions: an amnesty for those who had risen in revolt within the Cape Colony; a promise that the British would deny the franchise to Africans until after the Boer republics were returned to representative government; and additional financial support for reconstruction. The Peace ensured that there would be no significant change in the political relationship of Whites and Blacks in South Africa. ▷ **Boer Wars**

Vernon, Edward (1684–1757)
British admiral. He joined the navy in 1700, and also became an MP (1727–41). In 1739, during the War of **Jenkins' Ear**, he was sent to harry the Spaniards in the Antilles, and his capture of Portobello made him a national hero. During the Jacobite **Forty-Five Rebellion** Vernon's effective dispositions in the Channel successfully kept the standby Gallic reinforcements in their ports. He was nicknamed 'Old Grog', from his grogram coat, and in 1740 ordered the dilution of navy rum with water, the mixture being thereafter known as 'grog'.

Victoria (1819–1901)
Queen of Great Britain (1837/1901) and Empress of India (1876/1901). She was the only child of **George III**'s fourth son, Edward, and Victoria Maria Louisa of Saxe-Coburg, sister of Leopold I, King of Belgium. Taught by Lord **Melbourne**, her first Prime Minister, she had a clear grasp of constitutional principles and the scope of her own prerogative, which she resolutely exercised in 1839 by setting aside the precedent which decreed dismissal of the current ladies of the bedchamber, thus causing **Peel** not to take up office as Prime Minister. In 1840 she married Prince **Albert** of **Saxe-Coburg-Gotha**, and had four sons and five daughters. Strongly influenced by her husband, with whom she worked in closest harmony, after his death (1861) she went into lengthy seclusion, neglecting many duties, which brought her unpopularity and motivated a republican movement. However, with her recognition as Empress of India, and the celebratory golden (1887) and diamond (1897) jubilees, she rose high in her subjects' favour, and increased the prestige of the monarchy. She had strong preferences for certain prime ministers (notably **Melbourne** and **Disraeli**) over others (notably Peel and **Gladstone**), but did not press these beyond the bounds of constitutional propriety. At various points in her long reign she exercised some influence over foreign affairs, and the marriages of her children had important diplomatic, as well as dynastic, implications in Europe. She and was succeeded by her son, **Edward VII**.

Vikings

Raiders, traders, and settlers from Norway, Sweden and Denmark, who between the late 8c and the mid-11c conquered and colonized large parts of Britain, Normandy and Russia; attacked Spain, Morocco and Italy; traded with Byzantium, Persia and India; discovered and occupied Iceland and Greenland; and reached the coast of North America. As sea-borne raiders they gained a deserved reputation for brutality and destructiveness, but as merchants and settlers they played an influential and positive role in the development of medieval Europe. Their earliest overseas settlements were in the Orkney and Shetland Islands, which remained united to the Norwegian crown until 1472.
▷ **Canute; Danelaw; Normans; Rollo**

Vimy Ridge

An escarpment five miles north-east of Arras (Pas-de-Calais), and a strongly held part of the German defence line on the Western Front in **World War I**. It was successfully stormed during the Battle of Arras by the Canadian Corps of the British 1st Army (1917). This feat of arms had great symbolic significance in establishing Canada's identity as an independent nation.

Vortigern (5c)

Semi-legendary King of Britain. According to **Bede**, he recruited Germanic mercenaries led by Hengist and Horsa to help fight off the **Picts** after the final withdrawal of the Roman administration from Britain (AD409). Tradition has it that the revolt of these Ytroops opened the way for the Germanic conquests and settlements in England. ▷ **Angles; Britain, Roman; Jutes; Saxons**

W

Waitangi, Treaty of (1840)

The treaty that marked the formal assumption of sovereignty over New Zealand by a reluctant British government. Based on the fiction that Maori society resembled European in concepts of sovereignty and organization of government, it recognized Maori property rights in which they were promised undisturbed possession, gave the crown the sole right of purchase should they wish to sell, and bestowed upon them the rights and privileges of British subjects. The land question nevertheless remained a source of contention and warfare between settlers and Maoris for much of the 19c. ▷ **Maori Wars**

Wakefield, Edward Gibbon (1796–1862)

English colonial politician. Sentenced for abduction in 1827, he wrote in prison *A Letter from Sydney* (1829), which outlined his theory (expanded in several other books) of systematic colonization by the sale of crown lands at a price sufficient to oblige intending purchasers to work for wages while amassing capital. The intention was to re-create English society as a basis for future self-government, attracting landowners by ensuring a supply of respectable labour, both male and female, and assisting labourers to emigrate from the proceeds of the land sales. He influenced the South Australian Association (which founded South Australia in 1836) and, as secretary (1838) to Lord Durham, the **Durham Report** on Canada. He formed (1837) the New Zealand Association and sent a shipload of colonists there (1839) to force the British government to recognize it as a colony. With George William, 4th Baron Lyttleton, he founded (1850) the Anglican colony of Canterbury, where he emigrated in 1853.

Wallace, William (c.1274–1305)

Scottish knight and champion of the independence of Scotland. He routed the English Army at Stirling (1297), and took control of the government of Scotland as 'Guardian', but was defeated by **Edward I** at Falkirk (1298). He was eventually captured near Glasgow (1305), and was hanged, drawn, and quartered at Smithfield, London. Many legends collected around him due to his immense popular appeal as a national figure resisting foreign oppression.

Walpole, Sir Robert (1676–1745)
English politician. He became a Whig MP in 1701, and was made Secretary for War (1708) and Treasurer of the Navy (1710). Sent to the Tower for alleged corruption during the Tory government (1712), he was recalled by **George I**, and made a Privy Councillor and (1715) Chancellor of the Exchequer. After the collapse of the South Sea Scheme, he again became Chancellor (1721), and was widely recognized as 'Prime Minister', a title (unknown to the constitution) which he hotly repudiated. A shrewd manipulator of men, he took trouble to consult backbench MPs, and followed policies of low taxation designed to win their favour. He was regarded as indispensable by both George I and **George II**. His popularity began to wane in the 1730s over the Excise Scheme and also over his determination to avoid foreign wars. He did not fully recover from the outbreak of a war he had opposed in 1739, and resigned in 1742. His period in office is widely held to have increased the influence of the House of Commons in the constitution. He was created Earl of Orford. ▷ **South Sea Bubble**

Walsingham, Sir Francis (c.1530–90)
English statesman. He studied at Cambridge, became a diplomat, and was made a Secretary of State to **Elizabeth I** (1573–90), a member of the Privy Council, and knighted. A Puritan sympathizer, and a strong opponent of the Catholics, he developed a complex system of espionage at home and abroad, enabling him to reveal the plots of **Throckmorton** and **Babington** against the Queen, and was one of the commissioners to try **Mary, Queen of Scots** at Fotheringay. ▷ **Puritanism**

Walter, Hubert (c.1140–1205)
English churchman and statesman. He became Bishop of Salisbury (1189), and accompanied **Richard I, 'the Lionheart'** on the Third Crusade. Appointed Archbishop of Canterbury in 1193, he played key roles in raising the ransom to secure Richard's release from captivity, and in containing the rebellion of the King's brother, **John**. At the end of 1193, he became justiciar of England,

and was responsible for all the business of government until his resignation in 1198. On John's accession (1199), he became Chancellor, and was consulted on important matters of state.
▷ **Crusades**

War of 1812

The name given to the hostilities between the UK and the United States between 1812 and 1814. Its deepest causes went back to some unfulfilled provisions of the Peace of 1783, which secured American independence. However, war was eventually provoked by the persistent refusal of Britain to recognize American neutral and maritime rights. After 1793, in the course of the Anglo-French war, American trade was incessantly disrupted and American ships continually subjected to boarding and their crews to impressment. The most notorious of these incidents, the surrender of the USS *Chesapeake* to HMS *Leopard* in 1807, provoked commercial retaliation with President Thomas Jefferson's embargo policy. The failure of both this and the subsequent Non-Intercourse Act to alter British policies eventually left the USA no other option but to declare war, if independence was to mean anything at all. Ironically, war began as British policy was changed with the suspension of the Orders in Council, while the most decisive military engagement, the American victory at the Battle of New Orleans, occurred after peace had been made at the Treaty of **Ghent** (Dec 1814). Apart from this defeat, the British were militarily more effective, victorious with their Indian allies against American attempts to gain Canadian land, and even burning down the Capitol and the White House in Washington. The peace treaty marked a change in the attitude of Britain towards the USA, allowing a mutually beneficial commercial relationship to develop and for the USA marking the achievement of substantive, as well as formal, independence.

Warwick, Richard Neville, Earl of ('the Kingmaker') (1428–71)

English soldier and politician. He exercised great power during the first phase of the Wars of the **Roses**. Created Earl of Warwick in 1450, he championed the Yorkist cause. In 1460 he defeated and captured **Henry VI** at Northampton, had his cousin, Edward of York, proclaimed King as **Edward IV** (1461), and then destroyed the Lancastrian army at Towton. When Edward tried to assert his independence, Warwick joined the Lancastrians, forced the King to flee to Holland, and restored Henry VI to the throne (1470). He was defeated and killed by Edward IV at the Battle of Barnet. ▷ **Lancaster, House of; York, House of**

Washington, Treaty of (1871)

Treaty between the USA and Great Britain (whose delegation included the Canadian Prime Minister, John A Macdonald). The USA demanded compensation for the damage inflicted during the American Civil War by Confederate raiders using arms manufactured in Britain, together with arbitration of the boundary south of Vancouver Island and the possession of the strategic island of San Juan. Canada hoped to negotiate a trade agreement in return for the admission of US fishermen to her inshore waters. Macdonald was well aware that Britain, above all, wished to establish good relations with the USA and he was determined that Canadian interests should not suffer. While the USA secured compensation and a favourable settlement of the boundary question, Macdonald ensured that Canada gained free navigation of the rivers of Alaska (crucial for the **Hudson's Bay Company**) in exchange for free US use of the St Lawrence. Fishing and trade agreements were also negotiated between Canada and the USA which formed the basis for a consultative arrangement to resolve problems before they became international crises involving the British.

Waterloo, Battle of (18 June 1815)

The final defeat of **Napoleon I**, ending the **Napoleonic Wars** and the Emperor's last bid for power in the Hundred Days. A hard-fought battle, in which **Blücher**'s Prussian force arrived at the climax to support **Wellington**'s mixed Allied force. A number of crucial blunders by the French contributed to their defeat.

Wavell, Archibald Percival, 1st Earl (1883–1950)

British field marshal. He served in South Africa and India, became **Allenby**'s Chief-of-Staff in Palestine, and in 1939 he was given the Middle East Command. He defeated the Italians in North Africa, but failed against Rommel, and in 1941 was transferred to India, where he became Viceroy (1943). He was made field marshal and viscount (1943), earl (1947), Constable of the Tower (1948), and Lord-Lieutenant of London (1949). ▷ **World War II**

Webb, Sidney (James) (1859–1947) and
(Martha) Beatrice (1858–1943)
English social reformers, historians, and economists, married in 1892. Sidney became a lawyer, and joined the **Fabian Society**, where he wrote many powerful tracts. Beatrice interested herself in the social problems of the time. After their marriage they were committed to advancing the causes of **socialism** and trade unionism, publishing their classic *History of Trade Unionism* (1894), *English Local Government* (1906–29, 9 vols), and other works. They also started the *New Statesman* (1913). Sidney became an MP (1922), President of the Board of Trade (1924), Dominions and Colonial Secretary (1929–30), and Colonial Secretary (1930–1), and was created a baron in 1929.

Webster–Ashburton Treaty (1842)
An agreement between Britain and the USA which established the boundary between north-east USA and Canada. Among specific issues were disputed territory between Maine and New Brunswick and at the north end of Lake Champlain, navigation rights on the St John's River, and control of the Mesabi iron deposits. The treaty also established provisions for later joint action between the USA and Britain.

Wellesley (of Norragh), Richard (Colley), 1st Marquis
(1760–1842)
Irish administrator. He became an MP (1784), a Lord of the Treasury (1786), a marquis (1799), and Governor-General of India (1797–1805). Under his administration British rule in India became supreme: the influence of France was extinguished, and the power of the princes reduced by the crushing of Tippoo Sahib (1799) and the Marathas (1803). After his return to England, he became Ambassador to Madrid (1805), Foreign Minister (1809) and Lord-Lieutenant of Ireland (1821 and 1833).

Wellington, Arthur Wellesley, 1st Duke of (1769–1852)
Irish general and politician. He joined the British army in 1787, was sent to India with his regiment, and there defeated Tippoo Sahib, became Governor of Mysore, and broke the power of the Marathas. Knighted in 1804, he became an MP (1806), and Irish Secretary (1807). He defeated the Danes during the Copenhagen expedition (1807), and in the **Peninsular War** drove the French

out of Portugal and Spain, gaining victories at Talavera (1809), Salamanca (1812), and Toulouse (1814). For his role in this campaign he was given many honours, and created Duke of Wellington. After **Napoleon I**'s escape from Elba, he defeated the French at the Battle of **Waterloo**. He supported **Liverpool**'s government, and joined it as Master-General of the Ordnance (1818). He also became Constable of the Tower (1826) and army Commander-in-Chief (1827). His period as Prime Minister (1828–30) significantly weakened the Tory Party, which split over the question of **Catholic Emancipation** (1829), and was further weakened by disagreements over trade and reform. Wellington's opposition to parliamentary reform brought down his government, which was succeeded by the **Whigs**. He was Foreign Secretary under **Peel** (1834–5), retired from public life in 1846. ▷ **Napoleonic Wars**

Wesley, John (1703–91)
English evangelist and founder of Methodism. He was ordained deacon (1725) and priest (1728), and in 1726 became a fellow at Oxford and lecturer in Greek. He became leader of a small group which had gathered round his brother Charles, nicknamed the Methodists. The brothers went to Georgia (1735–8) as missionaries, but the mission proved a failure. In 1738, at a meeting in London, John experienced a personal religious 'conversion'; but his ensuing evangelical zeal caused most of the parish clergy to close their pulpits against him. This drove him into the open air at Bristol (1739), where he founded the first Methodist chapel, and then the Foundry at Moorfields, London, which became his headquarters. He spent much of his life travelling and preaching throughout the country, and also produced many religious works.

Wessex
A kingdom of the Anglo-Saxon heptarchy, with its main centres at Winchester and Hamwic (Southampton). Under **Alfred**, Wessex (by then incorporating Kent and Sussex) was the only English kingdom to withstand the onslaughts of the **Vikings**. Alfred's successors reconquered the **Danelaw**, and had united all England under a single monarchy by 954. ▷ **Anglo-Saxons; Mercia**

Westminster, Statute of (1931)
Legislation which clarified that Dominions in the **British Empire** were autonomous communities and effectively independent, though owing common allegiance to the crown. The statute closely

followed the formulation made by Arthur **Balfour** in the 1920s about the relationship of the Dominions to Britain and it also established a free association of members in the '**Commonwealth of Nations**'.

Westminster, Statutes of (1275, 1285 and 1290)

Part of a comprehensive programme undertaken by **Edward I** to reform English law and administration. The first statute (1275) was concerned mainly with criminal matters, notably compulsory trial by jury; the second (1285) covered many fields of law, and facilitated the creation of entailed estates; the third (1290) protected lords' feudal incidents.

Westminster Assembly

A body of clerics (120) and laymen (30) convened by the English **Long Parliament** in 1643 to arrange a religious settlement to replace the Church of England. Dominated by Presbyterians, it produced a directory of public worship to replace the Prayer Book, and the Westminster Confession of Faith. Its influence declined when the power of the army, which favoured toleration, increased after 1648. ▷ **Presbyterianism**

WEU (Western European Union)

An organization of western European nations, founded (1955) to coordinate defence and other policies. Its members are Belgium, France, Germany, Italy, Luxembourg, the Netherlands, Portugal, Spain and the UK. In the 1990s, it developed as the defence arm of the **EU**, bringing together the European members of **NATO**.

Whigs

A political party that emerged in 1679–80 as the group agitating for the exclusion of James, Duke of York (later **James VII and II**), on the grounds of his Catholicism. The name was probably a contraction of 'Whiggamores' — militant Scottish Presbyterians. The party benefited from the political changes of the **Glorious Revolution** of 1688 and, during its long period of dominance in British politics after 1714, drew much strength from defending 'the principles of 1688', which included limited monarchy and the importance of parliament. Whiggery is better seen as a general set of beliefs along these lines, rather than as a unified party. Most of its leaders were great landowners who used political patronage to create family-based groupings in parliament. The party was supported by many in the moneyed and commercial classes, and by Nonconformists who looked to the Whigs (usually mistakenly) to provide religious toleration. Whig fortunes waned in the late 18c, and Whigs became leading members of the new **Liberal Party** from the mid-19c. ▷ **Presbyterianism; Tories**

Whitby, Synod of (664)

A meeting before Oswiu, King of **Northumbria**, where the differences in organization between Roman and Celtic Christianity were debated. Roman concepts of church order prevailed, with the result that the two Christian traditions in Britain were eventually united in their acceptance of the authority and practices of Rome.

Wilberforce, William (1759–1833)

English politician, evangelist and philanthropist. He became an MP (1780), and in 1788 began the movement which resulted in the abolition of the slave trade in the British West Indies in 1807. He next sought to secure the abolition of all slaves, but declining health compelled him in 1825 to retire from parliament. He died, one month before the Slavery Abolition Act was passed in parliament. A lifelong friend of **Pitt**, 'the Younger', he was like him a strong opponent of reformers in the 1790s. His evangelical beliefs led him to urge the aristocracy to practise 'real Christianity', and to give a moral lead to the poor. ▷ **slave trade**

Wilkes, John (1727–97)

English politician and journalist. He studied at Leiden, became an MP (1757), and attacked the ministry in his weekly journal, *North Briton* (1762–3). He was imprisoned, released, then expelled from the house for libel. Re-elected on several occasions, and repeatedly expelled, he came to be seen as a champion of liberty, and an upholder of press freedom. In 1774 he became Lord Mayor of London, and in the same year finally gained readmission to parliament, where he remained until his retirement in 1790.

William I, 'the Conqueror' (c.1028–87)

Duke of Normandy and the first Norman King of England (1066/87). He was the illegitimate son of Duke Robert of Normandy. **Edward the Confessor**, who had been brought up in Normandy, most probably designated him as future King of England in 1051. When Harold Godwin, despite an apparent oath to uphold William's claims, took the throne as **Harold II**, William invaded with the support of the papacy, defeated and killed Harold at the Battle of **Hastings**, and was crowned King (25 Dec 1066). The key to effective control was military conquest backed up by aristocratic colonization, so that by the time of **Domesday Book** (1086), the leaders of Anglo-Saxon society south of the Tees had been almost entirely replaced by a new ruling class of **Normans**, Bretons and Flemings, who were closely tied to William by feudal bonds. He died while defending Normandy's southern border. ▷ **Anglo-Saxons; Norman Conquest**

William I, 'the Lion' (c.1142–1214)
King of Scots (1165/1214). He was the brother and successor of **Malcolm IV**. In 1173–4 he invaded Northumberland during the rebellion against **Henry II** of England, but was captured at Alnwick, and by the Treaty of Falaise (1174) recognized Henry as the feudal superior of Scotland. Despite his difficulties with England, he made Scotland a much stronger kingdom, and in 1192 Celestine III declared the Scottish Church free of all external authority save the Pope's. ▷ **David I**

William II, 'Rufus' (c.1056–1100)
King of England (1087/1100). He was the second surviving son of **William I, 'the Conqueror'**. His main goal was the recovery of Normandy from his elder brother, Robert Curthose, and from 1096, when Robert relinquished the struggle and departed on the First Crusade, William ruled the duchy as *de facto* duke. He also led expeditions to Wales (1095 and 1097); conquered Carlisle and the surrounding district (1092); and after the death of **Malcolm III, 'Canmore'**, exercised a controlling influence over Scottish affairs. Contemporaries condemned his government of England as arbitrary and ruthless. He exploited his rights over the Church and the nobility beyond the limits of custom, and quarrelled with Anselm, Archbishop of Canterbury. His personal conduct outraged many, for he was most likely a homosexual. He was killed by an arrow while hunting in the New Forest. It has been supposed that he was murdered on the orders of his younger brother, who succeeded him as **Henry I**, but his death was almost certainly accidental. ▷ **Crusades**

William III, 'of Orange' (1650–1702)

Stadholder of the United Provinces (1672/1702) and King of Great Britain (1689/1702). Born in The Hague, he was the son of William II of Orange by Mary, the eldest daughter of **Charles I** of England. In 1677 he married his cousin, Mary (1662–94), the daughter of **James VII and II** by Anne Hyde. Invited to redress the grievances of the country, he landed at Torbay in 1688 with an English and Dutch army, and forced James VII and II to flee; William and Mary were proclaimed rulers early the following year. He was defeated by James's supporters at Killiecrankie (17 July 1689) but overcame James at the Battle of the **Boyne** (1 July 1690), then concentrated on the War of the **Grand Alliance** against France (1689–97), in which he was finally successful. In later years, he had to withstand much parliamentary opposition to his proposals. He died, childless, the crown passing to Mary's sister, **Anne**. ▷ **Glorious Revolution**

William IV, 'the Sailor King' (1765–1837)

King of Great Britain and Ireland, and King of Hanover (1830/7). The third son of **George III**, he entered the navy in 1779, saw service in the USA and the West Indies, became Admiral in 1811, and Lord High Admiral in 1827–8. His elder brother having died, he succeeded **George IV** in 1830. Widely believed to have Whig leanings to his accession, he developed Tory sympathies, and did much to obstruct the passing of the first Reform Act (1832). He was the last monarch to use prerogative powers to dismiss a ministry with a parliamentary majority when he sacked **Melbourne** in 1834 and invited the **Tories** to form a government. He was succeeded by his niece, **Victoria**. ▷ **Reform Acts; Whigs**

William of Wykeham (Wickham) (1324–1404)

English churchman and statesman. Possibly the son of a serf, he rose to become the chief adviser of **Edward III** of England. He was appointed Keeper of the Privy Seal (1363), Bishop of Winchester (1367), and was twice Chancellor of England (1367–71 and 1389–91). He founded New College, Oxford, and Winchester College, both of which were fully established by the 1390s.

Williams, Roger (c.1604–83)

English colonist, founder of Rhode Island. A member of the Anglican church, his espousal of Puritan beliefs led him to emi-

318

grate in 1630 to the Massachusetts Bay colony. He refused to participate in the church in Boston, believing it had not separated from the English church, and moved to Salem where, after challenging the authority of the Puritan magistrates over matters of personal conscience, he was persecuted and eventually banished. He took refuge with the Indians, then purchased land from them on which he founded the city of Providence in 1636. His colony was a model of democracy and religious freedom; he went to England in 1643 and 1651 to procure a charter for it and served as its President (1654–7).

Williams, Shirley (Vivien Teresa) (1930–)

English politician. A former journalist, and Secretary of the Fabian Society (1960–4), she became a Labour MP in 1964. After many junior positions, she was Secretary of State for Prices and Consumer Protection (1974–6), and for Education and Science (1976–9). She lost her seat in 1979, became a co-founder of the Social Democratic Party in 1981, and the Party's first elected MP later that year. She lost her seat in the 1983 general election, but remained as the SDP's President (1982–7). She supported the merger between the SDP and the Liberal Party. ▷ **Labour Party; Liberal Party; Social Democratic Party**

Williams Thesis

Revolutionary argument postulated by Eric Williams in *Capitalism and Slavery* (1944) that British emancipation was more the consequence of 'laissez-faire' self-interest than imperial altruism. The idea that the abolition of the slave trade and slavery was simply the result of the high-minded idealism of the Abolitionists had been set in historical truth by books such as Reginald Coupland's *The British Anti-Slavery Movement* (1933); Williams argued cogently that while slavery and the slave trade had provided the necessary capital to finance the **Industrial Revolution** in England, by the beginning of the 19c the British West Indies sugar plantocracy with its expensive production, captive, monopolistic market and inefficient labour force had become an obstacle to a booming industrial society and its metropolitan, free-trading entrepreneurs.

Willibrord (658–739)

English monk. He was born in Northumbria and trained in Ripon Abbey; after working in Ireland, he and 11 others left for the

Netherlands as missionaries in 690. Responsible for converting much of the Netherlands to Christianity, the Merovingian and Carolingian Frankish kings legitimized his work in Friesland, which they welcomed as a stabilizing political influence in their interests. Willibrord visited Rome c.692 and 695, and was made Archbishop of the Frisians, based in Utrecht, in 694.

Wilson, Arnold (1884–1940)

British administrator. Having carried out surveying work in southern Persia as an Indian Army officer, he was appointed, by the British, to the commission charged with looking into the Ottoman–Persian Shatt al-Arab frontier dispute in 1913. He was a member of Cox's civil administration in 1915–16 and became (mid-1918) Acting Civil Commissioner, on Cox's departure to Tehran. Wilson's administration, although generally fair and efficient, was distinctly unsympathetic towards local, and particularly nationalist, aims. After **World War I**, he urged opposition both to the Anglo-French Declaration and to the notion of an Iraq run by a prince from the Sharifian family. His government appeared increasingly intolerant, giving rise to Iraqi fears that they had merely exchanged a Turkish master for a British, and that their political aspirations would be thwarted; this helped to bring about the insurrection of 1920. Later that year, Cox returned to Iraq, relieving Wilson of the task of carrying out the proposed constitutional programme for the country. He went on to become an MP, was arrested early in **World War II** because of alleged fascist sympathies and was killed in action, having volunteered as a rear-gunner in the RAF.

Wilson, Sir Henry Hughes (1864–1922)

British field marshal. He joined the Rifle Brigade in 1884, and served in Burma (1884–7) and South Africa (1899–1901). As Director of Military Operations at the War Office (1910–14), he elaborated plans for the rapid support of France in the event of war with Germany. By the end of **World War I**, he was Chief of the Imperial General Staff. Promoted field marshal and created a baronet (1919), he resigned from the army in 1922, and became an MP. His implacable opposition to the leaders of **Sinn Féin** led to his assassination on the doorstep of his London home.

Wilson (of Libya and of Stowlangtoft), Henry Maitland, 1st Baron
(1881–1964)

British field marshal. He fought in South Africa and in **World War I**, and at the outbreak of **World War II** was appointed Commander of British troops in Egypt. Having led the initial British advance in Libya (1940–1) and the unsuccessful Greek campaign (1941), he became Commander-in-Chief Middle East (1943) and Supreme Allied Commander in the Mediterranean theatre (1944). Wilson headed the British Joint Staff Mission in Washington (1945–7), and was raised to the peerage in 1946.

Wilson (of Rievaulx), (James) Harold, Baron (1916–)

English politician and Prime Minister of Britain. He became a lecturer in economics at Oxford in 1937. An MP in 1945, he was President of the Board of Trade (1947–51), and the principal opposition spokesman on Economic Affairs. An able and hard-hitting debater, in 1963 he succeeded **Gaitskell** as Leader of the **Labour Party**, then he became Prime Minister (1964–70). His economic plans were badly affected by balance of payments crises, leading to severe restrictive measures and devaluation (1967). He was also faced with the problem of Rhodesian independence, opposition to Britain's proposed entry into the Common Market, and an increasing conflict between the two wings of the Labour Party. Following his third general election victory, he resigned suddenly as Prime Minister and Labour leader in 1976. Knighted in 1976, he became a life peer in 1983. ▷ **EC; EEC; Rhodesia Crisis**

Windsor, House of

The name of the British royal family since 1917. This unequivocally English name resulted from a declaration by **George V**, a member of the House of **Saxe-Coburg-Gotha**. It was felt that a Germanic surname for the British monarchy was inappropriate during a war against Germany.

Wingate, Orde (Charles) (1903–44)

British general. He was commissioned in 1922, and served in the Sudan (1928–33) and Palestine (1936–9), where he helped create a Jewish defence force. In the Burma theatre (1942) he organized the Chindits — specially trained jungle-fighters who were supplied by air, and thrust far behind the enemy lines. He was killed in a plane crash in Burma. ▷ **World War II**

Winthrop, John (1588–1649)

English colonist. Educated at Cambridge, England, he became a lawyer, and in 1629 the first Governor of the Bay Company. He crossed the Atlantic to settle what would become Massachusetts and Massachusetts colony, and was re-elected Governor 12 times. His political and religious conservatism greatly influenced the political institutions that were formed in the Northern states of America.

witan (witenagemot)

The council (Old English, 'meeting of wise men') of the Anglo-Saxon kings, once regarded as the first English 'parliament'. It was not a popular assembly imposing constitutional restraints on kingship, but in essence an informal advisory body of great men. It nevertheless upheld the convention that kings should take into account the views of important subjects. ▷ **Anglo-Saxons**

Wolfe, James (1727–59)

British general. Commissioned in 1741, he fought against the **Jacobites** in Scotland (1745–6) and was sent to Canada during the **Seven Years War** (1756–63). In 1758 he was prominent in the capture of Louisbourg in Nova Scotia; the following year he commanded at the famous capture of **Quebec**, where he was killed.

Wollstonecraft, Mary (1759–97)

Pioneer advocate of women's rights. After working as a teacher and governess, she became a translator and literary adviser. In 1792 she published *Vindication of the Rights of Woman*, which advocated equality between the sexes, radical social change and economic independence for women. She also supported the French Revolution and her ideas were vilified by the authorities. After a failed first marriage, she married William Godwin in 1797 and died giving birth to a daughter, Mary (later Mary Shelley, author of *Frankenstein*).

Wolseley, Garnet Joseph, 1st Viscount (1833–1913)

British field marshal. He joined the army in 1852, and served in the Burmese War (1852–3), the **Crimean War** (where he lost an eye), the **Indian Uprising** (1857–8), and the Chinese War (1860). He put down the Red River Rebellion (1870) in Canada, and commanded in the Ashanti War (1873). After other posts in India,

Cyprus, South Africa and Egypt, he led the attempted rescue of General **Gordon** at Khartoum. He became a baron (1882) and, after the Sudan campaign (1884–5), a viscount. As army Commander-in-Chief (1895–1901), he carried out several reforms, and mobilized forces for the Boer War (1899–1902). ▷ **Boer Wars**

Wolsey, Thomas (c.1475–1530)
English cardinal and statesman. He was ordained in 1498, appointed chaplain to **Henry VII** in 1507, and became Dean of Lincoln. Under **Henry VIII**, he became Bishop of Lincoln, Archbishop of York (1514), and a cardinal (1515). Made Lord Chancellor (1515–29), he pursued legal and administrative reforms. He was Henry VIII's leading adviser, in charge of the day-to-day running of government. He aimed to make England a major power in Europe, and also had ambitions to become Pope, but his policy of supporting first Emperor Charles V (1523) then Francis I of France (1528) in the Habsburg–Valois conflict was unsuccessful, and high taxation caused much resentment. When he failed to persuade the Pope to grant Henry's divorce, he was impeached and his property forfeited. Arrested on a charge of high treason, he died while travelling to London.

Worcester, Battle of (3 Sep 1651)
The last battle of the **English Civil Wars**, fought between the English Army, supported by local militia, under Oliver **Cromwell** and an invading Scottish army led by **Charles II**, who had been crowned King of Scotland at Scone (1 Jan 1651). The English forces decisively overpowered their opponents and Charles was a fugitive for several weeks before escaping to Normandy to begin an exile in France, Germany and the Spanish Netherlands which lasted for almost nine years.

World War I (1914–18)
A war whose origins lay in the increasingly aggressive foreign policies as pursued by Austria-Hungary, Russia and, most significantly, Germany. The assassination of the heir to the Habsburg throne, Francis Ferdinand, at Sarajevo in Bosnia (28 June 1914), triggered the war which soon involved most European states following Austria's declaration of war on Serbia (28 July). Russia mobilized in support of Serbia (29–30 July); and Germany declared war on Russia (1 Aug), and on France (3 Aug). The German invasion of neutral Belgium (4 Aug) brought the British

into the war on the French side. Japan joined Britain, France and Russia under the terms of an agreement with Britain (1902, 1911), and Italy joined the Allies in May 1915. Turkey allied with Germany (Nov 1914), and they were joined by Bulgaria (Oct 1915). Military campaigning centred on France, Belgium and, later, Italy in Western Europe, and on Poland, western Russia and the Balkans in Eastern Europe. At the first Battle of Ypres, the French Army and the **British Expeditionary Force** prevented the Germans from from reaching the Channel ports. By the end of 1914, a static defence line had been established from the Belgian coast to Switzerland. The Allies attempted to break the stalemate by the **Gallipoli Campaign** aimed at re-supplying Russia and knocking out Turkey (Apr 1915–Jan 1916), but failed. On the eastern and south-eastern fronts, the Central Powers occupied Russian Poland and most of Lithuania, and Serbia was invaded. After staunch resistance, Serbia, Albania and, latterly, Romania were overrun. For three years, an Allied army was involved in a Macedonian campaign, and there was also fighting in Mesopotamia against Turkey. Naval competition had played a crucial role in heightening tension before 1914, but in the event, the great battle fleets of Germany and Britain did not play an important part in the war. The only significant naval encounter, at Jutland in 1916, proved indecisive. The Allies organized a large offensive for the Western Front in 1916, but were forestalled by the Germans, who attacked France at Verdun (Feb–July). To relieve the situation, the Battle of the Somme was launched, but proved indecisive. The Germans then unleashed unrestricted submarine warfare (Jan 1917) to cripple Britain economically before the USA could come to her aid. The USA declared war on Germany (2 Apr 1917) when British food stocks were perilously low, and the German submarine menace was finally overcome by the use of convoys. Tanks were used effectively by the Allies at the Battle of Cambrai (1916). In the spring of 1918 the Germans launched a major attack in the west, but after several months of success were driven back, with the USA providing an increasing number of much-needed troops. By Sep, the German Army was in full retreat, and signified its intention to sue for peace on the basis of President Wilson's **Fourteen Points**. By Nov, when the armistice was signed, the Allies had recaptured western Belgium and nearly all French territory. Military victories in Palestine and Mesopotamia resulted in a Turkish armistice (31 Oct 1918); Italian victories and a northward advance by Franco-British forces finished Austria-Hungary (and

Bulgaria). Estimated combatant war losses were: British Empire, just under 1 million: France, nearly 1.4 million; Italy, nearly $\frac{1}{2}$ million; Russia, 1.7 million; USA, 115 000; Germany 1.8 million; Austria-Hungary 1.2 million, and Turkey 325 000. About double these numbers were wounded. ▷ **Marne, Battle of the; Paris Peace Conference; Passchendaele, Battle of; reparations; Somme, Battle of the; Triple Entente; Versailles, Treaty of; Vimy Ridge, Battle of**

World War II (1939–45)

A war whose origins lay in three different conflicts which merged after 1941: **Hitler**'s desire for European expansion and perhaps even world domination; Japan's struggle against China; and a resulting conflict between Japanese ambitions and US interests in the Pacific. The origins of the war in Europe lay in German unwillingness to accept the frontiers laid down in 1919 by the Treaty of **Versailles** and the National Socialists' hegemonial foreign policy. After the German invasion of rump Bohemia-Moravia (Mar 1939), Britain and France pledged support to Poland. Germany concluded an alliance with the USSR (Aug 1939), and then invaded Poland (1 Sep). Britain and France declared war on Germany (3 Sep), but could not prevent Poland from being overrun in four weeks. For six months there was a period of 'phoney war', when little fighting took place, but the Germans then occupied Norway and Denmark (Apr 1940), and Belgium and Holland were invaded (10 May), followed immediately by the invasion of France. A combination of German tank warfare and air power brought about the surrender of Holland in four days, Belgium in three weeks, and France in seven weeks. Italy declared war on France and Britain in the final stages of this campaign. There followed the Battle of Britain, in which Germany tried to win air supremacy over Britain, but failed. As a result, German attempts to force Britain to come to terms came to nothing, not least because of Winston **Churchill**'s uncompromising stance. Germany launched submarine (U-boat) attacks against British supply routes, but then moved east and invaded Greece and Yugoslavia (Apr 1941) and, following an Italian military fiasco there, Greece. British military efforts were concentrated against Italy in the Mediterranean and North Africa. After early reverses for Italy, Rommel was sent to North Africa with the German Afrika Corps to reinforce Italian military strength, and fiercely-contested campaigning continued here for three years until Allied troops finally ejected German and Italian forces in mid-1943, invaded Sicily and then Italy itself, and forced Italy to make a separate peace (3 Sep 1943). In June 1941 Germany invaded her ally Russia along a 2 000 mile front, and German armies advanced in three formations: to the outskirts of Leningrad in the north, towards Moscow in the centre, and to the Volga River in the south. After spectacular early successes, the Germans were held up by bitter Soviet resistance, and by heavy winter snows and Arctic temperatures, for which they were completely unprepared. From Nov 1942 they were gradually driven back; Leningrad was under siege for nearly two and a half years (until Jan 1944), and about a third of its population died from starvation and disease. The Germans were finally driven out of the USSR (Aug 1944). A second front was launched against Germany by the Allies (June 1944), through the invasion of Normandy, and Paris was liberated (25 Aug). Despite German use of flying bombs and rockets against Allied bases, the Allies advanced into Germany (Feb 1945) and linked with the Russians on the River Elbe (28 Apr). The Germans surrendered unconditionally at Rheims (7 May 1945). In the Far East, Japan's desire for expansion, combined with a US threat of economic sanctions against her, led to her attack on Pearl Harbor and other British and US bases (7 Dec 1941), and the USA declared war against Japan the next day. In reply Japan's allies, Germany and Italy, declared war on the USA (11 Dec). Bitter fighting continued until 1945, when, with Japan on the retreat, the USA dropped two atomic bombs on Hiroshima and Nagasaki (6 and 9 Aug). Japan then surrendered 14 Aug. Casualty figures are not easy to obtain accurately, but approximately 3 million Russians were killed in action, 3 million died as prisoners of war, 8 million people died in occupied Russia, and about 3 million in unoccupied Russia. Germany suffered $3\frac{1}{4}$ million military casualties, around 6 million total casualties, and lost a million prisoners of war. Japan suffered just over 2 million military casualties and just over $\frac{1}{4}$ million civilian deaths. France lost a total of $\frac{1}{2}$ million dead, and Britain and her Commonwealth just over 600 000. The USA suffered just over 300 000 casualties. It is also estimated that in the course of the German occupation of a large part of Europe, about 6 million Jews were murdered in extermination and labour camps, along with a million or more other victims. ▷ **appeasement; Atlantic, Battle of the; Atlantic Charter; Britain, Battle of; Bulge, Battle of the; Casablanca Conference; D-Day; Desert Rats; El Alamein, Battle of; Free French; Lend-Lease Agreement; Munich Agreement; Normandy Campaign; North African Campaign;**

Nuremberg Trials; Paris Peace Conference; Potsdam Conference; Special Operations Executive; Yalta Conference

Wycliffe, John (c.1330–84)
English religious reformer. He taught philosophy at Oxford, then entered the Church, becoming Rector of Lutterworth, Leicestershire, in 1374. He was sent to Bruges to treat with ambassadors from the Pope about ecclesiastical abuses, but his views were found unacceptable, and he was prosecuted. He then attacked the Church hierarchy, priestly powers, and the doctrine of transubstantiation, wrote many popular tracts in English (as opposed to Latin), and issued the first English translation of the Bible. His opinions were condemned, and he was forced to retire to Lutterworth, where he wrote prolifically until his death. The characteristic of his teaching was its insistence on inward religion in opposition to the formalism of the time. His followers were known as '**Lollards**', and the influence of his teaching was widespread in England, in many respects anticipating the **Reformation**.

Y

Yalta Conference (4–11 Feb 1945)
A meeting at Yalta, in the Crimea, during **World War II**, between
Winston **Churchill**, Stalin and Roosevelt. Among matters agreed
were the disarmament and partition of Germany, the Russo-
Polish frontier, the establishment of the **UN**, and the composition
of the Polish government. In a secret protocol it was also agreed
that Russia would declare war on Japan after the war with Germany ended.

York, House of
The younger branch of the **Plantagenet Dynasty**, founded by
Edmund of Langley, the fourth son of **Edward III** and first Duke
of York, whence came three kings of England: **Edward IV**, who
usurped the Lancastrian king **Henry VI**; **Edward V**; and **Richard
III** killed at the Battle of **Bosworth Field**, and succeeded by **Henry
VII**, first of the Tudors. ▷ **Lancaster, House of; Roses, Wars of the;
Tudor, House of**

Yorktown Campaign (30 Aug–19 Oct 1781)
The final campaign of the **American Revolution**, in which the
British Army under General **Cornwallis** was trapped at Yorktown
in Virginia, by troops under George Washington and a French
fleet under Admiral de Grasse (1722–88). The defeat destroyed
the political will on the English side to continue the war. It brought
the fall of Lord **North**, Prime Minister since 1770, and opened the
way for peace negotiations.

Young Ireland
An Irish protest movement, founded in 1840, which produced
The Nation magazine, arguing for repeal of the Act of Union. It
set up an Irish Confederation in 1847, which returned several
nationalists to parliament, and an unsuccessful Young Ireland
rising took place in Tipperary (1848). ▷ **O'Connell, David; Union,
Acts of**

Ypres, Battle of (Oct–Nov 1914)
In **World War I** the halting of a German offensive to outflank the **British Expeditionary Force**. It left Ypres (Belgium) and its salient dominated on three sides by German-occupied heights.

Ypres, Battle of (Apr–May 1915)
A series of German attacks, using poison gas (chlorine) for the first time in warfare. It forced the British to shorten their defence line in the Ypres salient.

Z

Zambezi Expedition
An official British expedition (1858–64), led by David **Livingstone**, to investigate the potentiality of the Zambezi River for steamship communication with the interior of Africa, in order to promote the destruction of the **slave trade**, its replacement by 'legitimate' commerce, and the extension of missionary activity in the region. The expedition was a failure: the Zambezi was found to be non-navigable, Livingstone's relations with his associates were difficult and helped to thwart the scientific objectives, and the earliest missionary endeavours met with disaster.

Zionism
The movement which sought to recover for the Jewish people its historic Palestinian homeland (the *Eretz Israel*) after centuries of dispersion. The modern movement arose in the late 19c with plans for Jewish colonization of Palestine, and under Theodor **Herzl** also developed a political programme to obtain sovereign state rights over the territory. Gaining support after **World War I**, its objectives were supported by the British **Balfour Declaration** in 1917, as long as rights for non-Jews in Palestine were not impaired. After **World War II**, the establishment of the Jewish state in 1948 received **UN** support.

Zulu War (1879)

A war between British forces and the Zulu kingdom characterized by initial reverses for the British but final defeat for the Zulu. From the time of the arrival of Boer settlers in northern Natal in 1836, there had been uneasy border relations between white and black. The boundary was set at different times on the Tugela, Black Umfolosi and Buffalo Rivers, but Boer farmers continued to penetrate Zululand in search of land. A boundary commission was appointed (1878), but the colonial authorities refused to accept its recommendations because the High Commissioner, Sir Bartle Frere, considered that they were too favourable to the Zulu. When a party of Zulu crossed the Natal border to kidnap two wives of a Zulu chief, war was declared. After initial reverses at Isandlhwana and Rorke's Drift, the British forces under Sir Garnet **Wolseley** defeated the Zulu at Ulundi. **Cetewayo**, King of the Zulu, was exiled and Zululand was divided into 13 chieftaincies. The removal of the Zulu military threat encouraged the Boers to throw off British power in the Transvaal, leading to the first Boer War and the British defeat at **Majuba Hill** (1881).